TAKING SIDES

Clashing Views on Controversial

Issues in Business Ethics and Society

SIXTH EDITION

Clashing Views on Controversial

Issues in Business Ethics and Society

SIXTH EDITION

Selected, Edited, and with Introductions by

Lisa H. Newton
Fairfield University

and

Maureen M. Ford
Fairfield University

Dushkin/McGraw-Hill
A Division of The McGraw-Hill Companies

To our husbands—Victor J. Newton, Jr.,
and James H. L. Ford, Jr.

Photo Acknowledgement
Cover image: © 2000 by PhotoDisc, Inc.

Cover Art Acknowledgment
Charles Vitelli

Library of Congress Cataloging-in-Publication Data
Main entry under title:
Taking sides: clashing views on controversial issues in business ethics
and society/selected, edited, and with introductions by Lisa H. Newton and Maureen M. Ford.—6th
ed.
Includes bibliographical references and index.
1. Business ethics. I. Newton, Lisa H., *comp.* II. Ford, Maureen M., *comp.*
174.4
0-07-236003-8
95-83859

Printed on Recycled Paper

Preface

From the very beginning of critical thought, we find the distinction between topics susceptible of certain knowledge and topics about which uncertain opinions are available. The dawn of this distinction, explicitly entertained, is the dawn of modern mentality. It introduces criticism.

— Alfred North Whitehead
Adventures of Ideas (1933)

This volume contains 38 selections, presented in a pro and con format, that debate a total of 19 different controversial issues in business ethics. In this book we ask you, the reader, to examine the accepted practices of business in light of justice, right, and human dignity. We ask you to consider what moral imperatives and values should be at work in the conduct of business.

This method of presenting opposing views on an issue grows out of the ancient learning method of *dialogue*. Two presumptions lead us to seek the truth in a dialogue between opposed positions: The first presumption is that the truth is really out there and that it is important to find it. The second is that no one of us has all of it (the truth). The way to reach the truth is to form our initial opinions on a subject and give voice to them in public. Then we let others with differing opinions reply, and while they are doing so, we listen carefully. The truth that comes into being in the public space of the dialogue becomes part of our opinion—now a more informed opinion, and now based on the reasoning that emerged in the course of the airing of opposing views.

Each issue in this volume has an issue *introduction*, which sets the stage for the debate as it is argued in the YES and NO selections. Each issue concludes with a *postscript* that makes some final observations and points the way to other questions related to the issue. The introductions and postscripts do not preempt what is the reader's own task: to achieve a critical and informed view of the issue at stake. In reading an issue and forming your own opinion, you should not feel confined to adopt one or the other of the positions presented. There are positions in between the given views, or totally outside of them, and the *suggestions for further reading* that appear in each issue postscript should help you to continue your study of the subject. At the back of the book is a listing of all the *contributors to this volume*, which will give you information on the philosophers, business professors, businesspeople, and business commentators whose views are debated here.

Changes to this edition   This edition represents a considerable revision. There are 8 completely new issues: *Is Game Theory Devastating to Business Ethics?* (Issue 4); *Are Derivative Instruments Purchases Just Gambling?* (Issue 8); *Are Marketing and Advertising Fundamentally Exploitive?* (Issue 11); *Product Liability: Was Ford to Blame in the Pinto Case?* (Issue 12); *Should Patenting Life Be Forbidden?*

i

(Issue 15); *Should We Encourage International Trade in Tobacco Products?* (Issue 16); *Should We Export Pesticides to Developing Nations?* (Issue 17); and *Is CEO Compensation Justified by Performance?* (Issue 18). In addition, the YES selection for one of the issues has been replaced to bring the debate up to date: *Should Casino Gambling Be Prohibited?* (Issue 7). In all, there are 17 new selections.

A word to the instructor An *Instructor's Manual With Test Questions* (multiple-choice and essay) is available through the publisher for the instructor using *Taking Sides* in the classroom. A general guidebook, *Using Taking Sides in the Classroom*, which discusses methods and techniques for integrating the pro-con approach into any classroom setting, is also available. An online version of *Using Taking Sides in the Classroom* and a correspondence service for *Taking Sides* adopters can be found at http://www.dushkin.com/usingts/.

Taking Sides: Clashing Views on Controversial Issues in Business Ethics and Society is only one title in the Taking Sides series. If you are interested in seeing the table of contents for any of the other titles, please visit the Taking Sides Web site at http://www.dushkin.com/takingsides/.

Acknowledgments Praise and thanks are due to our families, without whose patience and support this volume would never have been completed. Special thanks go to those who responded to the questionnaire with specific suggestions for the sixth edition:

John Beck
Gonzaga University

George Bogaski
Mid-America Bible College

Kenneth M. Bond
Humboldt State University

Dennis Cooley
East Carolina University

Rita C. Hinton
Mississippi University for Women

Jay Taylor Keehley
Mississippi State University

Brian Mckenna
St. Xavier University

C. Eric Mount, Jr.
Centre College of Kentucky

Annette Rossignol
Oregon State Unviersity

Norman Runge
Wilmington College—New Castle

Edie Sturgeon
National University—San Diego

Lisa H. Newton
Fairfield University

Maureen M. Ford
Fairfield University

Contents In Brief

Contents

Free-market economist Adam Smith (1723–1790) states that if self-
interested people are left alone to seek their own economic advantage,
the result, unintended by any one of them, will be greater advantage for
all. German philosopher Karl Marx (1818–1883) and German sociologist
Friedrich Engels (1820–1895) argue that if people are left to their own self-
interested devices, those who own the means of production will rapidly
reduce everyone else to virtual slaves.

LaRue Tone Hosmer, a professor of corporate strategies, argues that
codes of ethics are ineffective in bringing about more ethical behavior on
the part of employees. Professor of philosophy Lisa H. Newton holds that
the formation and adoption of corporate codes are valuable processes.

Professor of business ethics Manuel Velasquez argues that ethical behavior and the development of the virtues that result in ethical behavior are the

best predictors of profit in business organizations. David M. Messick, a professor of ethics and decision in management, asserts that actual behavior, in business and in other areas of life, tends to be a nuanced combination of egotistical and justice-oriented profit-maximizing actions.

Robert C. Solomon, premier ethicist in contemporary scholarship, finds the use of game theory for business ethics "dangerous and demeaning," arguing that it reinforces a destructive obsession with measurable outcomes and a false sense of competition. He asserts that anyone who practices the kind of "rationality" stressed by game theory is a moral "monster." Professor of economics Ken Binmore states that the kind of game theory that Solomon condemns is not the kind in actual use and that game theory has a strong and useful role in business ethics.

PART 2   CURRENT ISSUES IN BUSINESS   77

Professor of medicine Arnold S. Relman argues that financial and technological pressures are forcing doctors to act like businessmen, with deleterious consequences for patients. Andrew C. Wicks, an assistant professor at the University of Washington School of Business, asserts that there are fundamental similarities between physician ethics and business ethics.

Philosopher Richard A. Spinello argues that the pharmaceutical industry should regulate its prices in accordance with the principles of distributive justice. The Pharmaceutical Manufacturers Association, an association of 93 manufacturers of pharmaceutical and biological products, argues that price controls are counterproductive in providing scarce goods for the consumer.

Michael A. Verespej, a writer for *Industry Week,* argues that a majority of employees are tolerant of drug testing. Jennifer Moore, a researcher of business ethics and business law, asserts that employers' concerns about drug abuse should not override employees' right to dignity and privacy.

PART 4   MOVING THE PRODUCT: MARKETING AND CONSUMER DILEMMAS   193

Issue 11.   Are Marketing and Advertising Fundamentally Exploitive?   194

Archbishop John P. Foley summarizes and comments on the 1997 report of the Pontifical Council for Social Communications, which charges that advertising can be deceptive and improperly influential on media editorial policy and states that it often promotes a lifestyle based on unbridled consumption. Professor of marketing Gene R. Laczniak contends that many of the Pontifical Council report's conclusions are overstated, only partially true, economically naive, and socially idealistic. While sympathetic to its aims, he argues that the Church's contribution to the debate is vitiated by such errors.

Issue 12.   Product Liability: Was Ford to Blame in the Pinto Case?   210

Investigative journalist Mark Dowie alleges that Ford Motor Company deliberately put an unsafe car—the Pinto—on the road, causing hundreds of people to suffer burn deaths and horrible disfigurement. James Neal, chief attorney for Ford Motor Company during the Pinto litigation, argues that there is no proof of criminal intent or negligence on the part of Ford.

PART 5   INTERNATIONAL OPERATIONS: GLOBAL OBLIGATIONS   239

Professor of business ethics Manuel Velasquez argues that since any business that tried to conform to moral rules in the absence of enforcement would cease to be competitive, moral strictures cannot be binding on such companies. Professor emeritus John E. Fleming asserts that multinational corporations tend to deal with long-term customers and suppliers in the goldfish bowl of international media and must therefore adhere to moral standards or lose business.

Susan S. Black, publisher of *Bobbin*, argues that customers will not tolerate goods made by slave labor, children, or women working in inhumane conditions. She maintains that customers are willing to pay more to make sure that the goods they buy were not made in sweatshops. Allen R. Myerson, a writer for the *New York Times*, looks at the economies of less developed countries and finds that allowing their citizens to work in sweatshops may be the only option these nations have to accumulate capital.

Jeremy Rifkin, president of the Foundation on Economic Trends, fears that genetic engineering extends human power over the rest of nature in ways that are unprecedented and whose consequences cannot be known. He urges a halt to such research, especially research whose aim is profit for the company that "owns" the results. William Domnarski, an intellectual property lawyer, finds the patenting of genes or genetic discoveries no different than patenting any other ideas. The purpose of patents is to reward and encourage useful invention, he argues, and there is no doubt that the modifications we introduce to the genetic material of plants and animals are useful to feed a starving world.

The International Tobacco Growers Association is ecstatic about the success in spreading tobacco growing into developing nations. The Association argues that tobacco is a product that is easier to grow than many other agricultural products and promises substantial economic progress for people who desperately need it. Associate professor Simon Chapman, assuming that the goal of reducing tobacco use worldwide takes first priority, suggests stopping the export of tobacco products and of tobacco-growing technology. He states that now that we have discovered the damage done by tobacco, it is wrong to spread that damage abroad for the sake of profit.

Professor Kenneth E. Goodpaster and professor Laura L. Nash state that due to its increasing population, the world will need all the food that can be grown to feed the people. This pertains mostly to the people of the developing world, where population growth is the highest. They concede that pesticides can be dangerous if abused but assert that the risks are outweighed by the certainty of death by starvation if pesticides are not used. Captain Jefferson D. Reynolds of the United States Air Force argues that developing countries lack the resources to protect their people from dangerous chemical exports. He considers pesticide exposure to be a major health problem, which is simply not getting the attention it deserves, and urges more regulation.

Professor of finance and business economics Kevin J. Murphy argues that chief executive officers (CEOs) are simply paid to do what they were hired to do—bring up the price of the stock to increase shareholder wealth. He concludes that for large increases in shareholder wealth, CEOs deserve large compensation. Professor of philosophy Lisa H. Newton finds the ultimate effect of large compensation packages on U.S. business to be negative. She asserts that the disparity between CEOs' wealth and the pay of their workers—let alone the poverty-stricken developing world—is unjust and a case of bad stewardship of resources.

Economics professors Thomas A. Carr and Sunder Ramaswamy and mathematics teacher Heather L. Pedersen describe three projects to promote sustainable use of rain forest products, which they argue help to preserve the forest and support the local economy. Investigative reporter Jon Entine asserts that most green marketing programs do nothing to slow forest destruction and, moreover, frequently result in the mistreatment of employees, vendors, and customers.

Introduction

The Study of Business Ethics: Ethics, Economics, Law, and the Corporation

Lisa H. Newton

Maureen M. Ford

This book is aimed at an audience of students who expect to be in business, who know that there are knotty ethical problems out there, and who want a chance to confront them ahead of time. The method of confronting them is an invitation to join in a debate, a contest of contrary facts and conflicting values in many of the major issues of the day. This introductory essay should make it easier to join in the arguments. Managing ethical policy problems in a company requires a wide background—in ethics, economics, law, and the social sciences—which this book cannot hope to provide. But since some background assumptions in these fields are relevant to several of the problems we examine in this volume, we will sketch out very briefly the major understandings that control them. There is ultimately no substitute for thorough study of the rules of the game and years of experience and practice; but an overview of the playing field may at least make it easier for you to understand the object and limitations of the standard plays.

Ethics

"Business ethics" is sometimes considered to be an oxymoron (a term that contradicts itself). Business and ethics have often been treated as mutually exclusive. But ethics is an issue of growing concern and importance to businesses, and we believe that many share our conviction that value questions are never absent from business decisions, that moral responsibility is the first characteristic demanded of a manager in any business, and that a thorough grounding in ethical reasoning is the best preparation for a career in business. The first imperative of business ethics is that it be taken seriously.

This book will not supply the substance of a course in ethics. For that you are directed to any of several excellent texts in business ethics or to any general text in ethics. *Taking Sides: Clashing Views on Controversial Issues in Business Ethics and Society* teaches ethics from the issue upward, rather than from the principle downward. You will, however, come upon much of the terminology of ethical reasoning in the course of considering these cases. For your reference,

Table 1

Fundamental Duties

	Beneficence—promoting human welfare	Justice—acknowledging human equality	Respect for Persons—honoring individual freedom
Basic fact about human nature that grounds the duty	Humans are animals, with vulnerable bodies and urgent physical needs, capable of suffering.	Humans are social animals who must live in communities and therefore must adopt social structures to maintain communities.	Humans are rational, free—able to make their own choices, foresee the consequences, and take responsibility.
Value realized in performance of the duty	Human welfare; happiness.	Human equality.	Human dignity; autonomy.
Working out of the duty in ethical theory	Best modern example is utilitarianism, from Jeremy Bentham and John Stuart Mill, who saw morality as that which produced the greatest happiness for the greatest number. Reasoning is consequential, aimed at results.	Best modern example is John Rawls's theory of justice as "fairness"; maintaining equality unless inequality helps everyone. Reasoning is deontological: morality derived from duty, not consequences.	Best modern example is Immanuel Kant's formalism, where morality is seen as the working out of the categorical imperative. Reasoning is deontological.
Samples of implementation of the duty in business	Protecting safety of employees; maintaining pleasant working conditions; contributing funds to the local community.	Obedience to law; enforcing fair rules; nondiscrimination; no favoritism; giving credit where credit is due.	Respect for employee rights; treating employees as persons, not just as tools; respecting differences of opinion.

a brief summary of the ethical principles and forms of reasoning most used in this book is found in Table 1.

Economics

Adam Smith

Capitalism as we know it is the product of the thought of Adam Smith (1723–1790), a Scottish philosopher and economist, and a small number of his European contemporaries. The fundamental capitalist act is the *voluntary exchange:*

two adults of sound mind and clear purposes meet in the marketplace, to which each repairs in order to satisfy some felt need. They discover that each has that which will satisfy the other's need—the housewife needs flour, the miller needs cash—and they exchange at a price such that the exchange furthers the interest of each. To the participant in the free market, the *marginal utility* of the thing acquired must exceed that of the thing traded, or else why make the deal? So each party to the voluntary exchange walks away from it richer.

Adding to the value of the exchange is the *competition* of dealers and buyers; because there are many purveyors of each good in the marketplace, the customer is not forced to pay exorbitant prices for things needed. (It is a sad fact of economics that to the starving man, the marginal value of a loaf of bread is very large, and a single merchant could become unjustly rich.) Conversely, competition among the customers (typified by an auction) makes sure that the available goods end up in the hands of those to whom they are worth the most. So at the end of the market day, everyone goes home not only richer (in real terms) than when they came—the voluntariness of the exchange ensures that— but also as rich as they could possibly be, since each had available all possible options of goods or services to buy and all possible purchasers of the goods or services brought to the marketplace for sale.

Sellers and buyers win the competition through *efficiency;* that is, through producing the best quality goods at the lowest possible price or through allotting their scarce resources toward the most valuable of the choices presented to them. It is to the advantage of all participants in the market, then, to strive for efficiency (i.e., to keep the cost of goods for sale as low as possible while keeping the quality as high as possible). Adam Smith's most memorable accomplishment was to recognize that the general effect of all this self-interested scrambling would be to make the most possible goods of the best possible quality available at the least possible price. Meanwhile, sellers and buyers alike must keep an eye on the market as a whole, adjusting production and purchasing to take advantage of fluctuations in *supply and demand*. Short supply will make goods more valuable, raising the price, and that will bring more suppliers into the market, whose competition will lower the price to just above the cost of manufacture for the most efficient producers. Increased demand for any reason will have the same effect. Should supply exceed demand, the price will fall to a point where the goods will be bought. Putting this all together, Smith realized that in a system of free enterprise, you have demonstrably the best possible chance of finding for sale what you want, in good quantity and quality and at a reasonable price. Forget benevolent monarchs ordering things for our own good, Smith suggested; in this system, we are led as by an *invisible hand* of enlightened self-interest to achieve the common good, even as we think we are being most selfish.

Adam Smith's theory of economic enterprise emerged in the natural law tradition of the eighteenth century. As was the fashion for that period, Smith presented his conclusions as a series of laws: the law of supply and demand, which links supply, demand, and price; the law that links efficiency with success; and, ultimately, the laws that link the absolute freedom of the market with the absolute growth of the wealth of the free-market country.

To these laws were added others, specifying the conditions under which business enterprise would be conducted in capitalist countries. The laws of *population* formulated by English clergyman and economist Thomas Malthus (1766–1834) concluded that population would always outstrip food production, ensuring that the bulk of humanity would always live at the subsistence level. Since Smith had already postulated that employers would purchase labor at the lowest possible price, it was a one-step derivation for English economist David Ricardo (1772–1823) to conclude that workers' *wages* would never exceed the subsistence level, no matter how prosperous industrial enterprise should become. From these capitalist theorists proceeded the nineteenth-century assumption that society would inevitably divide into two classes, a minority of fabulous wealth and a majority of subsistence-level workers.

These laws, like the laws of physics advanced at that time by Sir Isaac Newton (1642–1727) and the laws of psychology and government advanced at that time by John Locke (1632–1704), were held to be immutable facts of nature, true forever and not subject to change. No concept of progress, or of the historical fitness of a system to society at a point in time, was contemplated.

Karl Marx

Only within the last century and a half have we learned to think "historically." The notion of progress, the vision of a better future, and even the very idea that we might modify that future, in part by the discernment of historical trends, were unknown to the ancients and of no interest to medieval chroniclers. For Western political philosophy, history emerged as a factor in our understanding only with the work of the nineteenth-century German philosopher G. W. F. Hegel (1770–1831), who traced the history of the Western world as an ordered series of ideal forms, evolving one from another in logical sequence toward an ideal future. A young German student of Hegel's, Karl Marx (1818–1883), concluded from his study of philosophy and economics that Hegel had to be wrong: the phases of history were ruled not by ideas but by the *material conditions* of life, and their evolution one from another came about as the ruling class of each age generated its own revolutionary overthrow.

Marx's theory, especially as it applies to the evolution of capitalism, is enormously complex; for the purposes of this unit, it can be summarized simply. According to Marx, the *ruling class* in every age is the group that *owns the means of production* of the age's product. Throughout the seventeenth century, the product was almost exclusively agricultural, and the means of production was almost exclusively agricultural land: landowners were the aristocrats and rulers. With the coming of commerce and industry, the owners of the factories joined the ruling class and eventually dominated it. It was in the nature of such capital-intensive industry to concentrate within itself more capital: as Adam Smith had proved, its greater efficiency would drive all smaller labor-intensive industry out of business, and its enormous income would be put to work as more capital, expanding the domain of the factory and the machine indefinitely (at the expense of the cottage industry and the human being). Thus would the wealth of society concentrate in fewer and fewer hands, as the owners of the factories expanded their enterprises without limit into mighty industrial empires, dominated by machines and by the greed of their owners.

Meanwhile, all this wealth was being produced by a new class of workers, the unskilled factory workers. Taken from the ranks of the obsolete peasantry, artisans, and craftsmen, this new working class, the *proletariat,* expanded in numbers with the gigantic mills, whose "hands" they were. Work on the assembly line demanded no education or skills, so the workers could never make themselves valuable enough to command a living wage on the open market. They survived as a vast underclass, interchangeable with the unemployed workers (recently displaced by more machines) who gathered around the factory gates looking for jobs—*their* jobs. As Ricardo had demonstrated, they could never bargain for any wage above the subsistence level—just enough to keep them alive. As capitalism and its factories expanded, the entire population, except the wealthy capitalist families, sank into this hopeless, pauperized class.

So Marx saw Western society under capitalism as one that ultimately would be divided into a small group of fabulously wealthy capitalists and a mass of paupers, mostly factory workers. The minority would keep the majority in strict control through its hired thugs (the state—the army and the police), control rendered easier by thought control (the schools and the churches). The purpose of the ideology taught by the schools and the churches—the value structure of capitalism—was to show both classes that the capitalists had a right to their wealth (through the sham of liberty, free enterprise, and the utilitarian benefits of the free market) and a perfect right to govern everyone else. Thus, the capitalists could enjoy their wealth in good conscience and the poor would understand their moral obligation to accept the oppression of the ruling class with good cheer.

Marx foresaw, and in his writings attempted to help bring about, the disillusionment of the workers: there would come a point when the workers would suddenly ask, *Why* should we accept oppression all our lives? Their search for answers to this question would show them the history of their situation, expose the falsehood of the ideology and the false consciousness of those who believe it, show them their own strength, and lead them directly to the solution that would usher in the new age of socialism—the revolutionary overthrow of the capitalist regime. Why, after all, should they not undertake such a revolution? People are restrained from violence against oppression only by the prospect of losing something valuable, and, as Marx concluded, the industrialized workers of the world had nothing to lose but their chains.

As feudalism had been swept away, then, by the "iron broom" of the French Revolution, so capitalism would be swept away by the revolt of the masses, the irresistible uprising of the vast majority of the people against the minority of industrial overlords and their terrified minions—the armed forces, the state, and the church. After the first rebellions, Marx foresaw no lengthy problem of divided loyalties in the industrialized countries of the world. Once the scales had fallen from their eyes, the working-class hirelings of the army and police would quickly turn their guns on their masters and join their natural allies in the proletariat to create the new world.

After the revolution, Marx predicted, there would be a temporary "dictatorship of the proletariat," during which the last vestiges of capitalism would be eradicated and the authority to run the industrial establishment would be returned to the workers of each industry. Once the economy had been decentralized, to turn each factory into an industrial commune run by its own workers and each landed estate into an agricultural commune run by its farmers, the state as such would simply wither away. Some central authority would certainly continue to exist, to coordinate and facilitate the exchange of goods within the country (one imagines a giant computer, taking note of where goods are demanded, where goods are available, and where the railroad cars to take the goods from one place to the other are). But with no ruling class to serve and no oppression to carry out, there will be no need of the state to rule *people;* what is left will be confined to the administration of *things.*

Even as he wrote, just in time for the revolutions in Europe of 1848, Marx expected the end of capitalism as a system. Not that capitalism was evil in itself; Marx did not presume to make moral judgments on history. Indeed, capitalism was necessary as an economic system to concentrate the wealth of the country into the industries of the modern age. So, in Marx's judgment, capitalism had a respectable past and would still be necessary for awhile in the developing countries to launch their industries. But that task completed, it had no further role in history, and the longer it stayed around, the more the workers would suffer and the more violent the revolution would be when it came. The sooner the revolution, the better; the future belonged to communism.

As the collapse of the communist governments in Eastern Europe demonstrates (if demonstration were needed), the course of history has not proceeded quite as Marx predicted in 1848. In fairness, it might be pointed out that no other prophets of the time had any more luck with prognostications about the twentieth century. In any case, since Marx wrote, all participants in the debate on the nature and future of capitalism have had to respond to his judgments and predictions.

Law: Recovering for Damages Sustained

Life is full of misfortune. Ordinarily, if you suffer misfortune, you must put up with it and find the resources to deal with it. If your misfortune is my fault, however, the law may step in and make me pay for those damages, one way or another.

Through *criminal law,* the public steps in and demands punishment for an offense that is serious enough to outrage public feeling and endanger public welfare. If I knock you on the head and take your wallet, the police will find me, restore your wallet to you, and imprison or otherwise punish me for the crime.

Through *civil law,* if I do you damage through some action of mine, you may take me to civil court and ask a judge (and jury) to determine whether or not I have damaged you, if so by how much, and how I should pay you back for that damage. There are a number of forms of action under which you may make your claim; the most common for business purposes are *contract* and *torts*. If you and I agree to (or "contract for") some undertaking, and I back out of it after you have relied on our agreement to commit your resources to the undertaking, you have a right to recover what you have lost. In torts, if I simply injure you in some way, hurting you in health, life, or limb, or destroying your property, I have done you a wrong (*tort*, in French), and I must pay for the damage I have done. How much I will have to pay will depend (as the jury will determine) on (1) the amount of the damage that has been caused, (2) the extent to which I knew or should have known that my action or neglect to act would cause damage (my *culpability*), and (3) the extent to which *you* contributed to the damage, beyond whatever I did (*contributory negligence*).

Another kind of suit at law alleges *negligence,* which is a tort, on the part of a company, in that it made and put up for sale a product known to be defective and that the defect injured its users. To establish negligence, civil or criminal, four elements must be demonstrated: First, there must have been a *duty*—the party accused of negligence must have had a preexisting duty to the plaintiff. Second, there must have been a *breach of,* or failure to fulfill, that duty. Third, the plaintiff must have suffered an *injury*. And fourth, the breach of the duty must have been the *proximate cause* of the injury, or the thing that actually brought the injury about. Where negligence is alleged in a product liability case, it must be established that the manufacturer had a duty to make a product that could not do certain sorts of harm, that the duty was breached and the harm was caused, that nothing else was to blame, and that the manufacturer therefore must compensate the victim for the damage done.

Should companies ultimately be responsible for any harm that comes from the use of the products they profitably market and sell? Or should consumers be content to bear the responsibility for risks that they freely accept? Our ambivalence on this question as a society mirrors, and proceeds from, the ambivalence of the individual at the two poles of materialization of risk: when we are in a hurry, short of cash, or in need of a cigarette, then risky behavior looks to us to be our right, and we are resentful of the busybodies who would always have us play it safe. But when the risk materializes—when the accident or the disease happens—the perception of that risk (and the direction of that resentment) changes drastically. From the perspective of the hospital bed, it is crystal clear that the behavior was not worth the risk, that we never realized the behavior was risky, that we should have been warned, and that it was someone's duty to warn us. In that instantaneous change of perspective, three elements of negligence come into view: duty, breach, and injury. No wonder product liability suits are so common.

Yet the suit is a relatively recent phenomenon because of a peculiarity in the law. Until the twentieth century, a judge faced with a consumer who had been injured by a product (physically or financially) applied the principle of *caveat emptor*—"let the buyer beware"—and could ask the seller to pay damages only to the original buyer, and only if the exact defect in the product could be proven. For example, a defective kerosene lamp might explode and burn five people, but the exact defect (broken seam or shoddy wick) had to be brought into court or the case would be thrown out. In addition, the buyer could sue only the seller, not the manufacturer or designer, because the right to collect damages rested on the law of *contract*, not torts, and on the warrant of merchantability implied in the contractual relationship between buyer and seller. The cause of the action was understood to be a breach in that contract.

There matters stood until 1916, when an American judge allowed a buyer to sue the manufacturer of a product. A Mr. MacPherson had been injured when his car collapsed under him due to a defect in the wood used to build one of the wheels, and MacPherson went to court against the Buick Motor Company. The judge reasoned that the action was in torts, specifically "negligence," and not in contract, for a manufacturer is under a duty to make carefully any product that could be expected to endanger life, and this duty existed irrespective of any contract. So if MacPherson, or any future user of the product, was injured because the product was badly made, he could collect damages even if he had never dealt with the manufacturer in any way.

In the 1960s the automobile was still center stage in the arguments over the duties of manufacturers. Consumer advocate Ralph Nader's book *Unsafe at Any Speed* (1966) spearheaded the consumer rights movement with its scathing attack on General Motors and its exposé of the dangerous design of the Corvair. In response to the consumer activism resulting from that movement, Congress passed the Consumer Product Safety Act in 1972 and empowered the Consumer Product Safety Commission, an independent federal agency, to set safety standards, require warning labels, and order recalls of hazardous products. When three girls died in a Ford Pinto in 1978, the foundations of consumer rights against careless manufacturers were well established. What was new in the Ford Motor Company case was the allegation of *criminal* negligence—in effect, criminal homicide.

At present, product liability suits are major uncharted reefs in the navigational plans of American business. If a number of people die in a fire in a hotel, for instance, their families will often sue not only the hotel, for culpable negligence, but the manufacturers of the furniture that burned, alleging that it should have been fire-retardant; the manufacturers of the cushions on the furniture, alleging that they gave off toxic fumes in the fire; and the manufacturers of the chemicals that went into those cushions, alleging that there was no warning to the consumers on the toxicity of those chemicals in fire conditions. The settlements that can be obtained are used to finance the suit and the law firm that is managing it for the years that it will take to exhaust all the appeals. This phenomenon of unlimited litigation is relatively new on the American scene, and we are not quite sure how to respond to it.

The Corporation

The human being is a social animal. We exist in the herd and depend for our lives on the cooperation of those around us. Who are they? Anthropologists tell us that originally we traveled in extended families, then settled down into villages of intensely interlocked groups of families. With the advent of the

modern era, we have found our identities in family, village, church, and nation. Yet, in the great transformation of the obligations of the Western world
(see Henry Maine [1822–1888], *From Status to Contract*), we have abandoned the
old family-oriented care systems and thrown ourselves upon the mercy of secondary organizations: club, corporation, and state. The French sociologist Emile
Durkheim (1858–1917), in his classic work *Suicide,* suggested that following the
collapse of the family and the church, the corporation would be the association
in the future that would supply the social support that every individual needs
to maintain a moral life.

Can the corporation do that? Or is the corporation merely the organization that implements Adam Smith's self-interested pursuit of the dollar, with no
purpose but to maximize return on investment to the investors while protecting
them from unlimited liability?

On the other hand, once formed, and having become a major community
figure and employer, does the corporation have a right to exist that transcends at
least the immediate pursuit of money? The issue of so-called hostile takeovers
sends us back to the purpose and foundation of business enterprise in America. Let us review: When an entrepreneur gets a bright idea for how to make
money, he or she secures the capital necessary to run the business from investors (venture capitalists); uses that capital to buy the land, buildings, and
machinery needed to see the project through; hires the labor needed to do the
work; and goes into production. As the income from the enterprise comes in,
the entrepreneur pays the suppliers of raw materials; pays the workers; pays
the taxes, rent, mortgages, and utility bills; keeps some of the money for him-
or herself (salary); and then divides up the rest of the income (profit) among
the investors (probably including him- or herself) in proportion to the capital
they invested. Motives of all parties are presupposed: the entrepreneur wants
money; the laborers and the landlords want money; and the investors, who are
the shareholders in the company, want money. The investors thought that this
enterprise would yield them a higher return on their capital than any other investment available to them at the time; that is why they invested. However, this
is a free country, and people can move around. If the workers see better jobs,
they will take them; if a landlord can rent for more, the lease will be termi-
nated; and if the investors see a better place to put their capital, they will move
it. The determiner of the flow of capital is the rate of return, no more and no
less. Loyalty to the company, faithfulness to the corporation for the sake of the
association itself, is not on anyone's agenda—not on the worker's, certainly not
on the landlord's, and *most* certainly not on the shareholder's.

The shareholders are represented by a board of directors elected by them
to see that the company is run efficiently; that is, that costs are kept down and
income up to yield the highest possible return. The board of directors hires
management—the cadre of corporate officers headed by the president and/or
chief executive officer to do the actual running of the company. The corporate
officers thus stand in a *fiduciary* relationship to the shareholders; that is, they
are forbidden by the understandings on which the corporation is founded to
do anything at all except that which will protect and enhance the interests of
the shareholders. That goes for all the normal business decisions made by the

management; even the decision not to break the law can be seen as a prudent estimate of the financial costs of lawbreaking.

Yet our dealings with the business world, as citizens and as consumers, have always turned on recognition and support of the huge reliable corporations in established industries; not just coal and steel, which had certain natural limitations built into their consumption of natural resources, but the automobile companies, the airlines, the consumer products companies, and even the banks. Companies had "reputations" and "integrity," and they cultivated (and bought and sold) "good will." Consumers cooperated with the companies that catered to them in developing "brand loyalty." And, most important, those working in business cooperated with their employers in developing "company loyalty," which became a part of their lives, just as loyalty to one's tribe or nation was part of the lives of their ancestors. Is the company that sought our loyalty—and got it—just a scrap of paper, to disappear as soon as return on investment falls below the nearest competition? What part do we want corporations to play in our associative lives? If we want them to be any more than profit maximizers for the investors, what sorts of protections would we have to offer them, and what sorts of limitations should we put on their extra-profit-making activities?

Current Issues

Business ethics ultimately rests on a base of political philosophy, economics, and philosophical ethics. As these underlying fields change, new topics and approaches will surface in business ethics. For example, hostile takeovers did not take place very often in the regulatory climate that existed prior to the Reagan administration. The change in political philosophy introduced by his administration resulted in new business practices, which resulted in new ethical problems. Also, the work of John Rawls, a professor of philosophy at Harvard University, profoundly influenced our understanding of distributive justice and, therefore, our understanding of acceptable economic distribution in the society. The work currently being done in postmodern philosophy will change the way we see human beings generally and, hence, the activity of business.

No single work can cover all the issues of ethical practice in business in all their range and particularity, especially since, as above, we are dealing with a moving target. Our task here is much more limited. The purpose of this book is to allow you to grapple with some of the ethical issues of current business practice in the safety of the classroom, before they come up on the job where human rights and careers are at stake and legal action looms outside the boardroom or factory door. We think that rational consideration of these issues now will help you prepare for a lifetime of the types of problems that naturally arise in a complex and pluralistic society. You will find here no dogmas, no settled solutions to memorize. These problems do not have preset answers but require that you use your mind to balance the values in conflict and to work out acceptable policies in each issue. To employ business ethics, you must learn to think critically, to look beyond short-term advantages and traditional ways of doing things, and to become an innovator. The exercise provided by these debates should help you in this learning.

There is no doubt that businesspeople think that ethics is important. Sometimes the reasons why they think ethics is important have to do only with the long-run profitability of a business enterprise. There is no doubt that greater employee honesty and diligence would improve the bottom line or that strict attention to environmental and employee health laws is necessary to protect the company from expensive lawsuits and fines. But ethics goes well beyond profitability, to the lives that we live and the persons we want to be. What the bottom line has taught us is that the working day is not apart from life. We must bring the same integrity and care to the contexts of the factory and the office that we are used to showing at home and among our friends. An imperative of business ethics is to make of your business life an opportunity to become, and remain, the person that you know you ought to be—and as far as it is within your capability, to extend that opportunity to others.

In this book, we attempt to present in good debatable form some of the issues that raise the big questions—of justice, of rights, of the common good —in order to build bridges between the workaday world of employment and the ageless world of morality. If you will enter into these dialogues with an open mind, a willingness to have it changed, and a determination to master the skills of critical thinking that will enable you to make responsible decisions in difficult situations, you may be able to help build the bridges for the new ethical issues that will emerge in the next century. At the least, that is our hope.

On the Internet ...

Business Ethics Resources on WWW

Sponsored by the Centre for Applied Ethics, this page of business ethics resources links to corporate codes of ethics, business ethics institutions and organizations, and online papers and publications, as well as other elements.

http://www.ethics.ubc.ca/resources/business/

Critical Thinking Across the Curriculum Project

This site, sponsored by Longview Community College in Lee's Summit, Missouri, links to resources in critical thinking. They are divided into the core resources and discipline-specific resources.

http://www.kcmetro.cc.mo.us/longview/ctac/toc.htm

International Business Ethics Institute

The International Business Ethics Institute offers professional services to organizations interested in implementing, expanding, or modifying business ethics and corporate responsibility programs. Its mission is to foster global business practices that promote equitable economic development, resource sustainability, and democratic forms of government.

http://www.business-ethics.org

Economic and Game Theory

This site, by David K. Levine of the University of California–Los Angeles, uses the tools of modern economic and game theory to explore how the interaction of intelligent goal-seeking individuals determines social outcomes. The site includes general interest material, original research, and a list of further readings.

http://levine.sscnet.ucla.edu

PART 1

Capitalism and Corporations in Theory and Practice

*T*he nations of the Western European tradition tend to regard business as central to their citizens' lives and the meaning of their national life. But does business always represent what we want our countries to be about? This first section initially explores business theory. Should societies choose capitalism over other economic systems? This section also explores whether or not ethics and virtue have a place in the business world.

- Classic Dialogue: Can Capitalism Lead to Human Happiness?

- Are Corporate Codes of Ethics Just for Show?

- Does Ethics Matter in Business?

- Is Game Theory Devastating to Business Ethics?

ISSUE 1

Classic Dialogue: Can Capitalism Lead to Human Happiness?

YES: Adam Smith, from *An Inquiry into the Nature and Causes of the Wealth of Nations, vols. 1 and 2* (1869)

NO: Karl Marx and Friedrich Engels, from *The Communist Manifesto* (1848)

ISSUE SUMMARY

YES: Free-market economist Adam Smith (1723–1790) states that if self-interested people are left alone to seek their own economic advantage, the result, unintended by any one of them, will be greater advantage for all. He maintains that government interference is not necessary to protect the general welfare.

NO: German philosopher Karl Marx (1818–1883) and German sociologist Friedrich Engels (1820–1895) argue that if people are left to their own self-interested devices, those who own the means of production will rapidly reduce everyone else to virtual slaves. Although the few may be fabulously happy, all others would live in misery.

The rationale of capitalism is that an unintended coordination of self-interested actions will lead to the production of the greatest welfare of the whole. The logic proceeds thusly: As a natural result of free competition in a free market, quality will improve and prices will decline without limit, thereby raising the real standard of living of every buyer; to protect themselves in competition, sellers will be forced to innovate by discovering new products and new markets, thereby raising the real wealth of the society as a whole. Products improve without limit, wealth increases without limit, and society prospers.

But how does the common man—the "least advantaged" member of society—fare under capitalism? Not very well. The most efficient factories are those that hire workers at the lowest cost. And if all industry is accomplished by essentially unskilled labor and every worker can therefore be replaced by any other, then there is no reason to pay any worker beyond the subsistence wage. Therefore, only when free competition *fails* because the economy is expanding so rapidly that it runs out of labor can the working man's wages rise in a free market. According to capitalist theory, however, such a market imbalance—too few workers and therefore "artificially" high wages—will rapidly disappear because greater prosperity allows more of the working-class babies to survive to adulthood and enter into the workforce. Eighteenth-century economists Adam Smith, Thomas Malthus, and David Ricardo all agreed that as the society as a whole approaches maximum efficiency, all except the capitalists (the owners) approach the subsistence level of survival. So most of the accumulated wealth of the nation actually ends up in the hands of the employers, who enjoy the low prices of bread themselves while saving the money they would need to spend to keep their workers alive if the bread were more expensive.

This is where Karl Marx comes in. He focused not on the making of the wealth but on how the wealth is distributed—who gets it and who gets to enjoy it when it has been generated by the capitalist process. Marx found it unreasonable for the bulk of society's wealth to be languishing in the bank accounts of the super-rich. He argued that the welfare of the nation as a whole would be vastly increased if it could be shared systematically with the workers, which would allow them to join their employers as consumers of the manufactured goods of society. Lord John Maynard Keynes would later point out that such distribution would be an enormous spur to the economy; Marx, however, was more concerned that it would be a great gain in justice.

One empirical question that surrounds the issue of social justice in a free-market society is this: If the controllers of the wealth—the capitalists—are required to share it with the workers who produced it, will they not lose motivation to put their money at risk in productive enterprises? Other questions concern entitlement (aren't those who control the capital entitled to the entire return on it?) and the relative importance of liberty and equality as political values. As you read the following selections by Adam Smith and by Marx and Friedrich Engels, keep in mind that the debate is not bound by the historical controversies of Marx and his opponents; it goes to the core of contemporary notions of entitlement and justice.

Adam Smith  **YES**

An Inquiry into the Nature and Causes of the Wealth of Nations

Of the Division of Labour

The greatest improvement in the productive powers of labour, and the greater part of the skill, dexterity, and judgment with which it is anywhere directed or applied, seem to have been the effect of the division of labour.

The effects of the division of labour, in the general business of society, will be more easily understood by considering in what manner it operates in some particular manufactures. It is commonly supposed to be carried furthest in some very trifling ones; not perhaps that it really is carried further in them than in others of more importance: but in those trifling manufactures which are destined to supply the small wants of but a small number of people, the whole number of workmen must necessarily be small; and those employed in every different branch of the work can often be collected into the same workhouse, and placed at once under the view of the spectator. In those great manufactures, on the contrary, which are destined to supply the great wants of the great body of the people, every different branch of the work employs so great a number of workmen, that it is impossible to collect them all into the same workhouse. We can seldom see more, at one time, than those employed in one single branch. Though in such manufactures, therefore, the work may really be divided into a much greater number of parts than in those of a more trifling nature, the division is not near so obvious, and has accordingly been much less observed.

To take an example, therefore, from a very trifling manufacture, but one in which the division of labour has been very often taken notice of, the trade of the pin-maker; a workman not educated to this business (which the division of labour has rendered a distinct trade), nor acquainted with the use of the machinery employed in it (to the invention of which the same division of labour has probably given occasion), could scarce, perhaps, with his utmost industry, make one pin in a day, and certainly could not make twenty. But in the way in which this business is now carried on, not only the whole work is a peculiar trade, but it is divided into a number of branches, of which the greater part are likewise peculiar trades. One man draws out the wire, another straights it,

From Adam Smith, *An Inquiry into the Nature and Causes of the Wealth of Nations*, vols. *1 and 2* (1869). Notes omitted.

a third cuts it, a fourth points it, a fifth grinds it at the top for receiving the head; to make the head requires two or three distinct operations; to put it on is a peculiar business, to whiten the pins is another; it is even a trade by itself to put them into the paper; and the important business of making a pin is, in this manner, divided into about eighteen distinct operations, which in some man-ufactories arc all performed by distinct hands, though in others the same man will sometimes perform two or three of them. I have seen a small manufactory of this kind where ten men only were employed, and where some of them con-sequently performed two or three distinct operations. But though they were very poor, and therefore but indifferently accommodated with the necessary machinery, they could, when they exerted themselves, make among them about twelve pounds of pins in a day. There are in a pound upwards of four thousand pins of a middling size. Those ten persons, therefore, could make among them upwards of forty-eight thousand pins in a day. Each person, therefore, making a tenth part of forty-eight thousand pins, might be considered as making four thousand eight hundred pins in a day. But if they had all wrought separately and independently, and without any of them having been educated to this peculiar business, they certainly could not each of them have made twenty, perhaps not one pin in a day; that is, certainly, not the two hundred and fortieth, perhaps not the four thousand eight hundredth part of what they are at present capable of performing, in consequence of a proper division and combination of their different operations. . . .

This great increase of the quantity of work, which, in consequence of the division of labour, the same number of people are capable of performing, is owning to three different circumstances: first, to the increase of dexterity in every particular workman; secondly, to the saving of the time which is com-monly lost in passing from one species of work to another; and lastly, to the invention of a great number of machines which facilitate and abridge labour, and enable one man to do the work of many. . . .

It is the great multiplication of the productions of all the different arts, in consequence of the division of labour, which occasions, in a well-governed society, that universal opulence which extends itself to the lowest ranks of the people. Every workman has a great quantity of his own work to dispose of be-yond what he himself has occasion for: and every other workman being exactly in the same situation, he is enabled to exchange a great quantity of his own goods for a great quantity, or, what comes to the same thing, for the price of a great quantity of theirs. He supplies them abundantly with what they have oc-casion for, and they accommodate him as amply with what he has occasion for, and a general plenty diffuses itself through all the different ranks of the society.

Observe the accommodation of the most common artificer or day-labourer in a civilised and thriving country, and you will perceive that the number of people of whose industry a part, though but a small part, has been employed in procuring him this accommodation exceeds all computation. The woollen coat, for example, which covers the day-labourer, as coarse and rough as it may appear, is the produce of the joint labour of a great multitude of work-men. The shepherd, the sorter of the wool, the wool-comber or carder, the dyer, the scribbler, the spinner, the weaver, the fuller, the dresser, with many others, must all join their different arts in order to complete even this homely production. How many merchants and carriers, besides, must have been employed in transporting the materials from some of those workmen to others who often live in a very distant part of the country! How much commerce and navigation in particular, how many ship-builders, sailors, sail-makers, rope-makers, must have been employed in order to bring together the different drugs made use of by the dyer, which often come from the remotest corners of the world! What a variety of labour too is necessary in order to produce the tools of the meanest of those workmen! To say nothing of such complicated machines as the ship of the sailor, the mill of the fuller, or even the loom of the weaver, let us consider only what a variety of labour is requisite in order to form that very simple machine, the shears with which the shepherd clips the wool. The miner, the builder of the furnace for smelting the ore, the feller of the timber, the burner of the charcoal to be made use of in the smelting-house, the brickmaker, the bricklayer, the workmen who attend the furnace, the mill-wright, the forger, the smith, must all of them join their different arts in order to produce them. Were we to examine, in the same manner, all the different parts of his dress and household furniture, the coarse linen shirt which he wears next his skin, the shoes which cover his feet, the bed which he lies on, and all the different parts which compose it, the kitchen-grate at which he prepares his victuals, the coals which he makes use of for that purpose, dug from the bowels of the earth, and brought to him perhaps by a long sea and a long land carriage, all the other utensils of his kitchen, all the furniture of his table, the knives and forks, the earthen or pewter plates upon which he serves up and divides his victuals, the different hands employed in preparing his bread and his beer, the glass window which lets in the heat and the light and keeps out the wind and the rain, with all the knowledge and art requisite for preparing that beautiful and happy invention, without which these northern parts of the world could scarce have afforded a very comfortable habitation, together with the tools of all the different workmen employed in producing those different conveniences; if we examine, I say, all these things, and consider what a variety of labour is employed about each of them, we shall be sensible that without the assistance and co-operation of many thousands, the very meanest person in a civilised country could not be provided, even according to, what we very falsely imagine, the easy and simple manner in which he is commonly accommodated. Compared, indeed, with the more extravagant luxury of the great, his accommodation must no doubt appear extremely simple and easy; and yet it may be true, perhaps, that the accommodation of an European prince does not always so much exceed that of an industrious and frugal peasant, as the accommodation of the latter exceeds that of many an African king, the absolute master of the lives and liberties of ten thousand naked savages.

Of the Principle Which Gives Occasion to the Division of Labour

This division of labour, from which so many advantages are derived, is not originally the effect of any human wisdom, which foresees and intends that general opulence to which it gives occasion. It is the necessary, though very slow and gradual consequence of a certain propensity in human nature which has in view no such extensive utility; the propensity to truck, barter, and exchange one thing for another.

Whether this propensity be one of those original principles in human nature, of which no further account can be given; or whether, as seems more probable, it be the necessary consequence of the faculties of reason and speech, it belongs not to our present subject to inquire. It is common to all men, and to be found in no other race of animals, which seem to know neither this nor any other species of contracts.... But man has almost constant occasion for the help of his brethren, and it is in vain for him to expect it from their benevolence only. He will be more likely to prevail if he can interest their self-love in his favour, and show them that it is for their own advantage to do for him what he requires of them. Whoever offers to another a bargain of any kind, proposes to do this. Give me that which I want, and you shall have this which you want, is the meaning of every such offer; and it is in this manner that we obtain from one another the far greater part of those good offices which we stand in need of. It is not from the benevolence of the butcher, the brewer, or the baker, that we expect our dinner, but from their regard to their own interest. We address ourselves, not to their humanity but to their self-love, and never talk to them of our own necessities but of their advantages. Nobody but a beggar chooses to depend chiefly upon the benevolence of his fellow-citizens. Even a beggar does not depend upon it entirely. The charity of well-disposed people, indeed, supplies him with the whole fund of his subsistence. But though this principle ultimately provides him with all the necessaries of life which he has occasion for, it neither does nor can provide him with them as he has occasion for them. The greater part of his occasional wants are supplied in the same manner as those of other people, by treaty, by barter, and by purchase. With the money which one man gives him he purchases food. The old clothes which another bestows upon him he exchanges for other old clothes which suit him better, or for lodging, or for food, or for money, with which he can buy either food, clothes, or lodging, as he has occasion.

... Each animal is still obliged to support and defend itself, separately and independently, and derives no sort of advantage from that variety of talents with which nature has distinguished its fellows. Among men, on the contrary, the most dissimilar geniuses are of use to one another; the different produces of their respective talents, by the general disposition to truck, barter, and exchange, being brought, as it were, into a common stock, where every man may purchase whatever part of the produce of other men's talents he has occasion for....

Of Restraints Upon the Importation from Foreign Countries of Such Goods as Can Be Produced at Home

... The general industry of the society never can exceed what the capital of the society can employ. As the number of workmen that can be kept in employment by any particular person must bear a certain proportion to his capital, so the number of those that can be continually employed by all the members of a great society, must bear a certain proportion to the whole capital of that society, and never can exceed that proportion. No regulation of commerce can increase the quantity of industry in any society beyond what its capital can maintain. It can only divert a part of it into a direction into which it might not otherwise have gone; and it is by no means certain that this artificial direction is likely to be more advantageous to the society than that into which it would have gone of its own accord.

Every individual is continually exerting himself to find out the most advantageous employment for whatever capital he can demand. It is his own advantage, indeed, and not that of the society, which he has in view. But the study of his own advantage naturally, or rather necessarily, leads him to prefer that employment which is most advantageous to the society.

First, every individual endeavours to employ his capital as near home as he can, and consequently as much as he can in the support of domestic industry; provided always that he can thereby obtain the ordinary, or not a great deal less than the ordinary, profits of stock.

Thus, upon equal or nearly equal profits, every wholesale merchant naturally prefers the home trade to the foreign trade of consumption, and the foreign trade of consumption to the carrying trade. In the home trade his capital is never so long out of his sight as it frequently is in the foreign trade of consumption. He can know better the character and situation of the persons whom he trusts, and, if he should happen to be deceived, he knows better the laws of the country from which he must seek redress. In the carrying trade, the capital of the merchant is, as it were, divided between two foreign countries, and no part of it is ever necessarily brought home, or placed under his own immediate view and command. The capital which an Amsterdam merchant employs in carrying corn from Konigsberg to Lisbon, and fruit and wine from Lisbon to Konigsberg, must generally be the one half of it at Konigsberg and the other half at Lisbon. No part of it need ever come to Amsterdam. The natural residence of such a merchant should either be at Konigsberg or Lisbon, and it can only be some very particular circumstance which can make him prefer the residence of Amsterdam. The uneasiness, however, which he feels at being separated so far from his capital, generally determines him to bring part both of the Konigsberg goods which he destines for the market of Lisbon, and of the Lisbon goods which he destines for that of Konigsberg, to Amsterdam; and though this necessarily subjects him to a double charge of loading and unloading, as well as to the payment of some duties and customs, yet for the sake of having some part of his capital always under his own view and command, he willingly submits to this extraordinary charge; and it is in this manner that every country which has any considerable share of the carrying trade, becomes always the emporium, or general market, for the goods of all the different countries whose trade it carries on. The merchant, in order to save a second loading and unloading, endeavours always to sell in the home market as much of the goods of all those different countries as he can, and thus, so far as he can, to convert his carrying trade into a foreign trade of consumption. A merchant, in the same manner, who is engaged in the foreign trade of consumption, when he collects goods for foreign markets, will always be glad, upon equal or nearly equal profits, to sell as great a part of them at home as he can. He saves himself the risk and trouble of exportation, when, so far as he can, he thus converts his foreign trade of consumption into a home trade. Home is in this manner the centre, if I may say so, round which the capitals of the inhabitants of every country are continually circulating, and towards which they are always tending, though by particular causes they may sometimes be driven off and repelled from it towards more distant employments. But a capital employed in the home trade, it has already been shown, necessarily puts into motion a greater quantity of domestic industry, and gives revenue and employment to a greater number of the inhabitants of the country, than an equal capital employed in the foreign trade of consumption; and one employed in the foreign trade of consumption has the same advantage over an equal capital employed in the carrying trade. Upon equal, or only nearly equal profits, therefore, every individual naturally inclines to employ his capital in the manner in which it is likely to afford the greatest support to domestic industry, and to give revenue and employment to the greatest number of people of his own country.

Secondly, every individual who employs his capital in the support of domestic industry, necessarily endeavours so to direct that industry, that its produce may be of the greatest possible value.

The produce of industry is what it adds to the subject or materials upon which it is employed. In proportion as the value of this produce is great or small, so will likewise be the profits of the employer. But it is only for the sake of profit that any man employs a capital in the support of industry; and he will always, therefore, endeavour to employ it in the support of that industry of which the produce is likely to be of the greatest value, or to exchange for the greatest quantity either of money or of other goods.

But the annual revenue of every society is always precisely equal to the exchangeable value of the whole annual produce of its industry, or rather is precisely the same thing with that exchangeable value. As every individual, therefore, endeavours as much as he can both to employ his capital in the support of domestic industry, and so to direct that industry that its produce may be of the greatest value, every individual necessarily labours to render the annual revenue of the society as great as he can. He generally, indeed, neither intends to promote the public interest, nor knows how much he is promoting it. By preferring the support of domestic to that of foreign industry, he intends only his own security; and by directing that industry in such a manner as its produce may be of the greatest value, he intends only his own gain, and he is in this, as in many other cases, led by an invisible hand to promote an end which was no part of his intention. Nor is it always the worse for the society that it was no part of it. By pursuing his own interest he frequently promotes that of the society more effectually than when he really intends to promote it. I have never known much good done by those who affected to trade for the public good. It is an affectation, indeed, not very common among merchants, and very few words need be employed in dissuading them from it.

What is the species of domestic industry which his capital can employ, and of which the produce is likely to be of the greatest value, every individual, it is evident, can, in his local situation, judge much better than any statesman or lawgiver can do for him. The statesman, who should attempt to direct private people in what manner they ought to employ their capitals, would not only load himself with a most unnecessary attention, but assume an authority which could safely be trusted, not only to no single person, but to no council or senate whatever, and which would nowhere be so dangerous as in the hands of a man who had folly and presumption enough to fancy himself fit to exercise it.

To give the monopoly of the home market to the produce of domestic industry, in any particular art or manufacture, is in some measure to direct private people in what manner they ought to employ their capitals, and must, in almost all cases, be either a useless or a hurtful regulation. If the produce of domestic can be brought there as cheap as that of foreign industry, the regulation is evidently useless. If it cannot, it must generally be hurtful. It is the maxim of every prudent master of a family, never to attempt to make at home what it will cost him more to make than to buy. The tailor does not attempt to make his own shoes, but buys them of the shoemaker. The shoemaker does not attempt to make his own clothes, but employs a tailor. The farmer attempts to make neither the one nor the other, but employs those different artificers. All of them find it for their interest to employ their whole industry in a way in which they have some advantage over their neighbours, and to purchase with a part of its produce, or, what is the same thing, with the price of a part of it, whatever else they have occasion for.

What is prudence in the conduct of every private family, can scarce be folly in that of a great kingdom. If a foreign country can supply us with a commodity cheaper than we ourselves can make it, better buy it of them with some part of the produce of our own industry, employed in a way in which we have some advantage. The general industry of the country, being always in proportion to the capital which employs it, will not thereby be diminished, no more than that of the above-mentioned artificers, but only left to find out the way in which it can be employed with the greatest advantage. It is certainly not employed to the greatest advantage, when it is thus directed towards an object which it can buy cheaper than it can make. The value of its annual produce is certainly more or less diminished, when it is thus turned away from producing commodities evidently of more value than the commodity which it is directed to produce. According to the supposition, that commodity could be purchased from foreign countries cheaper than it can be made at home. It could, therefore, have been purchased with a part only of the commodities, or, what is the same thing, with a part only of the price of the commodities, which the industry employed by an equal capital would have produced at home, had it been left to follow its natural course. The industry of the country, therefore, is thus turned away from a more to a less advantageous employment, and the exchangeable value of its annual produce, instead of being increased, according to the intention of the lawgiver, must necessarily be diminished by every such regulation.

By means of such regulations, indeed, a particular manufacture may sometimes be acquired sooner than it could have been otherwise, and after a certain time may be made at home as cheap or cheaper than in the foreign country. But though the industry of the society may be thus carried with advantage into a particular channel sooner than it could have been otherwise, it will by no means follow that the sum total, either of its industry or of its revenue, can ever be augmented by any such regulation. The industry of the society can augment only in proportion as its capital augments, and its capital can augment only in proportion to what can be gradually saved out of its revenue. But the immediate effect of every such regulation is to diminish its revenue, and what diminishes its revenue is certainly not very likely to augment its capital faster than it would have augmented of its own accord, had both capital and industry been left to find out their natural employments.

Though for want of such regulations the society should never acquire the proposed manufacture, it would not, upon that account, necessarily be the poorer in any one period of its duration. In every period of its duration its whole capital and industry might still have been employed, though upon different objects, in the manner that was most advantageous at the time. In every period its revenue might have been the greatest which its capital could afford, and both capital and revenue might have been augmented with the greatest possible rapidity.

The natural advantages which one country has over another in producing particular commodities are sometimes so great, that it is acknowledged by all the world to be in vain to struggle with them. By means of glasses, hot-beds, and hot-walls, very good grapes can be raised in Scotland, and very good wine too can be made of them, at about thirty times the expense for which at least equally good can be brought from foreign countries. Would it be a reasonable law to prohibit the importation of all foreign wines, merely to encourage the making of claret and burgundy in Scotland? But if there would be a manifest absurdity in turning towards any employment thirty times more of the capital and industry of the country than would be necessary to purchase from foreign countries an equal quantity of the commodities wanted, there must be an absurdity, though not altogether so glaring, yet exactly of the same kind, in turning towards any such employment a thirtieth or even a three-hundredth part more of either. Whether the advantages which one country has over another be natural or acquired, is in this respect of no consequence. As long as the one country has those advantages and the other wants them, it will always be more advantageous for the latter rather to buy of the former than to make. It is an acquired advantage only which one artificer has over his neighbour who exercises another trade; and yet they both find it more advantageous to buy of one another than to make what does not belong to their particular trades.

Manifesto of the Communist Party

Aspectre is haunting Europe—the spectre of Communism. All the powers of old Europe have entered into a holy alliance to exorcise this spectre; Pope and Czar, Metternich and Guizot, French Radicals and German police-spies.

Where is the party in opposition that has not been decried as communistic by its opponents in power? Where the opposition that has not hurled back the branding reproach of Communism, against the more advanced opposition parties, as well as against its reactionary adversaries?

Two things result from this fact.

I. Communism is already acknowledged by all European Powers to be itself a Power.

II. It is high time that Communists should openly, in the face of the whole world, publish their views, their aims, their tendencies, and meet this nursery tale of the Spectre of Communism with a Manifesto of the party itself.

To this end, Communists of various nationalities have assembled in London, and sketched the following manifesto, to be published in the English, French, German, Italian, Flemish and Danish languages.

Bourgeois and Proletarians

The history of all hitherto existing society is the history of class struggles.

Freeman and slave, patrician and plebeian, lord and serf, guild-master and journeyman, in a word; oppressor and oppressed, stood in constant opposition to one another, carried on an uninterrupted, now hidden, now open fight, a fight that each time ended, either in a revolutionary re-constitution of society at large, or in the common ruin of the contending classes.

In the early epochs of history, we find almost everywhere a complicated arrangement of society into various orders, a manifold graduation of social rank. In ancient Rome we have patricians, knights, plebeians, slaves; in the Middle Ages, feudal lords, vassals, guild-masters, journeymen, apprentices, serfs; in almost all of these classes, again, subordinate gradations.

The modern bourgeois society that has sprouted from the ruins of feudal society, has not done away with class antagonisms. It has but established new

From Karl Marx and Friedrich Engels, *The Communist Manifesto* (1848).

classes, new conditions of oppression, new forms of struggle in place of the old ones.

Our epoch, the epoch of the bourgeoisie, possesses, however, this distinctive feature; it has simplified the class antagonisms. Society as a whole is more and more splitting up into two great hostile camps, into two great classes directly facing each other: Bourgeoisie and Proletariat.

From the serfs of the Middle Ages sprang the chartered burghers of the earliest towns. From this burgesses the first elements of the bourgeoisie were developed.

The discovery of America, the rounding of the Cape, opened up fresh ground for the rising bourgeoisie. The East-Indian and Chinese markets, the colonization of America, trade with the colonies, the increase in the means of exchange in commodities, generally, gave to commerce, to navigation, to industry, an impulse never before known, and thereby, to the revolutionary element in the tottering feudal society, a rapid development.

The feudal system of industry, under which industrial production was monopolized by closed guilds, now no longer sufficed for the growing wants of the new markets. The manufacturing system took its place. The guild-masters were pushed on one side by the manufacturing middle-class; division of labor between the different corporate guilds vanished in the face of division of labor in each single workshop.

Meantime the markets kept ever growing, the demand, ever rising. Even manufacturing no longer sufficed. Thereupon, steam and machinery revolutionized industrial production. The place of manufacture was taken by the giant, Modern Industry, the place of the industrial middle-class, by industrial millionaires, the leaders of whole industrial armies, the modern bourgeoisie.

Modern Industry has established the world-market, for which the discovery of America paved the way. This market has given an immense development to commerce, to navigation, to communication by land. This development has, in its turn, reacted on the extension of industry; and in proportion as industry, commerce, navigation, railways extended in the same proportion the bourgeoisie developed, increased its capital, and pushed into the background every class handed down from the Middle Ages.

We see, therefore, how the modern bourgeoisie is itself the product of a long course of development, of a series of revolutions in the modes of production and of exchange.

Each step in the development of the bourgeoisie was accompanied by a corresponding political advance of that class. An oppressed class under the sway of the feudal nobility, an armed and self-governing association in the medieval commune, here independent urban republic (as in Italy and Germany), there taxable "third estate" of the monarchy (as in France), afterwards, in the period of manufacturing proper, serving either the semi-feudal or the absolute monarchy as a counterpoise against the nobility, and in fact, cornerstone of the great monarchies in general, the bourgeoisie has at last, since the establishment of Modern Industry and of the world-market, conquered for itself, in a modern representative State, exclusive political sway. The executive of the modern State is but a committee for managing the common affairs of the whole bourgeoisie.

The bourgeoisie, historically, has played a most revolutionary part.

The bourgeoisie, wherever it has got the upper hand, has put an end to all feudal, patriarchal, idyllic relations. It has pitilessly torn asunder the motley feudal ties that bound man to his "natural superiors," and has left remaining no other nexus between man and man than naked self-interest, than callous "cash payment." It has drowned the most heavenly ecstasies of religious fervor, of chivalrous enthusiasm, of philistine sentimentalism, in the icy water of egotistical calculation. It has resolved personal worth into exchange value, and in place of the numberless indefeasible chartered freedoms, has set up that single, unconscionable freedom—Free Trade. In one word, for exploitation, veiled by religious and political illusions, it has substituted naked, shameless, direct, brutal exploitation.

The bourgeoisie has stripped of its halo every occupation hitherto honored and looked up to with reverent awe. It has converted the physician, the lawyer, the priest, the poet, the man of science, into its paid wage-laborers.

The bourgeoisie has torn away from the family its sentimental veil, and has reduced the family relation to a mere money relation.

The bourgeoisie has disclosed how it came to pass that the brutal display of vigor in the Middle Ages, which Reactionists so much admire, found its fitting complement in the most slothful indolence. It has been the first to show what man's activity can bring about. It has accomplished wonders far surpassing Egyptian pyramids, Roman aqueducts, and Gothic cathedrals; it has conducted expeditions that put in the shade all former Exoduses of nations and crusades.

The bourgeoisie cannot exist without constantly revolutionizing the instruments of production, and thereby the relations of production, and with them the whole relations of society. Conservation of the old modes of production in unaltered form, was, on the contrary, the first condition of existence for all earlier industrial classes. Constant revolutionizing of production, uninterrupted disturbance of all social conditions, everlasting uncertainty and agitation distinguish the bourgeois epoch from all earlier ones. All fixed, fast-frozen relations, with their train of ancient and venerable prejudices and opinions, are swept away, all newly-formed ones become antiquated before they can ossify. All that is solid melts into air, all that is holy is profaned, and man is at last compelled to face with sober senses, his real conditions of life, and his relations with his kind.

The need of a constantly expanding market for its products chases the bourgeoisie over the whole surface of the globe. It must nestle everywhere, settle everywhere, establish connections everywhere.

The bourgeoisie has through its exploitation of the world-market given a cosmopolitan character to production and consumption in every country. To the great chagrin of Reactionists, it has drawn from under the feet of industry the national ground on which it stood. All old-established national industries have been destroyed or are daily being destroyed. They are dislodged by new industries, whose introduction becomes a life and death question for all civilized nations, by industries that no longer work up indigenous raw material, but raw material drawn from the remotest zones; industries whose products are consumed, not only at home, but in every quarter of the globe. In place of the old wants, satisfied by the productions of the country, we find new wants, requiring for their satisfaction the products of distant lands and climes. In place of the old local and national seclusion and self-sufficiency, we have intercourse in every direction, universal inter-dependence of nations. And as in material, so also in intellectual production. The intellectual creations of individual nations become common property. National one-sidedness and narrow-mindedness become more and more impossible, and from the numerous national and local literatures there arises a world-literature.

The bourgeoisie, by the rapid improvement of all instruments of production, by the immensely facilitated means of communication, draws all, even the most barbarian, nations into civilization. The cheap prices of its commodities are the heavy artillery with which it batters down all Chinese walls, with which it forces the barbarians' intensely obstinate hatred of foreigners to capitulate. It compels all nations, on pain of extinction, to adopt the bourgeois mode of production; it compels them to introduce what it calls civilization into their midst, i.e., to become bourgeois themselves. In a word, it creates a world after its own image.

The bourgeoisie has subjected the country to the rule of the towns. It has created enormous cities, has greatly increased the urban population as compared with the rural, and has thus rescued a considerable part of the population from the idiocy of rural life. Just as it has made the country dependent on the towns, so it has made barbarian and semibarbarian countries dependent on the civilized ones, nations of peasants on nations of bourgeois, the East on the West.

The bourgeoisie keeps more and more doing away with the scattered state of the population, of the means of production, and of property. It has agglomerated population, centralized means of production, and has concentrated property in a few hands. The necessary consequence of this was political centralization. Independent, or but loosely connected provinces, with separate interests, laws, governments and systems of taxation, became lumped together in one nation, with one government, one code of laws, one national class-interest, one frontier and one customs-tariff.

The bourgeoisie, during its rule of scarce one hundred years, has created more massive and more colossal productive forces than have all preceding generations together. Subjection of Nature's forces to man, machinery, application of chemistry to industry and agriculture, steam-navigation, railways, electric telegraphs, clearing of whole continents for cultivation, canalization of rivers, whole populations conjured out of the ground—what earlier century had even a presentiment that such productive forces slumbered in the lap of social labor?

We see then: the means of production and of exchange on whose foundations the bourgeoisie built itself up, were generated in feudal society. At a certain stage in the development of these means of production and of exchange, the conditions under which feudal society produced and exchanged, the feudal organization of agriculture and manufacturing industry, in one word, the feudal relations of property became no longer compatible with the already developed productive forces; they became so many fetters. They had to be burst asunder; they were burst asunder.

Into their places stepped free competition, accompanied by a social and political constitution adapted to it, and by the economical and political sway of the bourgeois class.

A similar movement is going on before our own eyes. Modern bourgeois society with its relations of production, of exchange and of property, a society that has conjured up such gigantic means of production and of exchange, is like the sorcerer, who is no longer able to control the powers of the nether world whom he has called up by his spells. For many a decade past the history of industry and commerce is but the history of the revolt of modern productive forces against modern conditions of production, against the property relations that are the condition for the existence of the bourgeoisie and of its rule. It is enough to mention the commercial crises that by their periodical return put on trial, each time more threateningly, the existence of the entire bourgeois society. In these crises a great part not only of the existing products, but also of the previously created productive forces, are periodically destroyed. In these crises there breaks out an epidemic that, in all earlier epochs, would have seemed an absurdity—the epidemic of overproduction. Society suddenly finds itself put back into a state of momentary barbarism; it appears as if a famine, a universal war of devastation had cut off the supply of every means of subsistence; industry and commerce seem to be destroyed; and why? Because there is too much civilization, too much means of subsistence, too much industry, too much commerce. The productive forces at the disposal of society no longer tend to further the development of the conditions of bourgeois property; on the contrary, they have become too powerful for these conditions, by which they are fettered, and so soon as they overcome these fetters, they bring disorder into the whole of bourgeois society, endangering the existence of bourgeois property. The conditions of bourgeois society are too narrow to comprise the wealth created by them. And how does the bourgeoisie get over these crises? On the one hand by enforced destruction of a mass of productive forces; on the other, by the conquest of new markets, and by the more thorough exploitation of the old ones. That is to say, by paving the way for more extensive and more destructive crises, and by diminishing the means whereby crises are prevented.

The weapons with which the bourgeoisie felled feudalism to the ground are now turned against the bourgeoisie itself.

But not only has the bourgeoisie forged the weapons that bring death to itself; it has also called into existence the men who are to wield those weapons —the modern working-class—the proletarians.

In proportion as the bourgeoisie, i.e., capital, is developed, in the same proportion is the proletariat, the modern working-class, developed, a class of laborers, who live only so long as they find work, and who find work only so long as their labor increases capital. These laborers, who must sell themselves piecemeal, are a commodity, like every other article of commerce, and are consequently exposed to all the vicissitudes of competition, to all the fluctuations of the market.

Owing to the extensive use of machinery and to division of labor, the work of the proletarians has lost all individual character, and, consequently, all charm for the workman. He becomes an appendage of the machine, and it is only the most simple, most monotonous, and most easily acquired knack that is required of him. Hence, the cost of production of a workman is restricted, almost entirely, to the means of subsistence that he requires for his maintenance, and for the propagation of his race. But the price of a commodity, and also of labor, is equal to its cost of production. In proportion, therefore, as the repulsiveness of the work increases, the wage decreases. Nay more, in proportion as the use of machinery and division of labor increases, in the same proportion the burden of toil also increases, whether by prolongation of the working hours, by increase of the work enacted in a given time, or by increased speed of the machinery, etc.

Modern Industry has converted the little workshop of the patriarchal master into the great factory of the industrial capitalist. Masses of laborers, crowded into the factory, are organized like soldiers. As privates of the industrial army they are placed under the command of a perfect hierarchy of officers and sergeants. Not only are they the slaves of the bourgeois class, and of the bourgeois State, they are daily and hourly enslaved by the machine, by the over-looker, and, above all, by the individual bourgeois manufacturer himself. The more openly this despotism proclaims gain to be its end and aim, the more petty, the more hateful and the more embittering it is.

The less the skill and exertion or strength implied in manual labor, in other words, the more modern industry becomes developed, the more is the labor of men superseded by that of women. Differences of age and sex have no longer any distinctive social validity for the working class. All are instruments of labor, more or less expensive to use, according to their age and sex.

No sooner is the exploitation of the laborer by the manufacturer so far at an end, that he receives his wages in cash, than he is set upon by the other portions of the bourgeoisie, the landlord, the shopkeeper, the pawnbroker, etc.

The low strata of the middle class—the small trades-people, shopkeepers, and retired tradesmen generally, the handicraftsmen and peasants—all these sink gradually into the proletariat, partly because their diminutive capital does not suffice for the scale on which Modern Industry is carried on, and is swamped in the competition with the large capitalists, partly because their specialized skill is rendered worthless by new methods of production. Thus the proletariat is recruited from all classes of the population.

The proletariat goes through various stages of development. With its birth begins its struggle with the bourgeoisie. At first the contest is carried on by individual laborers, then by the workpeople of a factory, then by the operatives of one trade, in one locality, against the individual bourgeois who directly exploits them. They direct their attacks not against the bourgeois conditions of production, but against the instruments of production themselves; they destroy imported wares that compete with their labor, they smash to pieces machinery, they set factories ablaze, they seek to restore by force the vanished status of the workman of the Middle Ages.

At this stage the laborers still form an incoherent mass scattered over the whole country, and broken up by their mutual competition. If anywhere they unite to form more compact bodies, this is not yet the consequence of their own active union, but of the union of bourgeoisie, which class, in order to attain its own political ends, is compelled to set the whole proletariat in motion, and is moreover yet, for a time, able to do so. At this stage, therefore, the proletarians do not fight their enemies, but the enemies of their enemies, the remnants of absolute monarchy, the landowners, the non-industrial bourgeoisie, the petty bourgeoisie. Thus the whole historical movement is concentrated in the hands of the bourgeoisie; every victory so obtained is a victory for the bourgeoisie.

But with the development of industry the proletariat not only increases in number, it becomes concentrated in great masses, its strength grows, and it feels that strength more. The various interests and conditions of life within the ranks of the proletariat are more and more equalized, in proportion as machinery obliterates all distinction of labor, and nearly everywhere reduces wages to the same low level. The growing competition among the bourgeoisie, and the resulting commercial crises, make the wages of the worker ever more fluctuating. The unceasing improvement of machinery, ever more rapidly developing, makes their livelihood more and more precarious, the collisions between individual workmen and individual bourgeois take more and more the character of collision between two classes. Thereupon the workers begin to form combinations (Trades Unions) against the bourgeoisie; they club together in order to keep up the rate of wages; they found permanent associations in order to make provision beforehand for these occasional revolts. Here and there the contest breaks out into riots.

Now and then the workers are victorious, but only for a time. The real fruits of their battles lie, not in the immediate result, but in the ever expanding union of the workers. This union is helped on by the improved means of communication that are created by modern industry, and that place the workers of different localities in contact with one another. It was just this contact that was needed to centralize the numerous local struggles, all of the same character, into one national struggle between classes. But every class struggle is a political struggle. And that union, to attain which the burghers of the Middle Ages, with their miserable highways, required centuries, the modern proletarians, thanks to railways, achieve in a few years.

This organization of the proletarians into a class, and consequently into a political party, is continually being upset again by the competition between the workers themselves. But it ever rises up again, stronger, firmer, mightier. It compels legislative recognition of particular interests of the workers, by taking advantage of the divisions among the bourgeoisie itself. Thus the ten-hour bill in England was carried.

Altogether collisions between the classes of the old society further, in many ways, the course of development of the proletariat. The bourgeoisie finds itself involved in a constant battle. At first with the aristocracy; later on, with those portions of the bourgeoisie itself, whose interests have become antagonistic to the progress of industry; at all times, with the bourgeoisie of foreign countries. In all these battles it sees itself compelled to appeal to the proletariat, to ask for its help, and thus, to drag it into the political arena. The bourgeoisie itself, therefore, supplies the proletariat with its own elements of political and general education, in other words, it furnishes the proletariat with weapons for fighting the bourgeoisie.

Further, as we have already seen, entire sections of the ruling classes are, by the advance of industry, precipitated into the proletariat, or are at least threatened in their conditions of existence. These also supply the proletariat with fresh elements of enlightenment and progress.

Finally, in times when the class-struggle nears the decisive hour, the process of dissolution going on within the ruling class, in fact, within the whole range of old society, assumes such a violent, glaring character, that a small section of the ruling class cuts itself adrift, and joins the revolutionary class, the class that holds the future in its hands. Just as, therefore, at an earlier period, a section of the nobility went over to the bourgeoisie, so now a portion of the bourgeoisie goes over to the proletariat, and in particular, a portion of the bourgeois ideologists, who have raised themselves to the level of comprehending theoretically the historical movements as a whole.

Of all the classes that stand face to face with the bourgeoisie today, the proletariat alone is a really revolutionary class. The other classes decay and finally disappear in the face of Modern Industry; the proletariat is its special and essential product. . . .

In the conditions of the proletariat, those of old society at large are already virtually swamped. The proletarian is without property; his relation to his wife and children has no longer anything in common with the bourgeois family-relations; modern industrial labor, modern subjugation to capital, the same in England as in France, in America as in Germany, has stripped him of every trace of national character. Law, morality, religion, are to him so many bourgeois prejudices, behind which lurk in ambush just as many bourgeois interests.

All the preceding classes that got the upper hand, sought to fortify their already acquired status by subjecting society at large to their conditions of appropriation. The proletarians cannot become masters of the productive forces of society, except by abolishing their own previous mode of appropriation, and thereby also every other previous mode of appropriation. They have nothing of their own to secure and to fortify; their mission is to destroy all previous securities for, and insurances of, individual property.

All previous historical movements were movements of minorities, or in the interests of minorities. The proletarian movement is the self-conscious, independent movement of the immense majority, in the interest of the immense majority. The proletariat, the lowest stratum of our present society, cannot stir, cannot raise itself up, without the whole superincumbent strata of official society being sprung into the air.

Though not in substance, yet in form, the struggle of the proletariat with the bourgeoisie is at first a national struggle. The proletariat of each country must, of course, first of all settle matters with its own bourgeoisie.

In depicting the most general phases of the development of the proletariat, we traced the more or less veiled civil war, raging within existing society, up to the point where that war breaks out into open revolution, and where the violent overthrow of the bourgeoisie lays the foundation for the sway of the proletariat.

Hitherto, every form of society has been based, as we have already seen, on the antagonism of oppressing and oppressed classes. But in order to oppress a class, certain conditions must be assured to it under which it can, at least, continue its slavish existence. The serf, in the period of serfdom, raised himself to membership in the commune, just as the petty bourgeois, under the yoke of feudal absolutism, managed to develop into a bourgeois.

The modern laborer, on the contrary, instead of rising with the progress of industry, sinks deeper and deeper below the conditions of existence of his own class. He becomes a pauper, and pauperism develops more rapidly than population and wealth. And here it becomes evident that the bourgeoisie is unfit any longer to be the ruling class in society, and to impose its conditions of existence upon society as an over-riding law. It is unfit to rule, because it is incompetent to assure an existence to its slave within his slavery, because it cannot help letting him sink into such a state that it has to feed him, instead of being fed by him. Society can no longer live under this bourgeoisie, in other words, its existence is no longer compatible with society.

The essential condition for the existence, and for the sway of the bourgeois class, is the formation and augmentation of capital; the condition for capital is wage-labor. Wage-labor rests exclusively on competition between the laborers. The advance of industry, whose involuntary promoter is the bourgeoisie, replaces the isolation of the laborers, due to competition, by their revolutionary combination, due to association. The development of Modern Industry, therefore, cuts from under its feet the very foundation on which the bourgeoisie produces and appropriates products. What the bourgeoisie therefore produces, above all, are its own grave-diggers. Its fall and the victory of the proletariat are equally inevitable.

POSTSCRIPT

Classic Dialogue: Can Capitalism Lead to Human Happiness?

As a society, Americans have always prized liberty over equality. The attitude within the United States seems to be that the wealth of the society as a whole is the only legitimate goal of economic enterprise and that distribution for the sake of equity or charity is a side issue best left to churches and private charities. Americans have resisted attempts to socialize such basic needs as medicine, communications (e.g., the telephone companies), and economic security for the old, young, and infirm. In promoting capitalism, economists point to the failures of socialism in England and Sweden, and they cite the fall of communism in Eastern Europe and Russia.

The United States has built some safety nets: Social Security, Medicare and Medicaid, Aid to Dependent Children, and the like. But these and other elements of the welfare system have become a major political issue. People in the welfare system complain about its failure to provide adequately for those who need the most—babies and the infirm elderly, for example. Meanwhile, conservative members of Congress argue that welfare subsidies are costing the taxpayers too much. Can it be said that capitalism is "working" for people on welfare?

What about the "invisible hand" of Smith's free market; is it operating in the United States? Does America have true capitalism?

The last two decades of economic reform have seen the richest people in America absorbing more and more of the wealth and income while the poorest people have been becoming poorer. Should society strive to redistribute the productive assets of the country?

Suggested Readings

"The Search for Keynes: Was He a Keynesian?" *The Economist* (December 26, 1992).

John D. Bishop, "Adam Smith's Invisible Hand Argument," *Journal of Business Ethics* (March 1995), pp. 165–180.

Keith Bradsher, "As U.S. Urges Free Markets, Its Trade Barriers Are Many," *The New York Times* (February 7, 1992), p. A1.

Richard John Neuhaus, "The Pope Affirms the 'New Capitalism,'" *The Wall Street Journal* (May 2, 1991).

David Schweickart, *Against Capitalism,* rev. ed. (Cambridge University Press, 1993).

Adam Smith, *The Wealth of Nations* (Clarendon Press, 1976).

ISSUE 2

Are Corporate Codes of Ethics Just for Show?

YES: LaRue Tone Hosmer, from *The Ethics of Management* (Irwin Press, 1987)

NO: Lisa H. Newton, from "The Many Faces of the Corporate Code," in *The Corporate Code of Ethics: The Perspective of the Humanities*, Proceedings of the Conference on Corporate Visions and Values (Fairfield University, 1992)

ISSUE SUMMARY

YES: LaRue Tone Hosmer, a professor of corporate strategies, argues that codes of ethics are really only for show and that they are ineffective in bringing about more ethical behavior on the part of employees.

NO: Professor of philosophy Lisa H. Newton holds that the formation and adoption of corporate codes are valuable processes because they raise corporate awareness of ethical issues and because they can be a valuable part of the corporate action review process.

Business ethics, as an academic discipline and a corporate concern, is the product of the combination of two unlikely companions. Early in the twentieth century, what was called "business ethics" was in reality a set of agreements, created for and by businessmen, concerning the way they did business, and for the most part they were highly *un*ethical. These agreements demanded that you keep your salesman off the other guy's turf; that you refrain from introducing new products in direct competition with other members of the club; that you hire only white males, or at least make sure that only white males made it to the upper echelons of the company; and that you keep secret whatever you might know about your fellow businessmen's adulterated products or fictional tax returns. In short, like the "ethics" of any profession of the period, business ethics were the rules of the in-group—self-protective and self-serving.

Meanwhile, the ethics taught in colleges was linguistic and analytic. Professors taught only terms and their meanings, conversed only with themselves and their students, and were well aware that their teachings were of little use in the real world of business. Business ethics was not seen as a serious discipline.

However, starting in the late 1950s, scandals began to surface: price-fixing, unsafe products, and foreign bribes, for example. In response, the "social responsibility" movement, led primarily by the churches and a few crusading consumer advocates such as Ralph Nader, attempted to make business accountable to the general public for its practices. Businesses were told to get out of South Africa because of apartheid, to ensure product quality and safety, and to take responsibility for the environment. Although the business community's first response was to ignore the activists, some severe consequences—such as jail terms for some highly respected corporate officers, demonstrations, and hostile regulatory legislation—made it clear that some attention would have to be paid to ethics or at least to the *appearance* of ethics.

Businesspeople started thinking seriously about public accountability around the time when the armed conflict in Vietnam brought the ethics professors out of their classrooms and into the public arena. Philosophy developed a new, socially relevant branch of ethics, soon to be called "applied ethics," and by the early 1970s the ethicists of the applied branch were in dialogue with physicians over medical ethics, lawyers on legal ethics, and businesspeople on business ethics. Some familiarity with ethics is now required of most undergraduate business majors.

But does writing and teaching about ethics do any good? In the following selection, LaRue Tone Hosmer says no. He sees a fundamental problem with codes of ethics in that "ethics in management represents a conflict between the economic and the social performance of an organization." Accordingly, codes of ethics must be exercises in futility because they direct the corporation away from its primary function. Lisa H. Newton, arguing the contrary, asserts that the actual code is the least important element in the development of the corporate culture. She argues that the process of code development—principled, comprehensive, and participative—is the most valuable part of the development exercise.

Ask yourself, as you read these selections, is there a conflict between economic and social performance—that is, between business and ethics? Is *business ethics* an oxymoron?

Ethical Codes

Ethical codes are statements of the norms and beliefs of an organization. These norms and beliefs are generally proposed, discussed, and defined by the senior executives in the firm and then published and distributed to all of the members. Norms, of course, are standards of behavior; they are the ways the senior people in the organization want the others to act when confronted with a given situation. An example of a norm in a code of ethics would be, "Employees of this company will not accept personal gifts with a monetary value over $25 in total from any business friend or associate, and they are expected to pay their full share of the costs for meals or other entertainment (concerts, the theatre, sporting events, etc.) that have a value above $25 per person." The norms in an ethical code are generally expressed as a series of negative statements, for it is easier to list the things a person should not do than to be precise about the things a person should do.

The beliefs in an ethical code are standards of thought; they are the ways that the senior people in the organization want others to think. This is not censorship. Instead, the intent is to encourage ways of thinking and patterns of attitudes that will lead towards the wanted behavior. Consequently, the beliefs in an ethical code are generally expressed in a positive form. "Our first responsibility is to our customer" is an example of a positive belief that commonly appears in codes of ethics; another would be "We wish to be good citizens of every community in which we operate." Some company codes of ethics appear in [the two boxes that follow].

Do ethical codes work? Are they helpful in conveying to all employees the moral standards selected by the board of directors and president? Not really. The problem is that it is not possible to state the norms and beliefs of an organization relative to the various constituent groups—employees, customers, suppliers, distributors, stockholders, and the general public—clearly and explicitly, without offending at least one of those groups. It is not possible to say, for example, that a company considers its employees to be more important to the success of the firm than its stockholders, without putting the stockholders on notice that profits and dividends come second. Stockholders, and their agents at trust departments and mutual funds, tend to resent that, just as the employees

From LaRue Tone Hosmer, *The Ethics of Management* (Irwin Press, 1987), pp. 153–157. Copyright © 1987 by Irwin Press. Reprinted by permission.

would if the conditions were reversed. Consequently codes of ethics are usually written in general terms, noting obligations to each of the groups but not stating which takes precedence in any given situation.

THE ETHICS CODE OF JOHNSON AND JOHNSON, "OUR CREDO"

We believe our first responsibility is to the doctors, nurses and patients, to mothers and all others who use our products and services.

In meeting their needs everything we do must be of high quality.

We must constantly strive to reduce our costs in order to maintain reasonable prices.

Customers' orders must be serviced promptly and accurately.

Our suppliers and distributors must have an opportunity to make a fair profit.

We are responsible to our employees, the men and women who work with us throughout the world.

Everyone must be considered as an individual.

We must respect their dignity and recognize their merit.

They must have a sense of security in their jobs.

Compensation must be fair and adequate, and working conditions clean, orderly and safe.

Employees must feel free to make suggestions and complaints.

There must be equal opportunity for employment, development and advancement for those qualified.

We must provide competent management, and their actions must be just and ethical.

We are responsible to the communities in which we live and work and to the world community as well.

We must be good citizens—support good works and charities and bear our fair share of taxes.

We must encourage civic improvements and better health and education.

We must maintain in good order the property we are privileged to use, protecting the environment and natural resources.

Our final responsibility is to our stockholders.

Business must make a sound profit.

We must experiment with new ideas.

Research must be carried on, innovative programs developed and mistakes paid for.

New equipment must be purchased, new facilities provided and new products launched.

Reserves must be created to provide for adverse times.

When we operate according to these principles, the stockholders should realize a fair return.

Source: Company annual report for 1982, p. 5.

The basic difficulty with codes of ethics is that they do not establish priorities between the norms and beliefs. The priorities are the true values of a firm, and they are not included. As an example, let us say that one division in a firm is faced with declining sales and profits; the question is whether to reduce middle-management employment and cut overhead costs—the classic downsizing decision—but the code of ethics says in one section that we respect our employees and in another section that we expect "fair" profits. How do we decide? What is "fair" in this instance? The code of ethics does not tell us.

THE ETHICS CODE OF BORG-WARNER CORPORATION, "TO REACH BEYOND THE MINIMAL"

Any business is a member of a social system, entitled to the rights and bound by the responsibilities of that membership. Its freedom to pursue economic goals is constrained by law and channeled by the forces of a free market. But these demands are minimal, requiring only that a business provide wanted goods and services, compete fairly, and cause no obvious harm.

For some companies that is enough. It is not enough for Borg-Warner. We impose upon ourselves an obligation to reach beyond the minimal. We do so convinced that by making a larger contribution to the society that sustains us, we best assure not only its future vitality, but our own.

This is what we believe....

We believe in the dignity of the individual. However large and complex a business may be, its work is still done by people dealing with people. Each person involved is a unique human being, with pride, needs, values and innate personal worth. For Borg-Warner to succeed we must operate in a climate of openness and trust, in which each of us freely grants others the same respect, cooperation and decency we seek for ourselves.

We believe in our responsibility to the common good. Because Borg-Warner is both an economic and social force, our responsibilities to the public are large. The spur of competition and the sanctions of the law give strong guidance to our behavior, but alone do not inspire our best. For that we must heed the voice of our natural concern for others. Our challenge is to supply goods and services that are of superior value to those who use them; to create jobs that provide meaning for those who do them; to honor and enhance human life, and to offer our talents and our wealth to help improve the world we share.

We believe in the endless quest for excellence. Though we may be better today than we were yesterday, we are not as good as we must become. Borg-Warner chooses to be a leader—in serving our customers, advancing our technologies, and rewarding all who invest in us their time, money, and trust. None of us can settle for doing less than our best, and we can never stop trying to surpass what already have been achieved.

We believe in continuous renewal. A corporation endures and prospers only by moving forward. The past has given us the present to build on. But to follow our visions to the future, we must see the difference between traditions that give us continuity and strength, and conventions that no longer serve us—and have the course to act on that knowledge. Most can adapt after change has occurred; we must be among the few who anticipate change, shape it to our purpose, and act as its agents.

We believe in the commonwealth of Borg-Warner and its people. Borg-Warner is both a federation of businesses and a community of people. Our goal is to preserve the freedom each of us needs to find personal satisfaction while building the strength that comes from unity. True unity is more than a melding of self-interests; it results when values and ideals are also shared. Some of ours are spelled out in these statements of belief. Others include faith in our political, economic and spiritual heritage; pride in our work and our company; the knowledge that loyalty must flow in many directions; and a conviction that ownership is strongest when shared. We look to the unifying force of these beliefs as a source of energy to brighten the future of our company and all who depend on it.

Source: Company booklet, published 1982.

Let us look at two other examples very briefly. Another division in our company is in a market that has grown very rapidly and has now reached such a large size that direct distribution from the factory to the retail outlets would be much more economical. Our code of ethics says that we will "work closely with our suppliers and distributors, for they too deserve a profit," but perhaps we can reduce our prices to our customers, and gain a competitive advantage for ourselves, if we eliminate the wholesalers and ship directly. The code does not tell us how to choose between our distributors, our customers, and ourselves.

As a last example, we are fortunate in having within our company another division that also is growing rapidly; it needs to build a new manufacturing plant, but a town in an adjoining state has offered much more substantial tax concessions than the town in which we have operated for 60 years, and in which, let us assume, there is substantial unemployment and need for additional tax revenues. Our code of ethics says that we will be "good citizens" in every community in which we operate, but it does not explain how to choose between communities, or what being a "good citizen" really means.

Ethical dilemmas are conflicts between economic performance and social performance, with the social performance being expressed as obligations to employees, customers, suppliers, distributors, and the general public. Ethical codes can express a general sense of the obligation members of senior management feel towards those groups, but the codes cannot help a middle- or lower-level manager choose between the groups, or between economic and social performance. Should we reduce employment and increase our profits? Should we eliminate our wholesalers and cut our prices? Should we build in another city and reduce our taxes? Should we—and this is the reason I have included the code of ethics of Johnson and Johnson, Inc.—spend over $100 million removing Tylenol from the shelves of every store in the country after the non-prescription drug was found to have been deliberately poisoned in the Chicago area during 1982, causing the deaths of four individuals? James Burke, chairman of Johnson and Johnson, credits that code with guiding the actions of his company. "This document (the code of ethics) spells out our responsibilities to all our constituencies: consumers, employees, community, and stockholders. It served to guide all of us during the crisis, when hard decisions had to be made in what were often excruciatingly brief periods of time. All of our employees worldwide were able to watch the process of the Tylenol withdrawal and sub-sequent reintroduction in tamper-resistant packaging, confident of the way in which the decisions would be made. There was a great sense of shared pride in the knowledge that the Credo was being tested . . . and it worked!" I think that we can agree that the employees of Johnson and Johnson should be proud of the response of their firm, which put consumer safety ahead of company profits, but we also have to agree that that response, and that priority ranking, is not unequivocally indicated in the Credo of the company.

NO

Lisa H. Newton

The Many Faces of the Corporate Code

We seem to be in another of our code-writing phases. Interest in the development of corporate codes of ethics—by which term we encompass corporate Aspirations, Beliefs, Creeds, Guidelines and so on through the alphabet—has continued to rise since the 1970's, in tandem with the interest in the teaching and taking of ethics, in colleges and workplaces alike. In what follows, I take on some of the dominant themes in the codes of ethics literature, in an attempt to give a partial overview of the state of the art in the formulation of the corporate code.

The attempt turns out to be a study in multiple function. The much-recommended "corporate code of ethics" serves a diversity of functions, and must avoid a similar diversity of pitfalls. Some of these we will survey; to anticipate the end, we will discover that for maximum effectiveness and ethical validity, each code ought to meet three specifications:

1. In its *development and promulgation,* the code must enjoy the maximum participation of the officers and employees of the corporation (the principle of *participation*);
2. In its *content,* the code must be coherent with general ethical principles and the dictates of conscience (the principle of *validity*);
3. In its *implementation,* the code must be, and must be seen to be, coherent with the lived commitments of the company's officers (the principle of *authenticity*).

Clear and Present Need

Businesses ought to have codes of ethics, if for no other reason than to allay real doubts that businessmen are capable of morality at all. Leonard Brooks has recently taken note of the " ... crisis of confidence about corporate activity. Many corporate representations or claims have low credibility, including those made regarding financial dealings and disclosure, environmental protection, health and safety disclosures related to both employees and customers, and

From Lisa H. Newton, "The Many Faces of the Corporate Code," in *The Corporate Code of Ethics: The Perspective of the Humanities,* proceedings of the Conference on Corporate Visions and Values, sponsored by the Connecticut Humanities Council and Wright Investors' Service (Fairfield University, 1992). Copyright © 1992 by Lisa H. Newton. Reprinted by permission.

questionable payments." That is quite a list of things to be distrusted about. If we were looking for a blanket indictment of business, that one ought to cover the ballpark.[1] Or as Michael Hoffman and Jennifer Moore put it somewhat more concisely, it is the opinion of many of our wiser heads that " . . . business faces a true crisis of legitimacy."[2]

We cannot, *pace* Milton Friedman, leave the governance of the corporation to the forces of the market. While the market may bring about economic efficiency, Gerald Cavanagh points out, it cannot guarantee that corporate performance will be ethically and socially sensitive. Here the responsibility lies with the Board of Directors and top management, and it is "essential that board and management step up to the task," ascertain the ethical climate already prevailing and guide policy and decision in ethical directions. He adds as a final qualification that "while codes, structures and monitoring can encourage ethical decisions, it is even more important to have ethical people in the firm who want to make ethical judgments, know how to, and are not afraid to do so."[3] This is surely true: there is no structure or device in the universe, let alone within the capability of the American business community, that will keep people moral if they are determined to be immoral. But most people, at least most businesspeople, it seems are really neither one nor the other; they are prepared to be either, depending on the prevailing culture, and that is where the code can help.

There is nothing new in the aspiration to ethical codes. As early as 1961, Fr. Raymond Baumhart's survey of 2,000 business managers showed two-thirds of them interested in developing codes of ethics, which they thought would improve the ethical level of business practice.[4] By the seventies, public attention reinforced that view. George Benson traces the current effort on codes to the revelations on foreign and domestic bribery in government investigations 1973–1976, leading to the Foreign Corrupt Practices Act of 1977.[5] In the mid-seventies, W. Michael Blumenthal, then CEO of Bendix, went so far as to propose that the business executives of America organize a professional association to develop a comprehensive code of ethics for business with a review panel to enforce it. The idea died at the time, but might be worth following up at some point.[6] To this day, the most highly placed businessmen support the development of codes of ethics. In a survey conducted by Touche Ross in October, 1987, 1,082 respondents concluded that the most effective way to encourage ethical business behavior was the adoption of a code of ethics—outscoring the adoption of further legislation by 19%.[7] Nor is this support surprising. Ethics pays, not just in public relations but in company work. As the Business Roundtable, an association of Chief Executive Officers of major U.S. companies, concluded in 1988,

> It may come as a surprise to some that . . . corporate ethics programs are not mounted primarily to improve the reputation of business. Instead, many executives believe that a culture in which ethical concern permeates the whole organization is necessary to the self-interest of the company. . . . In the view of the top executives represented in this study, there is no conflict between ethical practices and acceptable profits. Indeed, the first is a necessary precondition for the second.[8]

To be sure, we can, at least in theory, behave like saints without a code to describe how we are behaving. But a written document reinforces an intention to be ethical—as a reminder, as a guide, and as a focus for the solidarity of the corporate officers in their attempts to run the company along the lines it lays down. And beyond this, there is the first concern mentioned: that the public is, probably justifiably, concerned over the proclivities of the business community and interested in seeing tangible proof of its intention to behave.

So a public commitment to ethics serves at least two functions: it addresses the concerns of the public and it reinforces (and clarifies) a bottom-line-justified interest in ethical behavior on the part of the officers. A third reason to take ethics seriously, address the subject explicitly, and articulate provisions to enforce it, is simple realism. As Freeman and Gilbert point out, as long as organizations are composed of human beings, no organizational task can proceed, nor can any cogent corporate strategy be formulated, without recognizing that these human beings have values. Their "First Axiom of Corporate Strategy," "Corporate strategy must reflect an understanding of the values of organizational members and stakeholders," is derived directly from the discovery that the human players in the corporate enterprise very often act in accordance with personal and cultural ethical imperatives, and that the corporation relegates itself to irrelevance if it fails to recognize this fact. Their second Axiom, "Corporate strategy must reflect an understanding of the ethical nature of strategic choice," acknowledges the interaction between corporate direction and private value. It is essential that the choices made by management in strategic planning meet the ethical standards implicit in the stakeholders' values.[9] The authors note the current fashion for describing strategy formulation as if persons did not exist, and point out at some length the errors of such attempts.[10]

Why Codes Fail

We sometimes take note of "widespread skepticism" as to the effectiveness of codes and the motivation behind their development. That skepticism bears some examination. Oddly, the doubts do not seem to have their roots in the business community, whose opinions are captured above. It seems to originate in the academic community of the business schools, possibly due to misunderstandings on the nature of valid corporate codes. LaRue Tone Hosmer states well the prevailing error:

> Ethical codes are statements of the norms and beliefs of an organization. These norms and beliefs are generally proposed, discussed, and defined by the senior executives in the firm and then published and distributed to all of the members. Norms, of course, are standards of behavior; they are the ways the senior people in the organization want the others to act when confronted with a given situation.[11]

Again,

> The beliefs in an ethical code are standards of thought; they are the ways that the senior people in the organization want others to think.[12]

With that understanding, no wonder that he must immediately insist that "[t]his is not censorship"! Although that insistence is hardly reinforced with his following, "the intent is to encourage ways of thinking and patterns of attitudes that will lead towards the wanted behavior."

And with both of those understandings in place, again it is not surprising that his evaluation of codes is negative: "Do ethical codes work? Are they helpful in conveying to all employees the moral standards selected by the board of directors and president? Not really."[13] The problem with the code he describes is not only that it is not effective—taking no essential account of the nature of the business, let alone the pre-existing commitments of the people to whom it is supposed to apply, how could it be?—but that it is not ethical. The basis for its norms is, it appears, completely subjective, founded on the whim of whoever happens to be in the executive offices the day that it occurs to a CEO to write a code of ethics; its application is coercive, being conceived by a more powerful group to apply to a less powerful group (but not to themselves); and there is no built-in check to see that it will actually help the company and its employees achieve the ends of the business. In short, it fails by any standards of reasonableness, and why on earth any firm would be interested in such a code is puzzling beyond the norm for such writings. (As Richard DeGeorge points out, we are occasionally willing to allow short lists of rules to be simply imposed on us, as long as the author is reliably known to be God. Senior officers, even CEO's, are not God.)[14]

While we have Hosmer's example before us, we may take the opportunity to extract some more general ethical principles from the critique. The code he describes was brought into existence by a few people in a few remote offices, enlisting the energies of none of the lower-ranking employees of the company. For this reason it fails on any measure of democracy, that understanding of governance that holds participation in policy formulation to be a part of justice; and it fails on any estimate of likely relevance to the situation of those excluded employees. The temptations that beset the stockman and secretary are best known to them, and it is inherently unwise to draw up rules without drawing on their experience. To avoid both sets of failures, it is essential to include as many employees as possible in the development process. This imperative we may call the *principle of participation.*

Second, the content of the code is completely unspecified save by reference to its authors—its provisions are those that strike the CEO and his golfing buddies as good, at the time they write it. Given their understandings of justice (see above and below), we are not inspired to confidence in their intuitions, but that is quite beside the point. Subjective presentations of this type can never qualify as imperatives with the authority of ethics. The provisions of a code must be reasoned, logically consistent, defended by reasoned argument, and coherent with the usual understandings of ethics: they must demonstrate respect for the individual, a commitment to justice, and sensitivity to the rights and interests of all parties affected by corporate action. We may call this requirement the *principle of validity.*

Third, it is assumed that the code is written by the senior officers, but that they themselves are not bound by it, and are therefore by implication perfectly free to ignore it or defy it if that is what they want to do. No liberty could be more destructive. People will do not as they are told, but as it is modeled to them; the company's values are trumpeted in the acts of the highest ranking employees, and need appear nowhere else. Again there is a violation of justice, in the development of a set of rules from which a privileged few shall be exempt, and again there is gross inattention to effectiveness. Whatever we may not know about codes, we know for sure that the real culture of a corporation will be embodied in the behavior of the senior officers, especially the CEO, and that it is imperative to secure the allegiance and the compliance of those persons for a code to be taken seriously; we may call this imperative the *principle of authenticity*. Hosmer's understanding of a corporate code violates all three principles, and condemns itself to ineffectiveness through its violations.

In the limiting case, then, a purported "code" can be no more than some authority's attempt to impose whimsical rules, which are bound to fail. A second type of code that is doomed to failure is the oracular code, confined to bare rules or ideals, no matter how derived or promulgated, with no commentary or explanation grounding the rule in experience.

> The difficulty with many codes is not that they prescribe what is immoral, but that they fail to be truly effective in helping members of the profession or company to act morally. To be moral means not only doing what someone says is right, but also knowing *why* what one does is right, and assuming moral responsibility for the action. How were the provisions of the code arrived at? On what moral bases do the injunctions stand?[15]

The standard instruction at the end of such codes, to discuss any dilemmas with the legal office, won't do it; they don't know morality. Implicit in this objection is a strong suggestion that the code must serve an educational function. This is correct; we will come back to this point.

A third and common way for codes to fail is through failure of the highest executives to take the provisions seriously, not only as they apply to themselves (the principle of authenticity, above), but as they apply to the company's management policies (especially "management by objectives") and other standard procedures. If the CEO honestly believes in the provisions, and takes the lead in modeling and enforcing them, if top management follows suit, and if the company's reward and punishment structure reinforces those provisions consistently, the code may well achieve its purpose even if it fails as a model of logical coherence. If they do not [do] so, there is very little chance that anyone else will either, at least when no one is watching. "Management needs to understand the real dynamics of its own organization. For example, how do people get ahead in the company? What conduct is actually rewarded, what values are really being instilled in employees?"[16] And the modeling and enforcement must be spread throughout the company. As Andy Sigler, CEO of Champion International and initiator of one of the best corporate codes in existence, put it, "Making speeches and sending letters just doesn't do it. You need a culture and peer pressure that spells out what is acceptable and isn't and why. It involves training, education, and follow-up."[17] For example, the institutionalization of any code must include protection from retaliation by supervisors against whistleblowers.[18] Kenneth Arrow would go further, arguing that any effective code must not only be fused into the corporate culture, but "accepted by the significant operating institutions and transmitted from one generation of executives to the next through standard operating procedures [and] through education in business schools."[19]

How Codes Succeed

The first condition for success is a commitment to the promotion of ethical behavior in a company—not to better public relations, nor to more certain deterrence of Federal inspectors, nor to the terror of an occasional bad apple, but to make the whole company a better and finer employer, producer, resident and citizen. For starters, the business community must take a leaf from the book of the professions, who have seen themselves as moral communities from the outset.[20] Like the professions, the corporation must take its status as a moral agent seriously. (There is almost a note of surprise in Leonard Brooks' observation that nowadays, there is a public expectation that if managers are caught *in flagrante delicto* [in the act of committing a misdeed], as they sometimes are, they will be punished. "This is a significant change because it is signalling that our society no longer regards the interests of the corporation or its shareholders to be paramount in importance. Neither corporate executives nor professionals can operate with impunity any longer, because society now expects them to be accountable.")[21] It certainly does.

From that basic commitment should follow a commitment to a process aimed at gathering that ethos from, and infusing it throughout, the entire company. Our first and third specifications, the principle of participation and the principle of authenticity, are two phases of that process commitment. The whole company (starting from the top) must commit itself to the development of the corporate code; the whole company (including the most junior members) must contribute to the process of deliberation; and the whole company (again, especially the top) must be, and feel, bound to obey and to exemplify it.

The imperative of validity is no more than a remote test of the coherence of the content. In accordance with the examples set by the professions, it is not essential for a code to be a model of academic ethics. The requirement that the code be in conformity with theory does not mean that the code must explicitly signal the kind of reasoning that validates it. Earlier in this enterprise academicians were perhaps too insistent, and codecrafters too self-conscious, on this point; earlier discussions of the issue of corporate and professional codes were known to break down on the issue of "consequentialist vs. deontological moral reasoning." Both are necessarily included in the development of a corporate ethic. As Robin and Reidenbach point out, maintaining a certain kind of "ethical profile" (e.g. strong customer orientation for a sales-driven industry) is absolutely essential for the bottom line—there is no more utilitarian requirement. Yet the "core values" extracted from that profile (e.g. "Treat customers with respect and honesty, ... the way you would want your family treated") can be derived from any system of primary duties, and are deontological in form and function. Any good formulation of a company's creed should be subject to verification by both kinds of moral reasoning.[22]

As Robin and Reidenbach emphasize, the code must be drawn to reflect the aims of the particular set of business practices with which the company is concerned. The ruling ideal of the code might equally be integrity of the practitioners, the excellence of craftsmanship, or the dedication to serve the client/customer, depending on the type of business it is. One of the first principles of "excellence" in the running of any company—the imperative to "stick to the knitting"—entails that a code for one industry, or one kind of company, need not apply with equal force to any others.

Along that line, be it noted that there are many reasons why a code cannot be all things to all people. Critics with certain key areas of interest, for instance, will often discover limits in codes that might not occur to the rest of us. Pat Werhane, for instance, complains that codes "usually tell the employee what he or she is not permitted to do, but they seldom spell out worker rights."[23] She goes on to argue that they tend to turn employees into legalists, obedient to the letter of the regulation but ignorant of its moral spirit.

The solution to both problems may lie in the shift of focus from dead rule to living dialogue. I am inclined to argue that the real value of the code does not lie in the finished product, rules with explanations that all must obey, but in the process by which it came to be. The first call for participation is an invitation to the employee to look into his conscience, discover his own moral commitments, and attempt to prioritize and formulate them. This may be the first time he has ever been asked to take on that job, and the educational value is enormous. The second phase of the participatory process includes the discovery of community consensus, a dialogue in which the employee must test his perceptions against those of others, re-examine and perhaps replace those that do not meet the test, and discover the defenses of those that do. However the code emerges, we will have much more articulate employees at the end of the process than we had at the beginning. And in this articulation is implicit genuine self-awareness: the employee now has his moral beliefs where he can see and get at them, and can be educated to apply them in new and creative ways should the situation around him change.

And it will change. Change was always a fact in the American business community, and very rapid, almost chaotic, change an occasional reality. Now, as Tom Peters points out, partly at his instigation, it has become a conscious policy. The continuation of that dialogue is needed especially as firms radically reorganize themselves, destroying the traditional departmental divisions and job descriptions. In the absence of traditional guides, all members of the corporation will need new and extraordinary norms to govern practice, and there is no substitute for a dialogical process in place as the change happens.[24]

Notes

1. Leonard J. Brooks, "Corporate Codes of Ethics," *Journal of Business Ethics* 8 (1989):117–129, p. 119.

2. W. Michael Hoffman and Jennifer Mills Moore, *Business Ethics,* second edition. New York: McGraw Hill, 1990, p. 2.

3. Gerald F. Cavanagh, *American Business Values,* second edition. Englewood Cliffs, New Jersey: Prentice-Hall, 1984, p. 159.

4. Raymond C. Baumhart, S. J., "How Ethical Are Businessmen?" *Harvard Business Review* 39 (July–August 1961):166–71.

5. George C. S. Benson, "Codes of Ethics," *Journal of Business* 8 (1989):305–319, p. 306.

6. W. Michael Blumenthal, "New Business Watchdog Needed," *The New York Times,* May 25, 1975, F1; and "R$_x$ for Reducing the Occasion of Corporate Sin," *Advanced Management Journal* 42 (Winter 1977):4–13.

7. Touche Ross, *Ethics in American Business: An Opinion Survey of Key Business Leaders on Ethical Standards and Behavior.* New York: Touche Ross, 1988, p. 14. The sample included only chief executive officers of companies with $500 million or more in annual sales, deans of business schools and members of Congress.

8. *Corporate Ethics: A Prime Business Asset.* New York: The Business Roundtable, 1988, p. 9.

9. R. Edward Freeman and Daniel R. Gilbert, Jr., *Corporate Strategy and the Search for Ethics.* Englewood Cliffs, New Jersey: Prentice-Hall, 1988, pp. 6–7.

10. *Loc. cit.* See also p. 138, and p. 197, n.25.

11. LaRue Tone Hosmer, *The Ethics of Management.* Homewood, Illinois: Irwin, 1987, p. 153.

12. *Ibid.* p. 154.

13. *Loc. cit.* p. 154.

14. Richard T. DeGeorge, *Business Ethics,* third edition. New York, Macmillan, 1990, p. 390.

15. DeGeorge, *op. cit.* p. 391.

16. William H. Shaw, *Business Ethics.* Belmont, California: Wadsworth Publishing Company, 1991, p. 175.

17. Andrew Sigler, CEO of Champion International, cited in "Businesses Are Signing Up for Ethics 101," *Business Week,* February 15, 1988, p. 56.

18. Leonard J. Brooks, "Corporate Codes of Ethics," *Journal of Business Ethics* 8 (1989):117–129, p. 124.

19. Kenneth J. Arrow, "Social Responsibility and Economic Efficiency," *Public Policy* 21 (Summer 1973):42.

20. Mark S. Frankel, "Professional Codes: Why, How, and With What Impact?" *Journal of Business Ethics* 8 (1989):109–115, p. 110.

21. Brooks, *op. cit.* p. 119.

22. Donald P. Robin and R. Eric Reidenbach, *Business Ethics: Where Profits Meet Value Systems.* Englewood Cliffs, New Jersey: Prentice-Hall, 1989, pp. 94–95.

23. Patricia H. Werhane, *Persons, Rights and Corporations.* Englewood Cliffs, New Jersey: Prentice-Hall, Inc. 1985, p. 159.

24. See Tom Peters, "Get Innovative or Get Dead (part one)," *California Management Review* 33 (Fall 1990):9–26.

POSTSCRIPT

Are Corporate Codes of Ethics Just for Show?

W hy might a corporation's management decide to develop a corporate code of ethics, to sponsor or join lectures and workshops on ethics, or to hire consultants to run "ethics training programs" for their middle managers? There are numerous possible answers to this question: The company may be in the headlines again for falsifying time sheets for government projects, and management wishes to project a righteous image before sentencing; employees may be stealing supplies and the employers want to make their people more moral in order to cut costs; or managers may simply believe that ethics as a principle is important to the company.

There may be no single answer to that question in any given case. Surely, given the fiduciary obligations of management to the shareholders, and given the expectations of the community, the managers will stress different motivations for community service at shareholders' meetings. This is probably as it should be; people are complex beings and operate from mixed motivations in most areas of life. There may be no need to insist on purity of motive before an ethics project begins. Motives, after all, come immediately under scrutiny in any consideration of ethics, and it is natural to search for ulterior ones. Whatever the motivation, are efforts to improve corporate behavior often successful? Should we promote the adoption of corporate codes of ethics in all, some, or no companies?

Suggested Readings

Peter Drucker, "What Is Business Ethics?" *The Public Interest* (Spring 1981).

Catherine C. Langlois and Bodo B. Schlegelmilch, "Do Corporate Codes of Ethics Reflect National Character? Evidence from Europe and the United States," *Journal of International Business Studies* (November 1990).

Maurica Lefebvre and Jang B. Singh, "The Content and Focus of Canadian Corporate Codes of Ethics," *Journal of Business Ethics* (October 1992).

Robert Solomon and Kristine Hanson, *It's Good Business* (Atheneum, 1985).

ISSUE 3

Does Ethics Matter in Business?

YES: Manuel Velasquez, from "Why Ethics Matters: A Defense of Ethics in Business Organizations," *Business Ethics Quarterly* (April 1996)

NO: David M. Messick, from "Why Ethics Is Not the Only Thing That Matters," *Business Ethics Quarterly* (April 1996)

ISSUE SUMMARY

YES: Professor of business ethics Manuel Velasquez argues that ethical behavior is more profitable, more rational, and more intrinsically valuable than unethical behavior. Following a line of argument pioneered by Plato and updated by game theorist Robert Axelrod and economist Robert Frank, Velasquez posits that ethical behavior and the development of the virtues that result in ethical behavior are the best predictors of profit in business organizations.

NO: David M. Messick, a professor of ethics and decision in management, counters that Velasquez's conclusions are oversimplified if they aim to predict that the rational businessperson will regularly follow ethical rules of conduct. He asserts that actual behavior, in business and in other areas of life, tends to be a nuanced combination of egotistical and justice-oriented profit-maximizing actions.

T he first complete work of philosophy ever written for the instruction of a nonprofessional audience was Plato's *Republic*, and its argument bears repeating: People ought to treat each other with justice and kindness, never taking advantage of another even when they are sure that the other can do nothing to retaliate, never seeking an unfair profit even when they know that they can get away with it. They ought to do this not for the sake of duty, for God, nor out of concern for the welfare of another. On the contrary, people should act virtuously out of concern for their own happiness and the welfare of their own souls. Plato claims that the worst misery comes from enslavement to the passions and that the passions are stirred into action mostly by the prospect of unjust gain or spiteful triumph. Therefore, to live a happy life, a person should live a life of justice and benevolence to others, not for the sake of the material rewards, but for the sake of the order of the soul—what one might call inner peace.

The twentieth century produced a Plato "rerun" in the form of the "prisoner's dilemma," a central construction of game theory. Game theory investigates paths to the maximization of advantage in structured adversarial situations, producing, for instance, the "war games" of the cold war era. In a prisoner's dilemma (explained more fully in the following selection by Manuel Velasquez), two parties are asked to make simultaneous moves in a situation where they cannot observe each other and where disturbingly familiar consequences follow from the wrong moves. If they "cooperate," agree upon and stick to the same story, they both win; if party A sticks to the agreement but party B defects, A loses big and B loses a little; if B sticks to the agreement and A defects, the rewards are reversed; if both defect, they both lose, but nowhere near as badly as the one who cooperates loses if the other defects. So when weighing the chances, each prisoner might conclude that she or he is better off defecting—at least that avoids the worst losses. The game is of infinite interest to strategists, for it mimics disarmament agreements on the international scene and all environmental agreements, national or international. (For instance, if all fishermen agree to use "dolphin-safe" methods of catching tuna, the price of all tuna will go up a little, but the dolphin will be saved, and the consumer, who likes dolphins, will not complain. But if one company decides to abandon these methods, it will be able to sell its tuna a little cheaper. Faced with a choice between more and less expensive tuna on the shelf, in the knowledge that saving the dolphins is now a lost cause since the less expensive tuna will surely crowd out the more expensive tuna, the consumer will take the less expensive, and those who stick by the agreement will lose market share.) When Robert Axelrod proved that cooperation—sticking to an agreement—maximizes interests of both parties in any realistic situation, philosophers took heart and hoped for a better future.

On the negative side, as David M. Messick asserts in the second selection, such proofs of rational behavior do not automatically control behavior, and the practicing corporate officer should not subject business decisions to such a rigorous, long-term formula. Many things other than that rational outcome matter, and evidence of "judgmental incoherence" in undergraduate choices is common in the field, as well as a good predictor of judgmental incoherence in careers to come. In short, people are messier than Plato or Axelrod ever dreamed.

As you read the following selections, remember that both authors are talking about choices that are made every day but that change the directions of lives and corporations. What sorts of calculations are uppermost in your mind as you choose—actions, careers, or lives?

Manuel Velasquez  **YES**

Why Ethics Matters: A Defense of Ethics in Business Organizations

In an article in the *Harvard Business Review* Amar Bhide and Howard H. Stevenson write that "Treachery, we found, can pay," and "There is no compelling economic reason to tell the truth or keep one's word."[1] Bhide and Stevenson are not the first to suggest that unethical behavior may be more profitable than ethical behavior. Over two thousand years ago, exactly the same claim was made by Thrasymachus, a character in Plato's *Republic* who concluded that while justice is for the simpleton, injustice is for the wise.

. . . Bhide and Stevenson are on the side of Thrasymachus. They assert that their claims are based on the empirical data provided by "extensive interviews." It is unclear just what this data is supposed to be, since they do not bother to provide it in their article. Perhaps they think that the readers of the *Harvard Business Review* might not be up to plowing through tables of numbers and statistics. Instead, what they provide are anecdotes and snippets of conversations taken, apparently, from their interviews with a variety of business people. These business people describe incidents where dishonesty or broken promises paid off and several are quoted as saying that many businesses "cavalierly break promises" yet suffer no sanctions. What Bhide and Stevenson's interviews clearly demonstrate is that many business people feel that unethical behavior in business often pays off.

But it is difficult to see what more we are supposed to learn from these stories and quotations since they seem to tell us what we already knew: that wrongdoing sometimes pays and that the good sometimes suffer. The real issue, however, and the issue that Plato's *Republic* addresses is this: is there any kind of systematic advantage to ethical behavior or any kind of systematic disadvantage to unethical behavior? That Platonic question is the issue I here want to address. In particular, I want to ask, is there any kind of systematic advantage that a business organization or business person has to gain from just behavior or is injustice truly more profitable? Like Bhide and Stevenson, however, I will address this question by appealing to some very unPlatonic empirical data....

Research on Prisoners Dilemmas

In a crucial passage in the *Republic,* one of Plato's characters suggests that norms of justice can be thought of as the outcome of a cooperative agreement among people. In a society that lacks norms of justice, he suggests, people inflict injustices on each other. People quickly conclude that they will be better off if everyone adheres to norms of justice. People consequently agree to cooperate in mutual adherence to norms of justice. However, each individual knows that he would be better off if he personally defected from following the norms that everyone else is following, "For no man who is worthy to be called a man would ever submit to such an agreement if he were able to resist; he would be mad if he did."

In this account, justice is characterized as creating the kind of situation that contemporary game theory calls a "prisoners dilemma." Prisoner's dilemmas are situations in which two parties are faced with a choice between two options: to cooperate in some course of action, or to not cooperate, that is, to defect. If both cooperate, they will both gain some benefit. If both defect, neither gets the benefit. If one cooperates while the other defects, the one who cooperates suffers a loss, while the one who defects gains a benefit....

The prisoner's dilemma gets its name from a story that is supposed to illustrate the kind of situation it represents. The story goes like this: Two thieves arrested for a crime vow not to betray each other. But the police put them in separate rooms, and tell each thief the same thing: "If your partner confesses and you keep silent, he goes free and you get 5 years in prison; if you confess and he keeps silent, you go free and he gets 5 years in prison. If you both confess, then you both get 3 years in prison. If you both keep silent, then we'll give you each 1 year in prison on a lesser charge."

The best outcome in a prisoner's dilemma is for both parties to cooperate. Mutual cooperation will leave them better off than if both defect. However, as early inquiries in game theory showed, if the parties are rational and self-interested, they will both choose to defect. Each party will reason as follows: "The other party will either cooperate or defect. If the other party cooperates, I will gain more by defecting than by cooperating; and, if the other party defects, I will also gain more by defecting than by cooperating. In either case, I will be better off by defecting than by cooperating." Since both parties reason in this self-interested way both end up defecting, and thus both end up losing out. Prisoner's dilemmas, in short, are situations in which the self-interested behavior of two parties leaves both worse off than cooperative behavior would.

Although prisoner's dilemmas technically involve only two parties, their lessons can be generalized to what are more accurately called "social dilemmas," situations in which several parties each face a prisoner's dilemma situation with respect to the other parties. The members of a commodity cartel, for example, will all benefit if all charge an agreed-upon high price for the commodity. But each member knows that if the others stick to the agreement, he has more to gain by selling the commodity at a lower price, while if the others do not stick to the agreement, he will also be better off selling at a lower price. Since all will reason this way, the cartel breaks down, prices fall, and all the members of the cartel end up worse off than if they had cooperated in the agreement. Studies have indicated that large groups in a social dilemma are rarely able to secure cooperation, especially if they expect not to interact frequently.

Prisoners dilemmas, in the form of social dilemmas, mirror many of the kinds of social situations with which our lives are filled, i.e., situations in which several people have a choice between cooperation or non-cooperation and in which the self-interested pursuit of non-cooperation leaves all worst off than cooperation. In addition to cartels, such situations include contracts and agreements or promises, honor systems, market competition, military arms races, the game of chicken, the provision of public goods, the "NIMBY" ("Not In My Back Yard") syndrome, the consumption of unowned resources, the free rider phenomenon, and, of course, ethics. Ethical norms can be interpreted as norms that put us in a prisoners' dilemma situation. For example, when two individuals talk with each other, they have a choice of cooperating in the norm of telling the truth, or they can try to take advantage of each other by lying to each other. When two individuals make an agreement, they have a choice of cooperating in the norm of keeping their word, or they can try to take advantage of each other by breaking the agreement. When individuals who each own a piece of property interact, they have a choice of cooperating in the norm against theft, or they can try to take advantage of each other by stealing each other's property. Being ethical, then, can be thought of as a kind of cooperation between individuals: it is cooperating in the moral norms that sustain our fundamental institutions such as the institution of language, of contract, and of property, and, more generally, the social conditions that make an orderly and flourishing human life possible. Being unethical, on the other hand, can be conceptualized as an attempt to take advantage of others by breaking the moral norms that others are following.

Seeing ethics in terms of the prisoner's dilemma suggests an explanation for two common observations business people make about ethics. First, business people often acknowledge that the business world would be a better place if everyone behaved ethically. This is what the prisoner's dilemma analysis of ethics would suggest since mutual cooperation in the norms of ethics is mutually beneficial; in particular we all gain the benefit of stable social institutions and an orderly and flourishing society if everyone cooperates in the moral norms that sustain these. But, secondly, business people just as often suggest, as Plato's Thrasymachus did, that ethical behavior in business is for suckers. And this, again, is what the prisoner's dilemma suggests since the person who sticks to ethics will lose out when she encounters a person who takes advantage of her by being unethical. The ethical person, then, is in a prisoner's dilemma and so appears to be at a disadvantage when dealing with an unethical one.

And, as a matter of fact, the central lesson of the prisoner's dilemma is that when individuals deal with each other in a prisoners dilemma situation, it is in each person's individual interest not to cooperate but to try to take advantage of the cooperation of the other party. Why, then, are people ever ethical? If, as Thrasymachus suggests, injustice pays off, why are people ever just? The Prisoner's Dilemma analysis raises in very stark form the question with which we began: why be ethical if getting away with being unethical pays better than being ethical?

Part of the explanation for why ethics matters lies in an unreal assumption we have so far been making. We have assumed that the people who meet in a prisoners dilemma interact with each other only once. In fact, as the prisoners dilemma analysis of ethics suggests, unethical behavior will pay off in a one-time meeting when the person who is taken advantage of cannot get back at the person who took advantage of her. This is perhaps the reason why ostensibly unethical behavior emerges in those exchanges in which parties interact only once, such as in the sale of cars or other big-ticket items, or exchanges in which the parties cannot identify each other, such as in freeway driving.

However, the situation is quite different when interactions are iterated and are between individuals who are known to each other; for example, when individuals have to deal with each other repeatedly or have on-going relationships with each other. When individuals can identify each other and have to deal with each other in repeated prisoner's dilemma situations, those who continue to try to take advantage of the other party can be made to suffer sustained losses, while those who learn to cooperate with the other party can make the largest gains.

The crucial factor that is at work when identifiable people deal with each other repeatedly, of course, is that when one party takes advantage of the other in one interaction, the injured party remembers this and can retaliate by doing the same in the next interaction. Through mutual retaliation, the parties can enforce cooperation, and a stable pattern of mutual cooperation can emerge. This phenomenon has been extensively studied in contemporary game theory. [Robert] Axelrod, in particular, has shown that in a series of repeated prisoners' dilemma encounters, the best strategy—called TIT FOR TAT—is for a party to co-operate initially but to retaliate with non-cooperation each subsequent time the other party fails to cooperate. Because of this continuous threat of retaliation, it is more rational for the parties to a series of repeated exchanges to cooperate with each other than to fail to cooperate. And cooperation, of course, brings with it the mutual advantages of mutually beneficial activities. Thus, where individuals have to deal with each other repeatedly, and where the threat of re-taliation is present, it is better to cooperate with the other party than to try to take advantage of them.

The implications of the prisoners' dilemmas research for ethics in busi-ness are fairly clear. Business interactions with its stakeholders—employees, customers, suppliers, creditors, and stockholders—are usually repetitive and on-going. Consequently, if a business attempts through unethical behavior to take advantage of these or other stakeholders in today's interaction, they can usu-ally find some way to retaliate against the business in tomorrow's interaction. The retaliation can consist of as simple an act as refusing to buy from, work for, or do business with the unethical party; or it may be a more complex form of retaliation such as sabotage, absenteeism, pilferage, organizing boycotts or other forms of getting others to refuse to do business with the unethical party, or getting even by inflicting other kinds of covert or overt injuries. Simply put, it is shortsighted for management to try to take advantage of these groups through unethical behavior. It is possible for a business to sometimes get away with unethical behavior, but in the long run, if interactions between identifiable parties are iterated and retaliation is a realistic option, unethical business behavior tends to be unprofitable and non-rational, while, ethical behavior will reap the rewards of mutual cooperation.

Although the threat of retaliation in repeated interactions goes some way toward explaining why ethics matters in business, still the explanation does not take us very far in making ethics more appealing. This is because the explanation assumes a negative motivation for ethical behavior. In effect it says that ethics is preferable because unethical behavior is punished. This provides a negative incentive for avoiding unethical behavior, but does not show that ethical behavior is itself an attractive option. A more satisfying justification of ethics would show that ethical behavior itself is desirable because it is beneficial. In fact, that was Plato's hope in the *Republic*. Plato aimed to show that ethical behavior was not merely a lesser evil, to be preferred over the greater evils that unethical behavior entailed, but that ethical behavior itself was advantageous.

In fact, a more positive explanation of why justice matters can be found in the work of the economist Robert Frank. Frank's research, like the prisoners' dilemma research, looks at situations in which people have a choice between cooperating with or taking advantage of others. Frank's analysis, however, is aimed at investigating whether it is better for a person to habitually cooperate with others or to habitually take advantage of others, when that person is living in a population of people some of whom habitually cooperate and some of whom habitually take advantage of others. Since, as I have argued, ethics is a kind of cooperation in the rules that support our fundamental social institutions, the question comes down to this: is it better to be habitually ethical or unethical in a society that consists of both ethical and unethical people? Plato, in the *Republic*, answered this question in the affirmative, arguing that the person who is habitually just will enjoy important reputational benefits.

Frank's studies provide ingenious support for Plato's claim that ethical behavior is itself beneficial. Frank uncovered two important facts about human behavior. First, he found that people send fairly reliable signals to each other regarding whether they habitually cooperate in keeping to rules and agreements, or whether they habitually attempt to take advantage of others. Signals of one's predisposition to be cooperative include visual cues such as facial expressions, auditory cues such as tone of voice, and past history such as is embodied in reports from others and in reputation. Frank's studies showed that people can accurately identify cooperative predispositions about 75 percent of the time, and can accurately identify non-cooperative predispositions about 60 percent of the time.

Secondly, Frank's studies showed that when people interact with each other and can choose the persons with whom they interact, they more often choose to interact with those whom they believe habitually cooperate in the rules of ethics and avoid those whom they believe will try to take advantage of them. That is, people try to avoid those who are unethical, and seek out those who are ethical.

Frank argued that these two factors—the ability to identify ethical and un-ethical predispositions, and the tendency to seek out those who are ethical and avoid those who are unethical— imply that it is more advantageous to be ha-bitually ethical than unethical. Because ethical people seek each other out and avoid unethical people, they will tend to increase the frequency of their dealings with each other. Ethical people will therefore increase the frequency with which they engage in mutually cooperative and thus mutually beneficial exchanges. On the other hand, unethical people will be avoided by ethical people and so they will be forced to deal with other unethical people. As a result, unethical people will tend to increase the frequency of their dealings with each other, and in these dealings each will try to take advantage of the other in a mutually destructive exchange. Frank's conclusion is that habitually ethical people will more often have mutually advantageous relationships with other ethical people while habitually unethical people will more often have mutually destructive relationships with other unethical people. In the long run, it turns out that habitually ethical people end up with larger gains than habitually unethical people.

Frank's research has clear implications for ethics in business. His find-ings imply that employees, for example, have fairly reliable ways of discovering whether a manager or even a team of managers is habitually ethical or uneth-ical. His research implies, further, that given the choice ethical employees will tend to seek to deal more with those whom they identify as ethical than with those who are unethical: that is, ethical employees will tend not to enter or to exit organizations when they learn those organizations are staffed by managers who deal unethically with their employees, and they will tend to enter and re-main loyal to organizations staffed by ethical managers. Unethical managers, on the other hand, will be left with the unethical remainder. Consequently, over the long run and for the most part, ethical managers will tend to have mu-tually cooperative interactions with ethically reliable employees and together with them will create mutually beneficial corporate enterprises, while unethi-cal managers will more often tend to find themselves in mutually destructive interactions with unethical employees and together with them create dysfunc-tional enterprises. Habitually ethical management is more advantageous over the long run, than habitually unethical management.

The prisoners' dilemma research is thus fairly supportive of the Platonic view that adherence to other-regarding norms of ethics confers benefits on the agent. First, adherence to other-regarding norms avoids injurious retaliation in on-going relationships with customers, employees, suppliers, and creditors. Sec-ond, habitual adherence to other-regarding norms will increase the frequency with which managers will find themselves in mutually beneficial interactions with ethical employees, while habitually unethical behavior will increase the frequency with which managers will find themselves in mutually destructive relationships with unethical employees. . . .

The research on distributive justice [the fairness of the way in which ben-efits and burdens are distributed among the members of a group] suggests that people desire distributive justice for itself and not merely for its external ad-vantages and that this desire is a powerful motivating force, often, but not always, even overriding personal advantage. This conclusion has important implications for profit-oriented business organizations, particularly insofar as the research shows that people's desire for justice will motivate them to take steps to ensure that justice prevails, even when this means foregoing advantages to themselves. It must matter to businesses, for example, that employees seek distributive justice in compensation and work assignments, and will take steps to ensure that work burdens are justly proportionate to compensation. In particular, if employees believe they are not being paid enough for the work they are doing in comparison to others, they will likely adjust their work output downward, perhaps by putting forth less effort, perhaps by taking days off from work, or perhaps by otherwise lowering their productivity. People outside a business will also react negatively to violations of distributive justice in ways that must matter to a business. Customers, for example, will turn against a company if they believe that it is unjustly charging more than it should for a product, as may happen, for example, when an essential commodity is in very short supply. Finally, it must matter to business that task performance is affected by the kind of distributive justice that prevails in an organization: compensation systems based on the principle of contribution create a competitive atmosphere in which resources and information are not shared, while compensation systems based on the principle of equality encourage cooperation and the sharing of resources and information. Clearly, then, distributive justice is intrinsically valuable to the employees, customers, and others with whom businesses deal, and for this reason it has to matter to businesses. . . .

The first studies on procedural justice found that dispute resolution processes in which the parties to a dispute are allowed to provide their own input into the process are seen as fairer than processes that deny parties any direct input. These studies also indicated that when processes embodied procedural justice, the institutions or processes themselves were respected and valued by the participants. Indicative of this was the fact that when decisions were made through processes that allowed for direct input, the decisions that emerged from the process were embraced and accepted as legitimate by the affected parties, to an extent not present when exactly the same decisions were made through processes that did not allow such input. Moreover, subsequent studies in a variety of social contexts showed that decision-making processes and institutions that allow affected parties direct input into the process, are judged to be more just than those which don't, and that such just processes and institutions, as well as the decisions reached through them are more likely to be accepted by affected parties, more likely to be seen as legitimate by the parties involved, and more likely to be complied with by the parties involved. Studies of workers, for example, have shown that when a system of employee evaluation allows workers to express their viewpoints and feelings and to communicate information about themselves and their work, they judge it to be more fair and are more likely to be satisfied with the process and more acceptant of their final evaluations regardless of whether the evaluations are low or high. Other studies have shown that employee evaluation systems are also judged as fair and valued when they are consistent and they communicate and rely on accurate information, factors that also contribute to acceptance of, and compliance with, processes and their outcomes. Some experimental models have suggested that the fairness of procedures is further determined by the extent to which they provide: adequate methods of selecting decision-makers, adequate procedures for setting and communicating the ground rules that will determine rewards, suitable methods of gathering and communicating the information on the basis of which the rules are applied, suitable decision-making mechanisms in the application of rules, safeguards against the abuse of power, procedures for appeals, and mechanisms for change that can represent the concerns of all participants.

The research on procedural justice has provided a number of additional indications that organizational participants respect and attribute intrinsic value to processes that are just. One set of studies showed that when employees feel that an organization's decision-making processes are just they exhibit lower levels of turnover and absenteeism, and higher levels of trust and commitment to the organization and to its management. And when employees believe an organization's decision-making processes and procedures are just, they are more willing to follow organizational leaders, more willing to do what they say and more willing to see their leadership as legitimate. In short, employees become committed to the just organization and remain loyal to it and willing to accept and follow its leaders. On the other hand, employees are repelled by the unjust organization and respond to organizational injustice with disaffection, disloyalty, and resistance to organizational leaders and their commands.

Organizations constituted of decision-making processes that are just, then, are valued by participants and endowed with respect. But is there any direct empirical evidence that just organizational procedures are valued for themselves instead of merely for the benefits they instrumentally provide their members? This is an extremely difficult question to answer with certainty, since it is possible that people value just processes because at some level they believe that just processes are likely to provide them with larger rewards than unjust ones. Nevertheless, there are some studies that indicate that people place some value on just procedures that is independent of the extent to which such procedures personally benefit them. Although certain studies have shown that just procedures have instrumental value for their participants, these same studies have demonstrated that just procedures are also imbued with noninstrumental or intrinsic value. For example, in one study, two groups of workers were both allowed to say what they thought would be an appropriate amount of work to perform in a given time. But while the amount of work for one group was adjusted in accordance with their input, the other group was told that although their input was being solicited, the amount of work they had to do had already been decided and their input would have no effect on the amount of work they would be asked to perform. A third, control group, was not allowed even to say what they thought would be an appropriate amount of work, and their work was simply assigned to them. Not surprisingly, this third group did not judge this process to be particularly fair. But the other two groups, even those who knew their input would have no effect on the outcome, rated the process as fair. Thus, procedures are judged to be fair, and so are desired, even apart from their instrumental value. It has been suggested, in fact, that procedural justice is desirable not for its instrumental value, but because it communicates that those who are treated justly (for example, those whose opinion or "voice" is solicited) are valued, respected, and accorded dignity. The empirical evidence we have, then, suggests that Plato was entirely right: justice is intrinsically desirable because it creates an intrinsically desirable organizational order, an order that communicates value, respect, and dignity, and so an order which elicits trust, organizational commitment and loyalty, which leads participants to attribute legitimacy to the organization's leaders and their decisions, and which leads participants to accept and implement organizational decisions. When an organization is constituted of processes that are seen as just, participants in the organization cleave to the organization itself: they embrace it, respect it, and are intensely loyal to it and its leadership....

Conclusion

We have argued, then, that Plato was right: justice is more profitable, more rational, and more intrinsically valuable than injustice, even in business. The research on prisoners' dilemmas shows that ethical behavior is more profitable and more rational than unethical behavior in terms of both the negative sanctions on unethical behavior and the positive rewards of ethical behavior; and the psychological research on justice shows that justice is intrinsically valuable, both from an outcome and from a process perspective, and so crucial for business organizations, particularly in terms of organizational effectiveness. There is, undoubtedly, much more to be said for ethics and justice in organizations. There is reason, for example, to suspect that the just organization is one in which morale is high and in which members are motivated to work harder and more productively at achieving organizational goals, and reason to suspect that the justice of an organization bears some significant relationship to its stability, i.e., its ability to maintain its essential functions though periods of stress and in turbulent environments. But enough has been said to show that Plato was correct and that Thrasymachus and his modern counterparts are wrong. Ethics in general and justice in particular matter tremendously for the profit-oriented self-interested business organization.

Note

1. Amar Bhide and Howard H. Stevenson, "Why be Honest if Honesty Doesn't Pay," *Harvard Business Review* (September-October 1990), pp. 121–29.

NO

David M. Messick

Why Ethics Is Not the Only Thing That Matters

Abstract: Ethics surely matters to people, but to ignore the fact that other things matter as well is to oversimplify human motivation and behavior. Human action is often the ungainly resolution of conflicts between ethical and egotistical impulses, and the challenge for moral psychology is to understand these conflicts and their resolution.

Professor [Manuel] Velasquez has written an eloquent essay defending the importance of ethics in business organizations. Much of his defense draws on the famous prisoner's dilemma and on psychological research dealing with distributive and procedural justice. His conclusion, that justice matters to people, in business organizations and elsewhere, is firmly supported by decades of psychological research.

But people are complex. While I agree with Professor Velasquez' conclusion, I must add that the story is more complicated than he implies. Ethics does matter to people, but so do a lot of other things including success, friendship, sex, money, prestige, love, power, and authority. Human motivation is a tumult of goals and desires that are often mutually incompatible. Psychologists and other behavioral scientists make a living by trying to understand how these potentially conflicting impulses get expressed in people's thoughts and deeds. Let me offer three illustrations of how ethics matters along with money, and, at the same time, illustrate how one might study the psychological processes that govern the conflicts between competing impulses.

1. For his dissertation research, van Avemaet (1974) conducted a study in which he had undergraduates perform a task that involved filling out questionnaires. The task was undertaken in a psychological laboratory with a purported second person whom the subjects never saw.

The subjects worked for either 45 or 90 minutes and completed either 6 or 3 questionnaires in this time period. When the subject had finished the questionnaires, the experimenter entered the room and stated that the other subject had had to leave immediately and was gone. The experimenter had $7.00 to pay the subjects, he continued, and had hoped to have the two students decide between themselves how to make the allocation. Now that the other had left, the pair could no longer make a joint decision, and the experimenter also had an appointment in just a few minutes and could not wait. Thus, the experimenter suggested that the subject take the entire $7.00, along with an envelope addressed to the other subject, and keep the amount of money to which he or she was entitled, and send the remainder to the other person.

Before giving the money (in 6 one dollar bills and change) and the envelope to the subject, the experimenter reminded the student of the amount of time he or she had spent and of the number of questionnaires completed. He also told the subject how much time and how many questionnaires the other person had logged. The crucial independent variable in this experiment was the information that was given to the subject about his and the others' accomplishments. The subject found out that he worked longer, shorter, or the same length of time as the other person, and that he completed more, fewer, or the same number of questionnaires.

The address on the envelope was actually the experimenter's apartment. What van Avemaet measured in the study was how much of the $7.00 that the subject sent to the other person in each experimental condition. The results can be summarized briefly as follows: When subjects had a claim to more than half the money *either* because they had worked longer or because they filled out more questionnaires, they kept most of the money. When the subjects had *no* claim to more than half and the other person did have on one or both dimensions, the subjects kept half the money. Clearly this pattern is unjust in that it displays a bias in favor of the subject. For instance, when subjects worked longer *and* did more than the other, they kept $4.68, on average. When the other did more and worked longer than the subject, the subjects kept $3.33 (not the $2.32 that they sent to the other in the symmetrical situation). The pattern of data displays a clear self-serving or egocentric bias that seems to imply that justice is irrelevant.

But not so fast. Of the 92 subjects who took the money and left the laboratory with it, 90 sent *some* money. Only 2 percent of the subjects, at most, adopted the purely selfish strategy of keeping all the $7 and forgetting about the other person. The data display a pattern of greed tempered by justice, or justice contorted by greed. The violations of justice are self-serving and predictable as are the deviations from simple greed. Greed and justice fuse into an ungainly shape that resists explanation by one principle alone.

2. One of the benefits of ethics that Professor Velasquez cites is the value of having an ethical reputation. Such a reputation evokes trust and attracts potential employees for whom trust and ethics matter. If these employees are better, in the sense of being cheaper, more honest, or more loyal than potential employees who do not value trust and ethics, then this is an economic advantage for being ethical (or for having the reputation of being ethical).

There may be more to it than this. Frank (forthcoming) presents evidence that less socially responsible firms must pay higher salaries than more socially responsible firms to attract employees. Frank's argument is that employees value social responsibility and view this quality as substitutable for salary. Thus, when asked if they would prefer a $30,000 per year job writing ads for Camel Cigarettes or for the American Cancer Society, 88% of the Cornell University seniors responding chose the latter. When asked how much they would have to be paid to switch jobs, the average pay differential was more than $24,000. These seniors claim that they would have to be paid 80% more, on average, to sell cigarettes than to sell health. This is the good news. The bad news is that there is a price for which most would be willing to switch. Again, what we witness is a trade-off that says that justice is important, but not supreme.

At least Frank's research suggests that it may be possible to put a price on ethics, to determine the economic value of a good reputation.

3. Research by Bazerman, Schroth, Shah, Diekmann, & Tenbrunsel (1994) indicates that this possibility may be an illusion. These investigators were interested in the value MBA students placed on procedural justice in comparison to salary, an issue obviously related to Frank's concern. The MBA students were asked to imagine that they were on the job market and that they were evaluating six offers of employment. Some of the subjects were instructed to evaluate the offers alone. Their task was merely to say whether they would accept the job or not. The other subjects had the offers presented in three pairs. Each pair contained one job that paid more but provided less procedural justice than the other. For example, part of the procedural justice instructions for the higher paying ($75,000) job of one of the pairs reads as follows:

> Decisions involving company policies such as training and job objectives are made by senior management. In general, new associates are not encouraged to voice their opinions or objections.

Instructions for the lower paying job ($60,000), with better procedural justice qualities, containing the following sentence:

> The firm encourages all consultants, both junior and senior, to voice their opinions for changes and improvements to the company's policies.

One of the firms provided an opportunity for junior associates to have a voice in policy making, whereas the other firm did not. Voice is a crucial ingredient in many theories of procedural justice, including those of Lind & Tyler (1988) and Thibaut & Walker (1975). The other two pairs varied the fairness of the firms' grievance procedures and interactional justice (Bies & Moag, 1986), respectively.

Two features of the results of this study are pertinent. There is evidence to support Velasquez' contention that ethics matters. Many students selected the lower paying job over the higher paying one, presumably because they valued procedural justice more than the salary difference. However, the strength of this preference depended on whether the students were evaluating the jobs singly or in pairs. Singly, 59% of the students said that they would accept the lower paying job in which they would have some voice, and only 36% said that they would accept the higher paying job without voice. When the jobs were offered in pairs, however, 55% of the students said they would take the higher paying job (without voice), only 33% said they would take the lower paying job (with voice), and 12% said they would accept neither. When evaluating the options singly, it appears that justice matters more than the salary difference; when evaluating pairs of jobs, it appears that the money matters more than justice. So how do we measure the economic value of justice?

This type of judgmental incoherence is not uncommon in psychological research. In fact much recent work has shown that the incoherence is systematic and lawful (Tversky, Sattah, & Slovic, 1988; Payne, Bettman, & Johnson, 1994). This work suggests that efforts to measure the value of justice may be ill-fated. Money matters as well as ethics and there may not be a simple answer to the question about how these two interests combine or trade off against each other.

Our last illustration and much other recent psychological research suggests that the expression of different, possibly conflicting interests and values in people's actions and judgments is highly context dependent. Whether need, equity, or equality is considered most important in a specific problem will hang on the details of the problem. One person's (perceived) justice may be another's wrong.

If we agree that ethics matters, along with a variety of other, occasionally incompatible interests, we may see some wisdom in the view that unethical actions may occur not because ethics does not matter, but because other factors matter more, or because mistakes are made. An understanding of how the psychology of judgment and decision making plays into ethics in organizations (Messick & Bazerman, in press) may complicate, but at the same time deepen our understanding of the ways in which ethics matters.

POSTSCRIPT

Does Ethics Matter in Business?

Shall I live a moral life? This is not the kind of question one can answer in a day, or a week, after reading some contrary views on the subject. It may be that the less we think about it, the more definitively it will be answered by our actions.

Corporations often develop "codes of conduct" or "vision statements," affirming a fundamental recognition of the importance of ethical behavior in business. Often it is unclear whether the code is intended to help people live more ethical lives, is a public relations ploy to impress neighbors and regulators in order to get more favorable treatment, or is designed as a legal lever to enable corporate executives to fire employees whose aggressive business practices become counterproductive. Some claim that corporate executives extol moral life only to keep the lowest-paid workers honest.

Suggested Readings

Amar Bhide and Howard H. Stevenson, "Why Be Honest If Honesty Doesn't Pay?" *Harvard Business Review* (September–October 1990).

R. Murray Lindsay, Linda M. Lindsay, and V. Bruce Irvine, "Instilling Ethical Behavior in Organizations: A Survey of Canadian Companies," *Journal of Business Ethics* (April 1996).

David M. Messick and Max H. Bazerman, "Ethics for the Twenty-First Century: A Decision Making Perspective," *Sloan Management Review* (1996).

James C. Wimbusch, Jon M. Shepard, and Steven E. Markham, "An Empirical Examination of the Relationship Between Ethical Climate and Ethical Behavior from Multiple Levels of Analysis," *Journal of Business Ethics* (December 1997).

ISSUE 4

Is Game Theory Devastating to Business Ethics?

YES: Robert C. Solomon, from "Game Theory as a Model for Business and Business Ethics," *Business Ethics Quarterly* (January 1999)

NO: Ken Binmore, from "Game Theory and Business Ethics," *Business Ethics Quarterly* (January 1999)

ISSUE SUMMARY

YES: Robert C. Solomon, premier ethicist in contemporary scholarship, finds the use of game theory for business ethics "dangerous and demeaning," arguing that it reinforces a destructive obsession with measurable outcomes and a false sense of competition. He asserts that anyone who practices the kind of "rationality" stressed by game theory is a moral "monster."

NO: Professor of economics Ken Binmore states that the kind of game theory that Solomon condemns is not the kind in actual use and that game theory has a strong and useful role in business ethics.

Ever since Albert Carr's 1968 article on "bluffing" in "Is Business Bluffing Ethical?" (*Harvard Business Review*), in poker and business, moral philosophers have argued about the role of cold-eyed, victory-oriented rational strategy in business. Of course, business negotiations require strategic thinking and allow for the possibility of conflicting interests. But is the calculating rationality of the poker game, or any game of strategy, the appropriate model for the business world?

Absolutely not, says Robert C. Solomon. Brushing aside Carr's protest that his essay was tongue-in-cheek, Solomon argues that too much of contemporary business theory, as opposed to practice, pretends that doing business is a zero-sum game and that only the clever and ruthless can do it successfully. For Solomon, that pretense misses the point of rationality; genuine self-interest; human sensitivity; aspiration; and, above all, the trust that is essential for all real (as opposed to game theory's fantasy) business dealings.

That is not all that Solomon finds wrong with game theory as a model for business transactions. Game theory is essentially a way of working out a set of assumptions numerically, with an air of mathematical exactitude. As such, it follows the general trend of business management practices to become more and more precise and mathematical, at least as described and advised in the business schools and scholarly journals. But business management is not about the numbers. Business management is about people, and business ethics especially aims to capture the human side of management, concludes Solomon.

Ken Binmore asks, "How do you justify game theory's insistence on absolute selfishness and mathematical exactitude in business matters?" He does not agree with those who say that game theory is accurate in assuming that humans are all terribly selfish, that business is an exact mathematical science, and that business therefore can be conducted no other way but on the precise workings out in any situation of the presupposition of universal selfishness. He also rejects Solomon's supposition that game theory is totally inappropriate for applications to business ethics. Instead, Binmore argues that game theory is nothing but a method for working out the implications, in iterated moves, of a set of assumptions. He believes that we can feed altruistic assumptions in business just as well as selfish ones and reach results that will incorporate altruism. In short, do not blame the numbers for the assumptions they track.

As you read the following selections, ask yourself these questions. As Binmore expounds game theory, is Solomon really being fair to game theory? What are the potentials and uses of game theory, if not in business, then in other areas of human endeavor? Even if game theory is not the best target, are we too beguiled by the flashers of numbers, statistics, trends, graphs, betas, and book values, and insufficiently sensitive to the human beings who abound in business? Are we too settled in basic assumptions about the self-interest of the individual and the self-interest of business so that we fail to see business as the cooperative, altruistic, socially responsive, and responsible practice it often is?

Robert C. Solomon

 **YES**

Game Theory as a Model for Business and Business Ethics

Abstract: Fifty years ago, two Princeton professors established game theory as an important new branch of applied mathematics. Game theory has become a celebrated discipline in its own right, and it now plays a prestigious role in many disciplines, including ethics, due in particular to the neo-Hobbesian thinking of David Gauthier and others. Now it is perched at the edge of business ethics. I believe that it is dangerous and demeaning. It makes us look the wrong way at business, reinforcing a destructive obsession with measurable outcomes and a false sense of competition. It falsely characterizes or insidiously advocates a style of human behavior that is utterly unacceptable. To put the matter quite crudely, a person who actually practiced the form of "rationality" advocated by game theory would be something of a monster.

We should not ask for more precision than a subject is capable of giving us.

— Aristotle, (384–322 B.C.E.) *Nicomachean Ethics* Bk. 1

Not that you won or lost—but how you played the game.

— Grantland Rice (1880–1954) "Alumnus Football"

After Albert Z. Carr compared doing business to playing poker in his infamous article, "Is Business Bluffing Ethical?" (*Harvard Business Review*, 1968), indignant executives and outraged business ethicists initiated what would turn out to be a long and tedious counter-offensive against the very idea that free enterprise was a kind of a "game" with its own rules, rules "different from the ethical ideals of civilized human relationships."[1] Predictably, Carr's critics emphasized the importance of integrity, honesty, hard work, trust, engagement in the community, and conscience, but their common point was that business needed a larger frame, a longer view and a stronger moral core than Carr's poker analogy suggested. (Carr himself rejected the game strategy metaphor, and is even said to have insisted that the article was tongue-in-cheek.) Many students and uncritical people in business nevertheless accept Carr's argument, in casual talk if not in theory or in practice.

Today, a somewhat broader metaphor has taken the stage and now invites our serious attention. It is not tongue-in-cheek. It does not present itself as a mere metaphor. It does not limit itself to a single, somewhat ill-reputed game such as poker. It is game theory, in general, and it has the best of credentials. Fifty years ago, two Princeton wizards (who, one might imagine, began by musing over their Friday night poker strategies) established game theory as an important new branch of applied mathematics. Game theory has become a celebrated discipline in its own right, and it now plays a prestigious role in the top business schools, in economics and sociology departments, in biology (especially ecology and evolutionary theory). More to the point, it has now made serious inroads into ethics, due in particular to the neo-Hobbesian thinking of David Gauthier and others.[2] Given its established prominence in business and economics and its appeal in ethics, it is easily understandable that it should now be perched at the edge of business ethics.

I have often said—and I admit that this is conscientiously polemical—that game theory has been a disaster in ethics, and now it threatens to become devastating to business ethics as well. It's not that the mathematical discipline itself is faulty. But formal thinking does not mix easily or comfortably with the sensitivities that are essential to ethics, and not all human activities are games, or anything like games. Out of fairness, I would want to distinguish between what I will call "refined" game theory and plain old "vulgar" game theory, especially since it is the most vulgar kind that is snapped up by most economists and too many business theorists.[3] It is not my intention to criticize the fundamentals of the theory itself, nor will I involve myself with the nuances of strategy. Rather, it is game theory as a model, or, more accurately, game theory as a *metaphor* of business activity that I want to object to, as strongly as possible. Not that I doubt that such theories sometimes apply to business activities and situations, but as a model of business as such, as a focal point and, too often, as the model of business, I believe that it is dangerous and demeaning. It makes us look the wrong way at business, reinforcing an already destructive obsession with easily measurable outcomes (namely "the bottom line") and an often false sense of competition. It represents (what some of its most avid followers would defend as) the most vulgar version of Hobbes, a version that Hobbes himself surely would not have accepted. It either falsely characterizes, or insidiously advocates, a style of human behavior that is utterly unacceptable. To put the matter quite crudely, a person who actually practiced the form of "rationality" advocated by game theory would be something of a monster. To think in terms of strategies of self-maximization, as opposed to unhesitatingly doing the right thing, is (as Bernard Williams put it, in a very different context) to have "one thought too many."[4]

Game theory, like mathematical models in physics, purports to help us to understand diverse and complex phenomena, in this case the supposedly rational behavior of that singularly abstract specimen of humanity, sometimes called "rational man" but better known as *homo economicus.* The model is "ideal"—in the standard sense of a fiction abstracted from a much more complex reality.

But such rationality is hardly an ideal as a model of human behavior in the same way that saintliness, for example, might be said to be. Or, for that matter, it is hardly an ideal as "rationality." Moreover, surely it should be noted (here briefly) that there is no subject, including sex, romance, relationships and death, on which most people are more *ir*rational than about money. Indeed, momentary reflection on peoples' savings habits, gambling compulsions, attitudes toward their jobs, the home shopping network, bargain hunting, and consumer spending in general makes this quite clear, all talk of "preferences" and "expected utilities" aside.

Moreover, game theory has distorted the very term "rationality" by co-opting and reducing its very rich meanings to one-dimensional strategic thinking. To be rational does not generally mean "to seek one's own advantage" or even, more generally still, "to seek to satisfy one's own preferences." Rationality does not simply refer to means-end ("instrumental") thinking. According to many authors, it rather refers precisely to those sorts of thinking that are not particularly self-involved, in which one does not take oneself to be a "special case" or an "exception."

Rationality, I would argue, is always culture-bound, both in its determination and its concerns. In one culture it may be rational to fear witches and in another it is rational to fear a nuclear accident. In one society rationality is determined through the use of certain procedures, in another, by appeal to a certain kind of result. In some societies, the appeal to authority, the consensus of the group, the wisdom of one's ancestors, constitutes rationality. In others, it is individual autonomy, deliberation and Bayesian decision theory [a theory that provides a solid theoretical foundation for thinking about problems of action and inference under uncertainty]. Rationality, I would argue, is very much a matter of "caring about the right things," a matter of ends and not a matter of means.[5] But game theory is not merely a description of (one conception of) rationality. It takes the form of a prescription, or a rather large set of prescriptions, about how it is "rational" to behave in a number of trying and challenging circumstances. Where there is no challenge, of course, there is no "game," but—and this is important—we should note how often and how easily (in this society) a situation is wrongly viewed as a challenge when it might more rationally be viewed as an invitation to cooperative and harmonious behavior, e.g., driving in rush hour or meeting together in an academic seminar.

Game theory tells the participants in various human endeavors—especially economic endeavors—just how to play "the game." But for most people, economics is not a game. It is a means of survival, "making a living," and to think of business as a game already falsifies the seriousness as well as the locus of that activity. A game is normally something divorced or detached from ordinary concerns, real payoffs, and penalties. Business, for most of us, constitutes many of our most ordinary concerns and has all-too-real payoffs and penalties. Business is not (usually) "played" at all, and it is rarely confined to a specific "field" (however the market might sometimes be described in such spatial terms). Its participants are not, for the most part, "players" but grudging breadwinners, and the artificial urge to "maximize" one's behavior hardly describes most peoples' attitude toward their work. Consumerism may have become a primary form of entertainment for many Americans but the means by which most Americans earn the money they spend is not, for most of them, entertaining or enjoyable. (Nor for that matter, is most of the spending itself.) Not that games by their nature must be enjoyed. But games, as games, are "played," and that suggests activity quite different from the rigors and pressures of everyday life. If some Sylvester Stallone or Hermann Kahn type argues that war is a game, I take it that what they mean is that it is something extraordinary, in which the normal rules of interaction are suspended. (The military uses the phrase "war games" for those just-practice maneuvers that are emphatically NOT real warfare and in which the usual roles of decency and fairness [more or less] obtain.) What counts as a game, and what it means to participate in a game, is a topic worthy of discussion, but such a discussion should precede, not lap at the heels of, game theory.[6]

Why would game theory appeal to business ethicists, indeed, how does it now come to fill an entire issue of one of the field's leading journals? The often-stated desire for (and current lack of) a rigorous business ethical theory and the intrinsic fascination with quasi-mathematical puzzles provides a partial answer.[7] But that business ethics—or for that matter ethics—needs a theory is by no means obvious. A more appropriate insight was anticipated by Aristotle, when he warned (in his *Nicomachean Ethics*) that we should not look for more precision in a subject than is appropriate. The problem with ethics, the subject that he was there introducing, is that it is a "sloppy" field of inquiry. I would argue that it requires, more than anything else, not a "theory" but a decent upbringing, a certain sensitivity, some compassion for human suffering —and only then some ability to calculate and measure "harms." Ethics develops with a keen sense of injustice, and not necessarily regarding one's own case, and only then might it come to involve the ability to generalize and formulate one or another conception of justice or fairness. If the practice of justice had awaited a satisfactory answer to Socrates' question, "what is justice?" we would all still be throwing rocks at one another. Ethics, first of all, requires not reflection but close attention to the nuances and intricacies of human relationships, only some of which are sometimes competitive and require strategy and tactics rather than tact, sympathy, mutual consideration and sharing. But from this short list of "preconditions" for ethics, it should be obvious that most of what counts as "ethical theory" is not of this kind at all, and many philosophers are not at all sympathetic to the idea that policy decisions, theories of justice and strategic interaction theories are meaningful only insofar as they presuppose some basic human emotional engagement. Game theory reinforces this resistance to fellow-feeling and replaces it, as in econometric theory, with cold numbers.

Ethics, they say, is the business of dispassionate reason, and, for many philosophers, the more formal the reasoning the better, the less contaminated by prejudices and bias. Feelings only interfere. The great ancestor of this position, with qualifications, is [Immanuel] Kant, but not only Kant. Even in "moral sentiment theory," there is the "ideal observer," who is very much still with us in ethics (long after the demise of the moral sentiments themselves). Thus in business ethics, it is still considered a virtue to talk about and judge matters in which they are not themselves involved or, all too often, informed. Game theory, as formal philosophy *par excellence,* might be viewed as one more vehicle for avoiding engagement. Game theory, by providing the precision that ethics through most of its waffly history has lacked, allows us to avoid the messiness of real-life political feuds, long-standing animosities, coercion and exploitation. Indeed, we have all heard it argued, rather unkindly, that moral philosophers—should one add an *ad hominem,* "especially game theorists"?— are not particularly adept at dealing with real suffering, or with injustice, or with relationships, except on an ethereally abstract level. But even without such (no doubt false) accusations, it can certainly be argued that game theory, with its emphasis on precision and procedure, by-passes those nagging and controversial questions about what it is that people do or ought to care about. Does it matter that the very heart of both business and ethics gets cut out in the process? . . .

Objections to Game Theory

In my book, *Ethics and Excellence,* I explored seven reasons why game theory, whatever its virtues, provides a poor model for business interaction as well as, in its unrefined versions, an appalling model of human nature.[8] I, too, often tend to slip between the refined and unrefined game theoretical models, but that, I think, is the insidiousness of the game theoretical flirtation. If my arguments serve only to force game theorists to further refine and clarify their models, I would consider my polemic worthwhile.

1. Game Theory and "Rationality"

Game theory too readily equates "rationality" with prudential self-interest in the face of competition and conflict. Of course, not all games are played "against" anything (including "nature"), and, so too, not all (or even most) business activities are competitive. But though the best game theorists allude to the possibility of cooperative games and point out the parallel in competitive altruistic contexts, it is illustrative that the game-type that dominates discussion and is most often chosen as a model for business is the prisoner's dilemma in its uncompromisingly competitive and even vicious versions. The paradigm here is insidious. The "rational" approach to a problem turns out to be self-interested and the solution is the "safe" one—better not to trust the other player because he or she might not trust you either. But if games (in general) are so conceived, cooperative games turn out to be preferable only because they are the safest games. They do not eliminate competitiveness or selfishness or distrust but rather emphasize strategies that minimize these. They assure mutually satisfying as well as optimal outcomes, but without rejecting the mind-set that provoked the problem. (Thus the Hobbesian conception of society by contract is argued to be the best solution to mutual hostility and fear.)[9] What is entirely missing is any sense of shared (as opposed to merely mutual) interests and dedication to anything larger or more meaningful than one's own interests.

Nick Rescher accuses traditional game theory of begging two questions; (1) whether rationality demands this prudential, safety-first approach and, (2) much more important, whether rationality demands the cultivation of personal advantage to the exclusion of the interests of others.[10] Philosophers have taken it as "paradoxical" that rational participants in a prisoner's dilemma fail to reach their mutually preferred result. A well-known game theorist, Anatole Rapaport, writes, "the paradox is that if both players make the rational choice, ... both lose."[11] Rescher denies the paradox: "There is in fact nothing paradoxical about this. It shows merely that the realization of a generally advantageous result may require the running of individual risks, and that the pursuit of other-disinterested prudence may produce a situation in which the general interest of the community is impaired."[12] But Rescher adds, "for these lessons we did not need to await modern game theory; the moralists of classical antiquity told us as much many years ago."[13] Indeed, they did, and this, in part, was the suspicion behind Aristotle's unsympathetic dismissal of profit-seeking commercial activity as "unnatural." But why should we, under the banner of "free enterprise," adopt as a model for business (much less for society) a self-fulfilling portrait of human nature so intrinsically unsocial and mutually so unsupportive?

2. Game Theory and Self-Interest

Game theory begins with the assumption that each player is trying to satisfy his or her own interests. Even where the assumption is so weak and so abstemious about human nature to insist only on the "interests" (not "self-interest") of the players, the notion of competitive self-interest inevitably sneaks back in. Refined game theorists insist that the notion of "interest" or "preference" here is not necessarily selfish; indeed it might include all sorts of altruistic desires, wanting to feed one's family or have money to give to the poor or to political candidates. But the slippage between this non-committal sense of "interest" and self-interest is fast and furious. One can see the slippage, for example, in John Rawls's characterization of "mutually disinterested rationality." I quote at some length:

> The assumption of mutually disinterested rationality, then, comes to this: the persons in the original position try to acknowledge principles which advance their system of ends as far as possible. They do this by attempting to win for themselves the highest index of primary social goods, since this enables them to promote their conception of the good most effectively whatever it turns out to be. The parties do not seek to confer benefits or to impose injuries on one another; they are not moved by affection or rancor. Nor do they try to gain relative to one another; they are not envious or vain. But in terms of a game, we might say: they strive for as high an absolute score as possible.[14]

The telling phrase, I think, is "attempting to win for themselves," and the problem with game theoretical thinking is that such phrases are never very far from or psychologically separable from self-interest. Indeed, even where the interests are *shared* interests, the model suggests that this is contingent rather than essential to the interests themselves. Consider, for example, acts done out of compassion, love or friendship.[15] Not that much of business is conducted in such intimate circumstances, but it could be argued that much of the recent emphasis on "dedication to the customer" and "teamwork" among employees is an effort to introduce truly shared interests into the business context. What is revealing about such interests is that they utterly resist game theoretical analysis.

Rawls tries to assure us that such efforts are "not envious or vain," but the very effort to "win for themselves the highest index" suggests that such assurances may themselves be in vain. It is curious that in the philosophical undressing that prepares no longer "encumbered" people for the "original position," they do not even know their own sex or abilities but nevertheless are left with the most ordinary and (I would argue) culturally induced emotions and motives (not to mention how much they supposedly know about game theory and the social sciences). Envy and vanity, far from being encumbrances, often appear to be primary determinants of liberal policy, indeed, of "fairness." Rawls tries to neutralize the idea of "ends," but nevertheless what emerges is difficult to defend without a relatively "thick" conception of human motivation. In the original position, Rawls argues, [people]

> do not know their conception of the good. This means that while they know that they have some rational plan of life, they do not know the details of this plan, the particular ends and interests which it is calculated to promote. How then can they decide which conceptions of justice are most to their advantage? ... they assume that they would prefer more primary social goods rather than less ... from the standpoint of the original position, it is rational for the parties to suppose that they do want a larger share, since in any case they are not compelled to accept more if they do not wish to.[16]

"It is rational ... to suppose that they do want a larger share"—this sounds a lot like "get the goods and then you can decide what to do with them." How many people in business, some of them ruthless, rationalize what can only be called their greed with the promise that, "afterward," they will engage in socially constructive, even idealistic behavior? Whereas the dominant question in business ethics, according to several illustrious theorists, is to just what extent it is possible to realistically minimize the long over-stated self-interested aspects of business.[17] Game theory does not address this concern but tends to undermine it, by stressing, despite denials, a "rational plan of life," namely the rationality of "a larger share."

3. Games and Keeping Score

In most games, we like to keep score. This is not an essential feature of games, but it does seem to be one of the most durable features of game theory. The best way to keep score is to have a dependable point system, a definite unit of worth. Not surprisingly, game theorists modeling society end up talking a great deal about money. Of course, here too the proper excuses are made, "money isn't the only or even the primary social good," "money is only a means and not an end" and so forth. But though the conversation may begin with talk about primary social goods, soon we have yet another example involving money. Economists, of course, do not apologize for this. Money-talk is their game, though they will admit (if pressed) that people do (at least occasionally) want things that money can't buy. But social theorists in general yield to the tendency to talk about money, too, if only because money is a readily measurable utility, an easily comparable measure, an apparently clear basis for comparison. Of course, even some unrefined theorists recognize that equal amounts of money do not have equal significance for different folks, and so the inescapable qualifications of marginal utility and the "utility of money" are (hesitantly) entered into the equation. But then the calculation proceeds as if all of this has been deftly settled with the simple declaration that we should "assume that these are the same." And when it's over, we can shift back to that very general talk about "primary social goods"—including such intangibles as health, freedom, self-esteem and peace of mind, as if the quantification of one carefully defined domain of the theory will extend ipso pipso to the rest.

But various ends are hard to compare (one person wants to win a downhill ski race, another wants to sleep in a hammock) and so success and "maximum utility" may be hard to measure. If we were to assign every end a monetary value however, and rate various preferences according to their exchange value on the market, we would indeed have a single scale on which to compare and evaluate ends and means and determine maximum utility. In practice, of course, we make such interpersonal utility comparisons all the time, and one might even trace the attempted "theory" of such comparisons back to Aristotle's discussion of "proportion" in distribution among unequals in Book V of his *Ethics*.[18] But the sad fact of the matter is that, in a "capitalist" (capital-minded) society, we are all prone to that lazy reductionism in which all or at least most things are compared according to their cost, narrowly construed. More to the point, corporate finance officers do this not from intellectual sloth but according to the rules of their profession. "Cost/benefit analysis" in business tends to be exclusively about dollars. Thus the victory of the economists, and the rise of what Karl Marx called "fetishism."

4. Game Theory and Altruism

Even where self-interest is not assumed as the basis of the game and the goal of each and every player, altruism gets treated as anomalous, at best a fringe benefit not to be taken for granted but at worst an intolerable interference with the workings of the game. (Imagine an extremely generous poker player, or one who did not want to take advantage of his unusually good hands, and you get the idea.) And so we assume self-interest if not selfishness, or worse, the unrefined game theorist promotes an extreme dichotomy between self-interest and altruism, to the great disadvantage of the latter. Moritz Schlick, for example, argues:

> The unrestrained development of such [altruistic] inclinations... can certainly not lead to the valuable, and will not, in fact, be considered moral. To

respect every desire of one's neighbor, to give in to every sympathetic impulse results, finally, neither in the highest measure of joy for the individual himself, nor indeed for the others; in such a case one no longer speaks of kindness, but of weakness.[19]

Rescher (who quotes Schlick with some sympathy) attacks this vision of presupposed selfishness throughout his book, insisting that it is a gross mistake to conceive of rationality in such a way that it conflicts with morality and the social good and to think of ethics in terms of "intelligent selfishness." He rejects the "prudentially safety-first-minded pursuit of personal advantage" that defines most game theory in favor of a theory of the "vicarious" sympathetic emotions. We obtain "utility" through our sympathy with others, experiencing joy at their successes, for instances, and not just from our own success. But even Rescher seems trapped in the old paradigm, which is a sign of its enduring strength. He distinguishes between "first order utility"—the satisfaction of one's own desires—and "second order utility"—one's satisfaction as the result of the satisfaction of another. But the very act of ordering (and the use of the word "vicarious") shows that Rescher too can't quite take seriously the idea of truly shared—not "vicarious"—satisfaction. So, too, even cooperative games presuppose just that notion of primary individual self-interest that I want us to reject, whether or not supplemented or made possible by simultaneously satisfying the interests of others. And the concept of the virtues—that is, as opposed to the skills required to play the game—gets lost here. This is what Rescher is aiming at when he attacks utilitarianism on the grounds that it insists that "everyone counts for one and only for one," which leaves no room, according to Rescher, for relationships, kinship and other forms of affection and association. Of course, a flexible utilitarian can readily incorporate the "vicarious" sentiments and second order utility into the "happiness calculus," but Rescher denies that the utilitarian can be so flexible. But my point is that the alternative to self-interested games is not altruism, much less self-sacrifice nor even vicarious satisfaction. It is the very notion of discrete "players" with discrete interests that I want to throw into question.

5. Game Theory and Goal-Oriented Behavior

Even the "modest" assumption that our behavior is "goal-oriented" is, I think, inaccurate and prejudicial. Ned McClennen, for instance, insists that he can "avoid making any essentialist assumptions about human nature" and requires only the modest assumption that people are goal-oriented.[20] (This is not to say anything about what goals they pursue, of course, nor is it even to suggest a more general Rawlsian consensus on fundamental goals.) But although one can hardly deny that we do have many goals in life, from wanting to get to the garbage can before the dog does to wanting to win a Nobel prize, the view that our activities are essentially goal-oriented is mistaken and, sometimes, tragic. "But certainly," someone is sure to protest, "nothing is more central to the 'Aristotelian' approach that you want to defend than the notion of teleology." And, indeed, that's so. But what Aristotle had in mind by "teleology" was quite different from what we mean (and game theorists in particular mean) by "goal-oriented." For one thing, the satisfaction of desire, while certainly not irrelevant to Aristotle's teleology, is not at all what he has in mind. But a more basic concern is that when one examines Aristotle's conception of the ingredients of the good life, the virtues and our various activities, it is evident that while these involve certain standards, it is not the satisfaction of those standards that motivates us, and one would be hard pressed to identify the "goals" (in our sense) that define most of those virtues. As for all of those activities, it is not as if they are all so goal-oriented either. Friendship is part of our telos but it is not, unless the concept is stretched entirely out of shape, goal-oriented. True, Aristotle begins the *Ethics* by insisting that "every art and science has its end," but if we look at friendship, it becomes clear that "goal-orientation" is not the only meaning of "having an end." What is the goal of friendship? Indeed, on Aristotle's analysis, the mutual pursuit of goals, concretely defined, indicates something less than real friendship. So, too, I want to suggest that the game-theoretical assumption of goal-orientation is misleading as a way of thinking about most human activities, including business.[21] Business, at its best, is a worthwhile and satisfying social activity, but this is hardly the "goal" of business. Although business activity is shot through with goals, objectives and strategies, business ("busy-ness") is defined by its activities, not by its goals—much less the narrow goal summarized as "the bottom line."

6. Games and "Externalities"

As argued earlier, the notion of games in the context of decision making is too contained. It is with good reason that game theorists refer to "externalities," for it is self-containment that defines most games. The football field has carefully drawn lines around it, and only a specified number of players are allowed on the field. Poker gets played with a conscientiously non-personalized deck of cards, and every player is "in" or "out." There is no waiting on the fringe to "see how the hand goes" before joining in. Life, on the other hand, is always open-ended. There need be no fixed number of players in most business deals, and business ethics has been conscientious in its insistence that the "playing field" of corporate business is not just the boardroom but the employees and customers and entire community, "stakeholders" and not necessarily insiders. Games are closed; the market is by its very nature open. Simply adding "players" to the game won't work, not because the complications are infinite (though sometimes it seems that way) but because human contexts change as we play with them, unlike the neatly painted board on which many games are played. There are never just 52 cards in the deck and never just *n* alternatives or players in the market, and the notion of "playing" a game radically changes when not only the spectators but a multitude of mere passers-by wander onto the playing field and have their lives desperately affected by the game.

7. Games and Rules

Games as we generally conceive of them are thought to be rule-defined.[22] But business as a practice is much larger than that. The rules come after. Business

ethics involves phronesis [practical wisdom, the ability to make the right decision in difficult circumstances], sensitivity and imagination, not just obeying
the rules. Of course there are rules (especially laws) and it is usually both unethical and imprudent to disobey them. But I think that it is essential to see
business and business life first of all as a practice, not a game (which is a very
specific and narrow kind of practice), in which general expectations and mutual agreements are established before there are any rules, much less laws. We
get taken in by "social contract"-type thinking, when in fact it is the established
practice that makes contracts possible—and rules sometimes necessary. But business has a lot longer history than business law, and, to be cryptic for lack of
space, rules, regulations and laws get formulated not before but after business
practices are established and, paradoxically, after the transgressions that they
are designed to prohibit.

Conclusion: Game Theory and Ideology

Let me end this discussion by insisting that game theory is not just a model
for business. Game theory is ideology. It is instructive. It provides the frame
within which participants in the practice operate, the lenses through which they
see what they are doing. "One should think of it this way." "This is how one
should behave." "One should expect that this is what will happen." Some of my
suspicion, accordingly, concerns how such a framework gets *used*, in defense of
what policies and practices, at whose expense, to whose benefit. It is all too easy
to show how a "rational" game strategy can eclipse extra-game considerations
of much greater importance. The very fact that game theoreticians have felt
compelled to show that their models are compatible with morals, or justice,
suggests that the purview of game theory is limited, problematically focused
or outside of the realm of ethics and social philosophy. It may be neat, even
elegant, but whether it is relevant to ethics or business ethics is worth serious
reflection and discussion.

Some of the recent wrinkles in game theory do indeed blunt my objections, and it might even be argued that game theory suitably refined can be
used to show us that we need to go beyond game theory.[23] But however cap-
tivating such paradoxes of formalism, it is a mistake to think that by solving
technical problems in a theory that is already off the mark we will thereby
resolve the criticism that it is indeed off the mark.[24] I am reminded of Peter
Geach's infamous witticism to the effect that no amount of evidence can compensate for a conceptual error. So, too, no amount of philosophical ingenuity
can compensate for what game theory excludes, namely, ethics.

Business, like most of human life, is motivated not by self-interest but by
a complex of what Adam Smith called fellow-feelings and sympathy, affection
and vulnerability, a sense of shame and a sense of honor, love and friendship,
animosity and resentment and a hundred more emotions and attitudes. We care
about what other people think of us. We care what we think of ourselves, and
"doing well" (in the neo-Hobbesian, game-theoretical sense rather than the Aristotelian *eudaimonia* [flourishing] sense) is the dominant factor in the way we
think of ourselves and the way we think of others close to us only in degenerate

cases. Game theory, even where it does not presuppose pure self-interest, misses the complexity of human behavior, even economic behavior. We are not, contrary to a well-known quip by Bertrand Russell, calculating creatures. To define rationality as maximizing the chances of getting what you want is to encourage (even if it does not entail) a life devoted to personal goal orientation and strategic calculation. That makes most virtues irrational if not unintelligible. To think always in terms of getting what you want, to think strategically, is to have "one thought too many," to be, as the saying goes, "too clever by half." Such a "rational" attitude to life is itself not only irrational but something much much worse.

Notes

1. Albert Z. Carr, "Is Business Bluffing Ethical?" *Harvard Business Review,* January–February, 1968. Some of these responses were published in the *Harvard Business Review,* May–June, 1968.

2. David Gauthier, *Morals by Agreement* (Oxford, 1986).

3. "Refinement," like many more ordinary concepts, has taken on a technical meaning in game theory. I am referring to the ordinary idea of "improved and sophisticated" (as opposed to "crude and undeveloped") here.

4. Not coincidentally, in tests of common decency (for example, the routine exercise of leaving an appropriate tip for a waitperson), economists as a group tend to do embarrassingly badly. Robert Frank, "Why Economists Make Bad Citizens" and (with T. Gilovich and D. Regan) "Does Studying Economics Inhibit Cooperation?" *Journal of Economic Perspectives* 7, no. 2 (Spring 1993): 159–171.

5. See my "Existentialism, Emotions, and the Cultural Limits of Rationality," *Philosophy East and West* 42, no. 4 (October 1992): 597–622.

6. Bernard Suits, *The Grasshopper* (Toronto: University of Toronto Press, 1978).

7. See, e.g., LaRue Tone Hosmer, "5 Years, 20 Issues, 141 Articles, and What?" *Business Ethics Quarterly* 6, no. 3 (July 1996): 325358.

8. *Ethics and Excellence,* (Oxford University Press, 1991).

9. Here I have benefited from T. C. Schelling, *The Strategy of Conflict* (Cambridge, 1960); Edward F. McClennen, "Morality as a Public Good," a manuscript read at the Society for Business Ethics meeting in Washington, D.C., December 1988, and Bernard Suit's delightful *Grasshopper* (Toronto, 1978).

10. Rescher, Nicholas, *Unselfishness* (University of Pittsburgh, 1975), pp. 38–39.

11. "Escape from Paradox," *Scientific American* 217 (1967): 51.

12. Rescher, p. 35.

13. Ibid.

14. John Rawls, *A Theory of Justice* (Harvard University Press, 1971), p. 144.

15. This, I take it, is what Nietzsche means by "what is done out of love is always beyond good and evil" (*Beyond Good and Evil,* §153), a phrase that does not have to be interpreted in the usual "immoralist" boot-in-the-face manner. Friedrich Nietzsche, *Beyond Good and Evil,* trans. Walter Kaufmann (New York: Random House, 1966), p. 90.

16. Rawls, p. 142.

17. See, for example, Edwin Hartman, *Organizational Ethics and the Good Life* (Oxford University Press, 1996).

18. John Harsanyi, (rf). I am indebted to David Sherman, unpublished.

19. Moritz Schlick, *Problems of Ethics,* trans. D. Rynin (New York: Dover, 1939), pp. 202–203.

20. Edward McClennen, "Foundational Explorations for a Normative Theory of Political Economy," in *Rationality and Dynamic Choice: Foundational Explorations* (Cambridge: Cambridge University Press, 1990).

21. For an excellent discussion of this non–goal-oriented concept of teleology in Aristotle, see Michael Stocker in Amelie Rorty, ed., *Essays on Aristotle* (University of California Press, 1980).

22. Ludwig Wittgenstein, *Philosophical Investigations.* See also Suits, *The Grasshopper.*

23. Mark Murphy, in correspondence, November 1996.

24. Jon Elster, in many books, including *Solomonic Judgments, Ulysses and the Sirens: Studies in Rationality and Irrationality,* and *Rational Choice,* brilliantly demonstrates the ways in which rationality breaks down. Nevertheless, he refuses to draw what would seem to be the obvious conclusion.

NO ⬅

Ken Binmore

Game Theory and Business Ethics

1. Introduction

As the author of one book on the elements of game theory and another on the possible applications to ethics (Binmore [3,4,5]), I suppose it is natural that I should be asked to reply to Robert Solomon's (13) claim that "game theory has been a disaster in ethics, and now it threatens to become devastating to business ethics as well." However, I find myself somewhat at a loss to know what to say, since the game theory he attacks is not practiced by any game theorists with whom I am familiar. At first, I thought this was because my friends and I were deemed to fall into the class of "refined" game theorists to whom Solomon is willing to grant grudging acceptance, but it turns out that their refinement lies in appealing to principles that contradict the essence of the game theoretic enterprise. My guess is therefore that the plain old "vulgar" game theory which he attacks is actually intended to be the same game theory for which John Harsanyi, John Nash, and Reinhard Selten were recently awarded the Nobel Prize. My strategy in replying will therefore have to be the same as those innocent men who are asked why they beat their wives. Instead of explaining why wife beating is a good idea, I shall have to insist that I don't beat my wife at all.

2. Solomon's Criticisms of Game Theory

After several pages of polemic, Solomon (12) reproduces seven criticisms of game theory from his book *Ethics and Excellence.* In this section I will respond to typical samples from each of these criticisms:

(1) In this criticism, he accuses game theorists of begging two questions: (a) Whether rationality demands a prudential, safety-first approach? (b) Whether rationality demands the cultivation of personal advantage to the exclusion of the interests of others? The first question perhaps relates to the misapprehension that game theory recommends the use of the maximin criterion outside zero-sum games. But even within a zero-sum game like Poker, few people would regard the enormous level of bluffing required by optional play to be either prudent or safety-first (Binmore [3]). Solomon believes that

game theorists must answer the second question in the affirmative, supporting this mistaken claim with various *ad hominen* remarks about the notorious selfishness of people in my profession. But rationality as understood by game theorists is entirely neutral about the goals of the players. For the utility theory of [John] Von Neumann and [Oskar] Morgenstern to be applicable, it is only necessary that the decisions a player makes are consistent with each other.

In fact, Bergstrom (2) recently used game theory to study interaction within the family on the assumption that brothers and sisters actively care about each other's welfare. In my view, the camaraderie that Solomon rightly believes to be so important for small-group interactions inside the firm has its origins in the instinctive strategies that our species evolved for use within kin games.

(2) This criticism is largely devoted to debunking John Rawls's (9) Theory of Justice. Solomon has some excuse for classifying Anatole Rapaport and David Gauthier as game theorists, since they actually talk about games in their books. However, both fail to clear the lowest hurdle that game theorists set for their profession: both maintain that it is rational to cooperate in the one-shot Prisoners' Dilemma. * But Rawls makes no pretense at being a game theorist. Behind the Rawlsian veil of ignorance, everybody is the same, and so Rawls is able to treat their predicament as a one-person decision problem. It is true that he resolves this decision problem using Von Neumann's maximum criterion, but game theorists do not endorse this idiosyncratic refusal to apply the standard methods of Bayesian decision theory [a theory that provides a solid theoretical foundation for thinking about problems of action and inference under uncertainty]. On the contrary, game theory recommends the use of maximum criterion only when two players have diametrically opposed interests. But such zero-sum games are as distant from the problem faced by the players in Rawls's original position as it is possible to get.

If Solomon wished to complain about the use of game theory behind the veil of ignorance, he would have done better to attack the widely cited ethical work of Harsanyi (6). Working independently of Rawls, he analyzed the result of using the original position to make moral judgments without appealing to unorthodox decision principles. Far from being led to Rawls' version of egalitarianism, Harsanyi concludes in favor of utilitarianism—the refutation of which was one of Rawls's (9) major aims in the Theory of Justice.

My own work criticizes both Harsanyi and Rawls for assuming that the hypothetical deal reached in the original position has the status of a binding contract (Binmore [5]). Without this assumption, the use of game-theoretic techniques leads to a conclusion much closer to Rawls than Harsanyi. If he had known of any of the literature that genuinely applies game theory to ethics, Solomon could therefore have directed his criticisms of Rawls at me. But I

---

* [The prisoners' dilemma is the story of two criminals who have been arrested for a heinous crime and are being interrogated separately. Each knows that if neither of them talks, the case against them is weak and they will be convicted and punished for lesser charges. If this happens, each will get one year in prison. If both confess, each will get 20 years in prison. If only one confesses and testifies against the other, the one who did not cooperate with the police will get a life sentence and the one who did cooperate will get parole—Ed.]

would be totally unmoved at game theory being criticized because its use leads to conclusions that Solomon dislikes. The principles of game theory are ethically neutral, like *modus ponens* in logic or $2 + 2 = 4$ in mathematics.

It is as silly to attack game theory because it leads to ethical conclusions that you don't like as to attack logic or mathematics for the same reason. If the conclusion is wrong, the place to look for a mistake is in the assumptions from which it is deduced. For example, Harsanyi's defense of utilitarianism shouldn't be rejected because he uses orthodox decision theory, but because he can't explain why anyone should feel constrained by the terms of his hypothetical contract. Similarly, my own work is vulnerable to criticism, not I hope because the analysis is wrong, but because of the highly speculative assumptions I make about our evolutionary heritage.

(3) This criticism charges game theorists with proceeding as though people care only about money. In reply, it is only necessary to observe that it was game theorists who were largely responsible for constructing modern utility theory because it was obvious to them that it is inadequate to model people as maximizers of money.

(4) In this criticism, game theorists are taken to task for neglecting the possibility that people may be altruistic. Here he seems to forget the footnote in which he praises Axelrod's (1) game-theoretic study of the evolution of reciprocal altruism. (Although it was not Axelrod who discovered the folk theorem of repeated game theory. Nor is it true that tit-for-tat is the "best" strategy even for the indefinitely repeated Prisoners' Dilemma. Later work shows that Axelrod's claims on this front are not robust.)

(5) Here game theorists are charged again with proceeding on the assumption that people are goal-oriented, but it is not clear why Ned McClennen (7,8) should be chosen for special mention since his theory of resolute choice is regarded as heretical by game theorists. (If McClennen were right on this subject, then Selten [10] would not be entitled to his Nobel Prize.) Let me repeat that game theorists simply assume that decisions are made consistently, and then appeal to various theorems for the conclusion that they then behave as though they were goal-oriented.

(6) This criticism would seem to apply to all mathematical modeling, since it lies in the assertion that the world is always more complicated than any specific model. His concern about the fact that it is not always clear in real-life games who should be counted among the players seems to be made in ignorance of the enormous literature within industrial organization on the entry and exit of players in games.

(7) In criticizing "social contract thinking," Solomon confuses the rules for sustaining an equilibrium in the game of life with the rules of the game of life itself. Of course established business practice should not be modeled as a game. It needs to be modeled as an equilibrium in a game. Similarly, to take up an earlier point, of course one should not model an ongoing business relationship as the one-shot Prisoners' Dilemma. But where are the game theorists who would make such an elementary blunder? We study implicit collusion in industries controlled by only a few firms using the theory of repeated games.

3. Game Theory and Ethics

Solomon's claim that game theory has been a curse to ethics seems particularly bizarre to someone who has been seeking to gain acceptance among moral philosophers for the view that we shall never understand how and why human morality evolved until we have learned to use game theory to put some flesh on the bones of David Hume's idea that its function is to coordinate behavior on one of the many equilibria in the complicated game of life that humans play. But never has such sweet music fallen on ears so deaf! Far from game theory proving a curse to moral philosophy, it is hard to find a moral philosopher who thinks that game theory has any relevance to his subject at all. I shall therefore conclude this brief note with some propaganda about the advantages of adopting my own game-theoretic approach to ethics.

Following Singer's (11) pioneering study, it seems to me that a scientific approach has no choice but to accept that our moral systems evolved along with the human race. According to Solomon, game theorists long ago forgot Hume's emphasis on the importance of the moral sentiments, but the natural origin of our ethical intuitions takes center stage when Singer discusses their evolution in terms of three "expanding circles"—kin selection, reciprocal altruism and group selection. The first and second of these were mentioned in passing in the previous section, but it is the third that I believe to be fundamental. Human groups that find efficient, nonconfrontational ways to solve the equilibrium selection will obviously expand in size or in number when compared with groups that fall into costly disputes over which equilibrium to select. In the long run, only the former groups will therefore survive.

In my own work, I argue that nothing more than these building blocks is necessary to explain the moral intuitions that we feel so forcefully (Binmore [4,5]). Along with the other game theorists who take this naturalistic line, I know perfectly well that my simple models don't take us very far. But we feel that the muddled platitudes of those who are unwilling to model at all take us nowhere at all. If an example is needed of the failure of traditional moral philosophy, let me recommend Solomon's (12) own *Reader's Digest* version of Aristotle's ideas. If a scientific discipline had made no progress in two thousand years, we would begin to doubt the soundness of the principles on which it was based. Perhaps we should begin to apply the same criteria to the traditional approach to ethics.

Bibliography

(1) R. Axelrod. *The Evolution of Cooperation.* New York: Basic Books, 1984.
(2) T. Bergstrom. "On the evolution of altruistic ethical rules for siblings." *American Economic Review* 85 (1985).
(3) K. Binmore. *Fun and Games.* Lexington, Mass.: D. C. Heath, 1991.
(4) K. Binmore. *Playing Fair: Game Theory and the Social Contract I.* Cambridge, Mass.: MIT Press, 1994.
(5) K. Binmore. *Just Playing: Game Theory and the Social Contract II.* Cambridge, Mass.: MIT Press, 1998.
(6) J. Harsanyi. *Rational Behavior and Bargaining Equilibrium in Games and Social Situations.* Cambridge: Cambridge University Press, 1977.

(7) E. McClennen. *Rationality and Dynamic Choice.* Cambridge: Cambridge University Press, 1990.
(8) E. McClennen. "Morality as a public good." *Business Ethics Quarterly* 9, no. 1 (1999).
(9) J. Rawls. *A Theory of Justice.* Oxford: Oxford University Press, 1972.
(10) R. Selten. "Reexamination of the perfectness concept for equilibrium points in extensive-games." *International Journal of Game Theory* 4 (1975): 25–55.
(11) P. Singer. *The Expanding Circle: Ethics and Sociobiology.* New York: Farrar, Strauss and Giroux, 1980.
(12) R. Solomon. *Ethics and Excellence.* Oxford: Oxford University Press, 1991.
(13) R. Solomon. "Game theory as a model for business and business ethics." *Business Ethics Quarterly* 9, no. 1 (1999).

POSTSCRIPT

Is Game Theory Devastating to Business Ethics?

Solomon and Binmore are engaged in a scholarly debate about a theory that, in spite of its popular name ("game"), has little to do with the popular life. But the larger debate is about the perceived inhumanity, or impersonality of the business world. It often seems that a corporate juggernaut simply cannot be reasoned with; its leaders believe that, because the books recommend a certain course of action as good for the shareholders, that action must be carried out, no matter the effect on the workers, the environment, or the law.

Part of the wider problem is the question of the corporate culture; part of it is the question of the moral individual caught up in the impersonal corporate context. What can be done? How can we give business a more human face?

Suggested Readings

Robert Axelrod, *The Evolution of Cooperation* (Basic Books, 1984).

Steven J. Brams, *The Theory of Moves* (Cambridge University Press, 1994).

Albert Z. Carr, "Is Business Bluffing Ethical?" *Harvard Business Review* (January–February 1968).

David Gauthier, *Morals By Agreement* (Oxford, 1986).

Nicholas Rescher, *Unselfishness* (University of Pittsburgh Press, 1975).

T.C. Schelling, *The Strategy of Conflict* (Cambridge University Press, 1960).

Robert Solomon, *Ethics and Excellence* (Oxford, 1991).

John von Neumann and Oscar Morgenstern, *Theory of Games and Economic Behavior* (Harvard University Press, 1944).

On the Internet ...

DUSHKIN ONLINE

Institute for Business and Professional Ethics

In addition to providing information about the DePaul University's Institute for Business and Professional Ethics, this site also offers ethics links, professional resources, an online journal of ethics, and an ethics calendar.

http://www.depaul.edu/ethics/

STAT-USA/Internet

This site, a service of the U.S. Department of Commerce, provides one-stop Internet browsing for business, trade, and economic information. It contains daily economic news, frequently requested statistical releases, information on export and international trade, domestic economic news and statistical series, and databases.

http://www.stat-usa.gov/stat-usa.html

PhRMA: America's Pharmaceutical Companies

PhRMA membership represents approximately 100 U.S. pharmaceutical companies that have a primary commitment to pharmaceutical research. Information on the effects of pharmaceutical price controls on research spending is one of the many topics covered at this site.

http://phrma.org

NumaWeb

This Numa Financial Systems site calls itself "the Internet's home page for financial derivatives." This site includes a reference index, a discussion forum, and links to many related sites.

http://www.numa.com/index.htm

PART 2

Current Issues in Business

*T*his section explores the topical issues in business, including two relatively new enterprises for business: the rapidly expanding medical field and the proliferation of casino gambling. The section closes with an issue on investing.

- Are Business and Medicine Ethically Incompatible?

- Are Pharmaceutical Price Controls Justifiable?

- Should Casino Gambling Be Prohibited?

- Are Derivative Instruments Purchases Just Gambling?

ISSUE 5

Are Business and Medicine Ethically Incompatible?

YES: Arnold S. Relman, from "What Market Values Are Doing to Medicine," *The Atlantic Monthly* (March 1992)

NO: Andrew C. Wicks, from "Albert Schweitzer or Ivan Boesky? Why We Should Reject the Dichotomy Between Medicine and Business," *Journal of Business Ethics* (vol. 14, 1995)

ISSUE SUMMARY

YES: Professor of medicine Arnold S. Relman argues that although doctors should not be businessmen, financial and technological pressures are forcing them to act like businessmen, with deleterious consequences for patients and for society as a whole.

NO: Andrew C. Wicks, an assistant professor at the University of Washington School of Business, challenges the perceived contrast between physician ethics and business ethics and suggests that a closer look will reveal fundamental similarities.

The heart of this issue may lie with the confusion between the two types of ethics involved: the *professional ethic* and the *market ethic*. The *professional,* or *fiduciary,* ethic, applicable to all professional-client relationships and all commercial fiduciary-beneficiary relationships, requires that the active party (professional or trustee) act *only in the interests of the other.* For example, doctors must act only in the interests of their patients, lawyers for their clients, pastors for their congregations (individually and collectively), and the managers of funds and trusts for those who have entrusted funds to them. By this ethic, boards of directors of publicly owned corporations must act only in the interests of the shareholders in the corporation.

The *market* ethic, in contrast, requires that each party protect *its own interests,* abstaining only from force and fraud as means to achieving an agreement. This adversarial ethic, best seen in labor negotiations and proceedings in a court of law, underlies the "voluntary transaction" on which the free market is based. The free market assumes a universe of rational free agents, each acting to maximize self-interest within a legal framework designed to protect the rights of all. Not all people fit that assumption—especially the very young, very old, sick, or disabled, or simply those who are very far away from the dealings—which is why there are fiduciary relationships.

The professional ethic of the physician is brief and simple, and it is reflected in the Hippocratic oath that is generally taken by those about to begin a medical practice:

> In whatsoever houses I enter, I will enter to help the sick, and I will abstain from all intentional wrongdoing and harm. . . . And whatsoever I shall see or hear in the course of my profession in my intercourse with men, if it be what should not be published abroad, I will never divulge, holding such things to be holy secrets. Now if I carry out this oath, and break it not, may I gain forever reputation among all men for my life and for my art.

There is much more to the oath than this, but the essence of the oath is as applicable now as it was 2,500 years ago when Hippocrates first established it; the essence is that the physician acts only for the benefit of the patient, attending to the patient's illnesses, comforting and reassuring him or her, tailoring diets and advice to the patient's particular case, and keeping her or his secrets in absolute confidence.

The relationship between the physician and the patient remained the same in the period between 500 B.C. and A.D. 1900. Sick people sought out healers, trusted their advice, often were helped by their ministrations, and, to the extent the patients were able, paid them for their services. In the twentieth century however, medicine began to be "professionalized": Licensing laws were established to eliminate quacks; legislation was enacted requiring licensed professionals to supervise a required professional education; professional organizations active in advancing the state of the art and protecting the professional image surfaced; and, generally, higher rates of reimbursement were charged by the physicians. Rapid advances in medical technology at midcentury sent medical costs beyond the reach of people with ordinary incomes and savings; third-party reimbursement—first from private insurers and then from the federal government (in the form of Medicare and Medicaid)—was introduced at the third quarter of the century and helped relieve the extraordinary burden on patients, but it also allowed the medical profession to prescribe ever more expensive technological cures, which sent health care costs through the roof.

As the twentieth century draws to a close, the consequences of these costs for the economy as a whole are becoming clear. "Cost-containment" measures that take medical care decisions out of the physician's private office and put them into the hands of corporate boards of health maintenance organizations (HMOs) and hospitals dominate medical progress at this point. But how does this affect the privacy aspect of the patient-physician relationship?

As you read these selections, ask yourself whether or not business is incompatible with the physician's ethic, as Arnold S. Relman seems to understand it. Does the reformulation proposed by Andrew C. Wicks make sense? Or do both writers miss the point? What do you see in the future for medical care in America?

79

Arnold S. Relman  **YES**

What Market Values Are
Doing to Medicine

From its earliest origins the profession of medicine has steadfastly held that physicians' responsibility to their patients takes precedence over their own economic interests. Thus the oath of Hippocrates enjoins physicians to serve only "for the benefit of the sick," and the oft-recited prayer attributed to Moses Maimonides, a revered physician of the twelfth century, asks God not to allow "thirst for profit" or "ambition for renown" to interfere with the physician's practice of his profession. In modern times this theme has figured prominently in many medical codes of ethics. The International Code of the World Medical Organization, for example, says that "a doctor must practice his profession uninfluenced by motives of profit." And in 1957, in its newly revised Principles of Medical Ethics, the American Medical Association [AMA] declared that "the principal objective of the medical profession is to render service to humanity." It went on to say, "In the practice of medicine a physician should limit the source of his professional income to medical services actually rendered by him, or under his supervision, to his patients."

Such lofty pronouncements notwithstanding, the medical profession has never been immune to knavery and profiteering. And, particularly in the days before biomedical science began to establish a rational basis for the practice of medicine, the profession has had its share of charlatans and quacks. Still, the highest aspiration of the medical profession—sometimes honored in the breach, to be sure—has always been to serve the needs of the sick. And that has been the basis of a de facto contract between modern society and the profession.

What are the terms of this contract? In this country, state governments grant physicians a licensed monopoly to practice their profession and allow them considerable autonomy in setting their educational and professional standards and their working conditions. The professional education of physicians is heavily subsidized, because tuition, even in the private medical schools, does not nearly cover the costs of educating medical students. Furthermore, the information, tools, and techniques that physicians use to practice their profession are usually developed through publicly supported research. Finally, hospitals provide physicians with the facilities and personnel and often even the specialized equipment they need to treat their hospitalized patients, thus relieving doctors of many of the kinds of overhead costs that businessmen must pay. Physicians have enjoyed a privileged position in our society, virtually assuring them of high social status and a good living. They have been accorded these privileges in the expectation that they will remain competent and trustworthy and will faithfully discharge the fiduciary responsibility to patients proclaimed in their ethical codes.

The Distinctions Between Medical Practice and Commerce

Now, if this description of a contract between society and the medical profession is even approximately correct, then clearly there are important distinctions to be made between what society has a right to expect of practicing physicians and what it expects of people in business. Both are expected to earn their living from their occupation, but the relation between physicians and patients is supposed to be quite different from that between businessmen and customers. Patients depend on their physicians to be altruistic and committed in advising them on their health-care needs and providing necessary medical services. Most patients do not have the expertise to evaluate their own need for medical care. The quality of life and sometimes life itself are at stake, and price is of relatively little importance, not only because of the unique value of the services rendered but also because patients usually do not pay out of pocket for services at the time they are received. Although most physicians are paid (usually by the government or an insurance company) for each service they provide, the assumption is that they are acting in the best interests of patients rather than of themselves. A fact that underscores the centrality of the patient's interests is that advertising and marketing in medical practice were until very recently considered unethical.

In contrast, in a commercial market multiple providers of goods and services try to induce customers to buy. That's the whole point. Competing with one another, businesses rely heavily on marketing and advertising to generate demand for services or products, regardless of whether they are needed, because each provider's primary concern is to increase his sales and thereby maximize his income. Although commercial vendors have an obligation to produce a good product and advertise it without deception, they have no responsibility to consider the consumer's interests—to advise the consumer which product, if any, is really needed, or to worry about those who cannot afford to buy any of the vendors' products. Markets may be effective mechanisms for distributing goods and services according to consumers' desires and ability to pay, but they have no interest in consumers' needs, or in achieving universal access.

In a commercial market, consumers are expected to fend for themselves in judging what they can afford and want to buy. *"Caveat emptor"* ["Let the buyer beware"] is the rule. According to classical market theory, when well-informed consumers and competing suppliers are free to seek their own objectives, the best interests of both groups are likely to be served. Thus, in commerce, market competition is relied upon to protect the interests of consumers. This is quite different from the situation in health care, where the provider of services protects the patient's interests by acting as advocate and counselor. Unlike the independent shoppers envisioned by market theory, sick and worried patients cannot adequately look after their own interests, nor do they usually want to. Personal medical service does not come in standardized packages and in different grades for the consumer's comparison and selection. Moreover, a sick patient often does not have the option of deferring his purchase of medical care or shopping around for the best buy. A patient with seizures and severe headache who is told that he has a brain tumor requiring surgery, or a patient with intractable angina and high-grade obstruction of a coronary artery who is advised to have a coronary bypass, does not look for the "best buy" or consider whether he really needs "top-of-the-line" surgical quality. If he does not trust the judgment and competence of the first surgeon he consults, he may seek the opinion of another, but he will very shortly have to trust someone to act as his beneficent counselor, and he will surely want the best care available, regardless of how much or how little his insurance will pay the doctor.

Some skeptics have always looked askance at the physician's double role as purveyor of services and patients' advocate. They have questioned whether doctors paid on a fee-for-service basis can really give advice to patients that is free of economic self-interest. One of the most caustic critiques of private fee-for-service medical practice was written early in this century by George Bernard Shaw, in his preface to *The Doctor's Dilemma*. It begins,

> It is not the fault of our doctors that the medical service of the community, as at present provided for, is a murderous absurdity. That any sane nation, having observed that you could provide for the supply of bread by giving bakers a pecuniary interest in baking for you, should go on to give a surgeon a pecuniary interest in cutting off your leg, is enough to make one despair of political humanity. But that is precisely what we have done. And the more appalling the mutilation the more the mutilator is paid....
>
> Scandalized voices murmur that... operations are necessary. They may be. It may also be necessary to hang a man or pull down a house. But we take good care not to make the hangman and the housebreaker the judges of that. If we did, no man's neck would be safe and no man's house stable.

Some contemporary defenders of fee-for-service evidently see no need to answer attacks like Shaw's. They reject the distinctions I have drawn between business and medical practice, claiming that medicine is just another market —admittedly with more imperfections than most, but a market nevertheless. They profess not to see much difference between medical care and any other important economic commodity, such as food, clothing, or housing. Such critics dismiss the notion of a de facto social contract in medical care. They assert that physicians and private hospitals owe nothing to society and should be free to sell or otherwise dispose of their services in any lawful manner they choose.

The Medical-Industrial Complex

Until recently such views had little influence. Most people considered medical care to be a social good, not a commodity, and physicians usually acted as if they agreed. Physicians were not impervious to economic pressures, but the pressures were relatively weak and the tradition of professionalism was relatively strong.

This situation is now rapidly changing. In the past two decades or so health care has become commercialized as never before, and professionalism in medicine seems to be giving way to entrepreneurialism. The health-care system is now widely regarded as an industry, and medical practice as a competitive business. Let me try briefly to explain the origins and describe the scope of this transformation.

First, the past few decades have witnessed a rapid expansion of medical facilities and personnel, leading to an unprecedented degree of competition for paying patients. Our once too few and overcrowded hospitals are now too numerous and on average less than 70 percent occupied. Physicians, formerly in short supply and very busy, now abound everywhere (except in city slums and isolated rural areas), and many are not as busy as they would like to be. Professionalism among self-employed private practitioners thrives when there is more than enough to do. When there isn't, competition for patients and worry about income tend to undermine professional values and influence professional judgment. Many of today's young physicians have to worry not only about getting themselves established in practice but also about paying off the considerable debt they have accumulated in medical school. High tuition levels make new graduates feel that they have paid a lot for an education that must now begin to pay them back—handsomely. This undoubtedly influences the choice of specialty many graduates make and conditions their attitudes toward the economics of medical practice.

Along with the expansion of health care has come a great increase in specialization and technological sophistication, which has raised the price of services and made the economic rewards of medicine far greater than before. With insurance available to pay the bills, physicians have powerful economic incentives to recruit patients and provide expensive services. In an earlier and less technologically sophisticated era most physicians were generalists rather than specialists. They had mainly their time and counsel to offer, commodities that commanded only modest prices. Now a multitude of tests and procedures provide lucrative opportunities for extra income. This inevitably encourages an entrepreneurial approach to medical practice and an overuse of services.

Another major factor in the transformation of the system has been the appearance of investor-owned health-care businesses. Attracted by opportunities for profit resulting from the expansion of private and public health insurance, these new businesses (which I call the medical-industrial complex) have built and operated chains of hospitals, clinics, nursing homes, diagnostic laboratories, and many other kinds of health facilities. Recent growth has been mainly in ambulatory and home services and in specialized inpatient facilities other than acute-care general hospitals, in part because most government efforts to control health-care costs and the construction of new facilities have been focused on hospitals. Nevertheless, the growth of the medical-industrial complex continues unabated. There are no reliable data, but I would guess that at least a third of all nonpublic health-care facilities are now operated by investor-owned businesses. For example, most nursing homes, private psychiatric hospitals, and free-standing therapeutic or diagnostic facilities are investor-owned. So are nearly two thirds of the so-called health-maintenance organizations, which now provide comprehensive prepaid medical care to nearly 35 million members.

Effects on Providers

This corporatization of health care, coupled with increasingly hostile and cost-conscious policies by private insurance companies and government, has had a powerful and pervasive effect on the attitudes of health-care providers —including those in the not-for-profit sector. Not-for-profit, nonpublic hospitals ("voluntary hospitals"), which constitute more than three quarters of the nonpublic acute-care general hospitals in the country, originally were philanthropic social institutions, with the primary mission of serving the health-care needs of their communities. Now, forced to compete with investor-owned hospitals and a rapidly growing number of for-profit ambulatory facilities, and struggling to maintain their economic viability in the face of sharp reductions in third-party payments, they increasingly see themselves as beleaguered businesses, and they act accordingly. Altruistic concerns are being distorted in many voluntary hospitals by a concern for the bottom line. Management decisions are now often based more on considerations of profit than on the health needs of the community. Many voluntary hospitals seek to avoid or to limit services to the poor. They actively promote their profitable services to insured patients, they advertise themselves, they establish health-related businesses, and they make deals with physicians to generate more revenue. Avoiding uninsured patients simply adds to the problems of our underserved indigent population and widens the gap in medical care between rich and poor. Promoting elective care for insured patients leads to overuse of medical services and runs up the national health-care bill.

Physicians are reacting similarly as they struggle to maintain their income in an increasingly competitive economic climate. Like hospitals, practicing physicians have begun to use advertising, marketing, and public-relations techniques to attract more patients. Until recently most medical professional societies considered self-promotion of this kind to be unethical, but attitudes have changed, and now competition among physicians is viewed as a necessary, even beneficial, feature of the new medical marketplace.

Many financially attractive opportunities now exist for physicians to invest in health-care facilities to which they can then refer their patients, and a growing number of doctors have become limited partners in such enterprises —for example, for-profit diagnostic laboratories and MRI [magnetic resonance imaging] centers, to which they refer their patients but over which they can exercise no professional supervision. Surgeons invest in ambulatory-surgery facilities that are owned and managed by businesses or hospitals, and in which they perform surgery on their patients. Thus they both are paid for their professional services and share in the profits resulting from the referral of their patients to a particular facility. A recent study in Florida revealed that approximately 40 percent of all physicians practicing in that state had financial interests in facilities to which they referred patients. The AMA, however, estimates that nationwide the figure is about 10 percent.

In other kinds of entrepreneurial arrangements, office-based practitioners make deals with wholesalers of prescription drugs and sell those drugs to their patients at a profit, or buy prostheses from manufacturers at reduced rates and sell them at a profit—in addition to the fees they receive for implanting the prostheses. In entering into these and similar business arrangements, physicians are trading on their patients' trust. This is a clear violation of the traditional ethical rule against earning professional income by referring patients to others or by investing in the goods and services recommended to patients. Such arrangements create conflicts of interest that go far beyond the economic conflict of interest in the fee-for-service system, and they blur the distinction between business and the medical profession.

Not only practitioners but also physicians doing clinical research at teaching hospitals are joining the entrepreneurial trend. Manufacturers of new drugs, devices, and clinical tests are entering into financial arrangements with clinicians engaged in testing their products—and the results of those studies may have an important effect on the commercial success of the product. Clinical investigators may own equity interest in the company that produces the product or may serve as paid consultants and scientific advisers, thus calling into question their ability to act as rigorously impartial evaluators. Harvard Medical School has wisely taken a stand against such arrangements, but unfortunately this obvious conflict of interest has so far been ignored, or at least tolerated, in many other institutions.

Business arrangements of this kind are also common in postgraduate education. Respected academic clinicians are frequently hired by drug firms to give lectures or write articles about the manufacturers' new products. The assumption, of course, is that these experts are expressing honest and dispassionate opinions about the relative merits of competing products, but such an assumption is strained by the realization that an expert is being handsomely paid by the manufacturer of one particular product in a market that is often highly competitive.

Similarly, drug manufacturers offer inducements to practicing physicians to attend seminars at which their products are touted, and even to institute treatment with a particular drug. In the former case the ostensible justification is furtherance of postgraduate education; in the latter it is the gathering of post-marketing information about a new drug. The embarrassing transparency of these subterfuges has recently caused pharmaceutical manufacturers to agree with the AMA that such practices should be curtailed.

In short, at every turn in the road physicians both in practice and in academic institutions are being attracted by financial arrangements that can compromise their professional independence.

Antitrust Medicine

The courts have significantly contributed to the change in atmosphere. For many years the legal and medical professions enjoyed immunity from antitrust law because it was generally believed that they were not engaged in the kind of commercial activity that the Sherman Act and the Federal Trade Commission Act were designed to regulate. In 1975 the Supreme Court ended this immunity (*Goldfarb v. Virginia State Bar*). It decided that the reach of antitrust law extended to the professions. Since then numerous legal actions have been taken against individual physicians or physicians' organizations to curb what government has perceived to be "anti-competitive" practices. Thus the courts and the Federal Trade Commission have prevented medical societies in recent years from prohibiting commercial advertising or marketing and from taking any action that might influence professional fees or legal business ventures by physicians.

Concerns about possible antitrust liability have caused the AMA to retreat from many of the anti-commercial recommendations in its 1957 code of ethics. The latest revisions of the ethical code say that advertising is permissible so long as it is not deceptive. Investments in healthcare facilities are also permissible, provided that they are allowed by law and disclosed to patients, and provided also that they do not interfere with the physician's primary duty to his or her patients. Reflecting the new economic spirit, a statement has been added that competition is "not only ethical but is encouraged." Indeed, the AMA goes even further, declaring that "ethical medical practice thrives best under free market conditions when prospective patients have adequate information and opportunity to choose freely between and among competing physicians and alternate systems of medical care." Thus an earlier forthright stand by organized medicine against the commercialization of medical practice has now been replaced by an uneasy ambivalence.

Very recently, however, the AMA seems to have reconsidered its position, at least with respect to some kinds of entrepreneurial activity. At its last meeting it adopted a resolution advising physicians not to refer patients to an outside facility in which the physician has an ownership interest—except when the facility was built in response to a demonstrated need and alternative financing for its construction was not available. It remains to be seen whether this advice will be heeded and whether the AMA will take a similar position on other commercial practices. It will also be interesting to see what response this modest stand in defense of professional ethics will elicit from the Federal Trade Commission.

The Government's Response

Government policy has also been ambivalent. The Reagan and Bush Administrations have staunchly supported competition and free markets in medicine under the delusion that this is a way to limit expenditures. The White House has therefore supported the Federal Trade Commission's antitrust policies and until recently has resisted all proposals for curbing entrepreneurial initiatives in health care. But expenditures are not likely to be limited in a market lacking the restraints ordinarily imposed by cost-conscious consumers who must pay for what they want and can afford. And if the competing providers in such a market have great power to determine what is to be purchased, then their competition inevitably drives up expenditures and the total size of the market. In business, success is measured in terms of increasing sales volume and revenues —the last thing we want to see in the health-care system. Despite its preference for market mechanisms, however, the Bush Administration recently abandoned ideology and supported legislation to regulate physicians' fees and to prevent physicians from referring their Medicare patients to diagnostic laboratories in which they have a financial interest. Regulations and new legislation to provide even stricter limits on physicians' investments in health-care facilities are currently under consideration in several states—not for ethical reasons but simply as measures to limit health-care spending. Clearly, cost control is now the highest priority in public policy.

Despite its recent willingness to intervene in limited ways to control costs generated by some of the entrepreneurial activities of physicians, the government has as yet shown little interest in interfering with the spreading commercialization of our health-care system. That should not be surprising, because private enterprise is now widely heralded as the answer to most economic problems. We hear much these days about the privatization of schools, highways, airports, jails, national parks, the postal service, and many other aspects of our society—and by this is meant not simply removal from government control but transfer to investor ownership. Business, it is said, can do a much better job of running most of these things than government, so why not turn them over to private enterprise? I do not want to debate this general proposition here, but medical care, I suggest, is in many ways uniquely unsuited to private enterprise. It is an essential social service, requiring the involvement of the community and the commitment of health-care professionals. It flourishes best in the private sector but it needs public support, and it cannot meet its responsibilities to society if it is dominated by business interests.

Why Should the Public Care?

If government is not concerned about the loss of social and professional values in our health-care system, should the American public care? I think it must. The quality and effectiveness of our medical care depend critically on the values and the behavior of its providers. If health care is not a business, then we should encourage our physicians to stand by their traditional fiduciary obligations, and we should enable, if not require, our voluntary hospitals to honor their commitments to the community.

If most of our physicians become entrepreneurs and most of our hospitals and health-care facilities become businesses, paying patients will get more care than they need and poor patients will get less. In a commercialized system the cost of health care will continue to escalate and yet we will not be assured of getting the kind of care we really need. In such a system we will no longer be able to trust our physicians, because the bond of fiduciary responsibility will have been broken. To control costs, government will be driven to adopt increasingly stringent regulations. Ultimately health care will have to be regulated like a public utility, and much greater constraints will be placed on physicians and hospitals than are now in place or even contemplated.

Our health-care system is inequitable, inefficient, and too expensive. It badly needs reform. The task will be arduous and the solution is far from clear, but I believe that the first step must be to gain a firm consensus on what we value in health care and what kind of a medical profession we want. The medical profession has held a privileged position in American society, based on the expectation that it will serve society's needs first of all. How can it hope to continue in that position if it loses the trust of the public? We cannot expect to solve our health-care problems unless we can count on the basic altruism of the profession and its sense of responsibility to patients and the general public welfare. American society and the medical profession need to reaffirm their de facto contract, because they will have to depend on each other as the United States painfully gropes its way toward a better system of health care.

Physicians have the power to make health-care reform possible. They know the system better than anyone, and if they want to, they can use its resources more prudently than they do now without any loss of medical effectiveness. It is primarily their decisions that determine what medical services will be provided in each case, and therefore what the aggregate expenditure for health care will be. If physicians remain free of conflicting economic ties, and if they act in a truly professional manner, medical facilities will probably be used more appropriately, regardless of their ownership or organization. In any case, no proposed reforms in the health-care system can ultimately be successful without a properly motivated medical profession. But if physicians continue to allow themselves to be drawn along the path of private entrepreneurship, they will increasingly be seen as self-interested businessmen and will lose many of the privileges they now enjoy as fiduciaries and trusted professionals. They will also lose the opportunity to play a constructive role in shaping the major reforms that are surely coming.

The medical profession is not likely to change its direction without help. The incentives that now encourage—indeed, in many cases require—physicians to act primarily as businessmen will have to be changed, and probably so will the configurations in which most physicians practice. In my opinion, a greater reliance on group practice and more emphasis on medical insurance that prepays providers at a fixed annual rate offer the best chance of solving the economic problems of health care, because these arrangements put physicians in the most favorable position to act as prudent advocates for their patients, rather than as entrepreneurial vendors of services. However, regardless of what structural changes in the health-care system are ultimately adopted, physicians hold the key. The sooner they join with government and the public in reaffirming the medical profession's ethical contract with society, the easier will be the task of reform and the greater the chance of its success.

NO ⬅

Andrew C. Wicks

Albert Schweitzer or Ivan Boesky? Why We Should Reject the Dichotomy Between Medicine and Business

As we contemplate the profound changes the Clinton administration will propose for health care, it is not surprising that numerous passionate and conflicting views exist on what direction to take. While investigating the full range of such perspectives is a task nearly as imposing as restructuring our ailing health care system, I do want to explore some key assumptions that frame how many people think about health care reform. These assumptions are tied to a broader sense that medicine and business are, and should remain, polar opposites—things which ought never to be mixed together or confused for fear that the results could be disastrous. More specifically, many scholars in medicine and medical ethics lament that medicine is increasingly becoming a business, and that the ethos of business will inevitably erode the moral identity of health care workers and dominate the physician-patient relationship.

... While I share much of the concern that is raised here, I will argue that this conceptualization of the issues is overly simplistic and that a more nuanced analysis is necessary. To make my argument I want to explore three questions:

1. What specific changes in medicine reflect the introduction of "business" thinking and are these changes desirable from an ethical standpoint?
2. How substantial are the differences between the ethics of medicine and the ethics of business?
3. Can the two ethical models, or aspects of them, be combined in a positive way?

As a vehicle to address these questions, I will focus on how we think about the models of medicine and business, specifically the ways in which ethical imperatives shape the activities of their respective practitioners and the missions of their institutions....

My approach to these issues will be that of an ethicist, trained to reflect on normative issues. I will not offer or defend specific policies or institutional

From Andrew C. Wicks, "Albert Schweitzer or Ivan Boesky? Why We Should Reject the Dichotomy Between Medicine and Business," *Journal of Business Ethics,* vol. 14 (1995), pp. 339–349. Copyright © 1995 by D. Reidel Publishing Co., Dordrecht, Holland, and Boston, U.S.A. Reprinted by permission of Kluwer Academic Publishers. Notes omitted.

arrangements, although my arguments will have direct relevance to the sorts of practical proposals that are being considered for health care. My underlying goal is to help reconceptualize how we think about both medicine and business, and in so doing, reshape how we approach the "American health care crisis."

The Costs of Commercialism

Among the more significant concerns that the commercialization of medicine raises are the following:

1. The market model doesn't "fit" medicine. Patients are vulnerable, they lack the knowledge to operate as effective consumers under a "caveat emptor" ["let the buyer beware"] model, and health care is an overridingly important good whose availability ought not to be determined by one's income or ability to pay.
2. The business model creates conflicts of interest in medicine, particularly between physicians and patients.
3. Allowing the market model to direct consumption is unacceptable: care would be focused on what pays rather than what is needed; market-thinking validates and supports the idea of "creating" needs rather than just meeting them; there would be incentive to overconsume which could possibly increase overall health care costs.
4. Thinking about health care as a business erodes the basis of a right to health care. That is, by thinking about health care as a commodity, rather than as a basic human right or special set of goods, it becomes more fitting to leave allocation and purchasing to market forces and individual ability to pay.
5. The growing ethos of commercialism erodes, or perhaps even renders inept, the Hippocratic tradition. By teaching physicians that they are business people we legitimate their self-interested aspirations, make patients equivalent to "customers" and, in so doing, undermine the sacred moral calling of physicians.

While I highlight these concerns and suggest they have merit, I also will argue that they create an overly simplistic picture. My strategy will be to expose some dubious assumptions which cloud our thinking on these matters. Among the assumptions embedded in the thinking of critics, such as Relman and Dougherty, are the following:

1. Medicine and business are ethically opposed and incompatible.
2. There can be no substantial mixture and/or balancing of the ethics of medicine and business [opening the door to commercialism and business will inevitably lead to its dominance over medicine].
3. The ethical problems associated with "medicine as a business" can be remedied only by rejecting the business framework.

The conceptions of business and medicine that are tied to these assumptions depict medicine as fundamentally about caring and healing. Physicians and other health care workers are compassionate, put the interests of their patients above their own, and are altruistic—i.e. there is a clear moral, perhaps even an "ultra" moral, content which defines their identity and shapes their activity. In contrast, business people are thought of as self-interested to the point of excluding any concern other than profit in their activities—i.e. they pursue only activities which serve their interest and maximize profits. The quintessential business person is greedy and driven by bottom line "business" considerations. Talk of concern for others or morality would, at best, be an after-thought, and at worst, only confuse the pursuit of their larger raison d'etre. As such, business activity is fundamentally amoral.

Let us examine these assumptions in turn. I will condense my critique of this reading of the two fields into four separate arguments.

Overestimating charity and altruism in health care workers.

This position makes too much of the charitable and altruistic nature of health care professionals. My purpose in saying this is not to question the integrity of the profession, or the extremely valuable moral traditions of medicine, but rather to temper the level of esteem in which we hold physicians. Due to the nature of the physician-patient relationship under a fee-for-service arrangement, it is in the self-interest of the physician not only to apply beneficial therapies, but to be overzealous. Providing aggressive and even excessive care to patients actually benefits the physician financially—to this extent, the well-being of the patient and the self-interest of the physician point generally in the same direction. One can also look to the stance of the majority of physicians and the AMA [American Medical Association] on such issues as HMO's, Medicare and Medicaid, and wholesale reform of the health care system to provide access for more patients as further evidence to question the degree to which physicians are self-effacing and charitable. Finally, one can point to the relatively high and rising salaries of physicians, the growth of medical specialists, the decline in indigent care, and the geographic maldistribution of physicians towards wealthier areas as further confirmation that we should be skeptical of imagining Albert Schweitzer or Mother Teresa when we call to mind the ordinary physician. Again, this is not to malign physicians or question their moral charge, rather, it is to give it a more sober and balanced interpretation.

The moral problems of introducing "business" into medicine aren't qualitatively different from those that currently exist in the "medical" model.

As I have already argued, the conflicts of interest which have been attached to the business model as areas of great concern, are present in the current system of health care delivery. The only difference is that while the "medical" model creates incentives to overtreat, the "business" model would lead physicians to undertreat. Even though both scenarios contain obvious conflicts many would argue that the former arrangement is clearly preferable to the latter. Yet, it has been persuasively argued that such a conclusion is far from obvious. First of all, there are substantial risks and harms which go along with overtreatment. Extra office visits may only hurt one's pocketbook, but unnecessary surgery, x-rays, or other invasive procedures can pose more serious physical harms to patients with little or no benefit. A recent report on the periodic use of unnecessary cesarean sections provides a disturbing reminder of just how common a phenomenon this may be. In addition, there are costs to society and third parties from overtreatment in the form of higher overall medical costs and fewer resources to offer more beneficial treatments to patients with clear and compelling needs. Finally, in this era of de facto rationing and fiscal scarcity, there is an implicit and indirect trade-off being made. When treatments are offered, others are being denied such that we must remember the harms of overtreatment are not simply to the patient and to society, but to other particular patients who have pressing medical needs that may not be met. . . .

Talking in grand metaphors/paradigms oversimplifies the problem.

Although I direct the next criticism at the commentators whom I challenge, it is also a criticism of my paper. By talking about "medicine" and "business" in global and unified models, we risk imposing a singular framework or paradigm onto a complex set of institutions and relationships. "Health care" and "medicine" include the interaction of patients with physicians, nurses, and nurse practitioners; it refers to interactions which take place in free clinics,— emergency rooms, private hospitals, public teaching hospitals, individual physician practices and HMO's; and it also connects with medical supply companies, pharmaceutical companies, insurance companies, and a range of other public and private institutions which play a variety of direct and indirect roles in the availability and delivery of health care. Talk of models is important and helps clarify a range of problems, yet it can also create new and less visible ones. The oppositional model of medicine and business tends to reinforce the idea of a singularity of norms and ideals, of context and organizational structure. Without tempering this image and accounting for the subtle and significant differences across these realms, such modeling can create arrangements which are not only inappropriate but dangerous. Indeed, I would argue that the differences that are encompassed between the various relationships and levels provides evidence that we need a more nuanced and balanced approach. The range of institutions, and the degree to which they are tied to the moral imperatives of medicine, should reinforce the idea that we are better off seeing the two models as on a continuum rather than as opposites.

Practical realities may force a marriage/combination.

Finally, if we are to construct a health care system which best fulfills the range of purposes we have for it, then it must be able to encompass a variety of objectives. A number of these objectives seem to require applying to medicine the skills, wisdom, and reflection of "business." There is a need to cut costs, reduce bureaucratic waste, spur innovation, recognize scarcity and turn what are now defacto trade-offs into conscious choices. We need to avoid the replication of services and expensive technologies across hospitals and research centers in close proximity; we need to educate physicians—at some level—to be more active gate-keepers of health services; and finally, we not only want to create greater access with reasonable cost, we want to temper public expectations and consumptive behavior—a key factor in the increased use and overall cost of health care. While this list is far from exhaustive, it illustrates the need for combining and perhaps even integrating the two models as well as the skills, wisdom, and imperatives of each. There are a number of ways to realize the ethical goals in practice, and we may be able to continue to keep the "business" and "medical" tasks distinct, but it seems clear that the two activities (and the ethics which emerge from them) can no longer be separated to the degree that they have been. In fact, one could argue that one of the key sources of this health care crisis is a failure to connect these two models, and more specifically, to ask the hard questions raised by fiscal scarcity.

In Search of a Better Model for Business

So far I have challenged the validity of the oppositional model based on practical limitations and reasons internal to the model itself. I want next to extend the argument by offering an alternative way of conceptualizing the ethics of medicine and business. I begin with a reconsideration and reconstruction of business ethics. In so doing, I seek to challenge how we think about the content of the terms "business" and "ethics", and as a result, how we think about medical ethics.

I take the description of business in the oppositional model outlined above as an accurate description of how many, and perhaps most, Americans approach the subject of business ethics. It is a model that economists have done a great deal to create and perpetuate. Business is about the pursuit of profit and self-interest—or more accurately, any form of self-beneficial activity that allows one to make a profit. Egoism and the valorization of greed drive business activity such that ethical considerations have no meaningful place, except as outside constraints placed on firms by consumers and the public (e.g. as boycotts, laws and regulations). This is not because people want businesses to ignore ethical issues, rather, it is due to the fact that competition, efficiency and the dynamics of the market leave no room for people to hold such ideals—those who do lose out. Why is this the case? In part, it has to do with assumptions about ethics. At its core, many assume ethics to be about altruism, about being kinder and gentler, about being charitable. Many associate ethical activity with looking out for others, putting their needs above one's own, doing the right thing for the right reasons. Ethics, we tend to think, requires denying self-interest. Thus, ethics and business cannot fit together: one activity upholds self-interest, while the other rejects it. In such a context, business ethics is necessarily an oxymoron and capitalism becomes all of the disturbing things that the movie *Wall Street* and the many narratives on the "Decade of Greed" made it out to be.

I want to challenge this viewpoint for a variety of reasons, many of which have been articulated by others. To do so, I will draw on examples of corporate activity, and specifically, one particular problem faced by Merck & Co., a prominent American pharmaceutical firm.

One obvious and common criticism is that this model gives us an extreme and unrealistic account of human beings. Few people are as greedy or purely self-interested as we assume Ivan Boesky, Michael Milken and others to have been. Human action stems from a variety of impulses and norms that have to do with our acculturation, sense of propriety, and other moral and social values. Self-interest is clearly one such impulse, and an important feature of human behavior, but its influence is far more complex as it is both shaped and balanced by a variety of other features. At the same time, few people are as pure of heart and single-mindedly self-effacing as Mother Teresa or Albert Schweitzer. Even when we perform the most apparently selfless acts, there is usually some element of "impure" motivation for selfish gain that accompanies it. Most human activity takes place in the realm in between, where there are a variety of motives and where practices have elements of both self-interest and regard for others. This is true for business as it is for other spheres or practices. The "self-interest" model should be rejected because it forces us to make crude and unrealistic assumptions about how people behave, glossing over the most interesting and complex part of life.

Second, the two realms problem sets the content of both ethics and business in ways which profoundly limit our ability to fit the two together. While economists have used some of Adam Smith's writings to argue for self-interest —better described as egoism or greed—as the crucial driving force of capitalism, their slant on the concept is defective. I have no argument against self-interest, but I would maintain that there is a vast difference between self-interest and selfishness or greed. The former allows room for consideration of the interests of others and competing moral interests (indeed, when it is constrained by other relevant moral values and virtues, we may call self-interest a moral concept). The same cannot be said for greed or selfishness, as the content of these notions is premised on rejecting any moral limits and competing norms. Thus, on this rehabilitated account, we can agree that self-interest has a prominent role in business, but only when it is constructed as a moral value which is shaped and limited by a variety of other moral considerations. Indeed, on this view, there is nothing odd about connecting or integrating self-interest with a range of other moral purposes for the organization or the individual.

It is equally important that we offer a more compelling account of ethics. Rather than highlighting altruism and charity, it would be more appropriate to focus on aspects of the moral life as respect for others, decency, trust, and justice or fair play. These concepts are arguably more relevant and appropriate concepts to use for interaction among strangers or for public and professional life. They are also less directly opposed to self-interest (particularly in the context of my rehabilitated definition). Indeed, on my redescription, not only is there nothing morally illegitimate about the pursuit of self-interest or financial gain, it may be described as a limited virtue. Thus, by taking a closer look at the content of both business and ethics it is apparent that how the terms are defined has a lot to do with the account of business ethics which emerges. When we use a more balanced and careful approach, ethics and business seem to fit together quite well.

Finally, I draw attention to particular corporations to illustrate the differences generated by this revised interpretation of business ethics. Consider the much publicized dilemma faced by Merck & Co. as they decided whether or not to develop and distribute a treatment for river blindness, a horrible illness which afflicted scores of people in the third world (particularly in parts of Africa, Central and South America).

> A Merck scientist discovered that a drug the company had developed to fight parasites in farm animals could possibly be adapted to kill the parasite which caused river blindness. The parasites, which grew to almost two feet in length once they entered the body via an insect bite, began as a relatively benign but offensive presence in nodules just under the skin. However, once they reproduced, creating millions of microscopic worms, victims experienced severe suffering that started with itching so terrible that some victims opted to commit suicide rather than continue to endure the pain. As the organisms spread, they often infiltrate the eyes, causing blindness. The idea of creating a drug to treat an illness that was so awful and affected so many was wonderful, except for the fact that none of the potential customers could pay for the drug. Merck faced the dilemma of whether to invest millions of dollars to develop the drug when there was little in the way of potential financial return. Its best case scenario involved gaining financial support from various private and public sources to help offset costs and to deliver the drugs, but such assistance had not been obtained. A key component of this situation is Merck's corporate philosophy:
>
>> We try never to forget that medicine is for the people. It is not for the profits. The profits follow, and if we have remembered that, they have never failed to appear. The better we have remembered it, the larger they have been.
>
> The company had assembled a world-class collection of scientists and workers who were not only among the most technically capable, but who were highly motivated. This motivation can be traced to their commitment to Merck's corporate philosophy, a credo which they took quite seriously and which they believed the company did as well. The drug development proved a success, but Merck's extensive efforts to get support for development and distribution failed. Transporting the drug was a further problem—sufferers lived in the bush where there were no established transportation networks. Thus, even if they opted to give the drug away, it would cost them roughly $20 million per year to get it to those in need. What should Merck do? Merck decided to give the drug away and pay to transport it to all countries who wanted the drug—forever.

While this is an extraordinary decision in itself, what is more important for our purposes is how we describe or interpret the situation. Under the "self-interest" model, the dilemma becomes a question of charity. Merck either pursues its larger goal of profit maximization and refuses to develop the drug because it won't generate enough income or good will to pay for the costs, or it decides to undertake a charitable activity. I would argue that this is a poor way to look at this case. A more constructive (and probably more accurate) way to look at it is as a test of Merck's mission statement. Just as their corporate mission statement exploded the dichotomy between business and ethics, so too was their decision a question of whether the company stood for the particular mixture of ethical and business imperatives that made up that philosophy. This is my final reason for dropping the "self-interest" model—because firms like Merck, and many others, reject it. These firms are finding ways to mix values and self-interest: starting with a commitment to serving a moral goal (e.g. patients, customers, or a variety of other "stakeholder" groups, i.e. those groups who can affect or who are affected by the activities of the corporation). Firms are finding that they can shape their guiding philosophy in terms of moral commitments, what many are calling value-driven management, and still have financially successful firms.

. . . Organizations don't have to be "charitable" or non-profit to undertake important communal projects or to serve moral ends. Ethics doesn't have to be about altruism or a singularity of intention to "do the right thing." Scientists at Merck and physicians in medical practice both display a moral commitment to a mission which we would be wrong to describe as largely "altruistic" or "charitable" because of the extent to which they benefit in the process, but it remains an important moral mission nonetheless. Indeed, I want to argue that it is vital that we distinguish this sort of activity (and the importance of the moral purposes served) from the endeavors of "greed" which the public has attributed to business's profit maximization philosophy. Within the prevailing profit maximization philosophy, moral concerns are, at best, seen as largely irrelevant to the purposes and activities of the firm and at worst, opposed to pursuing their "business" interests. Failure to draw such distinctions reinforces the idea that moral concerns are the domain of government or private citizens and have no place in "business". It leads us to perpetuate a world where corporations focus exclusively on one goal—the wealth, the material gain of its economic activity— while excluding virtually all others. It turns business into an activity which is more destructive and oppressive than creative and uplifting. . . .

From Opposition to Continuum: The Core Similarities of Business Ethics and Medical Ethics

I have now set the groundwork for pressing a larger argument about the similarity of business and medical ethics: both in terms of a larger mission or strategic statement of purpose, as well as the moral requirements of practitioners (i.e. physicians and managers respectively). While some have emphasized the altruism of physicians, I have argued that physicians have operated in a system where they can adopt the mantle of altruism without sacrificing their self-interest. Physicians make a good living caring for their patients, and although many have raised questions about the extent of their compensation, no one has questioned that physicians be well paid for serving their patients. Few people hold many illusions about the "altruism" of corporations, although many have provided vital support to charities, local communities, and other important causes. Thus, while altruism is more typically associated with physicians, it is hard to make a persuasive case for this being a prominent feature of either profession.

At the same time, I have argued that we should reject the other end of the spectrum, the model of business as driven by pure egoism and the unbridled pursuit of self-interest. As stakeholder firms and total quality management firms have found, doing so does not mean sacrificing financial success and firm survival, but can be seen as a key to securing both. A balanced reading of the business model and the content of "business" also lead us to want to reject this extreme as well. Insofar as this problem is not associated with medicine, except to the extent that it has been dominated by "business" thinking, I shall assume that my rejection of the greed model for business is sufficient to discredit this other pole of the oppositional model.

The common ground that emerges by closing off these two extremes and accepting the model I have articulated for business ethics is quite substantial. It is clear that physicians serve important moral goals by proclaiming their allegiance to the interests of patients and the general health of the community. Yet, while this is their "mission" statement, it is also not opposed to financial success and a reasonable standard of living. We argue about whether physicians are doing enough to help the poor, are being paid too much, or are sacrificing certain health needs of the community for their own benefit, but few reject that any viable picture of medicine contains elements of both models. Doctors are not about maximizing profits, but about serving patients—yet, like Merck, they recognize that in serving the patients, they will also be financially successful. The point is not to legitimize all self-regarding activities or collapse them into moral duties that are more other-regarding. Rather, it is to recognize that self-interest is a concept different from selfishness and greed, and that the former is perfectly compatible with serving other moral ends while the latter is not. Combining ethics and self-interest together is also about rehabilitating our view of medical (as well as business) ethics, moving away from the extreme of altruism and charity, and toward a view that makes trust, respect for others, decency, and a sense of fair play central concepts. Embracing this model does not entail watering down our expectations, lowering our standards, or legitimizing unacceptable behavior. Instead, it offers us a more complex view of the world and a more viable account of human activity that may well, ironically, allow us to have higher expectations of corporations and provide them with the means to meet those standards.

There are also important comparisons that some have drawn at the level of individual practitioners in medicine and business—between managers and physicians. It appears that there is a basic difference between the two fields in that physicians have one basic duty and serve one group, while managers have many duties and serve many groups. Whereas stakeholder theory has created obligations for managers to serve an array of interests, physicians have typically had one overriding duty: to serve the well-being of their patients. Yet, even in its prime, this dyadic model was over-simplistic. There have always been limits to this duty, particularly when there are compelling claims on behalf of communal health, legal constraints, the physician's own conscience, or the well-being of third parties. Further, if we accept Haavi Morreim's argument that the emergence of fiscal scarcity requires that we reject the dyadic model, and that the interests of a number of other groups and interests must be included, the role of physician begins to look a good deal more complex and more akin to that of the business manager in the stakeholder model. In practice, we may want to take steps to ensure that physicians focus primarily on the health and well-being of individual patients, yet they must also use the interests and claims of a wide variety of other stakeholder groups to shape and structure their activity. Just as managers used to think that it was enough to serve stockholders and operate in a role perhaps similar to physicians, the emergence of other compelling moral duties have pressed us to dramatically revise, if not disintegrate entirely, both models....

Conclusion

... While this discussion doesn't provide definitive answers, it seems possible to respond to my original three questions. *Is the introduction of "business" thinking creating drastic and/or dangerous changes in the practice of medicine?* First, based on the model I have defended and drawing on numerous scholarly sources and examples, it seems clear that "business" thinking and the business model need not be as corrosive as critics have made it out to be. Indeed, based on the reality of fiscal scarcity and the need to temper care for particular patients with a broader sense of justice, it seems evident that the influence of business may be a positive influence. *How substantial are the differences between the ethics of medicine and the ethics of business?* I have offered a sustained critique of the oppositional model which associated medicine with altruism and business with unmitigated self-interest, arguing that both are exaggerated and indefensible. In addition, I provided an alternative reconstruction of the two models ... which establishes core similarities between the two. This view explodes the oppositional image of medicine and business and places them on a continuum which is structured by these core similarities, but allows for significant differences between them. *Can the two models, or aspects of them, be molded together in a constructive way?* Not only can they be connected, but given the goals we have for health care, it seems essential that they be combined to construct a more useful system.

    ... [W]hile I suggest that we should continue to be skeptical about the effects of strict corporate control over the health care system and the willingness of companies to accept the sorts of ethical arguments I have articulated, health care institutions may be an ideal context in which to forge such a marriage. Medicine is an area where such interfaces of business and ethics—concerns about costs, innovation, and economics as well as the needs of particular patients and broader human welfare—can, and perhaps must, be connected in terms of the basic strategic identity of health care institutions if they are to serve our large goals. We may be able to draw on the ethics of medicine and the ethics of business to find a way out of the American health care crisis which avoids the pitfalls of the two "extreme" models with which we began.

Regardless of what one thinks of business ethics, or the ethos that pervades much of corporate America, it is clear that we can no longer entertain such global and simplistic dichotomies between medicine and business. Further discourse and the effort to create a promising direction for our health care system requires a more balanced and complex view of the situation, and acknowledgment that whatever directions we take must have substantial elements of both.

POSTSCRIPT

Are Business and Medicine Ethically Incompatible?

Currently, a variety of means to rein in what many consider to be the excesses of health maintenance organizations (HMOs) are being examined. Stories of medical benefits denied, of personal frustration and exorbitant personal expense, and of dreadful medical effects from unwise insurance dispositions regularly splash across the front pages. In some places, lawsuits have been filed against HMOs in which it is claimed that denial of reimbursement for a medical or surgical procedure that the patient cannot afford to pay for himself amounts to denial of that procedure and that *that* amounts to practicing medicine. Thus, if the HMOs are going to practice medicine, then they can be sued for malpractice when the results are bad. Whether or not these suits are successful will have a great impact on the health care industry.

At the state legislature level, state assemblies are now passing laws forbidding HMOs to deny certain benefits—most famously, a two-day hospital stay for new mothers. On one hand, such legislation clearly satisfies the desires of the constituency, which is outraged at the callous treatment of new mothers (i.e., releasing them shortly after they give birth). On the other hand, if HMOs are not very good at practicing medicine, how good can legislatures be? Medicine is an art and a science, not a political activity. Is there a better way to keep health care humane while keeping costs under control? Should the single-payer system be reexamined?

Suggested Readings

Daniel Callahan, *What Kind of Life: The Limits of Medical Progress* (Georgetown University Press, 1995).

Daniel Callahan, Ruud ter Meulen, and Eva Topinkova, eds., *A World Growing Old: The Coming Health Care Challenges* (Georgetown University Press, 1995).

Norman Daniels, *Seeking Fair Treatment: From the AIDS Epidemic to National Health Care Reform* (Oxford University Press, 1995).

Haavi Morreim, *Balancing Act: The New Medical Ethics of Medicine's New Economics* (Georgetown University Press, 1995).

ISSUE 6

Are Pharmaceutical Price Controls Justifiable?

YES: Richard A. Spinello, from "Ethics, Pricing and the Pharmaceutical Industry," *Journal of Business Ethics* (August 1992)

NO: Pharmaceutical Manufacturers Association, from "Price Controls in the Economy and the Health Sector," *Backgrounder* (April 1993)

ISSUE SUMMARY

YES: Philosopher Richard A. Spinello argues that the pharmaceutical industry should regulate its prices in accordance with the principles of distributive justice, with special attention to the needs of the least advantaged. If it does not, then government-imposed price controls may be necessary.

NO: The Pharmaceutical Manufacturers Association, an association of 93 manufacturers of pharmaceutical and biological products who support high manufacturing standards and ethical business practices, states that price controls are historically counterproductive in providing scarce goods for the consumer, especially in the health care sector.

How shall we distribute the scarce valuable products of our society? Current economic philosophies offer two alternatives: the free market and public provision. In a free market, tradable goods or money or services are exchanged between buyers and sellers at a rate that is acceptable to both. This system assumes that everyone can bring enough money or goods or services to the exchange to have their needs met. A public commodity, on the other hand, is available to all as needed; police protection is a good example of a public commodity. Where does health care and the products that are essential to health care fall in this division?

Before the 1900s, in the United States, physicians charged fees for visits, which the patient was expected to pay; all pharmaceuticals were sold at essentially what the market would bear; and the industry was profitable. The suffering of those who could not afford health care was occasionally relieved by private charities and by religious orders that set up hospitals for the poor. But on the whole, medical care and all that went with it was a marketable good.

In the twentieth century, several nations began to make health care available to all through public taxation, on the same basis as police and fire protection. The medical treatments available under socialized medicine, as it is called, included most of the treatments that were previously available only to those who could pay for them through the private sector.

The rationale for this extension of benefits was simple enough: we are all dependent for our prosperity on the productivity of the nation—that is, the productivity of its citizens—and that depends upon the national level of health. It makes sense to oppose disease and promote health with the same energy that is spent on opposing enemy armies and promoting sound fiscal policy. Early public health movements financed clean water and universal inoculations at public expense; medical treatments and drugs were a direct extension of this idea.

In nations that have socialized their health care provision, there have always been disputes over the acceptable boundaries of medical coverage: Should cosmetic surgery be covered? What about elaborate reconstructive surgery for the very old? Weight loss treatments? Psychiatric care, not including emergencies? However, treatment of disease—AIDS, for example—is always covered, and here is where the dispute begins.

The United States has never fully subscribed to socialized health care provision (or to socialized anything, for that matter), and there is no tax money allocated to underwrite the cost of manufacturing drugs. As part of its federal police power, the United States does have the legal apparatus to control prices of essential commodities if the lawmakers feel that these prices are unconscionably high. But are price controls to equalize access to essential medications justified?

The dispute centers on two points: First, do pharmaceutical companies have an obligation to take into account the needs of the poorest customers in setting their prices (in accordance with the principles of justice), or may they restrict sales to only those who can pay full price? Second, if price controls were established, would they work in practice to achieve the ends of justice, or would they bring about negative consequences such as the shutting down of drug research?

In the following selections, Richard A. Spinello argues that the principles of distributive justice justify the implementation of price controls. On the opposing side, the Pharmaceutical Manufacturers Association, in a paper prepared by Van Dyk Associates, Inc., a public policy consulting firm in Washington, D.C., reports that past attempts to administer price controls have all failed. As you read these selections, ask yourself what kind of arguments are being deployed by the disputants. Do the moral arguments advanced by Spinello carry enough weight to warrant a practical response? Do the empirical arguments advanced by the Pharmaceutical Manufacturers Association that price controls are ineffective in practice render the theoretical arguments irrelevant?

Richard A. Spinello

 **YES**

Ethics, Pricing and the
Pharmaceutical Industry

Introduction

A perennial ethical question for the pharmaceutical industry has been the aggressive pricing policies pursued by most large drug companies. Criticism has intensified in recent years over the high cost of new conventional ethical drugs and the steep rise in prices for many drugs already on the market. One result of this public clamor is that the pricing structure of this industry has once again come under intense scrutiny by government agencies, Congress, and the media.

The claim is often advanced that these high prices and the resultant profits are unethical and unreasonable. It is alleged that pharmaceutical companies could easily deliver less expensive products without sacrificing research and development. It is quite difficult to assess, however, what constitutes an unethical price or an unreasonable profit. Where does one draw the line in these nebulous areas? We will consider these questions as they relate to the pharmaceutical industry with the understanding that the normative conclusions reached in this analysis might be applicable to other industries which market *essential* consumer products. Our primary axis of discussion, however, will be the pharmaceutical industry where the issue of pricing is especially complex and controversial.

The Problem

Beyond any doubt, instances of questionable and excessive drug prices abound. Azidothymide or AZT is one of the most prominent and widely cited examples. This effective medicine is used for treating complications from AIDS. The Burroughs-Wellcome Company has been at the center of a spirited controversy over this drug for establishing such a high price—AZT treatment often costs as much as $6500 a year, which is prohibitively expensive for many AIDS patients, particularly those with inadequate insurance coverage. The company has steadfastly refused to explicate how it arrived at this premium pricing level, but

From Richard A. Spinello, "Ethics, Pricing and the Pharmaceutical Industry," *Journal of Business Ethics,* vol. 11 (August 1992), pp. 617–626. Copyright © 1992 by D. Reidel Publishing Co., Dordrecht, Holland, and Boston, U.S.A. Reprinted by permission of Kluwer Academic Publishers.

industry observers suggest that this important drug was priced to be about the same as expensive cancer therapy.[1] ...

Ethical Questions

The behavior of Burroughs and the tendency of most drug companies to charge premium prices for breakthrough medicines raises serious moral issues which defy easy answers and simple solutions. As Clarence Walton observed, "no other area of managerial activity is more difficult to depict accurately, assess fairly, and prescribe realistically in terms of morality than the domain of price" (1969, p. 209). This difficulty is compounded in the pharmaceutical industry due to the complications involved in ascertaining the true cost of production.

To be sure, every business is certainly entitled to a *reasonable profit* as a reward to its investors and a guarantee of long-term stability. But the difficulty is judging a reasonable profit level. When, if ever, do profits become "unreasonable?" It is even more problematic to determine if that profit is "unethical," especially if it is the result of premium prices.

Obviously, the issue of ethical or fair pricing assumes much greater significance when the product or service in question is not a luxury item but an essential one such as medicine. Few are concerned about the ethics of pricing a BMW or a waterfront condo in Florida. But the matter is quite different when dealing with vital commodities like food, medicine, clothing, housing, and education. Each of these goods has a major impact on our basic well-being and our ability to achieve any genuine self-fulfillment. Given the importance of these products in the lives of all human beings, one must consider how equitably they are priced since pricing will determine their general availability. Along these lines several key questions must be raised. Should free market, competitive forces determine the price of "essential" goods such as pharmaceuticals? Is it morally wrong to charge exceptionally high prices even if the market is willing to pay that price? Is it ethical to profit excessively at the expense of human suffering? Finally, how can we even begin to define what constitutes reasonable profits?

Also, the issue of pricing must be considered in the context of the pharmaceutical industry's lofty performance guidelines for return on assets, return on common equity, and so forth. On what authority are such targets chosen over other goals such as the widest possible distribution of some breakthrough pharmaceutical that can save lives or improve the quality of life? Pharmaceutical companies would undoubtedly contend that this authority emanates from the expectations of shareholders and other key stakeholders such as members of the financial community. In addition, these targets are a result of careful strategic planning that focuses on long-term goals.

But a key question persistently intrudes here. Should *other* viewpoints be considered? Should the concerns and needs of the sick be taken into account, especially in light of the fact that they have such an enormous stake in these issues? In other words, as with many business decisions, there appear to be stark tradeoffs between superior financial performance versus humane empathy and fairness. Should corporations consider the "human cost" of their objectives for excellent performance? And what role, if any, should fairness or justice play in pricing decisions? It is only by probing these difficult and complex questions that we can make progress in establishing reasonable norms for the pricing of pharmaceuticals.

... The strategic decisions of large organizations "inevitably involve social as well as economic consequences, inextricably intertwined" (Mintzberg, 1989, p. 173). Thus such firms are social agents whether they like it or not. It is virtually impossible to maintain neutrality on these issues and aspire to some sort of apolitical status. The point for the pharmaceutical industry and the matter of pricing seems clear enough. The refusal to take "non-economic" criteria into account when setting prices is itself a moral and social decision which inevitably affects society. Companies have a choice—either they can explicitly consider the social consequences of their decisions or they can be blind to those consequences, deliberately ignoring them until the damage is perceived and an angry public raises its voice in protest.

If companies do choose, however, to be attentive and *responsible* social agents they must begin to cultivate a broader view of their environment and their obligations. To begin with, they must treat those affected by their decisions as people with an important stake in those decisions. This stakeholder model, which has become quite popular with many executives, allows corporations to link strategic decisions such as pricing with social and ethical concerns. By recognizing the legitimacy of its stakeholders such as consumers and employees, managers will better appreciate all the negative as well as positive consequences of their decisions. Moreover, an honest stakeholder analysis will compel them to explore the financial and human implications of those decisions. This will enable corporations to become more responsible social agents, since explicit attention will be given to the social dimension of their various strategic decisions.

... According to Goodpaster and Matthews, the most effective solution to this and most other moral dilemmas is one "that permits or encourages corporations to exercise independent, non-economic judgment over matters that face them in their short- and long-term plans and operations" (1989, p. 161). In other words, the burden of morality and social responsibility does not lie in the marketplace or in the hand of government regulation but falls directly on the corporation and its managers.

Companies that do aspire to such moral and social responsibility will adopt *the moral point of view,* which commits one to view positively the interest of others, including various stakeholder groups. Moreover, the moral point of view assigns primacy to virtues such as justice, integrity, and respect. Thus, the virtuous corporation is analogous to the virtuous person: each exhibits these moral qualities and acts according to the principle that the single-minded pursuit of one's own selfish interests is a violation of moral standards and an offense to the community. The moral point of view also assumes that both the corporation and the individual thrive in an environment of cooperative interaction which can only be realized when one turns from a narrow self-interest to a wider interest in others.

Pricing Policies and Justice

This brings us back to the specific moral question of fair pricing policies for the pharmaceutical industry. The moral issue at stake here concerns justice and more precisely distributive justice. As we have remarked, justice has always been considered a primary virtue and thus it is an indispensable component of the moral point of view. According to Aristotle, justice "is not a part of virtue but the whole of excellence or virtue" (1962, p. 114). Thus, there can be no virtue without justice. This implies that if corporations are serious about assimilating the moral point of view and exercising their capacity for responsible behavior, they must strive to be just in their dealings with both their internal and external constituencies. Moreover, traditional discussions on justice in the works of philosophers such as Aristotle, Hume, Mill, and Rawls have emphasized distributive justice, which is concerned with the fair distribution of society's benefits and burdens. This seems especially relevant to the matter of ethical pricing policies.

Corporations which control the distribution of essential products such as ethical drugs like AZT can be just or unjust in the way they distribute these products. When premium prices are charged for such goods an artificial scarcity is created, and this gives rise to the question of how equitably this scarce resource is being allocated. The consequence of a premium pricing strategy whose objective is to garner high profits would appear to be an inequitable distribution pattern. As we have seen, due to the expensiveness of AZT and similar drugs they are often not available to the poor and lower middle class unless their insurance plans cover this expense or they can somehow secure government assistance which has not been readily forthcoming. However, if this distribution pattern can be considered unjust, what determines a just distribution policy?

There are, of course, many conceptions of distributive justice which would enable us to answer this question. Some stress individual merit (each according to his ability) while others are more egalitarian and stress an equal distribution of society's goods and services. Given a wide array of different theories on justice, where does the manager turn for some guidance and straightforward insights?

One of the most popular and plausible conceptions of justice is advanced by John Rawls in his well known work, *A Theory of Justice*. A thorough treatment of this complex and prolix work is beyond the scope of this essay. However, a concise summary of Rawls' work should reveal its applicability to the problem of fair pricing. Rawls' conception of justice, which is predicated on the Kantian idea of personhood, properly emphasizes the equal worth and universal dignity of all persons. All rational persons have a dual capacity: they possess the ability to develop a rational plan to pursue their own conception of the good life along with the ability to respect this same capacity of self-determination in others. This Kantian ideal underlies the choice of the two principles of justice in the original position. Furthermore, this choice is based on the assumption that the "protection of Kantian self-determination for all persons depends on certain formal guarantees—the equal rights and liberties of democratic citizenship— plus guaranteed access to certain material resources" (Doppelt, p. 278). In short, the essence of justice as fairness means that persons are entitled to an extensive system of liberties *and* basic material goods.

Unlike pure egalitarian theories, however, Rawls stipulates that inequities are consistent with his conception of justice so long as they are compatible with universal respect for Kantian personhood. This implies that such inequities should not be tolerated if they interfere with the basic rights, liberties, and material benefits all deserve as Kantian persons capable of rational self-determination. In other words, Rawls espouses the detachment of the distribution of primary social goods from one's merit and ability because these goods are absolutely essential for our self-determination and self-fulfillment as rational persons. These primary goods include "rights and liberties, opportunities and power, income and wealth" (Rawls, 1971, p. 92). Whatever one's plan or conception of the good life, these goods are the necessary means to realize that plan, and hence everyone would prefer more rather than less primary goods. Their unequal distribution in a just society should only be allowed if such a distribution would benefit directly the least advantaged of that society (the difference principle).

The key element in Rawls' theory for our purposes is the notion that there are material benefits everyone deserves as Kantian persons. The exercise of one's capacity for free self-determination requires a certain level of material well-being and not just the guarantee of abstract and formal rights such as freedom of expression and equal opportunity. Thus the primary social goods involve some material goods, like income and wealth. To a certain extent health care (including medicine) should be considered as one of the primary social goods since it is obviously necessary for the pursuit of one's rational life plan. Therefore, the distribution of health care should not be contingent upon ability and merit. Also it would be untenable to justify an inequitable distribution of this good by means of Rawls' difference principle. It is difficult to imagine a scenario in which the unequal distribution of health care in our society would be more beneficial to the least advantaged than a more equal distribution which would assure all consumers access to hospital care, medical treatment, medicines, and so forth. If we assume that the least advantaged (a group which Rawls never clearly defines) are the indigent who are also suffering from certain ailments, there is no advantage to any inequity in the distribution of health care. Unlike other primary goods such as income and wealth it cannot be distributed in such a way that a greater share for certain groups will benefit the least advantaged. In short, this is a zero sum game—if a person is deprived of medical treatment or pharmaceutical products due to premium pricing policies that person has lost a critical opportunity to save his life, cure a disease, reduce suffering, and so on.

Thus, at least according to this Rawlsian view of justice with its Kantian underpinnings, there seems to be little room for the unequal distribution of a vital commodity such as health care in a just society. It follows, then, that the just pharmaceutical corporation must be far more diligent and consider very carefully the implications of pricing policies for an equitable distribution of its products. The alternative is government intervention in this process, and as we have seen, this has the potential to yield gross inefficiencies and ultimately be self-defeating. If these corporations charge premium prices and garner excessive profits from their pharmaceutical products, the end result will be the deprivation of these goods for certain classes of people. Such a pricing pattern systematically worsens the situation of the least advantaged in society, violates the respect due them as Kantian persons, and seriously impairs their capacity for free self-determination.

It should be emphasized, however, that this concern for justice does not imply that pharmaceutical companies should become charities by distributing these drugs free of charge or at prices so low they must sustain meager profits or even losses. To be sure, their survival, long-term stability, and ongoing research are also vital to society and can only be guaranteed through substantial profits. Thus, the demand for justice which we have articulated must be balanced with the need to realize key economic objectives which guarantee the long-term stability of this industry. As Kenneth Goodpaster notes, "the responsible organization aims at congruence between its moral and nonmoral aspirations" (1984, p. 309). In other words, it does not see goals of justice and economic viability as mutually exclusive, but will attempt to manage the joint achievement of both objectives.

We are arguing, then, that pharmaceutical companies should seek to balance their legitimate concern for profit and return on investment with an equal consideration of the crucial importance of distributive justice. There must be an explicit recognition that for the afflicted certain pharmaceutical products are critical for one's well-being; hence they are as important as any primary social good and are deserved by every member of society. As a result these products should be distributed on the widest possible basis, but in a way that permits companies to realize a realistic and reasonable level of profitability.

It is, of course, quite difficult to define a "reasonable level of profitability." In many respects the definition of "reasonable" is the crux of the matter here. Unfortunately, as outsiders to the operations of drug companies we are ill prepared to judge whether development costs for certain drugs are inflated or truly necessary. As a result, these corporations must be trusted to arrive at their own definition of a reasonable profit, given the level of legitimate costs involved in researching and developing the drug in question. But we can look to some case histories for meaningful examples that would serve as a guide to a more general definition. One of the most famous controversies over drug prices concerned the Hoffman-LaRoche corporation and the United Kingdom in which the government's Monopoly Commission alleged that Hoffman-LaRoche was charging excessive prices for valium and librium in order to subsidize its research and preserve its monopoly position. In the course of the prolonged deliberations between the British government and the company reasonable profits were defined as "profits no higher than is necessary to obtain the 'desired' performance of industry from the point of view of the economy as a whole."[2] In general, then, under normal circumstances reasonable profits for a particular product should be consistent with the average return for the industry. Exceptions might be made to this rule of average returns if the risks and costs of development are inordinately and unavoidably high.

Thus, based on this Rawlsian ideal of justice I propose the following thesis regarding ethical pricing for pharmaceutical companies: for those drugs which are truly essential the just corporation will aim to charge prices that will assure the widest possible distribution of these products consistent with a reasonable level of profitability. In other words, these companies will seek to minimize the deprivation of material benefits which are needed by all persons for their self-realization by imposing restraints on their egocentric interests in premium prices and excessive profits.... Moreover, we must present some sort of methodology for reaching this determination.

... The more critical the product and the less likely it will be affordable to certain segments of society, the more prominent should be the consideration given to distributive justice in pricing policy deliberations. Justice cannot be the exclusive concern in these deliberations, but must be given its proportionate weight depending upon the way in which the questions in this framework are addressed. Thus, as pricing decisions duly consider factors such as production and promotion costs, etc., they should also take into account the element of distributive justice. Clearly, however, drugs that are less important for society because they deal with less serious ailments should not be subject to the same demands of justice as those for diseases which are truly life threatening or debilitating. Hence drug companies should have much more flexibility in pricing medicines for these less critical ailments....

This analysis does not by any means eliminate the frustrations regarding ethical pricing which were cited earlier by Walton. We can offer no definitive, quantitative formulae or comprehensive criteria to assure that pricing in this industry will always be fair and just. As with most moral decisions, much will depend on the individual judgment and moral sensitivity of the managers making those decisions.... It seems beyond doubt that responsible and fair pricing in the pharmaceutical industry is a serious moral imperative, since for so many consumers it is a matter of well-being or infirmity and perhaps even life or death.

We might consider once again the wisdom of Aristotle on this topic of justice. In the *Nicomachean Ethics* he writes that "we call those things 'just' which produce and preserve happiness for the social and political community" (1962, p. 113). If corporations respond to the demands of justice for the sake of the common good, it will help promote the elusive goal of a just community and a greater harmony between the corporation and its many concerned stakeholders.

Notes

1. Holzman, D.: 1988, 'New Wonder Drugs at What Price?', *Insight* (March 21), pp. 54–55. For more recent data on drug prices see 'Maker of Schizophrenia Drug Bows to Pressure to Cut Costs', *The New York Times* (Dec. 6, 1990), pp. A1 and D3.

2. 'F. Hoffman-LaRoche and Company A.G.', Harvard Business School Case Study in Matthews, Goodpaster, Nash (eds.), *Policies and Persons* (McGraw Hill Book Company: N.Y., 1985).

References

Aristotle: 1962, *Nicomachean Ethics,* trans. by M. Oswald (Library of Liberal Arts, Bobbs Merrill Company, Inc., Indianapolis).

Doppelt, G.: 1989, 'Beyond Liberalism and Communitarianism: Towards a Critical Theory of Social Justice', *Philosophy and Social Criticism* 14 (No. 3/4).

Goodpaster, K.: 1984, 'The Concept of Corporate Responsibility', in T. Regan (ed.), *Just Business: New Introductory Essays in Business Ethics* (Random House, New York).

Goodpaster, K. and Matthews, J.: 1989, 'Can a Corporation Have a Conscience', in K. Andrews (ed.), *Ethics in Practice* (Harvard Business School Press, Boston).

Mintzberg, H.: 1989, 'The Case for Corporate Social Responsibility', in A. Iannone (ed.), *Contemporary Moral Controversies in Business* (Oxford University Press, New York).

Rawls, J.: 1971, *A Theory of Justice* (Harvard University Press, Cambridge).

Walton, C.: 1969, *Ethos and the Executive* (Prentice Hall, Inc., Englewood Cliffs, N.J.).

**Pharmaceutical Manufacturers
Association**

Price Controls in the Economy
and the Health Sector

Executive Summary

The current national focus on health care reform has revived discussion of price controls as a possible policy instrument.

Such discussion is predictable because health-sector costs consistently have risen faster than the general rate of price inflation and—in part because of unintended inflationary consequences created by health-reform programs of the 1960s—have tended to be resistant to government efforts to date to contain them. If, as anticipated, current contemplated reform includes dramatic expansion of health system access, additional pressures for cost containment will be created.

This brief paper examines experience with price controls historically and, then, since World War II in the U.S. health sector. Major points:

1. Price controls have been attempted in many times and places dating back 40 centuries. Except in those times and places where national unity and consensus made controls easily enforceable—for instance, in World War II Great Britain where the country quite literally was fighting for its survival—they generally have failed. Moreover, when controls have been ended, inflation typically has equalled or exceeded the rate which would have been reached without controls. In the meantime, economic growth has been inhibited.

2. Controls, when applied, quickly create artificial scarcities, resource misallocations, and black markets. Large bureaucratic structures are required for administration. Problems of enforcement and equity arise. Since controls interfere with normal market mechanisms, issues of fairness (both to consumers and producers) quickly present themselves. Public support for controls quickly erodes.

3. In the United States, those government officials who have administered price controls universally counsel against their further use. These judgments are made, typically, on practical as well as theoretical bases.

4. In the health sector, the federal government has made numerous attempts since World War II to freeze or selectively control costs. None of these efforts has slowed a steady rise in health sector inflation.
5. The experience with overall drug-price controls has been limited in this country to Nixon-era controls. Their effect, however, was the same as with controls generally. Prices rose sharply after their relaxation.
6. Internationally, drug price controls also have proved ineffective. Additionally, they have reduced research into breakthrough drugs in countries where they have been adopted.
7. New health-sector price controls could be expected to create the same effects that prior controls have done. Alternative means of health-sector cost containment are available and already have been applied on a limited basis. All would be felt only over a longer period.

Summary: When faced with near-term general or sectoral inflation, national leaders often have turned to price controls. Such controls create enormous distortions and in the end do not quell inflation. Imperfect but applicable means of cost containment suggest themselves in the current effort toward health care reform....

Clear Lessons from the Experience of the United States and Other Nations With Price Controls

From Hammurabi, Babylonia, and the Roman Empire to the 1970s experiences of the United States, Japan, Canada, and Australia, price controls have been tried. And in every single instance, with the possible exception of wartime Britain, they have been found wanting. They basically did not work. Their only certain result in any country has been to reduce production. And such losses in production usually mean a profit squeeze, less investment in plant and equipment and in R&D [research and development], and less growth in the future.

Another lesson learned: All the great monetary stabilizers of this century have been classical economists who insisted upon balanced budgets and government living within its means at home and abroad, without borrowing from the central bank or printing more paper money of its own.

Not one resorted to price controls because all knew from previous history that price controls, freezes and "rollbacks" simply produced scarcities and artificial distortions.

Treasury Secretary Lloyd Bentsen, while Vice Chairman of the Congressional Joint Economic Committee in 1978, chaired a hearing in which he noted that one of the problems he had seen with wage and price controls was that there were so many ways that they could be evaded. His assessment:

"Mandatory wage and price controls don't stop inflation any more than the Maginot line stopped the defeat of the French Army. And they are not going to protect the American consumer from all of the hurt and the damage of inflation.... The Joint Economic Committee ... found that the mere prospect of controls ... resulted in a substantial increase to the consumers of this country and additional inflation because of manufacturers increasing prices in anticipation of the wage demands that resulted...."

Price Controls in The U.S. Health Sector

Since World War II the federal government has made several attempts to control health care costs, either by freezing prices across the board or by imposing selective controls on individual sectors such as hospitals or physicians. None of these initiatives has slowed the steady rise in what Americans are paying for health care through taxes, through private insurance, or out of their own pockets.

Throughout this period, any savings achieved by controls in one sector have been offset by increased spending in others. Economies achieved by shorter patient stays in hospitals have been erased by higher payments for nursing home and home health care. Hospitals barred from adding new beds have poured the money into new outpatient facilities and expensive diagnostic equipment. Placing a ceiling on prices that doctors could charge for treatments or office visits simply has produced a larger number of treatments or office visits. Indeed, Medicare administrators drawing up a new "resource-based" schedule of allowable physician fees have factored into their calculations the assumption that doctors automatically would offset half the reduction in their rates of payment by an increase in billings.

No scheme yet tried has produced actual dollars-and-cents savings. No scheme could—short of central government control of all health care costs and spending. And were that attempted, it would produce ... shortages, dislocations, and other problems....

This section will examine... health care price controls initiated at the federal level in the last 50 years, and show how and why they failed. (The wage-price stabilization program during the Korean War is not discussed because professional fees, such as doctor bills and hospital charges, were excluded from controls.) It will then sketch alternative cost control initiatives mounted in the private sector, often with government support, that offer more hope for moderating health care inflation than does price regulation....

The Steady Expansion of Federally-Funded Health Services

... [I]n the U.S. experience, price controls have not stemmed the growth of health care spending. As a government program, price controls necessarily exist in a political environment where other pressures are operating in the direction of greater spending. Each year, Congressional budgetmakers make significant cuts in Administration Medicare and Medicaid requests—almost always through cuts to providers. Yet each year, actual payments increase.

Why is it that, despite the "success" of PPS [Prospective Payment System] in halving the growth of inpatient hospital costs (the single largest segment of the Medicare program), total spending for hospital care by Medicare and Medicaid has doubled in the seven years after PPS over the seven years before—from $230 billion to $460 billion?

Why has total federal spending for Medicaid increased by 73 percent in just the last two years while Medicare spending was rising far less rapidly?

The answer: At the same time the government was administering its price controls, it was taking other actions that raised its health care costs. Example:

- In the same legislation in which Congress froze physician fees, it required Medicaid to cover more children and more low income pregnant women and extended Medicare to mammographies.
- At the same time it reduced provider fees for Medicare, it was mandating states to cover expensive and medically-questionable treatments under Medicaid, for which it provides half the funds.
- At the same time it was implementing the RVS fee schedule [a revised payment system for Medicare physicians, begun in 1992], Congress significantly extended Medicare benefits for nursing homes, home health and hospice care.

The same political thinking that makes price controls attractive to them makes it hard for policymakers to restrain themselves from sweetening government health benefits packages to enlist Congressional and interest-group support. This bit of history is instructive in view of the declared objective of the Clinton Administration to extend health insurance to the 37 million uninsured while at the same time reducing health care costs.

Price Controls on Pharmaceuticals

Conclusions about the wisdom of price controls in the pharmaceutical sector must be drawn primarily from the experience of other countries. The United States has had only one experience with such controls—during the wage-price freeze of the Nixon Administration. Most other industrialized countries have long tried to regulate drug prices and outlays as part of their broader programs of national health insurance. Only the United States and Denmark leave pricing to the competitive marketplace.

The U.S. Experience

The Nixon Administration Wage and Price Stabilization programs tried to control drug prices, with these results:

- In the three years prior to the program, the drug component of the Consumer Price Index had risen only 3 percent, considerably less than health care cost inflation generally.
- During the period of controls (April, 1971 through October, 1974) the Index increased by only 1.5 percent.
- As soon as controls were lifted, however, the typical "catch-up" effect was seen. Between 1975 and 1977, drug prices rose almost 12 percent. When the last impacts of price controls had faded from the economy, prices were probably higher than they would have been without controls.

Controls also were ineffective in curbing spending on drugs.

In the three years before they were instituted, patient drug costs rose by an average of $378 million a year. During the three control years, they rose $515 million a year. In the three years after, they rose $600 million a year....

Effects of Drug Price Controls Beyond Prices

... [I]t is clear that price controls on drugs in other countries have uniformly failed to accomplish their goal. It also is clear why controls, which are supposed to hold down spending, have had the opposite effect. If government decides for a pharmaceutical company how much it can charge for its products, the company has little incentive to conduct the extremely expensive search for truly innovative and breakthrough therapies. The odds against a drug in development making it to market are 5,000 to 1. Even when a drug advances to where it is actually tested in clinical trials on patients, the odds against its being marketed are 10 to 1. Unless there is pricing freedom, the financial reward is just not worth the risk.

Many firms in nations with strict price controls largely have abandoned the search for breakthrough drugs. Funds that might have been used for research have been shifted to increased promotion and marketing of existing drugs, seeking increased demand as a way of maintaining revenues in the face of controlled prices. Foreign firms also engage in low-risk research and development to come up [with] "new" drugs that are not innovative, and only marginally better than existing therapies, but are nonetheless eligible for higher controlled prices than the older drugs in their inventory.

A study of the French pharmaceutical industry, which was responsible for only 3 world class drugs between 1975 and 1989, concluded that "the calibre of research [has] deteriorated because severe price control has encouraged French companies to give priority to small therapeutic improvements which are useful in price negotiations." Of Japan, Dr. Heinz Redwood, a British researcher and policy analyst, says "There is a pronounced tendency to develop 'Japanese drugs for Japan' rather than for world health care. This is largely the result of the Japanese system of price regulation... which grants very high prices for new drugs, whilst putting heavy pricing pressure on older drugs."

In Italy, the Ruoppolo Commission, created to revamp the price control system to give greater encouragement to innovative activity, reported that:

> "The virtual freezing of the price of old products... has acted as a decisive incentive in the search by companies for new registrations in order to obtain more up-to-date prices; and then, by means of appropriate promotion, induce a prescription shift from the old to the new [drug]."

Were price controls to touch off the same syndrome here, it could have a profound effect not only on the nature of this country's pharmaceutical industry but on world health. The international community depends on innovative U.S. industry to provide it with new medicines. Almost 50 percent of the new drugs effective enough to be marketed globally in the past 20 years have been developed in the U.S. In biotechnology and immunology, it is 70 percent.

What Will Happen If New Price Controls Are Placed on Health Care?

Given previous experience with price controls generally, and on what has happened when they have been imposed in different forms upon the U.S. health care system, it is not difficult to speculate what will happen if federal policymakers impose what have been called "interim cost containment measures" to hold the line on prices for the period—probably several years—that will pass before a new national health insurance system can be passed into law, implemented by regulations, survive the inevitable court challenges, and actually begin to operate throughout the country.

1. Investment funds that would have flowed into the development of new medical technology, new cures for disease and other advances will be diverted to other, more economically attractive channels.
2. The economic incentive to enter the health care field will decline, eventually leading to a shortage of physicians and other trained personnel.
3. Providers will continue to find ways to "game" the system, reducing hoped-for savings. To counter this, government will impose increasing supervision, restrictions, and paperwork on the activities of health care professionals.
4. The quality of health care will suffer. Physicians will spend less time with patients and there will be fewer drugs in hospital formularies. Shortages and waiting lists will develop as they have in other countries. Those who can afford it will try to preserve their current quality of care by creating a separate, privately-funded privileged system of health care as exists in Britain. This alternative system in turn will draw the best professionals and force the quality of care given the rest of us lower.
5. The inherent contradiction between universal system access and simultaneous cost containment inevitably will lead to de facto rationing of care. The Medicaid experience is instructive here. As Medicaid has become the largest item in their budgets, many states have severely restricted reimbursement under the program. Many doctors have responded by refusing to take Medicaid patients. To expand eligibility for Medicaid, the state of Oregon has had to adopt a rationing system, barring payment for whole categories of treatments. Similarly, Great Britain denies expensive surgery to patients over a certain age.

Alternative to Controls Which Could Contain Costs

Health care costs can be contained without the distortions created by controls.

Most of the measures listed below now are being practiced in the health care system—many with the support and encouragement of government. Others are readily available. Strong incentives to use these measures would occur under "managed competition" schemes for health care reform.

- Expansion of Health Maintenance Organizations, group practice associations, and other organizations under which health care practitioners have no incentives to perform unneeded services.
- Expansion of Preferred Provider Organizations and other arrangements in which physicians give up higher fees for an assured caseload.
- Greater emphasis on prevention, early intervention, wellness, and lifestyle changes to lower the incidence of disease and the necessity for surgery.
- Requiring second opinions before surgery and other expensive services.
- Living wills, which give terminal patients the right to appoint someone to decide when to stop the use of high-cost technology whose only purpose is to prolong life according to its clinical definition.
- Drug utilization review systems, that are consistent with the principles developed by the American Medical Association, the American Pharmaceutical Association, and the Pharmaceutical Manufacturers Association. Such systems detect and correct inappropriate prescribing practices as well as fraud and abuse.
- Encouraging medical innovation, including the development of cost-effective therapies such as drugs as a cure for major diseases and a substitute for surgery.
- Greater research on the "outcomes" of alternative treatments, to spread knowledge among physicians about the most effective treatments and therapies.
- Education of patients so they can work more knowledgeably with their doctors. Patient information should be more widely available on computer networks.
- Tort reform to reduce the practice of "defensive" medicine to avoid malpractice suits which, according to the American Medical Association, costs the health care system $15 billion a year.
- Measures to reduce redundancy of expensive technologies and equipment in the same markets—i.e., where several hospitals and clinics in the same area invest in the same costly technologies whereas demand might justify only one such facility.
- The imposition of substantial deductibles and/or co-payments on the insured so as to require patients to make prudent choices about health expenditures. (A Rand Corporation study has shown that patients, when required to write a check on each physician visit, make visits with less frequency.)
- Voluntary industry measures to limit drug-price increases, with or without antitrust waivers, with provision for monitoring by credible third-party agency.

None of the above measures, of course, can be expected to produce immediate and dramatic reductions in health-sector inflation—particularly if implemented while health-sector access simultaneously is being dramatically expanded. Nor can they counteract and overcome those factors which plague the U.S. health system more greatly than those of other Western countries: High rates of poverty, violent crime, homelessness, aging, AIDS and drug abuse.

The aforementioned measures are appropriate ways of maintaining quality while reducing costs. Any government involvement should be designed to increase incentives to adopt such measures.

But the government cannot have it both ways by adopting incentives for the marketplace to manage care *and* government price controls on the components of care. To manage care, providers and insurers must invest significant fiscal and human resources into restructuring, expanding and monitoring health care delivery. Why invest when price controls will likely reward those providers who were most inefficient in the old fragmented system? Attempts to solve the data needs equity issues and enforcement rules would further slow enactment of proper incentives.

At the same time, however, it can be predicted with relative certainty that, given past international and U.S. experience, health-sector as well as other price controls—even when applied short-term—lead to distortions and, over time, do not result in net cost reductions.

POSTSCRIPT

Are Pharmaceutical Price Controls Justifiable?

The United States is more committed to the free market than any other developed nation. Consequently, the arguments advanced by the Pharmaceutical Manufacturers Association against pharmaceutical price controls tend to be accepted for all cases: attempts to regulate the market must fail. According to the laws of the market, if we try to support prices (as with the products of American farms), we will drive buyers from the market and tempt inefficient suppliers to stay in, both of which tend to drive prices *down*. Without price supports, prices would likely recover on their own as enthusiastic buyers outbid each other for the reduced amount of product. On the other hand, as in the case of pharmaceuticals, if we try to control prices, we will drive suppliers from the market and truncate the healthy process of competition that would have brought prices down naturally. Meanwhile, the company's reward for, and means for, pursuing research into better drugs would be destroyed.

But the principles of justice, which govern us as surely as the laws of supply and demand, require that we make our economic arrangements keeping in mind the fate of the least advantaged among us. Does the market do that? Which do we hold more dear, the liberty of the market or justice in distribution? As Spinello notes, people who have AIDS are dying. Is it likely that this fact will eventually persuade pharmaceutical manufacturers to accept price controls?

Suggested Readings

Judy Chaconas, "Providers Offer Prescription for Medicaid Drug-Pricing Law," *Trustee* (December 1991).

Joseph A. DiMasi et al., "The Cost of Innovation in the Pharmaceutical Industry," *Journal of Health Economics* (vol. 10, 1991).

David Hanson, "Report on Drug R & D Fuels Attack on Prices," *Chemical and Engineering News* (March 8, 1993).

Office of Technology Assessment, *Pharmaceutical R & D: Costs, Risks and Rewards* (Government Printing Office, 1993).

David Pryor, "Drugs *Must* Be Made Affordable," *The New York Times* (March 7, 1993), p. F13.

Pamela Zurer, "NIH Weighs Role in Drug Pricing," *Chemical and Engineering News* (December 21, 1992).

ISSUE 7

Should Casino Gambling Be Prohibited?

YES: William A. Galston and David Wasserman, from "Gambling Away Our Moral Capital," *The Public Interest* (Spring 1996)

NO: William R. Eadington, from "The Proliferation of Commercial Gaming in America," *The Sovereign Citizen* (Fall 1994)

ISSUE SUMMARY

YES: Political theorist William A. Galston and research scholar David Wasserman argue that there are significant moral objections to widespread casino gambling: gambling is deleterious to family and social life, and gambling losses fall on the most vulnerable members of society. Worse, legalizing gambling masks the need for adequate taxing to meet social responsibilities.

NO: Professor of economics William R. Eadington counters that gambling is a normal extension of commercial activity and it can safely promote the welfare of the host areas. He is less concerned about the reported downside of the gaming enterprise.

Is gambling wrong? If so, why? Many argue that there is no overt coercion: gamblers happily spend their money. There is no injustice: the poor are not deprived as a result. There is no exploitation of the person (the effective objection against prostitution) unless the person is the gambler himself or herself, willingly exploited. So why not use casino gambling to support America's cities?

Formed over the course of the last century, growing to wealth and splendor with the expansion of heavy manufacturing and the American domination of the world markets following World War II, American cities attracted hundreds of thousands of immigrants in search of jobs, education, and a better life for themselves and their families. While the good times lasted, waves of immigrants educated their children and watched them move up into the mobile middle class and the suburban lifestyle. When the bad times came, the last of those waves of immigrants, notably the African Americans and Hispanics from the South and the Caribbean, were stranded in cities without jobs, without ways up or out, and without hope.

Can casino gambling help this situation? What other hope is there? The present initiatives to introduce casino gambling to U.S. cities and the issue here result from two stubborn facts.

First, no traditional economic remedy will help American cities. The services we demand that cities provide are too expensive to support with any available enterprise that might choose a city location. Manufacturing is gone, lost to technology and foreign competition, and the new "information" industries will not employ the city's discontented crowds, feed its hungry, or care for its sick.

Second, gambling has shown itself to be a cow of almost infinite cash. No coercive collection mechanisms are needed to transfer money from private pockets to the public good; people choose freely—and happily—to gamble, lavishly spending their own money at the gaming tables, in a way that they will never choose to pay their taxes. Costs are low and revenues are spectacular. For instance, the Mashantucket Pequot Indians in Connecticut, who set up a casino on their reservation in 1992, now support and educate every member of that once destitute tribe with its income. The tribe also contributes handsomely to Native American cultural foundations; employs hundreds of non-Native American residents of the state, and on top of those contributions, transfers to the state of Connecticut $130 million each year as quid pro quo for its monopoly on slot machines. Many see no downside: the sources of all this cash, the gamblers, are happy to give it up.

Why not lead the cow to the people who really need the milk? American inner cities are dying for lack of jobs and money; casinos supply both, without adding to the tax burden of the marginal industries and dwindling middle class that remains within the city boundaries. The argument ertainly seems compelling.

Not everyone agrees. Columnist William Safire cites singer/songwriter Kenny Rogers's "The Gambler": "You have to know when to hold 'em, know when to fold 'em..." "On the issue of casino gambling—its promotion of a false something-for-nothing philosophy, its corruption of both parties' politics with millions in Big Gambling cash—I am folding my hand" (*The New York Times* [March 29, 1999]). Tracking the association of casino gambling with the growth in addictive gambling, divorce, jail, bankruptcy, and increased tax costs to pay for all of this unhappiness, Safire concludes, "Good ends do not justify bad means," and he recommends that government put an end to casino gambling—or at least get out of the business of promoting it. Other critics worry about the growth of crime, especially about the participation in the industry of organized crime; they cite the evils of compulsive gambling and the possible additional drain that impoverished gamblers may put on social services. Who is right? Remember, as you read the following selections, that no one can really know for certain how far the market for gaming can continue to expand and what the ripple effects of casinos will be on America's aging urban centers. Appropriately, the introduction of largescale casino gambling to cities carries a risk; it makes gamblers of us all, whatever we decide.

William A. Galston and
David Wasserman

Gambling Away Our Moral Capital

During the past generation, there has been a dramatic expansion of legalized gambling. Beginning with New Hampshire in 1964, 37 states and the District of Columbia have instituted lotteries. As recently as 1988, only two states allowed casino gambling. Today, 24 states do so, as do a number of Native American reservations. And gambling has become very big business. Total wagers reached nearly half a trillion dollars in 1994. Gross revenues from gambling have surged —to $40 billion annually, from only $10 billion a decade ago. Casino gambling has quadrupled; lottery revenues have registered a sixfold increase; and gambling on Indian reservations, nonexistent until the late 1980s, now brings in more than $3 billion each year. State governments drain off about one-third of total lottery wagers to finance public-sector activities....

It may seem churlish and retrograde to raise moral objections against gambling, especially given its deep roots in American history. Indeed, as historian Jackson Lears has suggested, it's possible to construct a moral case in its favor. Gambling may be justified as a source of intense experience, against the grain of our otherwise routinized urban lives; as a temporary release from the bonds of reality and responsibility into a realm of fantasy and imagination; as the expression of an anti-utilitarian spirit (gambling is not really about accumulating money). Gambling can even be seen as a much-needed counterweight to a smug Protestant ethic. According to this argument, gambling helps us to focus on chance as a way of experiencing the world and instructs us in the lack of a direct link between effort, merit, and success. Besides, it may be asked, what's the difference between gambling and the kind of economic risk-taking that has always been celebrated as part of America's "go-getter" culture of striving?

Some arguments against gambling do seem puritanical or overly fastidious. Few of us regard ourselves as having so stringent a duty to preserve our assets that we refrain from squandering even small amounts of money on trivial pursuits. But we can take a more relaxed view of our stewardship obligations and still regard gambling as a vice. While we may have no objection to small wagers guided by informed judgment or skilled play, we must also recognize the danger of recklessness and compulsion in almost any form of gambling. The same qualities that make gambling so attractive—its intensity and fantasy— make it potentially destructive.

Moreover, the rejection of a smug Protestant ethic may mask an elitist contempt for bourgeois striving. While gambling allows people of all social classes to display what Lears terms a "fine, careless disregard for utilitarian standards," it is a display that is unbecoming in a society with egalitarian ambitions and very costly for the poorer members of that society. Anti-utilitarianism is particularly destructive for individuals with limited resources.

We hardly need gambling to display a healthy respect for the vicissitudes of fortune or the limitations of individual effort. We can acknowledge the uncertainty of life by mitigating its effects, through individual or social insurance schemes: by steeling ourselves against it, through a stoic regulation of our desires, hopes, and fears; or by living more fully in its shadow, giving over more of our lives to the enjoyment of the present moment. It is hardly necessary, and arguably perverse, to recognize the role of chance in our lives by increasing its sway.

But if gambling is a vice, why isn't capitalism? There are several reasons: While gambling is at best zero-sum, entrepreneurship creates advantages for others and for society as a whole. While stock markets do represent opposing gambles on price movements, they also provide essential liquidity for market systems. Even futures—apparently a pure gamble—allow risk-averse individuals to hedge against market fluctuations. There are also important differences of individual motivation and behavior between gambling and business risk-taking: The entrepreneur is focused on the future; the gambler, on the present. The entrepreneur innovates; the gambler at best calculates. The entrepreneur is compelled to think about ways of satisfying the needs of others; the gambler is not. The attempt to equate the two invites us to abandon, as sanctimonious or hypocritical, those very aspects of entrepreneurship that make it morally defensible. We should reject the invitation. The riverboat gambler is a dangerous icon just because he appeals to the darker side of capitalism.

Gambling and Civil Society

Gambling is even more problematic when it is viewed in a social context: when we look at who gambles, in what social settings, with what impact on other social institutions. First, expenditures on the most widespread form of gambling, state lotteries, are clearly regressive. In *Selling Hope,* a comprehensive review of contemporary state lotteries, Charles Clotfelter and Philip Cook found that "the relatively poor spend a much larger fraction of their income on lottery tickets than the relatively affluent." For example, a 1984 study of the Maryland lottery found that players with incomes over $50,000 spent an average of $2.57 a week on lottery tickets, while those with incomes under $10,000 spent $7.30.

While regressivity appears to be less acute for casino play—one study of Las Vegas found that expenditures increased disproportionately with income, and one study of Atlantic City found only slight regressivity—this difference may vanish as casinos become more accessible. Researchers have consistently found that members of minority groups and people with less education gamble more. In Maryland in 1984, 41 percent of blacks with incomes under $10,000 spent at least $10 a week on lottery tickets, compared to only 8 percent of whites in the same income class. These findings suggest that gambling losses fall disproportionately on some of the more vulnerable members of society.

Second, gambling is increasingly asocial. As gambling expert A. Alvarez observes:

> Back in the 1980s, the center of the casinos was the "table games"—blackjack, roulette, baccarat, craps, poker—games that involve some social exchange with other people—players, dealers, croupiers—and varying degrees of skill.... Gradually, however, casinos have cut back on the space allotted to table games and filled it with slot machines.... But compared to traditional forms of gambling, playing the slots is an autistic activity—mindless, solitary, and addictive—and its popularity is growing at a terrible speed.

We are now gambling alone as well as bowling alone, and the peculiar social function of gambling—as Alvarez describes it, "the only place where people from the straight world could rub shoulders with gangsters and not get in trouble"—is becoming an anachronism.

Third, the growing appeal and accessibility of gambling to middle class and poor families appears to have done less to domesticate gambling than to coarsen family life. While Alvarez is struck by the increasingly Disney-like face of Las Vegas—a proliferation of "pirate battles, jousting knights, and exploding volcanoes"—other observers are struck by the inappropriateness of the moral suggestions children receive and act out. Iowa State University professors Corly Peterson and Allison Engel observed unsupervised children carrying plastic cups filled with quarters, parked in front of interactive video games, looking like their cuptoting parents sitting in front of video slot machines... kids betting dollar bills on mechanical horse race games... kids rushing from video screen to video screen until their money was gone.

Even in the rare supervised child-care centers, they found, "the atmosphere... mimics the visual stimulation of a casino."

Fourth, the rise in the popularity of gambling not only reflects but also reinforces a loss of confidence in hard work as a source of social advancement. The flight of blue-collar jobs, the trend toward downsizing, and the vagaries of the service sector have all contributed to a sharp decline in the proportion of Americans who believe that hard work pays off, from 60 percent in 1960 to 33 percent by the 1980s. As Alvarez observes, "When work is no longer a reliable route to prosperity, a big kill in the lotteries or the slots becomes the one hope of escape from the economic trap." It is certainly possible to exaggerate the impact of gambling on the work ethic and the impact of cynicism about the work ethic on the current popularity of gambling. But the emphasis on luck as a route to prosperity should be especially troublesome to governments involved in the promotion of gambling.

Marketing Vice

This litany of concerns does not make the case for outlawing all forms of gambling. The costs of criminalizing it are likely to be very high, and the moral posture of the state in issuing such a wholesale condemnation is questionable.

But these concerns do suggest that states should not encourage gambling or make their own functions dependent on its proliferation. Indeed, many of these concerns are exacerbated by state sponsorship.

The practical impact of state sponsorship is troubling if uncertain. Although several studies have found large increases in compulsive and problem gambling following the introduction of state lotteries or casinos, the reliability of these findings is limited by inconsistency and vagueness in the definition of "compulsive" and "problem" gambling and by the possibility that much of the apparent increase is due to increased awareness and increased reporting. Similarly, we do not know for sure how much the state's endorsement of spendthrift ways in lottery promotion adds to the powerful social forces that subvert the inculcation of thrift and industry in the most beleaguered communities in the United States—forces such as the loss of working-class jobs and the perverse incentives of the present welfare system.

But claims about adverse consequences by no means exhaust the moral objections to state sponsorship of gambling. The more important objections, we think, concern the propriety of the state's role as gambling promoter. Even if it were appropriate for individuals to express, through gambling, their recognition of the role of chance in their lives, it would be unseemly for the state to do so. The state's promotion of gambling belies its commitment to reducing the influence of morally arbitrary factors on the lives of its citizens and to supporting the virtues of thrift, hard work, and responsibility. Consider the messages conveyed by state-sponsored ads promoting lottery sales:(1)

> Playing the lottery is exciting; you'll be bored if you don't: "It's the Pick/It's a Kick/Come on in and try your luck. You can't buy more excitement for a buck."

> Playing the lottery is smart; you can't win if you don't play: "Imagine this.... The numbers are picked. Your numbers. And suddenly, your life has changed. Suddenly you're rich. Could it happen? Absolutely! But, you have to do more than just imagine. You have to play."

> Playing will give you quick, even instant, results; no more need to defer gratification: "Just One Ticket... and it Could Happen to You."

> Playing the lottery is the way to get set for life: "The Rich. Join Them."

Those who believe that statecraft is "soulcraft" have good grounds for objecting to government promulgation of such messages. But even those who believe that families and religious communities are responsible for inculcating the virtues of thrift and industry should be appalled at the denigration of those virtues in state lottery advertising.

Some critics regard it as wrong for anyone to offer a vanishingly small chance of a huge windfall to people mired in poverty. It is particularly objectionable for that offer to come from the state. Even if we disagree about the extent of the state's obligation to reduce privation and ignorance, we should agree that it has an obligation not to exploit them.

Public and Private Vice

Equally disturbing is the deliberate exploitation of poverty to finance public projects that should be paid for by taxes if undertaken at all. As Fairfield University philosophy professor Lisa Newton has said:

> There is an ironic justice in the fact that our eagerness to legalize casino gambling for the sake of the revenues follows directly from our unwillingness to assess ourselves a fair and adequate amount in taxes. The problems with our public character dovetail with the problems in our private character.

Defenders of state-sponsored gambling deny that the use of lotteries to raise public funds is a sign of public vice. They insist that this is a time-honored practice, frequently employed in early American communities and fully consistent with republican civic virtue. But this defense overlooks the huge differences between today's lotteries and their predecessors.

Unlike current state lotteries, early American lotteries were public-spirited and progressive. A typical colonial lottery was instituted to finance specific public works projects, such as bridges or roads, and participation was seen more as a charitable contribution than a form of gambling. For example, lotteries supported the reconstruction of Boston's Faneuil Hall and new buildings for Harvard, Princeton, and Yale. For decades after the Declaration of Independence, nearly all states sponsored lotteries, in 1793, President George Washington helped promote one to finance improvements in the District of Columbia.

In contrast, present-day lotteries have become a permanent revenue source for the states and a permanent pastime for their citizens; their operations are contracted out to professional gambling firms, their economic burden is regressive rather than progressive, and their customers are largely indifferent to their objectives. Although the political approval of state lotteries has often been secured by promising to earmark their revenues for government functions such as public education and care for the elderly, the actual use of lottery revenues has rarely, if ever, been so constrained. When lottery revenues are indeed earmarked for specific projects, they are often ones that the legislature would balk at funding by direct taxation. And those who purchase lottery tickets are less likely to be rich citizens with a strong moral or economic interest in the uses to which the revenues are put than poor citizens with little say or interest in their uses.

The resurgence of legal gambling also raises classic issues of public morality. The willingness of the state to legalize and sponsor gambling has introduced large amounts of new special interest money into our politics. With contributions totaling $2 million at the national level during the 1993–1994 election cycle, gambling-financed political-action committees are now in the same league as the National Rifle Association. At the state level, proponents of casino gambling have been able to outspend opponents by as much as 50 to 1; this has led recently to major corruption scandals in Louisiana, Missouri, Arizona, Kentucky, South Carolina, and West Virginia. In Florida, backers of a pro-gambling referendum spent almost as much as the state's two gubernatorial candidates combined. It is time to ask ourselves how much civic corruption we are willing to tolerate.

William R. Eadington

 **NO**

The Proliferation of Commercial Gaming in America

Commercial gaming has arrived in America in the 1990s. To understand this, it is worthwhile to begin by examining the phenomenal success of the Foxwood's Casino and High Stakes Bingo in Ledyard, Connecticut. This is an Indian casino, owned by the 260 tribal members of the Mashantuckett Pequot Indian tribe, which opened in February, 1992. The amount of revenue generated by the casino in gaming winnings—customer expenditures on table games —in its first year of operation exceeded $200 million. In their second year of operation, after they negotiated with the Governor of Connecticut for the right to have slot machines and an exclusive franchise on casinos in Connecticut in exchange for a minimum $100 million payment to the State, their gaming winnings will approach $500 million. In their third year of operation—1994— when they have doubled their size, their gross gaming revenues could approach $700 million. At that point, they will be generating almost as much revenue as all the casinos in Reno, Nevada.

For another comparison, if you were to take all the movie theaters in America, the Foxwood's Casino is already generating about 10% as much in revenue as is generated in all ticket sales to all movie theaters in this country. Furthermore, because of its monopoly status in New England, the casino's profit margins are likely to be approximately 50%. That is for a tribe that ten years ago only had three people living on the reservation.

The gaming industry in America is going through an unprecedented proliferation and expansion that carries with it some amazing stories, of which the Ledyard situation is one. It also poses some fascinating and quite complex challenges to public policy, with regard to the impact that gambling is likely to have on society.

We are in the midst of a near total reversal of legal commercial gaming opportunities for American citizens in terms of their presence and accessibility. We are actually in the midst of a phenomenon that is occurring world wide.

From William R. Eadington, "The Proliferation of Commercial Gaming in America," *The Sovereign Citizen*, no. 1 (Fall 1994). Copyright © 1994 by Nichols College Institute for American Values. Reprinted by permission.

I would like to address a number of questions that relate to this phenomenon. Generally the questions are:

- Why is this occurring at this particular point in time?
- What are the dimensions of the gaming industries that are emerging?
- Where are these changes likely to carry us?
- What challenges will society have to confront as gambling becomes more and more present, and more and more pervasive in modern society?

As with many other facets of society, the following axiom is a useful starting point. To understand where we are today, we must first have an understanding of where we have been and how we have evolved to the current situation. Then we must try to see the directions implied by the current momentum to project what the situation will be like over the next couple of decades.

If one looks back as recently as 1910, we could note that gambling In America was virtually illegal almost everywhere. 1910 is interesting because that was the year that Nevada made casinos illegal. It was the year that New York made pari-mutuel wagering and race track wagering illegal. The only legal gambling one could find that year was on race tracks in Kentucky and in parts of Maryland. Everywhere else in America, gambling was illegal.

A half century later, in the year 1960, gambling was still largely prohibited in America. There were, as of yet, no lotteries. Casinos could be found only in Nevada, but Nevada, clearly, in the eyes of the rest of the country, was an outlaw state, which had created an environment to allow outlaws to legitimize themselves in the casino business. Wagering on racing had proliferated to about twenty states. However, people in the racing industry had a tendency to claim they were not in the gambling business; rather, they were in the business of improving the bloodlines and breed stock of thoroughbred horses, and if wagering on horses could be used as a way to subsidize the improvement of the quality of horses in this country, all the better.

That was the extent of legal gaming. There was a lot of illegal gambling, to be sure, but it was often viewed with a very critical eye. It was often cited as being the major source of income for organized crime, and a common view of gambling at the time could be summed up by an article written by Robert Kennedy, soon to become Attorney General of the United States. The article was entitled, "A Two Dollar Bet Means Murder". That seemed to summarize the public attitude towards gambling as late as the 1960s.

Churches, governments and good citizens agreed that gambling was evil, or at least that gambling was not something that should be accepted and brought into society. What were the substantive reasons? It was felt that gambling corrupted officials and law enforcement; it undermined the Protestant ethic of linkages between hard work and reward. And gambling could destroy lives through compulsive gambling, which would also lead to thefts, embezzlement, suicides, or worse. In total, gambling was considered a thoroughly unwholesome activity. That did not mean it was not fun for customers, however.

The contrast with the status of commercial gaming in the 1990s, however, is striking. Lotteries, which did not exist at all in America in 1960, can now be found in thirty-seven states and the District of Columbia. More than eighty percent of Americans can walk down to their local convenience store and purchase a lottery ticket. In 1992 lottery sales in America were over $21 billion, and after payment of prizes to winners, lotteries generated gross revenues of about $10 billion to the various states that had them. Casinos, as late as 1989 still could only be found in two places in the United States, in Nevada and in Atlantic City. Yet only four years later, one could gamble legally casino style in Nevada and Atlantic City, New Jersey; in mining town small stakes casinos in South Dakota and Colorado; on riverboats in Iowa, Illinois and Mississippi, and soon Louisiana, Missouri and Indiana. Or one could go [to] Indian casinos in Connecticut, Michigan, Minnesota, Wisconsin, South Dakota, Washington, Arizona, California, Colorado, New York, and soon in Mississippi, Louisiana, Texas and Rhode Island. All of this has transpired in a period of four years.

There has also been an expansion of non-casino casino style gambling, in the form of slot machines, video poker machines, or—in the euphemistically more acceptable name—video lottery terminals. The spread of gaming devices has been quite rapid, with their introduction into bars and taverns or other age restricted locations in the states of Montana, South Carolina, South Dakota, Oregon, Louisiana, West Virginia and Rhode Island. It has also recently been considered by the legislature of the state of Massachusetts, among others.

What does the casino industry do? How big an industry is casino gaming? And how does it affect peoples lives?

In 1992, the gross winnings for the various gaming industries in the United States, including lotteries, casinos, race tracks, charitable gambling and Indian gaming, were nearly $30 billion. That is the total expenditure of all customers on various gambling products. This also reflects total player losses after payment of winnings, as well as gross revenues on gaming to the various operators and purveyors of gambling services. This is approximately 0.6% of disposable income in the United States; roughly one-dollar out of every $150 spent in America is spent on gambling. This represents about five times as much money as Americans spend on going out to the movies: it represents about the same amount of income that is earned by all stock brokerages and securities firms in America; it represents approximately one-fourth of the gross revenues of all attorneys in America. Gambling is not a small business, it is substantial in its revenues and in its presence in society, and it is in the midst of a phenomenal expansion.

What has happened to social attitudes concerning gambling, and why are we seeing this phenomenon occurring now, at this very point in time?

There have historically been three main arguments in opposition to gambling. All of these arguments have been undermined by trends in the past three decades. The arguments are as follows:

1. Gambling leads to political corruption and brings organized crime into the mainstream of society.

However, as has been discovered time and again, political corruption and the infiltration of organized crime into gambling occurs more often when gambling is illegal, or where it is set up legally with considerable discretion given to public officials who can essentially sell the economic rents from gambling to the highest bidders. Gambling, especially when it is presented with a high degree of competent and professional regulation, can be run without scandal, and it can be run by individuals and organizations who themselves have a high degree of honesty and integrity with regard to their business dealings. It can be run without the kind of corruption that had dominated the quasi-legal or illegal gambling that used to be the major form of gambling in this country.

Lotteries, which have been run predominantly by governments, have had virtually no scandal in the 25 years that they have existed. Indeed, lotteries have also taught Americans how to gamble more than any other single activity, certainly more than such personalities as Jimmy the Greek, and more than casinos. Lotteries have played a very important role in this phenomenon, both by teaching people that gambling can be fun—even though lotteries themselves are far less interesting and entertaining than casino style gambling—but they have also demonstrated that gambling can be run with a high degree of honesty.

In New Jersey, the integrity of the regulatory process and the competence and integrity of the gaming operations has been there almost from the start, with relatively few lapses. Nevada has had a long learning process where its casino industry has gone from one of questionable integrity to one of fairly decent integrity with competent and professional operations and regulation.

2. Gambling is immoral.

Gambling has been considered as sinful by many religions. In earlier times, the church and the state would argue a person should not gamble because it is not good for people; it runs against family values; it undermines a husband's work values and long term objectives of achieving prosperity through hard work and meeting family responsibilities.

Why has this changed? In the last thirty years the church and the state have become major purveyors of gambling services. They have co-opted themselves out of the ability to take a strong moral position with regard to gambling. For many churches and charities, gambling—in the form of bingo and pull-tab tickets—have become a major revenue source.

Governments have turned to lotteries as a major revenue generator, arguing, in a world of increasing demand on public services, they cannot increase taxes not without risking their political futures. They also claim gambling is really a free tax. It is a tax that is voluntary because people choose to gamble. Therefore, governments have gone through the process of taking an illegal activity—gambling—legalizing it through lottery, and attempting to hold an exclusive franchise on their gambling monopoly so that they could maximize revenue for the state out of lottery profit. One has to be only slightly cynical to suggest that this may not be the appropriate role of government in preying on the propensities of its citizens to participate in an activity many still consider immoral.

Another factor relating to the moral arguments against gambling is that if one examines the challenges of the modern world, which is characterized by such terrible moral dilemmas and controversies over policy aimed at such things as abortion, AIDS, genocide, homosexuality, homelessness, and drug abuse, the moral questions posed by these broader issues make the morality of gambling seem quaint in comparison, or perhaps even anachronistic.

3. Gambling creates compulsive gamblers.

The third argument against gambling, compulsive gambling, is a real issue. Society is gaining greater understanding over time of this phenomenon. Among those factors that have improved our understanding of compulsive gambling in recent years is that it is an affliction that affects only a small percentage of the population, estimated at between one and five percent of the adult population. It is unclear whether compulsive gambling is a psychological or a physiological phenomenon. It is also unclear whether it is truly an addiction or merely an irresponsibility, an immaturity, on the part of those who are so cursed. But society has chosen more and more to take the attitude that if most people want to gamble, and if most people can do so responsibly, than gambling should not be prohibited for the majority, just to protect a small minority who might be at fault anyway, and for whom prohibition of gambling might not stop them from destroying themselves through gambling or some other vice anyway.

In summary, society has changed its attitude from "gambling is wrong, gambling is a sin", to one of saying "It's ok to gamble". The policy questions have shifted from "Should we gamble or not?" to "Who gets to benefit by being the purveyors of gambling services?" With regard to this point, we have seen the various claimants come forward. The claimants on gambling are the following groups, all of whom are well deserving. Governments have said that they should be the purveyors of gambling services because clearly they must deal with the fiscal crisis that is pervasive throughout this country, and clearly the demands for public services cannot be met through continuing tax increases on the middle class and the poor. So if government gets to run gambling, they can generate important tax revenues, and turn around and spend it in a fashion that is beneficial for society.

A second group of claimants—charities—respond to this argument with the claim that, if we allow government to take the revenues from gambling, it is like throwing it into a black hole. Nothing good seems to come out of government. They can absorb as much income as they can without resolving their crises. Rather, society should let charities be the purveyors of gambling services. Charities throughout Canada, and charities in certain states in the United States such as North Dakota or Minnesota, have become major purveyors of gambling services. In Minnesota, for example—a state of about four million people—charitable organizations and not-for-profit organizations in 1990 grossed about $250 million from their legal charitable gambling, after payment of prizes. They certainly are in the gambling business, and their argument is, "Let us have the revenues from gambling because we will spend them directly on things of definite and distinct value for the community; as charities, we know how to do good things."

Another set of groups who are purporting to be the legitimate claimants to the right to offer gambling are cities, or regions, in partnership with private sector gambling corporations. We have seen a bit of this in Connecticut, with attempts to legalize casinos in Hartford and Bridgeport, and we have seen legalization of a number of casinos in the Midwest, on the basis that their communities need jobs; their communities need investments; their communities need to stimulate economic development and tourism. The way they do this is to try to capture the same kinds of economic benefits that have accrued to Nevada and—to a lesser extent—New Jersey. The argument is, if the state would authorize a casino or casinos, private sector firms in partnership with political jurisdictions will create jobs; they will create investments; they will bring in tourists to the area; and everybody will benefit.

The fourth group of claimants are the Indian tribes in America. There is little doubt that, among all the minorities who have been treated in various ways by government programs over time, Indians have probably been the least effectively treated. The worst of the welfare cases in America have been Indian stories. After a combination of the emergence of Indian sovereignty as a well-defined right and a quirky law—the Indian Gaming Regulatory Act of 1988—along with some quite opportunistic situations that evolved for certain tribes, Indian gaming has become the most powerful economic development tool ever to develop for Indian tribes in America. Some tribes—such as the Mashantuckett Pequot of Connecticut—are becoming wealthy beyond their wildest expectations because of being at the right place at the right time with a set of circumstances that could be fully exploited.

Of the various claimants, one should probably concentrate on private sector casino development in league with cities, which is probably going to be the most important one over time. What are the jurisdictions who are legalizing casinos trying to do, and how effective are they likely to be? The motivation for places such as New Orleans, Kansas City, St. Louis, Davenport, Biloxi/Gulfport, Chicago, Bridgeport, Hartford and in Canada, Windsor and Montreal and Winnipeg have been to attempt to capture the economic benefits from casinos in the same manner as Nevada has done. These cities have looked at Las Vegas, which is a very interesting city for a number of reasons. They argue that they should be able to achieve the same successes.

Las Vegas is a city that most people would have claimed in 1960 was "all mobbed up". The common perception outside of Nevada was that Las Vegas was a city run for mobsters, by mobsters, in a very corrupt political system. However, Las Vegas is a city that for each of the last three decades has been among the five fastest growing metropolitan areas in the United States. It is a city that now has the ten largest hotels in the world. In terms of number of rooms, Las Vegas has more hotel rooms than both New York and London. Las Vegas is probably the best large convention city in the world today. They have the ability to accommodate over 100,000 visitors at one time. Las Vegas is also evolving in the same general direction as Orlando, Florida, with the construction of major amusement parks at a number of destination resort casino properties. In fact, the term "Las Orlando", has been used more and more commonly in recent years, and the term is actually getting to the point where one wonders whether the term Las Orlando, is an attempt to describe Las Vegas as a variant of Orlando, or an attempt to describe Orlando as a variant of Las Vegas.

The process of a rush to legalization of gambling has pointed out some very interesting patterns, and indeed, weaknesses in the American system. The first such weakness is that the American political system can be very myopic. It tends to concentrate on a single issue and run with that issue as long as it can. With regard to gambling, the dominant policy consideration used to be organized crime. That was the only point of debate: the concern that gambling inevitably led to involvement by organized crime and consequent political corruption.

If one examines the way that New Jersey wrote its Casino Control Act in 1977, and tries to see what their concerns were as embodied in the Act, it becomes very clear. The concerns of the Casino Control Act were to keep organized crime out of the casino gaming business, because that is its natural tendency. And that was the dominant way of thinking about commercial gaming until the late 1980s, especially with regard to casinos. And then—all of a sudden—concerns about organized crime diminished; they seemed to pass into posterity, into nostalgia. What replaced it was the primacy of economic benefits to be derived from gaming. Gambling's greatest social value is in creating economic benefits; thus, state after state has moved toward the legalization of gambling to capture those economic benefits.

There is a second weakness inherent in the American political system. This is the belief that if legislation works well in one place, it can work just as well in another jurisdiction, even though the safeguards may be slightly more relaxed and the circumstances somewhat different. There has been a very interesting and clear evolution in the legalization of casino style gambling in America. If we examine the third jurisdiction to legalize casinos, after Nevada and Atlantic City, we find it in a little place called Deadwood, South Dakota. Deadwood is about thirty miles from Mount Rushmore, and its population is about 1600 people. It is a small, remote, rural area. Deadwood peaked economically in the 1890s as a mining town, and it has not had much economic stimulus ever since. It is most famous for being the town where Wild Bill Hickock was shot in the back while playing poker, holding a hand of aces and eights, now known as the "dead man's" hand. The tourist attraction of Deadwood was the tomb of Wild Bill in Boot Hill, buried next to Calamity Jane.

In the 1980s, the town of Deadwood was literally falling apart. The city fathers argued the only way Deadwood could be saved would be to create a revenue source that will allow them to put some money aside for historic preservation of Deadwood. They were able to convince the voters of South Dakota in the 1988 election to authorize small stakes limited casino gambling in Deadwood. Five dollar maximum wagers were allowed, and no license could have more than thirty slot machines or table games. In November, 1989, Deadwood opened its first casinos and became the third jurisdiction in America to have casinos. Within a year every business in Deadwood had become a casino, and every other business was pushed out. In one sense, it was phenomenally successful; in another sense it was a disaster. People would travel six or eight hours to get to the slot machines of Deadwood.

Shortly thereafter, Iowa set up constrained riverboat gaming legislation that would allow no more than five dollar maximum wagers, and a person could lose no more than $200 per excursion. There was a belief among the good people of Iowa that the evils of gambling would show up if large wagers were allowed and if people were allowed to lose too much money in any given visit. Therefore, they legislated against it. They also allocated three percent of the gross winnings from their casinos for compulsive treatment programs, so that any social damage created by the casinos would be taken care of. They also mandated that—at least when the river was not frozen—gambling would have to take place on the riverboats while they were floating on the water. The belief—or symbolism—was that if all the sinning from gambling was taking place on the Mississippi River, then those sins, as they work their way back to shore, would be washed pure by the time they reached shore so as to not infect the good people of Iowa.

So Iowa and South Dakota set the tone for responsible, remote, small stakes gambling. But what happened next? Illinois is right across the river from Iowa and so they decided they did not want Iowa to get all the gaming revenues from their citizens, so they passed a riverboat gaming bill as well. However, they failed to put in the maximum wager limitation, or the maximum loss limitation, and they even allowed casino credit about which Iowa would shudder at the thought. Within nine months after Iowa passed its legislation, Illinois had copied it.

Further down the Mississippi River, in the state of Mississippi, the legislature argued that they also should have riverboat gambling; but they carried it one step further. They legislated that their riverboats did not have to go out and sail on the river. Indeed, after the law was passed, the Attorney General of Mississippi offered an opinion that Mississippi gaming boats do not even need to have motors on the boats. Indeed, they did not even have to be boats. A license holder in Mississippi can build a casino as long as it sits over the water. So, in an analogy to Darwinian evolution, we have seen casinos crawl out of the rivers and position themselves on the banks of rivers to become land-based casinos.

By the time riverboats worked their way into Louisiana, not only were the riverboats getting closer to the shore; they were getting closer to the cities. Louisiana, over a period of a little over a year, passed legislation that authorized riverboats within New Orleans, a major metropolitan area. They also passed non-casino gaming legislation that allowed video lottery terminals in bars, taverns, truck stops and off-track betting parlors throughout the state. Then in 1992, they passed legislation for a land-based monopoly casino in the center of New Orleans, right in the heart of its tourism area.

Thus, there has been a very rapid evolution from harmless, distant, remote gambling, to wide-open urban style gambling, bringing for the first time casinos to where many people live. This has been part of a process that has moved very quickly. It is also being copied in a lot of other jurisdictions. Every new jurisdiction, in order to be competitive, takes the position that they have to be more aggressive than the previous competing jurisdiction which legalized. So as legislation has moved one step further each time, casinos and their presence have become less constrained, less remote, less socially responsible.

The Indian gaming issue—which has been more influenced through the courts—accelerates the process of legalization. If Indians have casinos in particular jurisdictions, the entire public policy debate changes, because once Indians have casinos, the debate in the state, as has already occurred in Connecticut, is no longer, "Should we have casinos?" Rather, the important questions shift to "Who should have the casinos?", "Who should benefit from them?", and "Where should they be located?"

So, at this point in time, America confronts a situation where the momentum for the spread of gambling is, in my opinion, still just beginning. The United States casino and gaming market could be characterized as being terribly under-supplied. That under-supply is being addressed in a variety of ways, and at a very rapid pace.

How much growth remains in the gaming industry in America? In the United States, as mentioned earlier, commercial gaming is nearly a $30 billion a year industry. That represents an expenditure of about $110 per capita.

How much can such expenditures grow? To gain some insight into that question, we can examine the experience of New South Wales, Australia, the largest Australian state, home of Sydney, the country's largest city. In many respects, Australia is similar to America. With regard to gambling, there is generally widely available and accessible gambling in New South Wales. Per capita expenditures in New South Wales are about $570, about four times that of America when corrected for exchange rate differences.

How large can the American gaming industry get? It is not unreasonable to project an industry with gross revenues of $100 billion to $125 billion at maturity with current population and current real income. It can expand by a factor of about four or five just by addressing the question of under-supply of gaming facilities in America. If this process continues unconstrained, we could go from about 300,000 slot machines in America, to about three million, within a decade or so.

One of the issues with this type of projection is, could this really occur? The one thing that is working to bring it about is, if one examines the reasons why politicians are legalizing gaming, especially casino style gaming, one sees the rationale shrouded in economic justifications. Legislatures legalize casinos because of jobs. As Mayor Richard Daly of Chicago said, "Why do we want casinos in Chicago? Jobs, jobs, jobs."

POSTSCRIPT

Should Casino Gambling Be Prohibited?

Two major cities in Connecticut, Hartford and Bridgeport, have both considered the introduction of casino gambling. Thirty-seven states and the District of Columbia have lotteries; in 1993, those lotteries sold $25.1 billion in tickets. Many regions have instituted, or are considering instituting, riverboat casinos or other restricted gaming establishments. Nonprofit institutions have long supported themselves with gambling; can the private sector be far behind? Underlying the entire debate is the tension of passing time: the market for gambling cannot be infinite, and each casino that opens draws revenue that the next cannot tap. And video lotteries (casinos on the Internet), which bring income to no location whatsoever, threaten all gambling establishments.

Life is a gamble, and risk is a part of our daily lives. The questions before us are not, in that sense, new. But they are certainly more complex, and they will demand our full attention in the next decade. America's cities need more help than anyone knows how to give them. Are the gambler's solutions the best solutions?

Suggested Readings

"Canada: 'A Gamble'," *The Economist* (June 18, 1994).

"Gambling May Yield Revenue Windfall," *Aviation Week and Space Technology* (August 15, 1994).

Francis X. Clines, "Gambling, Pariah No More, Is Booming Across America," *The New York Times* (December 5, 1993).

Susan B. Garland, "Clinton vs. The Sin Lobby: All Bark," Government Lobbyists, *Business Week* (July 18, 1994).

Robert Goodman, "Legalized Gambling as a Strategy for Economic Development," *United States Gambling Study* (March 1994).

Dan Parker, "Night Moves—When an Industry Runs Around the Clock (Weekends and Holidays) It Leaves Workers and Families Run-down and Stressed Out," *The Atlantic City Press* (June 14, 1993).

Timothy P. Ryan, Patricia J. Connor, Janet F. Speyerer, *The Impact of Casino Gambling in New Orleans* (Division of Business and Economic Research, University of New Orleans, LA, May 1990).

Gerald Slusher, *The Casino Industry and Its Impact on Southern New Jersey* (Division of Economic Development, Atlantic City, NJ, January 1991).

Frank Wolfe, "Inherited Talents," *Forbes 400* (October 17, 1994).

ISSUE 8

Are Derivative Instruments Purchases Just Gambling?

YES: Frank Partnoy, from *F.I.A.S.C.O.: The Inside Story of a Wall Street Trader* (Penguin Books, 1999)

NO: Merton H. Miller, from *Merton H. Miller on Derivatives* (John Wiley & Sons, 1997)

ISSUE SUMMARY

YES: Frank Partnoy, former trader and salesman at Morgan Stanley, makes a case that the financial instruments known as "derivatives" are wildly risky and generally good only for making large commissions for the salesmen who push them on unwary insurance companies and pension funds.

NO: Merton H. Miller, a Nobel prize–winning economist, contends that derivatives allow financial players to hedge their bets more efficiently, and in doing so they make the world a safer place.

Derivatives are financial instruments whose returns are linked to the performance of an underlying asset, such as mortgages, bonds, currencies, or commodities. Although the commodities market has been around a long time and has had its share of criticism over the years, it operates on agreed contracts, contracts for the purchase of a commodity (eggs, coffee, pork bellies) at least grounded in reality and recognizable in ordinary life. If you buy futures in eggs, for instance, speculating that the price will go up at some future date, but you forget to sell as the market moves, when your date arrives, so will your eggs. This might become a big problem if you are not in need of a truckload of eggs. This possibility tends to regulate the futures commodities markets. The possibility of the commodity being delivered takes buying futures out of the realm of "gambling": the intent of the contract at purchase time (to make a profit by an advantageous trade) is, according to the law, limited by the words of the contract and the existence of a real commodity.

But derivatives operate without such an agreed contract; they are risk bets to hedge against changes in the marketplace. While derivatives are linked to performance of underlying assets, such as mortgages or bonds, that linkage has nothing to do with the way they operate. Take the case of Orange County, California, which went into default because its speculators bought derivative securities linked to movements in a multiple of the difference between Swiss and U.S. interest rates. As the Swiss and U.S. interest rates changed, so did the amount of difference between them; as the direction of the U.S. interest rates changed versus the Swiss, Orange County won or lost its bets on (a multiple of) the amount of the change. If the interest rates had moved in the right direction, the yield on the investment would have been very high. As it happened, U.S. interest rates were raised by the Federal Reserve to clamp down on inflation for most of 1994 and the first months of 1995. That was the wrong direction for Orange County; the rate hikes sent the value of Orange County's portfolio on a downward spiral (keep in mind if the yield is high, so are the risks.)

What should be done to prevent this type of disaster? Some suggest telling the states and counties exactly what they can and cannot buy. Instead, Arthur Levitt, the chairman of the Securities and Exchange Commission, has asked state and local governments to monitor those who manage and invest the taxpayers' money. It is not now known if that request will be sufficient to protect local governments from uninformed or unscrupulous investment advisors.

As you read the following selections, keep in mind the reasons for the stock and commodities markets in the first place—to help business and farmers raise cash—but always to help investors to make a profit. Contrast these with the objectives in the management of public funds (security and liquidity). The history of these markets, especially of the events that led to their present regulation, suggest that the stock market, especially in the complex areas of options, futures, and derivatives in general, is a financial and ethical minefield. This may help you understand the ethical complexities of the exchanges, their investment houses, banks, and financial advisors. The investment houses are all in the business of giving professional advice (with the client's interest at heart) and selling products to the public with their own profit foremost. How can these two goals be compatible? The public in many cases has little or no understanding of the products and the risks involved and depends on these professionals to give them good advice.

What weight should be given the values of freedom and justice in investment activities? Should government curb, with careful regulation, the activities of those investment experts who manage the public money—more than those who speculate for their own profit or for the profit of private clients? Why, or why not? When looking at government regulation of the financial markets, think about what it could do to the choices for investors and the ability to raise money by those who wish to expand or gain from these markets. Can government do a better job of protecting the public till than a well-trained professional who knows the local territory? Can, or should, government save one from oneself or save the community from the consequences of its own bad judgment? If so, how can this be done most effectively?

Frank Partnoy  **YES**

F.I.A.S.C.O.

Keeping tabs on the derivatives obituaries column is nearly a full-time job these days, especially with the recent surge in activity. By the time you read this, the market is likely to be more than $100 trillion (it was estimated at $65–80 trillion as of mid-1998), headed for the astronomical $1 quadrillion mark. I can't resist the urge to abuse the late Senator Everett Dirksen's famous quote: a quadrillion here and a quadrillion there and pretty soon you're talking about some serious money.

⟨❦⟩

... Derivatives, once again, are a horror show. The structured notes and leveraged swaps that rocked the financial markets with billion-dollar losses in 1994–95 are back. The same specters that haunted, and then broke Barings, and Orange County, and took a slice out of Procter & Gamble have returned from the dead. And in my opinion, the sequel is even more scary.

Derivatives remain unseen, yet ubiquitous. Time bombs are ticking away, concealed in the underbelly of our investment portfolios. Whether you realize it or not, most of you investors continue to have exposure to derivatives, typically through investments in mutual funds (yes, even Fidelity) and pension funds (yes, even TIAA/CREF). I was not happy to discover that my new hometown, sleepy San Diego, has a $3.3 billion public-employee pension fund chock full of derivatives. I own derivatives, indirectly, through a mutual fund I bought, and I'll bet you own them, too. If you still don't believe me, just call your mutual fund manager or read your prospectus. And get ready to weep.

Of course, Wall Street isn't weeping one tear. Derivatives continue to be hugely profitable for bankers, in part because fund managers who buy derivatives will pay a premium to take on risks they can hide from shareholders, and in part because other buyers don't fully understand what they are buying. Derivatives have helped Wall Street to its best year ever—bonuses were up more than 30 percent last year. Sellers of derivatives are ecstatic. Many buyers are happy, for now; ignorance is bliss. Yet 70 percent of derivatives professionals say they expect big losses in the coming year.

Opinion about derivatives remains sharply divided. George Soros, billionaire trader, warns that derivatives traders cause instability that will "destroy society." ... [I believe that] derivatives carry hidden seeds of destruction, and that no one truly understands their risks....

Asian Fallout

Much of the [recent] derivatives action... has been in Asia, where the derivatives market is estimated to be in the tens of trillions of dollars, though no one really knows how big it is. Market participants are worried, and Hong Kong pension fund regulators even proposed forbidding derivatives use. Japan and the Asian "tigers"—Korea, Indonesia, Malaysia, the Philippines, Singapore, Taiwan, Thailand—were doing just fine until the summer of 1997. On July 2, 1997, Thailand, which had pegged its currency, the baht, to a basket of foreign currencies, based on Thailand's trade with other countries, finally had to eliminate the peg. The baht plunged more than 17 percent against the U.S. dollar that day, just as the Mexican Peso had collapsed on December 20, 1994. The effects were cataclysmic.

[For instance, there was a] mouth-watering Thai baht structured note.... That note, and similar foreign exchange-linked notes, were issued by highly-rated corporations and government sponsored enterprises, such as General Electric Credit Corporation and the Federal Home Loan Banks. The notes looked safe, and paid a deliciously high coupon. But if you were an unlucky holder of a Thai baht structured note on July 2, 1997, you were suffering from more than mild digestive problems. A mountain of pink bismuth powder couldn't block the financial dysentery as the note ripped through the innards of your balance sheet, faster than a plate of bad paed ped.

The other Asian tigers followed Thailand into the dumpster. Asian banks had been feasting, like the fat Mexican banks of the early 1990s, making leveraged bets on their own markets and currencies using equity swaps, total return swaps, options, futures, forwards, and more complex derivatives. Now, they faced annihilation. Within months, the foreign currency value of investments in East Asia dropped by 50 percent or more.

Structured notes and swaps did far more than cause localized commercial collywobbles in Asia. They ensured that the ripple effects of the baht devaluation would reach well beyond the domestic markets. If a butterfly flapping its wings in Thailand can affect weather in the U.S., imagine what a currency devaluation can do. Individual investors, money managers, even hedge fund operators throughout the world were hurting.

Most of the derivatives causing the pain were "over-the-counter" rather than traded on any exchange. That means, for example, that Asian banks engaging in swaps had a counterparty, typically a U.S. or European bank, who expected repayment on the swap, just as I would expect repayment if you and I had bet $10 on whether the Asian markets would falter. In other words, the Asian banks and companies hadn't lost money to any centralized exchange; they had lost money to other companies, primarily Western banks. The bottom line was that if the Asian banks went bust, their counterparties might lose the entire amounts the Asian banks owed.

The over-the-counter nature of these derivatives trades created enormous potential for loss. For example, banking regulators warned that U.S. banks had more than $20 billion of exposure to Korea. One Korean investment firm, SK Securities Company, had bet with J. P. Morgan that the Thai baht would rise relative to the Japanese yen, and when the baht collapsed, SK owed J. P. Morgan about $300 million. Other banks—including Citicorp, Chase Manhattan, and Bankers Trust—each disclosed more than a billion dollars of exposure to Asia. This exposure to a counterparty's inability or unwillingness to repay is called "credit risk." Credit risk is a banal non-issue irrelevant to a counterparty until a so-called credit event actually occurs; then, credit risk is a central issue mattering all too much. Credit risk from derivatives was a major reason the U.S. was so concerned about rescuing Asia (and its banking counterparties) from financial meltdown.

One man who was suffering more than most during this period of financial indigestion in Asia was Victor Niederhoffer, the celebrated, and often barefooted, squash/derivatives maestro and hedge fund manager extraordinaire. Niederhoffer's imbroglio illustrates the interconnectedness of modern capital markets, and the amazing velocity of investments in derivatives.

In June 1997, Niederhoffer was on top of the world. His excellent autobiography, *The Education of a Speculator,* was selling well, and he was managing more than $100 million of investments, including much of his own considerable wealth. He was both popular and respected, and had an incredible track record: returns of 30 percent per year for fifteen years, with a 1996 return of 35 percent.

Unfortunately, Niederhoffer also had made a big bet on the baht. And when the Thai butterfly flapped its wings, he lost about $50 million, almost half of his fund.

Derivatives traders who lose $50 million, or more, seem to follow a pattern. I used to fall into that pattern playing blackjack in Las Vegas. Perhaps you've had a similar experience. You play a hand of blackjack for $100, thinking it wouldn't kill you to lose that much money. You lose the hand. Then, you play another hand, thinking it wouldn't be a big deal to lose $200. Besides, maybe you'll win the hand and get back to even. You lose that hand, too. Then, you lose another hand, and another hand, and another. Pretty soon, you're down $500, an amount of money you really would prefer *not* to lose. What do you do? Do you quit? Or course not. You do the opposite. You increase your wagers, and start betting to get even. That's the pattern. You look up to the eye-in-the-sky, and a little voice in your head trembles, "If only I could win that money back, *then* I would stop gambling. Forever."

Imagine adding five zeros to that $500. What does that voice sound like, now? It might sound awfully depressing if the $50 million was your money. But what if the money was, in the words of Justice Louis Brandeis, "other people's money"? Suddenly betting to get even doesn't seem foolish at all. Wouldn't you double-down, at least once, for $50 million of *someone else's* money? Why not? If you win, you're even and no one will ever care about your temporary loss. And if you lose, do you really think it matters much if you lose another $50 million of someone else's money. After the first $50 million, you've pretty much guaranteed that special someone won't be inviting you to Thanksgiving dinner.

So Niederhoffer, like others before him—Nick Leeson of Barings, Joseph Jett of Kidder, Peabody, Yasuo Hamanaka of Sumitomo, Toshihide Iguchi of Daiwa—began betting to get even, taking on additional risk in the hope that he could make back enough money to overcome his losses on the baht. Academics would refer to Niederhoffer, at this point in his life, as a rogue trader.

He had recovered a bit of the Thai loss by September, but was still down about 35 percent for the year. Going into October, Niederhoffer began doubling down by selling put options on the Standard & Poor's 500 index futures contract. This was a truly gutsy move. The S & P 500 index futures contract allows speculators to make leveraged bets on the performance of the S & P 500 index, an index that tracks 500 large stocks. You can sell put options on this contract in the same way you can sell put options on any other instrument.

... A put option is the right to sell some underlying financial instrument or index at a specified time and price. In the trader's parlance, or Corvette lingo, if you bought a put option, you might pay $1,000 today for the right to sell a Corvette for $40,000 some time during the next month. You would make money if the price of Corvettes dropped. If the price of a Corvette dropped to $30,000, you would make $10,000—the $40,000 you could sell a Corvette for, using the put option, minus the $30,000 you could buy a Corvette for in the market (less the $1,000 premium you had paid).

Whereas the buyer of a put option wants the price to go down, the seller of a put option wants the price to stay the same or go up—but definitely, *please*, not to go down. The more the price goes down, the more the seller of the put option must pay the buyer. In our example, if the price of Corvettes dropped to $30,000, and we had sold put options on 100 Corvettes, we would lose $900,000 ($1 million less the $100,000 premium we had received). The strategy of selling put options does not carry the one benefit Morgan Stanley touted for some of the riskier products it sold: "downside limited to size of initial investment." In this case, you could lose *more* than everything. A put seller's downside is limited only by the size of his or her imagination (and the fact that prices don't usually drop below zero.)

Niederhoffer was looking OK through the weekend of October 25–26. October had not been an especially eventful month, the publication of my book notwithstanding. Niederhoffer was waiting, hoping the options would expire worthless so he could keep the premium and get back closer to even. Remember, he wanted the market to stay the same or go up—but definitely, *please*, not to go down.

On Monday, October 27, 1997, the U.S. stock market plummeted 554 points, or about 7 percent. The S & P index fell 64.67 points to 876.97. It had been almost exactly 10 years since the stock market crash of 1987, dubbed "Black Monday," October 19, 1987. A 7 percent drop didn't meet the definition of market crash, and it certainly couldn't match Black Monday. But for Niederhoffer, that Monday delivered a death blow. By noon, he was broke.

By Wednesday, his funds had been liquidated. The $100 million-plus of his investors' money was gone.

Take a guess at who Niederhoffer's investors were? That's right, believe it or not, my hometown favorite, the $3.3 billion San Diego public-employee pension fund was right there in the thick of it with Niederhoffer's other put option sellers. Well done, San Diego!

Merton H. Miller on Derivatives

Financial derivatives, for those who may have been too preoccupied with their own concerns to notice, come these days in basically three different flavors, like the quarks in nuclear physics.

Historically, the first derivatives to burst on the scene in their modern form were exchange-traded futures and options in the early 1970s, in Chicago, naturally (though their ancestry traces back to Holland in the seventeenth century and, surprisingly, to Japan at about the same time). Next in time came so-called swaps. Swaps are contracts in which, as the name suggests, two counterparties exchange payment streams, typically a floating interest-rate stream for a fixed-interest rate stream or a stream in dollars for a stream in marks or yen. Finally, and most recently, has come an explosive revival in so-called "structured notes" that might, to take one wild example, let a Brazilian firm, say, borrow at 5% in U.S. dollars plus the amount by which the returns on the Brazilian stock market exceed that on the Mexican market. These customized structured deals, admittedly, may sometimes strike outsiders as a bit bizarre, but the fact remains that the use of derivatives of all three flavors has grown rapidly over the last twenty years. And why is that?

Their use has grown, I insist, because they have satisfied an important business need. They have allowed firms and banks, at long last, to manage effectively and at low cost, business and financial risks that have plagued them for decades, if not for centuries.

But despite what I and most other economists, at least of the Chicago variety, see as the social benefits of these financial derivatives, they have, let us face it, also been getting a very bad press recently. Everyone by now surely has read about Procter and Gamble, that sweet little old Ivory soap company that dropped $150 million or so on derivatives, and about the big German conglomerate, Metallgesellschaft, that supposedly dropped ten times that amount on oil futures. Derivatives horror stories have created the impression that derivatives have brought us close to a financial Chernobyl that threatens to bring the whole economy down around our ears unless derivatives are brought under strict government control and supervision.

The Real Threat: Derivatives or Central Banks?

So, before going any further, let me emphasize that no serious danger of a derivatives-induced financial collapse really exists. Note, however, how I have carefully phrased that: no *derivatives-induced* financial collapse. Firms will continue to lose money on bad judgment and bad derivatives deals, just as they always have in deals on ordinary assets like stocks and real estate. And a major crack in one of the world's financial markets is always possible. But crashes in financial markets are not exogenous calamities like earthquakes. They are *policy* disasters, tracing not to transactions between *private-sector* parties, but to the deliberately deflationary actions of a central bank somewhere, usually overreacting to its previous policy errors in the other direction.

A classic example, of course, has been the turmoil in the U.S. bond market since the spring of 1994 after our Federal Reserve System suddenly nudged up short-term interest rates. And why did the Fed feel it had to nudge them up? Because the Fed had previously driven short rates far too low, hoping that lower short rates would lead to lower long rates which in turn, the Fed hoped, would pull the U.S. economy more rapidly out of recession. That announced policy of driving interest rates down gave the banks, the hedge funds, and the big institutional investors generally what seemed a surefire, money-coining strategy: borrow short and lend long. The low short rates kept their cost of borrowing small and the Fed's fears of throttling the then still-weak economic expansion would keep them low. Prices of long-term bonds, then, could go only one way: up. For more than a year, those leveraged bets on falling long-term interest rates paid off handsomely.

But the Fed eventually discovered, or should I say rediscovered, that the short-term rate could be held below its warranted level only by rapidly expanding the money supply and risking a resurgence of price inflation. The Fed thereupon suddenly stepped on the monetary brakes by raising short-term interest rates, hoping that its anti-inflation rhetoric would keep the more inflation-sensitive long-term rates from rising. But the Fed guessed wrong. Long-term rates rose right along with short-term rates and blood began to flow on Wall Street (and in Orange County). So far, the fallout on the U.S. real economy from the Fed's monetary tightening has been small. But more tightening may be on the way and we must not become complacent. We need only look to the mismanagement by the Federal Reserve System in the early 1930s to see how much permanent damage a central bank can inflict on an economy.

The Current State of Derivatives Regulation

For what further comfort it may offer to those worried about the dangers from unregulated derivatives, let me also assure them that derivatives already are very extensively regulated. The futures exchanges, for example, are regulated (and very heavy-handedly) by the Commodities Futures Trading Commission, or CFTC, one of the largest producers of bureaucratic red tape this side of Japan. The securities broker/dealer firms like Goldman Sachs or Salomon Brothers are regulated by the Securities and Exchange Commission, or SEC, an agency with a world-recognized reputation as a tough cop.

On that score, however, some critics, including our U.S. General Accounting Office, have complained recently that while the SEC may regulate the dealer firms and their capital requirements, the agency has no special or specific requirements for their derivatives operations. But if you know how the derivatives business is structured in Wall Street these days, that line of argument by our GAO makes no real sense. The name of the game in the derivatives business is *credit quality.* Nobody will deal swaps with you if you can't convince them that you have adequate capital, or unless you post substantial collateral if you don't. For further reassurance to the particularly credit-sensitive sector of the market, moreover, some of the big brokerage firms have even split parts of their derivatives business off into separate subsidiaries, with dedicated capital of their own. These "subs" have received triple-A credit ratings from the private credit-rating agencies like Moody's and Standard & Poors, agencies who do a more stringent capital and credit analysis, incidentally, than the SEC ever has or ever could. And far from suggesting any looming capital inadequacy, the ratings of the subs, in fact, are actually higher than that of the banks that do most of the derivatives business.

Those banks, moreover, which currently account for about 70% of the derivatives business, are themselves heavily regulated, to say the least. The derivatives activities of every bank dealer are regulated by at least one, and sometimes by as many as three separate regulators. The bank officers often find themselves saying good-bye to one group of examiners going out the back door just as another group is being ushered in at the front door.

The S&L Crisis and the Supposed Dangers of Inadequate Regulation

But if derivatives, as I insist, are already adequately (or more than adequately) regulated, how do I answer people who say we've heard that same talk about overregulation back in the early 1980s when the savings and loan industry was insisting that *its* regulation was adequate. And look what happened.

But are the two cases really parallel? Very definitely not. The so-called deregulation of S&Ls in the early 1980s was less a matter of allowing free market magic to do its work than an attempt by Congress to prolong the life of an industry that a truly free market would have ended years before. The industry was not allowed to die a natural death because residential housing and everything connected with it had become a sacred cow of U.S. politics. Congress in the 1930s and even more so in the years after World War II was encouraging U.S. citizens to buy homes and finance them with thirty-year fixed-rate mortgages from local savings and loan associations funded by insured deposits. By the mid 1960s however, as inflation and hence interest rates began to rise in the United States, the S&Ls found themselves having to pay 6% or more to keep from losing their deposits, while the thirty-year fixed-rate mortgages on their books had been made years before at 4 to 5%. By the late 1970s, in fact, as inflation accelerated, more of the industry had become technically insolvent on a mark-to-market basis.

At that point, rather than face up to closing down the politically potent local S&L industry and bailing out their federally insured depositors with tax money, Congress gave the S&Ls one last chance to stay alive, by allowing them to invest in more than just the mortgages on single-family homes, their traditional market niche. They could now invest in commercial real estate, luxury condos, and resort properties, a form of diversification which, by itself, might not have been so troublesome. But the S&Ls were allowed to support commercial property developments of that kind, without having to face the normal market tests for funding such risky ventures. Congress, in the dark of night (that is to say without holding hearings or any public debate), had raised the limit on government guaranteed deposit accounts of S&Ls from $10,000 to $100,000 per *account*. Not per individual or per family, but per account. In today's prices that would be equivalent to close to $200,000 per account, a non-trivial sum. S&Ls could thus raise virtually unlimited funds for speculative property development merely by offering to pay fifty or seventy-five basis points above the going deposit rate. Deposit brokers would then funnel them money from all over the country. The depositors didn't ask any questions about how the S&Ls hoped to earn those extra fifty or seventy-five basis points. Why should they care? The U.S. government was guaranteeing their deposits.

To cite the S&L bailouts as grounds for regulating derivatives is thus not only to miss the point of that government-spawned disaster, but is doubly ironic. Financial derivatives, if they had only been more readily available in the early 1980s, could have kept the S&L industry viable as a residential housing lender without massive life support from subsidized deposits. If maturity mismatch between floating-rate deposits and fixed-rate mortgages is your problem, then interest-rate swaps and futures and options can be your solution. Indeed, that is precisely the direction in which what's left of the S&L industry is going at the moment. The industry has also been helped, of course, by the development of variable-rate mortgages and even more by its ability to securitize its locally raised mortgages by bundling them into mortgage pools. Those pools in turn, serve as inputs to still another class of derivatives securities, the so-called CMOs or collateralized mortgage obligations. CMOs support many new strategies for controlling interest-rate risks, though, alas, also some new ways for the unskilled or the unlucky to lose big chunks of money.

Derivatives and the Safety of the Banking System

Not only are the S&Ls much safer institutions today, thanks to derivatives, than they were in the past, but so too are the commercial banks. Despite all the hullabaloo in the press, and all the bad publicity surrounding derivatives, banks are safer today, not riskier. And for several reasons.

For one thing, the customers in a bank's derivatives book are now much better credit risks, on the whole, than those in their regular loan portfolio. Top-rated, blue-chip clients had been leaving the banks steadily for many years in favor of public-market funding, especially commercial paper. Swaps and options have brought them back. And even for some of the banks' so-so, intermediate credits, swaps strengthen a bank's hand on long-term fixed rate credits. They let a bank pull the plug on a firm when its condition is just beginning to deteriorate, without having to wait for an actual default.

The swaps and options book, moreover, is typically highly diversified whereas banks' commercial portfolios are often heavily concentrated by region, or by industry (like Continential Bank and its oil credits) or by foreign country (like Citibank and its Latin American credits). And, of course, as noted earlier for the S&Ls, a bank's swaps and derivatives book can be managed to control interest-rate risk. If more of a bank's customers want to take the floating-rate side than want the fixed-rate side of interest-rate swaps, the bank simply lays off the excess directly with other dealers who happen to have the reverse position. Or, I am happy to say, the bank can make an offsetting transaction using exchange-traded financial futures, like the Eurodollar futures of the Chicago Mercantile Exchange, or CME.

But if swaps and derivatives have really made the financial system safer, not riskier, as I have claimed, why are we hearing so many calls these days for more regulation? Part of the answer, I suspect, comes from misunderstanding by the public and the financial press about how serious the risks really are.... A telltale sign of how deep those misunderstandings go is the almost universal practice of citing the nominal size of swaps outstanding and treating that number as if it were the amount at risk. Last year the conventional number was $8 trillion, this year it's $12 trillion. But whether eight or twelve, it's a huge amount. If it really did measure the risk exposure, it would be hard to blame people for being worried.

Those multitrillion dollar numbers, however, are just bookkeeping entries, or better, score-keeping entries, not transaction amounts. And similarly for interest-rate swaps. What gets swapped is *not* the trillions of principal amount, but only the *interest* on the principal, which is an order of magnitude smaller. And even that is an overstatement, because only the *difference* between the fixed and the floating rates is exchanged, which cuts it in half again. So we're talking not about $12 trillion at risk, but something like 1 to 2% of that amount, which is certainly not trivial, but it's not terribly frightening either, given the elaborate risk-control programs installed by all the major banks and dealers.

POSTSCRIPT

Are Derivative Instruments Purchases Just Gambling?

What is happening in the financial markets? Are derivatives a safe hedge in large portfolios to reduce the risks of institutional investors? Is this true, and does it apply to the small investor in a mutual fund who buys derivatives as a hedge from loss? Experienced investment advisors characterize the risk-taking "day traders" as "the folks who missed the bus to Atlantic City (and its gambling casinos)." Would a comparison to poker or blackjack at the many casinos around the country be a better way of describing the stock and commodities markets and the many investment advisors, with their "unique" investment instruments, who operate in these markets? Can the Securities and Exchange Commission (SEC) and/or the government keep these markets from being "casinos" without eliminating the "free market" system upon which they operate?

The derivatives question may best be seen as part of a larger question: In a free market economy is self-regulation and consumer choice sufficient to protect the public, or must the government take responsibility for protecting the common good?

Suggested Readings

Tim W. Ferguson, "The Dynamite and the Derivatives," *The Wall Street Journal* (February 28, 1995).

Roger Lowenstein, "Will Orange County Squeeze California?" *The Wall Street Journal* (June 15, 1995).

Suzanne McGee, "Derivatives Could Hedge Career Growth," *The Wall Street Journal* (August 24, 1995).

Donald G. Simonson, "Vignettes from the Derivatives 'Crisis,'" *United States Banker* (September 1994).

Jeffrey Taylor, "Securities Firms Agree to Set Controls on Derivatives," *The Wall Street Journal* (March 9, 1995).

R. S. Wurman, A. Siegel, and K. M. Morris, *The Wall Street Journal Guide to Understanding Money and Markets* (Prentice Hall, 1990).

Employee Incentives and Career Development

This site is dedicated to the proposition that effective employee compensation and career development is an effective tool in obtaining, maintaining, and re-taining a productive workforce. It contains links to pay-for-knowledge, incentive systems, career development, wage and salary compensation, and more.

http://www.snc.edu/socsci/chair/336/group1.htm

WorkNet@ILR

The School of Industrial and Labor Relations at Cornell University offers this site consisting of an index of Internet sites relevant to the field of industrial and labor relations; a list of centers, institutes, and affiliated groups; and an electronic archive that contains full-text documents on the glass ceiling, child labor, and more.

http://www.ilr.cornell.edu/workplace.html

WorkNet: Alcohol and Other Drugs in the Workplace

This site of the Canadian Centre on Substance Abuse provides news, databases, bibliographies, resources, and research on alcohol and other drugs in the workplace.

http://www.ccsa.ca/wise.htm

The National Employee Rights Institute

The National Employee Rights Institute (NERI) is a nonprofit organization that was founded to assist individuals, both employed and unemployed, in under-standing, enforcing, and expanding their rights in the workplace.

http://www.nerinet.org

PART 3

Human Resources: The Corporation and the Employee

*T*he workforce is changing. Employees in the United States and Canada, and to a lesser extent elsewhere in the world, are becoming very diverse: many ethnic groups are represented in the workplace, women and men are approaching equality in numbers in most fields, and an array of protected conditions—such as age, ethnicity, disability, and religious persuasion—are making corporate life complicated for employers. Employees are more aware of their rights and more willing to demand that their employers honor them than they've ever been. What can business do to protect the rights of this diverse group while protecting its own economic interests?

- Does Blowing the Whistle Violate Company Loyalty?

- Should Concern for Drug Abuse Overrule Concerns for Employee Privacy?

ISSUE 9

Does Blowing the Whistle Violate Company Loyalty?

YES: Sissela Bok, from "Whistleblowing and Professional Responsibility," *New York University Education Quarterly* (Summer 1980)

NO: Robert A. Larmer, from "Whistleblowing and Employee Loyalty," *Journal of Business Ethics* (vol. 11, 1992)

ISSUE SUMMARY

YES: Philosopher Sissela Bok asserts that although blowing the whistle is often justified, it does involve dissent, accusation, and a breach of loyalty to the employer.

NO: Robert A. Larmer, an associate professor of philosophy, argues that attempting to stop illegal or unethical company activities may be the highest type of company loyalty an employee can display.

Whistle-blowing occurs when an employee discovers a wrong at his or her place of employment and exposes it, thereby saving lives or a great deal of money, but almost always at great expense to him- or herself. Since the readings that follow are theoretical, some specific cases might be useful. In "The Whistle Blowers' Morning After," *The New York Times* (November 9, 1986), N. R. Kleinfeld portrays five of the early whistle-blowers, some of whom have become famous as case studies in business schools across the country. Each one has an interesting story to tell; each claims that if he had it to do over again he would, for he likes living with a clear conscience. But each has also paid a price: great stress, sometimes ill health, career loss, financial ruin, and/or loss of friends and family.

Charles Atchinson blew the whistle on the Comanche Park nuclear plant in Glen Rose, Texas, a power station that was unsafe. It cost him his job, plunged him into debt, and left emotional scars on his family. Kermit Vandivier, who blew the whistle on the B. F. Goodrich Aircraft Brakes scandal, also lost his job. He has since begun a new career as a journalist. James Pope claimed that the Federal Aviation Administration (FAA) found in 1975 an effective device, known as an airborne collision avoidance system, that would prevent mid-air crashes; but it chose instead to pursue an inferior device it had had a hand in developing. Mr. Pope was "retired" early by the FAA. The most famous whistle-blower of all may be A. Ernest Fitzgerald, the U.S. Air Force cost analyst who found huge cost overruns on Lockheed cargo planes that were being developed for the Air Force. After his revelations, he was discharged from the Air Force. He fought for 13 years to be reinstated, which he was, at full rank, in 1982. For some first-hand accounts by Fitzgerald, see *Pentagonists: An Insider's View of Waste, Mismanagement, and Fraud in Defense Spending* (Houghton Mifflin, 1989) and *The High Priests of Waste* (W. W. Norton, 1972). The common thread of these stories is that when someone detected a wrong and properly reported it, he was demoted, labeled a troublemaker, and disciplined or fired, even when the evidence was very much in his favor. All of them, incidentally, initially believed in their organizations, and not only were all of them sure that they were acting in an ethical manner, but they also believed that they would be thanked for their efforts and diligence.

Professors Myron Peretz Glazer and Penina Migdal Glazer, in *The Whistle Blowers: Exposing Corruption in Government and Industry* (Basic Books, 1989), tell the story of 55 whistle-blowers—why they did what they did, and what the consequences were for themselves and their families. The Glazers found that the dominant trait in these whistle-blowers was a strong belief in individual responsibility. As one of the spouses of a whistle-blower stated, "A corrupt system can happen only if the individuals who make up that system are corrupt. You are either going to be part of the corruption or part of the forces working against it. There isn't a third choice. Someone, someday, has to take a stand; if you don't, maybe no one will. And that is wrong."

The Glazers write that the strong belief in individual responsibility that drove these ethical resisters was often supported by professional ethics, religious values, or allegiance to a community. But the personal costs of public disclosure were high, and the results were less than satisfactory. In some cases the accused corporations made no changes. The whistle-blowers, however, had to recreate careers, relocate, and settle for less money in new jobs. For most resisters, the worst part was the devastating months or even years of dislocation, unemployment, and temporary jobs. In response to a question posed by the Glazers, 21 of the whistle-blowers advised other potential whistle-blowers to "forget it" or to "leak the information without your name attached." If blowing the whistle is unavoidable, however, then "be prepared to be ostracized, have your career come to a screeching halt, and perhaps even be driven into bankruptcy."

As you read the following selections by Sissela Bok and Robert A. Larmer, think about these cases and others you may have heard about. Consider the motivations involved in whistle-blowing and whether they reflect loyalty or disloyalty to the company. How would you view an instance of whistle-blowing if you or your company were the target? Who deserves the greatest consideration in potential whistle-blowing situations: the individual, the company, or the public?

Sissela Bok

 **YES**

Whistleblowing and Professional Responsibility

W histleblowing" is a new label generated by our increased awareness of the ethical conflicts encountered at work. Whistleblowers sound an alarm from within the very organization in which they work, aiming to spotlight neglect or abuses that threaten the public interest.

The stakes in whistleblowing are high. Take the nurse who alleges that physicians enrich themselves in her hospital through unnecessary surgery; the engineer who discloses safety defects in the braking systems of a fleet of new rapid-transit vehicles; the Defense Department official who alerts Congress to military graft and overspending: all know that they pose a threat to those whom they denounce and that their own careers may be at risk.

Moral Conflicts

Moral conflicts on several levels confront anyone who is wondering whether to speak out about abuses or risks or serious neglect. In the first place, he must try to decide whether, other things being equal, speaking out is in fact in the public interest. This choice is often made more complicated by factual uncertainties: Who is responsible for the abuse or neglect? How great is the threat? And how likely is it that speaking out will precipitate changes for the better?

In the second place, a would-be whistleblower must weigh his responsibility to serve the public interest against the responsibility he owes to his colleagues and the institution in which he works. While the professional ethic requires collegial loyalty, the codes of ethics often stress responsibility to the public over and above duties to colleagues and clients. Thus the United States Code of Ethics for Government Servants asks them to "expose corruption wherever uncovered" and to "put loyalty to the highest moral principles and to country above loyalty to persons, party, or government."[1] Similarly, the largest professional engineering association requires members to speak out against abuses threatening the safety, health, and welfare of the public.[2]

From Sissela Bok, "Whistleblowing and Professional Responsibility," *New York University Education Quarterly,* vol. 11 (Summer 1980), pp. 2–7. Copyright © 1980 by Sissela Bok. Reprinted by permission.

A third conflict for would-be whistleblowers is personal in nature and cuts across the first two: even in cases where they have concluded that the facts warrant speaking out, and that their duty to do so overrides loyalties to colleagues and institutions, they often have reason to fear the results of carrying out such a duty. However strong this duty may seem in theory, they know that, in practice, retaliation is likely. As a result, their careers and their ability to support themselves and their families may be unjustly impaired.[3] A government handbook issued during the Nixon era recommends reassigning "undesirables" to places so remote that they would prefer to resign. Whistleblowers may also be downgraded or given work without responsibility or work for which they are not qualified; or else they may be given many more tasks than they can possibly perform. Another risk is that an outspoken civil servant may be ordered to undergo a psychiatric fitness-for-duty examination,[4] declared unfit for service, and "separated" as well as discredited from the point of view of any allegations he may be making. Outright firing, finally, is the most direct institutional response to whistleblowers.

Add to the conflicts confronting individual whistleblowers the claim to self-policing that many professions make, and professional responsibility is at issue in still another way. For an appeal to the public goes against everything that "self-policing" stands for. The question for the different professions, then, is how to resolve, insofar as it is possible, the conflict between professional loyalty and professional responsibility toward the outside world. The same conflicts arise to some extent in all groups, but professional groups often have special cohesion and claim special dignity and privileges.

The plight of whistleblowers has come to be documented by the press and described in a number of books. Evidence of the hardships imposed on those who chose to act in the public interest has combined with a heightened awareness of professional malfeasance and corruption to produce a shift toward greater public support of whistleblowers. Public service law firms and consumer groups have taken up their cause; institutional reforms and legislation have been proposed to combat illegitimate reprisals.[5]

Given the indispensable services performed by so many whistleblowers, strong public support is often merited. But the new climate of acceptance makes it easy to overlook the dangers of whistleblowing: of uses in error or in malice; of work and reputations unjustly lost for those falsely accused; of privacy invaded and trust undermined. There comes a level of internal prying and mutual suspicion at which no institution can function. And it is a fact that the disappointed, the incompetent, the malicious, and the paranoid all too often leap to accusations in public. Worst of all, ideological persecution throughout the world traditionally relies on insiders willing to inform on their colleagues or even on their family members, often through staged public denunciations or press campaigns.

No society can count itself immune from such dangers. But neither can it risk silencing those with a legitimate reason to blow the whistle. How then can we distinguish between different instances of whistleblowing? A society that fails to protect the right to speak out even on the part of those whose warnings turn out to be spurious obviously opens the door to political repression. But from the moral point of view there are important differences between the aims, messages, and methods of dissenters from within.

Nature of Whistleblowing

Three elements, each jarring, and triply jarring when conjoined, lend acts of whistleblowing special urgency and bitterness: dissent, breach of loyalty, and accusation.

Like all dissent, whistleblowing makes public a disagreement with an authority or a majority view. But whereas dissent can concern all forms of disagreement with, for instance, religious dogma or government policy or court decisions, whistleblowing has the narrower aim of shedding light on negligence or abuse, or alerting to a risk, and of assigning responsibility for this risk.

Would-be whistleblowers confront the conflict inherent in all dissent: between conforming and sticking their necks out. The more repressive the authority they challenge, the greater the personal risk they take in speaking out. At exceptional times, as in times of war, even ordinarily tolerant authorities may come to regard dissent as unacceptable and even disloyal.[6]

Furthermore, the whistleblower hopes to stop the game; but since he is neither referee nor coach, and since he blows the whistle on his own team, his act is seen as a violation of loyalty. In holding his position, he has assumed certain obligations to his colleagues and clients. He may even have subscribed to a loyalty oath or a promise of confidentiality. Loyalty to colleagues and to clients comes to be pitted against loyalty to the public interest, to those who may be injured unless the revelation is made.

Not only is loyalty violated in whistleblowing, hierarchy as well is often opposed, since the whistleblower is not only a colleague but a subordinate. Though aware of the risks inherent in such disobedience, he often hopes to keep his job.[7] At times, however, he plans his alarm to coincide with leaving the institution. If he is highly placed, or joined by others, resigning in protest may effectively direct public attention to the wrongdoing at issue.[8] Still another alternative, often chosen by those who wish to be safe from retaliation, is to leave the institution quietly, to secure another post, and then to blow the whistle. In this way, it is possible to speak with the authority and knowledge of an insider without having the vulnerability of that position.

It is the element of accusation, of calling a "foul," that arouses the strongest reactions on the part of the hierarchy. The accusation may be of neglect, of willfully concealed dangers, or of outright abuse on the part of colleagues or superiors. It singles out specific persons or groups as responsible for threats to the public interest. If no one could be held responsible—as in the case of an impending avalanche—the warning would not constitute whistleblowing.

The accusation of the whistleblower, moreover, concerns a present or an imminent threat. Past errors or misdeeds occasion such an alarm only if they still affect current practices. And risks far in the future lack the immediacy needed to make the alarm a compelling one, as well as the close connection to particular individuals that would justify actual accusations. Thus an alarm can be sounded about safety defects in a rapid-transit system that threaten or will shortly threaten passengers, but the revelation of safety defects in a system no longer in use, while of historical interest, would not constitute whistleblowing. Nor would the revelation of potential problems in a system not yet fully designed and far from implemented.[9]

Not only immediacy, but also specificity, is needed for there to be an alarm capable of pinpointing responsibility. A concrete risk must be at issue rather than a vague foreboding or a somber prediction. The act of whistleblowing differs in this respect from the lamentation or the dire prophecy. An immediate and specific threat would normally be acted upon by those at risk. The whistleblower assumes that his message will alert listeners to something they do not know, or whose significance they have not grasped because it has been kept secret.

The desire for openness inheres in the temptation to reveal any secret, sometimes joined to an urge for self-aggrandizement and publicity and the hope for revenge for past slights or injustices. There can be pleasure, too—righteous or malicious—in laying bare the secrets of co-workers and in setting the record straight at last. Colleagues of the whistleblower often suspect his motives: they may regard him as a crank, as publicity-hungry, wrong about the facts, eager for scandal and discord, and driven to indiscretion by his personal biases and shortcomings.

For whistleblowing to be effective, it must arouse its audience. Inarticulate whistleblowers are likely to fail from the outset. When they are greeted by apathy, their message dissipates. When they are greeted by disbelief, they elicit no response at all. And when the audience is not free to receive or to act on the information—when censorship or fear of retribution stifles response—then the message rebounds to injure the whistleblower. Whistleblowing also requires the possibility of concerted public response: the idea of whistleblowing in an anarchy is therefore merely quixotic.

Such characteristics of whistleblowing and strategic considerations for achieving an impact are common to the noblest warnings, the most vicious personal attacks, and the delusions of the paranoid. How can one distinguish the many acts of sounding an alarm that are genuinely in the public interest from all the petty, biased, or lurid revelations that pervade our querulous and gossip-ridden society? Can we draw distinctions between different whistleblowers, different messages, different methods?

We clearly can, in a number of cases. Whistleblowing may be starkly inappropriate when in malice or error, or when it lays bare legitimately private matters having to do, for instance, with political belief or sexual life. It can, just as clearly, be the only way to shed light on an ongoing unjust practice such as drugging political prisoners or subjecting them to electroshock treatment. It can be the last resort for alerting the public to an impending disaster. Taking such clear-cut cases as benchmarks, and reflecting on what it is about them that weighs so heavily for or against speaking out, we can work our way toward the admittedly more complex cases in which whistleblowing is not so clearly the right or wrong choice, or where different points of view exist regarding its legitimacy—cases where there are moral reasons both for concealment and for disclosure and where judgments conflict....

Individual Moral Choice

What questions might those who consider sounding an alarm in public ask themselves? How might they articulate the problem they see and weigh its injustice before deciding whether or not to reveal it? How can they best try to make sure their choice is the right one? In thinking about these questions it helps to keep in mind the three elements mentioned earlier: dissent, breach of loyalty, and accusation. They impose certain requirements—of accuracy and judgment in dissent; of exploring alternative ways to cope with improprieties that minimize the breach of loyalty; and of fairness in accusation. For each, careful articulation and testing of arguments are needed to limit error and bias.

Dissent by whistleblowers, first of all, is expressly claimed to be intended to benefit the public. It carries with it, as a result, an obligation to consider the nature of this benefit and to consider also the possible harm that may come from speaking out: harm to persons or institutions and, ultimately, to the public interest itself. Whistleblowers must, therefore, begin by making every effort to consider the effects of speaking out versus those of remaining silent. They must assure themselves of the accuracy of their reports, checking and rechecking the facts before speaking out; specify the degree to which there is genuine impropriety; consider how imminent is the threat they see, how serious, and how closely linked to those accused of neglect and abuse.

If the facts warrant whistleblowing, how can the second element—breach of loyalty—be minimized? The most important question here is whether the existing avenues for change within the organization have been explored. It is a waste of time for the public as well as harmful to the institution to sound the loudest alarm first. Whistleblowing has to remain a last alternative because of its destructive side effects: it must be chosen only when other alternatives have been considered and rejected. They may be rejected if they simply do not apply to the problem at hand, or when there is not time to go through routine channels or when the institution is so corrupt or coercive that steps will be taken to silence the whistleblower should he try the regular channels first.

What weight should an oath or a promise of silence have in the conflict of loyalties? One sworn to silence is doubtless under a stronger obligation because of the oath he has taken. He has bound himself, assumed specific obligations beyond those assumed in merely taking a new position. But even such promises can be overridden when the public interest at issue is strong enough. They can be overridden if they were obtained under duress or through deceit. They can be overridden, too, if they promise something that is in itself wrong or unlawful. The fact that one has promised silence is no excuse for complicity in covering up a crime or a violation of the public's trust.

The third element in whistleblowing—accusation—raises equally serious ethical concerns. They are concerns of fairness to the persons accused of impropriety. Is the message one to which the public is entitled in the first place? Or does it infringe on personal and private matters that one has no right to invade? Here, the very notion of what is in the public's best "interest" is at issue: "accusations" regarding an official's unusual sexual or religious experiences may well appeal to the public's interest without being information relevant to "the public interest."

Great conflicts arise here. We have witnessed excessive claims to executive privilege and to secrecy by government officials during the Watergate scandal in order to cover up for abuses the public had every right to discover. Conversely, those hoping to profit from prying into private matters have become adept at invoking "the public's right to know." Some even regard such private matters as threats to the public: they voice their own religious and political prejudices in the language of accusation. Such a danger is never stronger than when the accusation is delivered surreptitiously. The anonymous accusations made during the McCarthy period regarding political beliefs and associations often injured persons who did not even know their accusers or the exact nature of the accusations.

From the public's point of view, accusations that are openly made by identifiable individuals are more likely to be taken seriously. And in fairness to those criticized, openly accepted responsibility for blowing the whistle should be preferred to the denunciation or the leaked rumor. What is openly stated can more easily be checked, its source's motives challenged, and the underlying information examined. Those under attack may otherwise be hard put to defend themselves against nameless adversaries. Often they do not even know that they are threatened until it is too late to respond. The anonymous denunciation, moreover, common to so many regimes, places the burden of investigation on government agencies that may thereby gain the power of a secret police.

From the point of view of the whistleblower, on the other hand, the anonymous message is safer in situations where retaliation is likely. But it is also often less likely to be taken seriously. Unless the message is accompanied by indications of how the evidence can be checked, its anonymity, however safe for the source, speaks against it.

During the process of weighing the legitimacy of speaking out, the method used, and the degree of fairness needed, whistleblowers must try to compensate for the strong possibility of bias on their part. They should be scrupulously aware of any motive that might skew their message: a desire for self-defense in a difficult bureaucratic situation, perhaps, or the urge to seek revenge, or inflated expectations regarding the effect their message will have on the situation. (Needless to say, bias affects the silent as well as the outspoken. The motive for holding back important information about abuses and injustice ought to give similar cause for soul-searching.)

Likewise, the possibility of personal gain from sounding the alarm ought to give pause. Once again there is then greater risk of a biased message. Even if the whistleblower regards himself as incorruptible, his profiting from revelations of neglect or abuse will lead others to question his motives and to put less credence in his charges. If, for example, a government employee stands to make large profits from a book exposing the inequities in his agency, there is danger that he will, perhaps even unconsciously, slant his report in order to cause more of a sensation.

A special problem arises when there is a high risk that the civil servant who speaks out will have to go through costly litigation. Might he not justifiably try to make enough money on his public revelations—say, through books or public speaking—to offset his losses? In so doing he will not strictly speaking have *profited* from his revelations: he merely avoids being financially crushed by their sequels. He will nevertheless still be suspected at the time of revelation, and his message will therefore seem more questionable.

Reducing bias and error in moral choice often requires consultation, even open debate[10]: methods that force articulation of the moral arguments at stake and challenge privately held assumptions. But acts of whistleblowing present special problems when it comes to open consultation. On the one hand, once the whistleblower sounds his alarm publicly, his arguments will be subjected to open scrutiny; he will have to articulate his reasons for speaking out and substantiate his charges. On the other hand, it will then be too late to retract the alarm or to combat its harmful effects, should his choice to speak out have been ill-advised.

For this reason, the whistleblower owes it to all involved to make sure of two things: that he has sought as much and as objective advice regarding his choice as he can *before* going public; and that he is aware of the arguments for and against the practice of whistleblowing in general, so that he can see his own choice against as richly detailed and coherently structured a background as possible. Satisfying these two requirements once again has special problems because of the very nature of whistleblowing: the more corrupt the circumstances, the more dangerous it may be to seek consultation before speaking out. And yet, since the whistleblower himself may have a biased view of the state of affairs, he may choose not to consult others when in fact it would be not only safe but advantageous to do so; he may see corruption and conspiracy where none exists.

Notes

1. Code of Ethics for Government Service passed by the U.S. House of Representatives in the 85th Congress (1958) and applying to all government employees and office holders.

2. Code of Ethics of the Institute of Electrical and Electronics Engineers, Article IV.

3. For case histories and descriptions of what befalls whistleblowers, see Rosemary Chalk and Frank von Hippel, "Due Process for Dissenting Whistle-Blowers," *Technology Review* 81 (June–July 1979); 48–55; Alan S. Westin and Stephen Salisbury, eds., *Individual Rights in the Corporation* (New York: Pantheon, 1980); Helen Dudar, "The Price of Blowing the Whistle," *New York Times Magazine,* 30 October 1979, pp. 41–54; John Edsall, *Scientific Freedom and Responsibility* (Washington, D.C.: American Association for the Advancement of Science, 1975), p. 5; David Ewing, *Freedom Inside the Organization* (New York: Dutton, 1977); Ralph Nader, Peter Petkas, and Kate Blackwell, *Whistle Blowing* (New York: Grossman, 1972); Charles Peter and Taylor Branch, *Blowing the Whistle* (New York: Praeger, 1972).

4. Congressional hearings uncovered a growing resort to mandatory psychiatric examinations.

5. For an account of strategies and proposals to support government whistleblowers, see Government Accountability Project, *A Whistleblower's Guide to the Federal Bureaucracy* (Washington, D.C.: Institute for Policy Studies, 1977).

6. See, e.g., Samuel Eliot Morison, Frederick Merk, and Frank Friedel, *Dissent in Three American Wars* (Cambridge: Harvard University Press, 1970).

7. In the scheme worked out by Albert Hirschman in *Exit, Voice and Loyalty* (Cambridge: Harvard University Press, 1970), whistleblowing represents "voice" accompanied by a preference not to "exit," though forced "exit" is clearly a possibility and "voice" after or during "exit" may be chosen for strategic reasons.

8. Edward Weisband and Thomas N. Franck, *Resignation in Protest* (New York: Grossman, 1975).

9. Future developments can, however, be the cause for whistleblowing if they are seen as resulting from steps being taken or about to be taken that render them inevitable.

10. I discuss these questions of consultation and publicity with respect to moral choice in chapter 7 of Sissela Bok, *Lying* (New York: Pantheon, 1978); and in *Secrets* (New York: Pantheon Books, 1982), Ch. IX and XV.

Robert A. Larmer

 **NO**

Whistleblowing and Employee Loyalty

W histleblowing by an employee is the act of complaining, either within the corporation or publicly, about a corporation's unethical practices. Such an act raises important questions concerning the loyalties and duties of employees. Traditionally, the employee has been viewed as an agent who acts on behalf of a principal, i.e., the employer, and as possessing duties of loyalty and confidentiality. Whistleblowing, at least at first blush, seems a violation of these duties and it is scarcely surprising that in many instances employers and fellow employees argue that it is an act of disloyalty and hence morally wrong.[1]

It is this issue of the relation between whistleblowing and employee loyalty that I want to address. What I will call the standard view is that employees possess *prima facie* duties of loyalty and confidentiality to their employers and that whistleblowing cannot be justified except on the basis of a higher duty to the public good. Against this standard view, Ronald Duska has recently argued that employees do not have even a *prima facie* duty of loyalty to their employers and that whistleblowing needs, therefore, no moral justification.[2] I am going to criticize both views. My suggestion is that both misunderstand the relation between loyalty and whistleblowing. In their place I will propose a third more adequate view.

Duska's view is more radical in that it suggests that there can be no issue of whistleblowing and employee loyalty, since the employee has no duty to be loyal to his employer. His reason for suggesting that the employee owes the employer, at least the corporate employer, no loyalty is that companies are not the kinds of things which are proper objects of loyalty. His argument in support of this rests upon two key claims. The first is that loyalty, properly understood, implies a reciprocal relationship and is only appropriate in the context of a mutual surrendering of self-interest. He writes,

> It is important to recognize that in any relationship which demands loyalty the relationship works both ways and involves mutual enrichment. Loyalty is incompatible with self-interest, because it is something that necessarily requires we go beyond self-interest. My loyalty to my friend, for example, requires I put aside my interests some of the time.... Loyalty depends on ties that demand self-sacrifice with no expectation of reward, e.g., the ties of loyalty that bind a family together.[3]

From Robert A. Larmer, "Whistleblowing and Employee Loyalty," *Journal of Business Ethics,* vol. 11 (1992), pp. 125–128. Copyright © 1992 by D. Reidel Publishing Co., Dordrecht, Holland, and Boston, U.S.A. Reprinted by permission of Kluwer Academic Publishers.

The second is that the relation between a company and an employee does not involve any surrender of self-interest on the part of the company, since its primary goal is to maximize profit. Indeed, although it is convenient, it is misleading to talk of a company having interests. As Duska comments,

> A company is not a person. A company is an instrument, and an instrument with a specific purpose, the making of profit. To treat an instrument as an end in itself, like a person, may not be as bad as treating an end as an instrument, but it does give the instrument a moral status it does not deserve...[4]

Since, then, the relation between a company and an employee does not fulfill the minimal requirement of being a relation between two individuals, much less two reciprocally self-sacrificing individuals, Duska feels it is a mistake to suggest the employee has any duties of loyalty to the company.

This view does not seem adequate, however. First, it is not true that loyalty must be quite so reciprocal as Duska demands. Ideally, of course, one expects that if one is loyal to another person that person will reciprocate in kind. There are, however, many cases where loyalty is not entirely reciprocated, but where we do not feel that it is misplaced. A parent, for example, may remain loyal to an erring teenager, even though the teenager demonstrates no loyalty to the parent. Indeed, part of being a proper parent is to demonstrate loyalty to your children whether or not that loyalty is reciprocated. This is not to suggest any kind of analogy between parents and employees, but rather that it is not nonsense to suppose that loyalty may be appropriate even though it is not reciprocated. Inasmuch as he ignores this possibility, Duska's account of loyalty is flawed.

Second, even if Duska is correct in holding that loyalty is only appropriate between moral agents and that a company is not genuinely a moral agent, the question may still be raised whether an employee owes loyalty to fellow employees or the shareholders of the company. Granted that reference to a company as an individual involves reification and should not be taken too literally, it may nevertheless constitute a legitimate shorthand way of describing relations between genuine moral agents.

Third, it seems wrong to suggest that simply because the primary motive of the employer is economic, considerations of loyalty are irrelevant. An employee's primary motive in working for an employer is generally economic, but no one on that account would argue that it is impossible for her to demonstrate loyalty to the employer, even if it turns out to be misplaced. All that is required is that her primary economic motive be in some degree qualified by considerations of the employer's welfare. Similarly, the fact that an employer's primary motive is economic does not imply that it is not qualified by considerations of the employee's welfare. Given the possibility of mutual qualification of admittedly primary economic motives, it is fallacious to argue that employee loyalty is never appropriate.

In contrast to Duska, the standard view is that loyalty to one's employer is appropriate. According to it, one has an obligation to be loyal to one's employer and, consequently, a *prima facie* duty to protect the employer's interests. Whistleblowing constitutes, therefore, a violation of duty to one's employer and needs strong justification if it is to be appropriate. Sissela Bok summarizes this view very well when she writes

> the whistleblower hopes to stop the game; but since he is neither referee nor coach, and since he blows the whistle on his own team, his act is seen as a violation of loyalty. In holding his position, he has assumed certain obligations to his colleagues and clients. He may even have subscribed to a loyalty oath or a promise of confidentiality. Loyalty to colleagues and to clients comes to be pitted against loyalty to the public interest, to those who may be injured unless the revelation is made.[5]

The strength of this view is that it recognizes that loyalty is due one's employer. Its weakness is that it tends to conceive of whistleblowing as involving a tragic moral choice, since blowing the whistle is seen not so much as a positive action, but rather the lesser of two evils. Bok again puts the essence of this view very clearly when she writes that "a would-be whistleblower must weigh his responsibility to serve the public interest *against* the responsibility he owes to his colleagues and the institution in which he works" and "that [when] their duty [to whistleblow] . . . *so overrides loyalties to colleagues and institutions,* they [whistleblowers] often have reason to fear the results of carrying out such a duty."[6] The employee, according to this understanding of whistleblowing, must choose between two acts of betrayal, either her employer or the public interest, each in itself reprehensible.

Behind this view lies the assumption that to be loyal to someone is to act in a way that accords with what that person believes to be in her best interests. To be loyal to an employer, therefore, is to act in a way which the employer deems to be in his or her best interests. Since employers very rarely approve of whistleblowing and generally feel that it is not in their best interests, it follows that whistleblowing is an act of betrayal on the part of the employee, albeit a betrayal made in the interests of the public good.

Plausible though it initially seems, I think this view of whistleblowing is mistaken and that it embodies a mistaken conception of what constitutes employee loyalty. It ignores the fact that

> the great majority of corporate whistleblowers . . . [consider] themselves to be very loyal employees who . . . [try] to use 'direct voice' (internal whistleblowing), . . . [are] rebuffed and punished for this, and then . . . [use] 'indirect voice' (external whistleblowing). They . . . [believe] initially that they . . . [are] behaving in a loyal manner, helping their employers by calling top management's attention to practices that could eventually get the firm in trouble.[7]

By ignoring the possibility that blowing the whistle may demonstrate greater loyalty than not blowing the whistle, it fails to do justice to the many instances where loyalty to someone constrains us to act in defiance of what that person believes to be in her best interests. I am not, for example, being disloyal to a friend if I refuse to loan her money for an investment I am sure will bring her financial ruin; even if she bitterly reproaches me for denying her what is so obviously a golden opportunity to make a fortune.

A more adequate definition of being loyal to someone is that loyalty involves acting in accordance with what one has good reason to believe to be in that person's best interests. A key question, of course, is what constitutes a good reason to think that something is in a person's best interests. Very often, but by no means invariably, we accept that a person thinking that something is in her best interests is a sufficiently good reason to think that it actually is. Other times, especially when we feel that she is being rash, foolish, or misinformed we are prepared, precisely by virtue of being loyal, to act contrary to the person's wishes. It is beyond the scope of this paper to investigate such cases in detail, but three general points can be made.

First, to the degree that an action is genuinely immoral, it is impossible that it is in the agent's best interests. We would not, for example, say that someone who sells child pornography was acting in his own best interests, even if he vigorously protested that there was nothing wrong with such activity. Loyalty does not imply that we have a duty to refrain from reporting the immoral actions of those to whom we are loyal. An employer who is acting immorally is not acting in her own best interests and an employee is not acting disloyally in blowing the whistle.[8] Indeed, the argument can be made that the employee who blows the whistle may be demonstrating greater loyalty than the employee who simply ignores the immoral conduct, inasmuch as she is attempting to prevent her employer from engaging in self-destructive behaviour.

Second, loyalty requires that, whenever possible, in trying to resolve a problem we deal directly with the person to whom we are loyal. If, for example, I am loyal to a friend I do not immediately involve a third party when I try to dissuade my friend from involvement in immoral actions. Rather, I approach my friend directly, listen to his perspective on the events in question, and provide an opportunity for him to address the problem in a morally satisfactory way. This implies that, whenever possible, a loyal employee blows the whistle internally. This provides the employer with the opportunity to either demonstrate to the employee that, contrary to first appearances, no genuine wrongdoing had occurred, or, if there is a genuine moral problem, the opportunity to resolve it.

This principle of dealing directly with the person to whom loyalty is due needs to be qualified, however. Loyalty to a person requires that one acts in that person's best interests. Generally, this cannot be done without directly involving the person to whom one is loyal in the decision-making process, but there may arise cases where acting in a person's best interests requires that one act independently and perhaps even against the wishes of the person to whom one is loyal. Such cases will be especially apt to arise when the person to whom one is loyal is either immoral or ignoring the moral consequences of his actions. Thus, for example, loyalty to a friend who deals in hard narcotics would not imply that I speak first to my friend about my decision to inform the police of his activities, if the only effect of my doing so would be to make him more careful in his criminal dealings. Similarly, a loyal employee is under no obligation to speak first to an employer about the employer's immoral actions, if the only response of the employer will be to take care to cover up wrongdoing.

Neither is a loyal employee under obligation to speak first to an employer if it is clear that by doing so she placed herself in jeopardy from an employer who will retaliate if given the opportunity. Loyalty amounts to acting in another's best interests and that may mean qualifying what seems to be in one's own interests, but it cannot imply that one take no steps to protect oneself from the immorality of those to whom one is loyal. The reason it cannot is that, as has already been argued, acting immorally can never really be in a person's best interests. It follows, therefore, that one is not acting in a person's best interests if one allows oneself to be treated immorally by that person. Thus, for example, a father might be loyal to a child even though the child is guilty of stealing from him, but this would not mean that the father should let the child continue to steal. Similarly, an employee may be loyal to an employer even though she takes steps to protect herself against unfair retaliation by the employer, e.g., by blowing the whistle externally.

Third, loyalty requires that one is concerned with more than considerations of justice. I have been arguing that loyalty cannot require one to ignore immoral or unjust behaviour on the part of those to whom one is loyal, since loyalty amounts to acting in a person's best interests and it can never be in a person's best interests to be allowed to act immorally. Loyalty, however, goes beyond considerations of justice in that, while it is possible to be disinterested and just, it is not possible to be disinterested and loyal. Loyalty implies a desire that the person to whom one is loyal take no moral stumbles, but that if moral stumbles have occurred that the person be restored and not simply punished. A loyal friend is not only someone who sticks by you in times of trouble, but someone who tries to help you avoid trouble. This suggests that a loyal employee will have a desire to point out problems and potential problems long before the drastic measures associated with whistleblowing become necessary, but that if whistleblowing does become necessary there remains a desire to help the employer.

In conclusion, although much more could be said on the subject of loyalty, our brief discussion has enabled us to clarify considerably the relation between whistleblowing and employee loyalty. It permits us to steer a course between the Scylla of Duska's view that, since the primary link between employer and employee is economic, the ideal of employee loyalty is an oxymoron, and the Charybdis of the standard view that, since it forces an employee to weigh conflicting duties, whistleblowing inevitably involves some degree of moral tragedy. The solution lies in realizing that to whistleblow for reasons of morality is to act in one's employer's best interests and involves, therefore, no disloyalty.

Notes

1. The definition I have proposed applies most directly to the relation between privately owned companies aiming to realize a profit and their employees. Obviously, issues of whistleblowing arise in other contexts, e.g., governmental organizations or charitable agencies, and deserve careful thought. I do not propose, in this paper, to discuss whistleblowing in these other contexts, but I think my development of the concept of whistleblowing as positive demonstration of loyalty can easily be applied and will prove useful.

2. Duska, R.: 1985, 'Whistleblowing and Employee Loyalty', in J. R. Desjardins and J. J. McCall, eds., *Contemporary Issues in Business Ethics* (Wadsworth, Belmont, California), pp. 295–300.

3. Duska, p. 297.

4. Duska, p. 298.

5. Bok, S.: 1983, 'Whistleblowing and Professional Responsibility', in T. L. Beauchamp and N. E. Bowie, eds., *Ethical Theory and Business,* 2nd ed. (Prentice-Hall Inc., Englewood Cliffs, New Jersey), pp. 261–269, p. 263.

6. Bok, pp. 261–2, emphasis added.

7. Near, J. P. and P. Miceli: 1985, 'Organizational Dissidence: The Case of Whistle-Blowing', *Journal of Business Ethics* 4, pp. 1–16, p. 10.

8. As Near and Miceli note 'The whistle-blower may provide valuable information helpful in improving organizational effectiveness ... the prevalence of illegal activity in organizations is associated with declining organizational performance' (p. 1).
    The general point is that the structure of the world is such that it is not in a company's long-term interests to act immorally. Sooner or later a company which flouts morality and legality will suffer.

POSTSCRIPT

Does Blowing the Whistle Violate Company Loyalty?

Whistle-blowing is a difficult choice. What would you do when faced with such a choice? The corporation is not the only setting for whistle-blowers. Would you report a friend for drug abuse, cheating on exams, or stealing? How do you weigh the possibility of damage being done to the community against the security of your own career (some damage done to many people versus much damage done to a few people)? If you see only painful consequences if you blow the whistle, does that settle the problem—or does simple justice and fidelity to law have a claim of its own?

Should we, as a society, protect the whistle-blower with legislation designed to discourage corporate retaliation? Richard T. DeGeorge and Alan F. Westin, two of the earliest business ethics writers to take whistle-blowing seriously, agree that companies should adopt policies that preclude the need for employees to blow the whistle. "The need for moral heroes," DeGeorge concludes in *Business Ethics,* 2d ed. (Macmillan, 1986), "shows a defective society and defective corporations. It is more important to change the legal and corporate structures that make whistle blowing necessary than to convince people to be moral heroes." In *Whistle Blowing: Loyalty and Dissent in the Corporation* (McGraw-Hill, 1981), Westin writes, "The single most important element in creating a meaningful internal system to deal with whistle blowing is to have top leadership accept this as a management priority. This means that the chief operating officer and his senior colleagues have to believe that a policy which encourages discussion and dissent, and deals fairly with whistle-blowing claims, is a good and important thing for their company to adopt.... They have to see it, in their own terms, as a moral duty of good private enterprise."

Suggested Readings

Tim Barnett, Ken Bass, and Gene Brown, "Religiosity, Ethical Ideology, and Intentions to Report a Peer's Wrongdoing," *Journal of Business Ethics* (November 1996), pp. 1161–1174.

Terry Morehead Dworkin and Janet P. Near, "A Better Statutory Approach to Whistle-Blowing," *Journal of the Society for Business Ethics* (January 1997), pp. 1–16.

Kenneth Kernaghan, "Whistle-Blowing in Canadian Governments: Ethical, Political and Managerial Considerations," *Optimum* (1991–1992).

ISSUE 10

Should Concern for Drug Abuse Overrule Concerns for Employee Privacy?

YES: Michael A. Verespej, from "Drug Users—Not Testing—Anger Workers," *Industry Week* (February 17, 1992)

NO: Jennifer Moore, from "Drug Testing and Corporate Responsibility: The 'Ought Implies Can' Argument," *Journal of Business Ethics* (vol. 8, 1989)

ISSUE SUMMARY

YES: Michael A. Verespej, a writer for *Industry Week,* argues that workers are the hardest hit when their coworkers use drugs, and he suggests that, for this reason, a majority of employees are tolerant of drug testing.

NO: Jennifer Moore, a researcher of business ethics and business law, asserts that a right is a right and that any utilitarian concerns that employers can cite to justify drug testing should not override the right of the employee to dignity and privacy on the job.

In 1928 U.S. Supreme Court justice Louis Brandeis defined the right of privacy as "the right to be let alone, the most comprehensive of rights and the right most valued by civilized men." The constitutional origins of that right are hazy, found variously in the Fourth Amendment (prohibiting illegal searches and seizures), the Fifth Amendment (prohibiting compulsory testimony), and parts of the Ninth Amendment. But the U.S. Constitution only limits *government* action, and worried Americans increasingly find that their employers can be a more dangerous threat to their privacy.

What right does an employee have to be "let alone" by his or her employer? Historically, none at all. Dictatorial employers had no qualms about making and enforcing rules governing not only job performance but dress and personal behavior on the job as well. Many also had rules for off-the-job behavior. School boards, for example, routinely enforced rules that required teachers to abstain from smoking and drinking, to attend church regularly, and to limit courting to one day a week. But with the advent of organized labor, the freedom of the employer to dictate the employee's lifestyle off the job almost disappeared. On-the-job requirements also ceased to be absolute. Although certain obvious safety rules could be enforced (such as prohibiting alcohol on the job and requiring that safety equipment be worn), the presumption was that rules should not be extended beyond necessity. Until very recently, we had seemed to be approaching an understanding that the employee's choices of amusements and associations off the job were sacrosanct and that his or her personal style of dress and grooming on the job could be regulated only to the extent that such appearances were reasonably job-related.

Then came drugs. Unlike alcohol, drugs can be easily concealed in one's clothing and cannot be detected on a person's breath after they are consumed. Seasoned foremen who would have no trouble spotting the slurred speech and wobbly walk caused by alcohol may not be able to detect drug use in their employees. The effect of drug use on judgment and behavior, especially for such people as pilots, bus drivers, and military personnel, can and does cause deaths.

While many may agree that this fact alone justifies testing for on-the-job drug use, there are many factors that complicate the issue. First, the only tests currently available to determine drug use are seriously invasive (unlike the Breathalyzer test for alcohol, for instance). In practice, the tester must take a blood sample from the worker or require the worker to give up a urine sample. The blood test requires a needle stick that some find painful and terrifying, and the urination must be observed to ensure that the test is valid—at an imaginable cost in embarrassment to the worker and to the observer. Second, the tests cannot distinguish between drug-use behavior on the job and off the job. Marijuana smoked on a Friday night may show up in urine that is expelled on the following Tuesday. So the worker subjected to testing at random may find his off-the-job activities severely restricted by the tests. To be sure, no one is interested in condoning off-the-job drug use, but the move from on-the-job regulation to 24-hour regulation is an unintended consequence that raises further legal and ethical issues.

Third, the tests are not always accurate. Most employers have a policy that if an employee fails one drug test, he or she can take another in order to ensure accuracy. If the employee fails twice, he or she is out. But the tests are only 90 to 95 percent accurate, at best. That means that 1 out of 10, or at best 1 out of 20, will yield a false positive (the employee will appear to have drugs in his or her system). One out of 100, or at best 1 out of 400, will yield a false positive upon retest of a false positive. But some firms have thousands of workers. Is it fair to impose a testing routine that commits gross injustice once in 100 cases —or even only once in 400 cases?

As you read the following selections by Michael A. Verespej and Jennifer Moore, ask yourself how society ought to balance the conflicting demands of privacy for the worker and safety for society. Given the doubts surrounding the practice, is routine randomized drug testing justified? On the other hand, given the terrible dangers that attend drug use on the job, can society afford to do without it?

Michael A. Verespej  **YES**

Drug Users—Not Testing—
Anger Workers

Drug testing by companies still elicits an emotional response from employees. But it's a far different one from four years ago.

Back then, readers responding to an IW [*Industry Week*] survey angrily protested workplace drug testing as an invasion of privacy and argued that drug testing should be reserved for occasions in which there was suspicion of drug use or in an accident investigation.

Today's prevailing view, based on a recent IW survey covering essentially the same questions, stands as a stark contrast. Not only do fewer employees see drug testing as an invasion of privacy, but a significantly higher percentage think that companies should extend the scope of drug testing to improve safety and productivity in the workplace.

Why aren't employees as leery of workplace drug testing as they were four years ago?

First, both the numbers and the comments suggest that employees and managers are less worried that inaccurate drug tests will brand them as drug users. Just 19.3% of those surveyed say that they consider drug testing an invasion of privacy, compared with 30% in the earlier survey.

Second, the tight job market appears to have made non-drug-users resent the presence of drug users in the workplace. Third, in contrast to four years ago, employees and managers are more concerned about the potential safety problems that drug users cause them than whatever invasion of privacy might result from a drug test. The net result: Unlike four years ago, employee thinking is now in sync with the viewpoints held for some time by top corporate management. "Job safety and performance are more important than the slight invasion of privacy caused by drug testing," asserts Lee Taylor, plant manager at U.S. Gypsum Co.'s Siguard, Utah, facility. "Freedom and privacy end when others are likely to be injured," adds the president of a high-tech business in Fort Collins, Colo.

G. A. Holland, chief estimator for a Bloomfield, Conn., construction firm, agrees: "Drug testing may be an invasion of privacy, but, because drug use puts others in danger, [drug testing] is an acceptable practice. The safety of employees overrides the right to privacy of another." Adds D. S. McRoberts, manager of a Green Giant food-processing plant in Buhl, Idaho: "The risks employees put themselves and their peers under when they use drugs justify testing."

Perhaps the most blunt response comes from Louis Krivanek, a consulting engineer with Omega Induction Services, Warren, Mich.: "I certainly wouldn't ride with a drinking alcoholic. Why should I work with a drug addict not under control?"

And the anti-drug-user attitude is not just a safety issue, either. "Drug users are also a financial risk to the employer," declares John Larkin, president of Overland Computer, Omaha, Nebr. "It's time to begin thinking about the health and welfare of the company," says William Pence, vice president and general manager of Kantronics Inc., Lawrence, Kans. "Drug testing is simply a preventive measure to ensure the future stability of a company."

The competitive factor also appears to be influencing workers' viewpoints. "A drug-free environment must exist if the quality of product and process is to be continuously improved," writes one employee.

"Productivity and company survival are too important to trust to an employee with a drug problem," says Jack VerMeulen, director of quality assurance at C-Line Products, Des Plaines, Ill. "Employees are a company's most valuable assets, and those assets must perform at the peak of their ability. Test them." One could argue that workers—and managers—have simply become conditioned to drug testing in the workplace because it is no longer the exception, but the rule. After all, 56% of the managers responding to the survey—twice as many as four years ago—say their companies have drug-testing programs in place.

But the real reason for the change in opinion appears to be that four years of day-in, day-out experience with workplace drug problems have made managers and employees less tolerant of users. The attitude appears to be: Drug users are criminals and shouldn't be protected by the absence of a drug-testing program.

"Users are, by definition, criminals," declares Nick Benson, senior automation engineer at Babcock & Wilcox, Lynchburg, Va. "Drug users are breaking the law," states Naomi Walter, a data-processing specialist at Gemini Marketing Associates, Carthage, Mo. "So why let them get an advantage?"

Layoffs and plant and store closings are also behind the new lack of tolerance for the drug user. "I believe that if a company is paying a person to work for them," says one IW reader, "that person should be drug-free. A job is a privilege, not a right."

❦

That lack of tolerance is reflected in significantly changed ideas of who in the workplace should be tested for drug use. A significantly higher percentage of respondents think that more workers should be tested at random or that *all* employees should be tested.

More than 45% of IW readers—compared with 29.6% four years ago—say that drug tests should be conducted at random. And 70.5% think all employees should be required to take drug tests. Only 60% felt that way in the last IW drug-testing survey. Not surprisingly, then, the percentage of readers who would take a drug test and who think that employers should be able to test employees for drug use is now 93%; it was 88% four years ago.

But several attitudes haven't changed. Workers and managers still think that when companies use drug testing, they should be required to offer rehabilitation through employee-assistance programs, that management should be tested as well as employees, and that alcohol problems are equally troublesome. "Employers should be prepared to help—not just fire someone if the drug or alcohol abuse is exposed," says H. A. Dellicker, programming manager at Siemens Nixdorf, Burlington, Mass. "You need a properly monitored rehabilitation program."

Readers are just as adamant that if the majority of employees is to be tested, then everyone should be included—all the way up to the CEO. "Drug testing should be conducted on all employees, from top management down to the lowest position," asserts Sharon Hyitt, a drafting technician at Varco Pruden Buildings, Van Wert, Ohio. And IW readers contend that any drug-testing program should test for alcohol abuse as well. "Drug testing stops short," argues a reader in Muncie, Ind. "Alcoholism is more widespread in our workplace and just as destructive."

A plant superintendent in Ohio agrees and laments, "Alcohol is the most abused drug in our workplace, but it is not covered under our testing program. While the 'heavy' drugs get the spotlight because of the violence associated with their distribution, alcohol does the most damage in the workplace."

A product-testing engineer agrees, "Alcohol should be included in the tests and then perhaps lunch-time drinking would decrease. Why is it O.K. for those who have three-martini lunches to come back to work and try to function?"

NO ☜

Drug Testing and Corporate Responsibility: The "Ought Implies Can" Argument

In the past few years, testing for drug use in the workplace has become an important and controversial trend. Approximately 30% of Fortune 500 companies now engage in some sort of drug testing or screening, as do many smaller firms. The Reagan administration has called for mandatory testing of all federal employees. Several states have already passed drug testing laws; others will probably consider them in the future. While the Supreme Court has announced its intention to rule on the testing of federal employees within the next few months, its decision will not settle the permissibility of testing private employees. Discussion of the issue is likely to remain lively and heated for some time.

Most of the debate about drug testing in the workplace has focused on the issue of privacy rights. Three key questions have been: Do employees have privacy rights? If so, how far do these extend? What kinds of considerations outweigh these rights? I believe there are good reasons for supposing that employees do have moral privacy rights,[1] and that drug testing usually (though not always) violates these, but privacy is not my main concern in this paper. I wish to examine a different kind of argument, the claim that because corporations are responsible for harms committed by employees while under the influence of drugs, they are entitled to test for drug use.

This argument is rarely stated formally in the literature, but it can be found informally quite often.[2] One of its chief advantages is that it seems, at least at first glance, to bypass the issue of privacy rights altogether. There seems to be no need to determine the extent or weight of employees' privacy rights to make the argument work. It turns on a different set of principles altogether, that is, on the meaning and conditions of responsibility. This is an important asset, since arguments about rights are notoriously difficult to settle. Rights claims frequently function in ethical discourse as conversation-stoppers or non-negotiable demands.[3] Although it is widely recognized that rights are not absolute, there is little consensus on how far they extend, what kinds of considerations should be allowed to override them, or even how to go about

From Jennifer Moore, "Drug Testing and Corporate Responsibility: The 'Ought Implies Can' Argument," *Journal of Business Ethics,* vol. 8 (1989), pp. 279–287. Copyright © 1989 by D. Reidel Publishing Co., Dordrecht, Holland, and Boston, U.S.A. Reprinted by permission of Kluwer Academic Publishers.

settling these questions. But it is precisely these thorny problems that proponents of drug testing must tackle if they wish to address the issue on privacy grounds. Faced with the claim that drug testing violates the moral right to privacy of employees, proponents of testing must either (1) argue that drug testing does not really violate the privacy rights of employees;[4] (2) acknowledge that drug testing violates privacy rights, but argue that there are considerations that override those rights, such as public safety; or (3) argue that employees have no moral right to privacy at all.[5] It is not surprising that an argument that seems to move the debate out of the arena of privacy rights entirely appears attractive.

In spite of its initial appeal, however, I will maintain that the argument does not succeed in circumventing the claims of privacy rights. Even responsibility for the actions of others, I will argue, does not entitle us to do absolutely anything to control their behavior. We must look to rights, among other things, to determine what sorts of controls are morally permissible. Once this is acknowledged, the argument loses much of its force. In addition, it requires unjustified assumptions about the connection between drug testing and the prevention of drug-related harm.

An "Ought Implies Can" Argument

Before we can assess the argument, it must be set out more fully. It seems to turn on the deep-rooted philosophical connection between responsibility and control. Generally, we believe that agents are not responsible[6] for acts or events that they could not have prevented. People are responsible for their actions only if, it is often said, they "could have done otherwise". Responsibility implies some measure of control, freedom, or autonomy. It is for this reason that we do not hold the insane responsible for their actions. Showing that a person lacked the capacity to do otherwise blocks the normal moves of praise or blame and absolves the agent of responsibility for a given act.

For similar reasons, we believe that persons cannot be obligated to do things that they are incapable of doing, and that if they fail to do such things, no blame attaches to them. Obligation is empty, even senseless, without capability. If a person is obligated to perform an action, it must be within his or her power. This principle is sometimes summed up by the phrase "ought implies can". Kant used it as part of a metaphysical argument for free will, claiming that if persons are to have obligations at all, they must be autonomous, capable of acting freely.[7] The argument we examine here is narrower in scope, but similar in principle. If corporations are responsible for harms caused by employees under the influence of drugs, they must have the ability to prevent these harms. They must, therefore, have the freedom to test for drug use.

But the argument is still quite vague. What exactly does it mean to say that corporations are "responsible" for harms caused by employees? There are several possible meanings of "responsible". Not all of these are attributable to corporations, and not all of them exemplify the principle that "ought implies can". The question of how or whether corporations are "responsible" is highly complex, and we cannot begin to answer it in this paper.[8] There are, however, four distinct senses of "responsible" that appear with some regularity in the argument. They can be characterized, roughly, as follows: (a) legally liable; (b) culpable or guilty; (c) answerable or accountable; (d) bound by an obligation. The first is purely legal; the last three have a moral dimension.

Legal Liability

We do hold corporations legally liable for the negligent acts of employees under the doctrine of *respondeat superior* ("let the master respond"). If an employee harms a third party in the course of performing his or her duties for the firm, it is the corporation which must compensate the third party. *Respondeat superior* is an example of what is frequently called "vicarious liability". Since the employee was acting on behalf of the firm, and the firm was acting through the employee when the harmful act was committed, liability is said to "transfer" from the employee to the firm. But it is not clear that such liability on the part of the employer implies a capacity to have prevented the harm. Corporations are held liable for accidents caused by an employee's negligent driving, for example, even if they could not have foreseen or prevented the injury. While some employee accidents can be traced to corporate negligence,[9] there need be no fault on the part of the corporation for the doctrine of *respondeat superior* to apply. The doctrine of *respondeat superior* is grounded not in fault, but in concerns of public policy and utility. It is one of several applications of the notion of liability without fault in legal use today.

Because it does not imply fault, and its attendant ability to have done otherwise, legal liability or responsibility **a** cannot be used successfully as part of an "ought implies can" argument. Holding corporations legally liable for harms committed by intoxicated employees while at the same time forbidding drug-testing is not inconsistent. It could simply be viewed as yet another instance of liability without fault. Of course, one could argue that the notion of liability without fault is itself morally unacceptable, and that liability ought not to be detached from moral notions of punishment and blame. This is surely an extremely important claim, but it is beyond the scope of this paper. The main point to be made here is that we must be able to attribute more than legal liability to corporations if we are to invoke the principle of "ought implies can". Corporations must be responsible in sense **b**, **c**, or **d**—that is, *morally* responsible —if the argument is to work.

Moral Responsibility

Are corporations morally responsible for harms committed by intoxicated employees? Perhaps the most frequently used notion of moral responsibility is sense **b**, what I have called "guilt" or "culpability".[10] I have in mind here the strongest notion of moral responsibility, the sense that is prevalent in criminal law. An agent is responsible for an act in this sense if the act can be imputed to him or her. An essential condition of imputability is the presence in the agent of an intention to commit the act, or *mens rea*.[11] But does an employer whose workers use drugs satisfy the *mens rea* requirement? The requirement probably would be satisfied if it could be shown that the firm intended the resulting harms, ordered its employees to work under the influence of drugs, or even, perhaps (though this is less clear) turned a blind eye to blatant drug abuse in the workplace.[12] But these are all quite farfetched possibilities. It is reasonable to assume that most corporations do not intend the harms caused by their employees, and that they do not order employees to use drugs on the job. Drug use is quite likely to be prohibited by company policy. If corporations are morally responsible for drug-related harms committed [by] employees, then, it is not in sense **b**.

Corporations might, however, be morally responsible for harms committed by employees in another sense. An organization acts through its employees. It empowers its employees to act in ways in which they otherwise would not act by providing them with money, power, equipment, and authority. Through a series of agreements, the corporation delegates its employees to act on its behalf. For these reasons, one could argue that corporations are responsible, in the sense of "answerable" or "accountable" (responsibility **c**), for the harmful acts of their employees. Indeed, it could be argued that if corporations are not morally responsible for these acts, they are not morally responsible for any acts at all, since corporations can only act through their employees.[13] To say that corporations are responsible for the harms of their employees in sense **c** is to say more than just that a corporation must "pay up" if an employee causes harm. It is to assign fault to the corporation by virtue of the ways in which organizational policies and structures facilitate and direct employees' actions.[14]

Moreover, corporations presumably have the same obligations as other agents to avoid harm in the conduct of their business. Since they conduct their business through their employees, it could plausibly be argued that corporations have an obligation to anticipate and prevent harms that employees might cause in the course of their employment. If this reasoning is correct, corporations are morally responsible for the drug-related harms of employees in sense **d**—that is, they are under an obligation to prevent those harms. The "ought implies can" argument, then, may be formulated as follows:

1. If corporations have obligations, they must be capable of carrying them out, on the principle of "ought implies can".
2. Corporations have an obligation to prevent harm from occurring in the course of conducting their business.
3. Drug use by employees is likely to lead to harm.
4. Corporations must be able to take steps to eliminate (or at least reduce) drug use by employees.
5. Drug testing is an effective way to eliminate/reduce employee drug use.
6. Therefore corporations must be permitted to test for drugs.[15]

The Limits of Corporate Autonomy

This is surely an important argument, one that deserves to be taken seriously. The premise that corporations have an obligation to prevent harm from occurring in the conduct of their business seems unexceptionable and consistent with the actual moral beliefs of society. There is not much question that drug use by employees, especially regular drug use or drug use on the job, leads to harms of various kinds. Some of these are less serious than others, but some are very serious indeed: physical injury to consumers, the public, and fellow employees —and sometimes even death.[16]

Moreover, our convictions about the connections between responsibility or obligation and capability seem unassailable. Like other agents, if corporations are to have obligations, they must have the ability to carry them out. The argument seems to tell us that corporations are only able to carry out their obligations to prevent harm if they can free themselves of drugs. To prevent corporations from drug testing, it implies, is to prevent them from discharging their obligations. It is to cripple corporate autonomy just as we would cripple the autonomy of an individual worker if we refused to allow him to "kick the habit" that prevented him from giving satisfactory job performance.

But this analogy between corporate and individual autonomy reveals the initial defect in the argument. Unlike human beings, corporations are never fully autonomous selves. On the contrary, their actions are always dependent upon individual selves who are autonomous. Human autonomy means self-determination, self-governance, self-control. Corporate autonomy, at least as it is understood here, means control over others. Corporate autonomy is essentially derivative. But this means that corporate acts are not the simple sorts of acts generated by individual persons. They are complex. Most importantly, the members of a corporation are frequently not the agents, but the objects, of "corporate" action. A good deal of corporate action, that is, necessitates doing something not only *through* corporate employees, but *to* those employees.[17] The act of eliminating drugs from the workplace is an act of this sort. A corporation's ridding itself of drugs is not like an individual person's "kicking the habit". Rather, it is one group of persons making another group of persons give up drug use.

This fact has important implications for the "ought implies can" argument. The argument is persuasive in situations in which carrying out one's obligations requires only *self*-control, and does not involve controlling the behavior of others. Presumably there are no restrictions on what one may do to oneself in order to carry out an obligation.[18] But a corporation is not a genuine "self", and there *are* moral limits on what one person may do to another. Because this is so, we cannot automatically assume that the obligation to prevent harm justifies employee drug testing. Of course this does not necessarily mean that drug testing is *unjustified*. But it does mean that before we can determine whether it is justified, we must ask what is permissible for one person or group of persons to do to another to prevent a harm for which they are responsible.

Are there any analogies available that might help to resolve this question? It is becoming increasingly common to hold a hostess responsible (both legally and morally) for harm caused by a drunken guest on the way home from her party. In part, this is because she contributes to the harm by serving her guest alcohol. It is also because she knows that drunk driving is risky, and has a general obligation to prevent harm. What must she be allowed to do to prevent harms of this kind? Persuade the guest to spend the night on the couch? Surely. Take her car keys away from her? Perhaps. Knock her out and lock her in the bathroom until morning? Surely not.

Universities are occasionally held legally and morally responsible for harms committed by members of fraternities—destruction of property, gang rapes, and injuries or death caused by hazing. What may they do to prevent such harms? They may certainly withdraw institutional recognition and support from the fraternity, refusing to let it operate on the campus. But may they expel students who live together off-campus in fraternity-like arrangements? Have university security guards police these houses, covertly or by force? These questions are more difficult to answer.

We sometimes hold landlords morally (though not legally) responsible for tenants who are slovenly, play loud music, or otherwise make nuisances of themselves. Landlords are surely permitted to cancel the leases of such tenants, and they are justified in asking for references from previous landlords to prevent future problems of this kind. But it is not clear that a landlord may delve into a tenant's private life, search his room, or tap his telephone in order to anticipate trouble before it begins.

Each of these situations is one in which one person or group of persons is responsible, to a greater or a lesser degree, for the prevention of harm by others, and needs some measure of control in order to carry out this responsibility.[19] In each case, there is a fairly wide range of actions which we would be willing to allow the first party, but there are some actions which we would rule out. Having an obligation to prevent the harms of others seems to permit us some forms of control, but not all. At least one important consideration in deciding what kinds of actions are permissible is the *rights* of the controlled parties.[20] If these claims are correct, we must examine the rights of employees in order to determine whether drug testing is justified. The relevant right in the case of drug testing is the right to privacy. The "ought implies can" argument, then, does not circumvent the claims of privacy rights as it originally seemed to do.

The Agency Argument

A proponent of drug testing might argue, however, that the relation between employers and employees is significantly different from the relation between hosts and guests, universities and members of fraternities, or landlords and tenants. Employees have a special relation with the firm that employs them. They are *agents,* hired and empowered to act on behalf of the employer. While they act on the business of the firm, it might be argued, they "are" the corporation. The restrictions that apply to what one independent agent may do to another thus do not apply here.

But surely this argument is incorrect, for a number of reasons. First, if it were correct, it would justify anything a corporation might do to control the behavior of an employee—not merely drug testing, but polygraph testing, tapping of telephones, deception, psychological manipulation, whips and chains, etc.[21] There are undoubtedly some people who would argue that some of these procedures are permissible, but few would argue that all of them are. The fact that even some of them appear not to be suggests that we believe there are limits to what corporations may do to control employees, and that one consideration in determining these limits is the employees' rights.

Secondly, the argument implies that employees give up their own autonomy completely when they sign on as agents, and become an organ or piece of the corporation. But this cannot be true. Agency is a moral and contractual relationship of the kind that can only obtain between two independent, autonomous parties. This relationship could not be sustained if the employee ceased to be autonomous upon signing the contract. Employees are not slaves, but autonomous agents capable of upholding a contract. Moreover, we expect a certain amount of discretion in employees in the course of their agency. Employees are not expected to follow illegal or immoral commands of their employers, and we find them morally and legally blameworthy when they do so. That we expect such independent judgment of them suggests that they do not lose their autonomy entirely.[22]

Finally, if the employment contract were one in which employees gave up all right to be treated as autonomous human beings, then it would not be a legitimate or morally valid contract. Some rights are considered "inalienable" —people are forbidden from negotiating them away even if it seems advantageous to them to do so. The law grants recognition to this fact through anti-discrimination statutes, minimum wage legislation, workplace health and safety standards, etc. Even if I would like to, I may not trade away, for example, my right not to be sexually harassed or my right to know about workplace hazards.

Again, these arguments do not show that drug testing is unjustified. They do show, however, that *if* drug testing is justified, it is not because the "ought implies can" argument bypasses the issue of employee rights, but because drug testing does not impermissibly violate those rights.[23] To think that obligation, or responsibility for the acts of others, can circumvent rights claims is to misunderstand the import of the "ought implies can" principle. The principle tells us that there is a close connection between obligation or responsibility and capability. But it does not license us to disregard the rights of others any more than it guarantees us the physical conditions that make carrying out our obligations possible. It may well prove that employees' right to privacy, assuming they have such a right, is secondary to some more weighty consideration. I take up this question briefly below. What has been shown here is that the issue of the permissibility of drug testing will not and cannot be settled *without* a close scrutiny of privacy rights. If we are to decide the issue, we must eventually determine whether employees have privacy rights, how far they extend, and what considerations outweigh them—precisely the difficult questions the "ought implies can" argument sought to avoid.

Is Drug Testing Necessary?

The "ought implies can" argument also has another serious flaw. The argument turns on the claim that forbidding drug testing prevents corporations from carrying out their obligation to prevent harm. But this is only true if drug testing is *necessary* for preventing drug-related harm. If it is merely one option among many, the forbidding drug testing still leaves a corporation free to prevent harm in other ways. For the argument to be sound, in other words, premise 5 would have to be altered to read, "drug testing is a necessary element in any plan to rid the workplace of drugs."

But it is not at all clear that drug testing *is* necessary to reduce drug use in the workplace. Its necessity has been challenged repeatedly. In a recent article in the *Harvard Business Review,* for example, James Wrich draws on his experience in dealing with alcoholism in the workplace and suggests the use of broadbrush educational and rehabilitative programs as alternatives to testing. Corporations using such programs to combat alcohol problems, Wrich reports, have achieved tremendous reductions in absenteeism, sick leave, and on-the-job accidents.[24] Others have argued that impaired performance likely to result in harm could be easily detected by various sorts of performance-oriented tests— mental and physical dexterity tests, alertness tests, flight simulation tests, and so on. These sorts of procedures have the advantage of not being controversial from a rights perspective.[25]

Indeed, many thinkers have argued that drug testing is not only unnecessary, but is not even an effective way to attack drug use in the workplace. The commonly used and affordable urinalysis tests are notoriously unreliable. They have a very high rate both of false negatives and of false positives. At best the tests reveal, not impaired performance or even the presence of a particular drug, but the presence of metabolites of various drugs that can remain in the system long after any effects of the drug have worn off.[26] Because they do not measure impairment, such tests do not seem well-tailored to the purpose of preventing harm—which, after all, is the ultimate goal. As Lewis Maltby, vice president of a small instrumentation company and an opponent of drug testing, puts it,

> . . . [T]he fundamental flaw with drug testing is that it tests for the wrong thing. A realistic program to detect workers whose condition put the company or other people at risk would test for the condition that actually creates the danger.[27]

If these claims are true, there is no real connection between the obligation to prevent harm and the practice of drug testing, and the "ought implies can" argument provides no justification for drug testing at all.[28]

Conclusion

I have made no attempt here to determine whether drug testing does indeed violate employees' privacy rights. The analysis . . . above suggests that we have reason to believe that employees have some rights. Once we accept the notion of employee rights in general, it seems likely that a right to privacy would be among them, since it is an important civil right and central for the protection of individual autonomy. There are also reasons, I believe, to think that most drug testing violates the right to privacy. These claims need much more defense than they can be given here, and even if they are true, this does not necessarily mean that drug testing is unjustified. It does, however, create a *prima facie* case against drug testing. If drug testing violates the privacy rights of employees, it will be justified only under very strict conditions, if it is justified at all. It is worth taking a moment to see why this is so.

It is generally accepted in both the ethical and legal spheres that rights are not absolute. But we allow basic rights to be overridden only in special cases in which some urgent and fundamental good is at stake. In legal discourse, such goods are called "compelling interests".[29] While there is room for some debate about what counts as a "compelling interest", it is almost always understood to be more than a merely private interest, however weighty. Public safety might well fall into this category, but private monetary loss probably would not. While more needs to be done to determine what kinds of interests justify drug testing, it seems clear that if testing does violate the basic rights of employees, it is only justified in extreme cases—far less often than it is presently used. Moreover, we believe that overriding a right is to be avoided wherever possible, and is only justified when doing so is *necessary* to serve the "compelling interest" in question. If it violates rights, then drug testing is only permissible if it is necessary for the protection of an interest such as public safety and if there is no other, morally preferable, way of accomplishing the same goal. As we have seen above, however, it is by no means clear that drug testing meets these conditions. There may be better, less controversial ways to prevent the harm caused by drug use; if so, these must be used in preference to drug testing, and testing is unjustified. And if the attacks on the effectiveness of drug testing are correct, testing is not only unnecessary for the protection of public safety, but does not serve any "compelling interest" at all.

What do these conclusions tell us about the responsibility of employers for preventing harms caused by employees? If it is decided that drug testing is morally impermissible, then there can be no duty to use it to anticipate and prevent harms. Corporations who fail to use it cannot be blamed for doing so. They cannot have a moral obligation to do something morally impermissible. Moreover, if it turns out that there is no other effective way to prevent the harms caused by drug use, then it seems to me we may not hold employers morally responsible for those harms. This seems to me unlikely to be the case— there probably are other effective measures to control drug abuse in the work-place. But corporations can be held responsible only to the extent that they are permitted to act. It would not be inconsistent, however, to hold corporations legally liable for the harms caused by intoxicated employees under the doctrine of *respondeat superior,* even if drug testing is forbidden, for this kind of liability does not imply an ability to have done otherwise.

Notes

1. Employees do not, of course, have legal privacy rights, although the courts seem to be moving slowly in this direction. Opponents of testing usually claim that employees have *moral* rights to privacy, even if these have not been given legal recognition. See, for example, Joseph Des Jardins and Ronald Duska, "Drug Testing in Employment", in *Business Ethics: Readings and Cases in Corporate Morality,* 2nd edition, ed. W. M. Hoffman and J. M. Moore (McGraw-Hill, forthcoming).

2. See, for example, "Work-Place Privacy Issues and Employer Screening Policies," Richard Lehr and David Middlebrooks, *Employee Relations Law Journal* 11, 407. Lehr and Middlebrooks cite the argument as one of the chief justifications for

drug testing used by employers. I have also encountered the argument frequently in discussion with students, colleagues, and managers.

3. Ronald Dworkin has referred to rights as moral "trumps". This kind of language tends to suggest that rights overwhelm all other considerations, so that when they are flourished, all that opponents can do is subside in silence. Rights are frequently asserted this way in everyday discourse, and in this sense rights claims tend to close, rather than open, the door to fruitful ethical dialogue.

4. In his article "Privacy, Polygraphs, and Work," *Business and Professional Ethics Journal* 1, Fall, 1981, 19, George Brenkert has developed the idea that my privacy is violated when some one acquires information about me that they are not entitled, by virtue of their relationship to me, to have. My mortgage company, for example, is entitled to know my credit history; a prospective sexual partner is entitled to know if I have any sexually transmitted diseases. Thus their knowledge of this information does not violate my privacy. One could argue that employers are similarly entitled to the information obtained by drug tests, and that drug testing does not violate privacy for this reason. A somewhat different move would be to argue that testing does not violate privacy because employees give their "consent" to . . . drug testing as part of the employment contract. For a sustained attack on these and other Type 1 arguments, see Joseph Des Jardins and Ronald Duska, "Drug Testing in Employment".

5. One might defend this position on the ground that the employer "owns" the job and is therefore entitled to place any conditions he wishes on obtaining or keeping it. The problem with this argument is that it seems to rule out *all* employee rights, including such basic ones as the right to organize and bargain collectively, or the right not to be discriminated against, which have solid legal as well as ethical grounding. It also implies that ownership overrides all other considerations, and it is not at all clear that this is true. One might take the position that by accepting a job, an employee has agreed to give up all his rights save those actually specified in the employment contract. But this makes the employment contract look like an agreement in which employees sell themselves and accept the status of things without rights. And it overlooks the fact that we believe there are some things ("inalienable" rights) that persons ought not to be permitted to bargain away. Alex Michalos has discussed some of the limitations of the employment contract in "The Loyal Agent's Argument", in *Ethical Theory and Business,* 2nd edition, ed. Tom L. Beauchamp and Norman E. Bowie (Englewood Cliffs, NJ: Prentice-Hall, 1983), p. 247.

6. The term "responsibility" is deliberately left ambiguous here. Several different meanings of it are examined below.

7. See Immanuel Kant, *Critique of Practical Reason,* trans. Lewis White Beck (Indianapolis: Bobbs-Merril, 1956), p. 30.

8. In this paper I have tried to avoid getting embroiled in the question of whether or not corporations are themselves "moral agents", which has been the question to dominate the corporate responsibility debate. The argument I offer here does, I believe, have important implications for the problem of corporate agency, but does not require me to take a stand on it here. I am content to have those who reject the notion of corporations as moral agents read my references to corporate responsibility as shorthand for some complex form of individual or group responsibility.

9. One example would be negligent hiring, which is an increasingly frequent cause of action against an employer. Employers can also be held negligent if they give orders that lead to harms that they ought to have foreseen. Domino's Pizza is now under suit because it encouraged its drivers to deliver pizzas as fast as possible, a policy that accident victims claim should have been expected to cause accidents.

10. This understanding of moral responsibility often seems to overshadow other notions. In an article on corporate responsibility, for example, Manuel Velasquez concludes that because corporations are not responsible in this sense, they are "not responsible for anything they do". "Why Corporations Are Not Responsible For Anything They Do", *Business and Professional Ethics Journal* 2, Spring, 1983, 1.

11. There is also an *actus reus* requirement for this type of responsibility—that is, the act must be traceable to the voluntary bodily movements of the agent. Obviously, corporations do not have bodies, but the people who work for them do. The question, then, has become when may we call an act by one member of the corporation a "corporate act". If it is possible to do so at all, the decisive feature is probably the presence of some sort of corporate "intention." This is why I focus on intention here, and why intention has been central to the discussion of corporate responsibility.

12. There are some, like Velasquez, who hold that a corporation can never satisfy the *mens rea* requirement because this would require a collective mind. If this were true, the argument would collapse at the outset. Others believe that a *mens rea* can be attributed to corporations metaphorically, if it can be shown that company policy includes an "intention" to harm, and it is this model I follow here.

13. There are, of course, those who take precisely this position. See Velasquez, "Why Corporations Are Not Responsible For Anything They Do".

14. See, for example, Peter French, *Collective and Corporate Responsibility* (New York: Columbia University Press, 1984).

15. It is tempting to conclude from this argument that drug testing is not only permissible, but obligatory, but this is not the case. The reason why it is not provides a clue to one of the major weaknesses of the argument. Drug testing would be obligatory only if it were *necessary* for the prevention of harm due to drug use, but it is not clear that this is so. But [it] also means that it is not clear that corporations are deflected from their duty to prevent harm by a prohibition against drug testing. See below for a fuller discussion of this problem.

16. For example, it has been claimed that employees who use drugs cause four times as many work-related accidents as do other employees. The highly publicized Conrail crash in 1987 was determined to be drug-related. Of course there are harms to the company itself as well, in the form of higher absenteeism, lowered productivity, higher insurance costs, etc. But since these types of harm raise the question of what a company may do to preserve its self-interest, rather than what it may do to prevent harms to others for which they are responsible, I focus here on harm to employees, consumers, and the public.

17. In our eagerness to assign "corporate responsibility", this fact has frequently been overlooked. This in turn has led, I believe, to an oversimplified view of corporate action. I discuss this problem more fully in a paper in progress entitled "The Paradox of Corporate Autonomy".

18. It is an interesting question whether there are limitations on what individuals can do to themselves to control their own behavior. What about individuals who undergo hypnosis, or who have their jaws wired shut in order to lose weight? Are they violating their own rights? Undermining their own autonomy? It could be argued plausibly that these kinds of things are not permissible, on the Kantian ground that we have a duty not to treat ourselves as merely as means to an end. Of course, if there are such restrictions, it makes the "ought implies can" argument as applied to corporations even weaker.

19. None of these analogies is perfect. In the case of the hostess and guest, for example, the guest is clearly intoxicated. This is rarely true of employees who are tested for drugs; if the employee were visibly intoxicated, there would be no need to test. Moreover, in the hostess/guest case the hostess contributes directly to the

intoxication. There are important parallels, however. In each case one party is held morally (and in two of the cases, legally) responsible for harms caused by others. Moreover, the first parties are responsible in close to the same way that employers are responsible for the acts of their employees: they in some sense "facilitate" the harmful acts, they have some capacity to prevent those acts, and they are thus viewed as having an obligation to prevent them. One main difference, of course, is that employees are "agents" of their employers. . . .

20. There are other, utility-related considerations, as well—for example, harm to employees who are unjustly dismissed, a demoralized workforce, the costs of testing, etc. I concentrate here on rights because they have been the primary focal point in the drug testing debate.

21. The assumption here is that persons are entitled to do whatever they wish to themselves. See Note 18.

22. See Michalos, "The Loyal Agent's Argument".

23. Some violations of right, of course, are permissible. . . .

24. James T. Wrich, "Beyond Testing: Coping with Drugs at Work", *Harvard Business Review* Jan.–Feb. 1988, 120.

25. See Des Jardins and Duska, "Drug Testing in Employment", and Lewis Maltby, "Why Drug Testing is a Bad Idea", *Inc.* June 1987. While other sorts of tests also have the potential to be abused, they are at least a direct measurement of something that an employer is entitled to know—performance capability. Des Jardins and Duska offer an extended defense of this sort of test.

26. See Edward J. Imwinkelreid, "False Positive", *The Sciences,* Sept.–Oct. 1987, 22. Also David Bearman, "The Medical Case Against Drug Testing", *Harvard Business Review* Jan.–Feb. 1988, 123.

27. Maltby, "Why Drug Testing is a Bad Idea", pp. 152–153.

28. It could still be argued that drug testing *deters* drug use, and thus has a connection with preventing harm, even though it doesn't directly provide any information that enables companies to prevent harm. This is an important point, but it is still subject to the restrictions discussed in the previous section. Not everything that has a deterrent value is permissible. It is possible that a penalty of capital punishment would provide a deterrent for rapists, or having one's hand removed deter shoplifting, but there are very few advocates for these penalties. Effectiveness is not the only issue here; rights and justice are also relevant.

29. The principle that fundamental rights may not be overridden by the state unless doing so is necessary to serve a "compelling state interest" is a principle of constitutional law, but it also reflects our moral intuitions about when it is appropriate to override rights. The legal principle would not apply to all cases of drug testing in the workplace because many of these involve private, rather than state, employees. But the principle does provide us with useful guidelines in the ethical sphere. Interestingly, Federal District Judge George Revercomb recently issued an injunction blocking the random drug testing of Justice Department employees on the ground that it did not serve a compelling state interest. Since there was no evidence of a drug problem among the Department's employees, the Judge concluded, there is no threat that would give rise to a compelling interest. See "Judge Blocks Drug Testing of Justice Department Employees", *New York Times* July 30, 1988, 7.

POSTSCRIPT

Should Concern for Drug Abuse Overrule Concerns for Employee Privacy?

In the controversy over drug testing, the two sides seem to be reasoning from different moral principles and to different consequences. The proponents of randomized drug testing cite the principle of Least Harm: left to themselves to take drugs, the workforce is likely to turn out terribly harmful results—damaged products, derailed trains, and the pervasive negligence that makes products unsafe and the workplace dangerous.

The opponents of drug testing, however, find more harm than good resulting from drug testing. Given the potential for error, good employees will be not only fired but stigmatized; the morale of the workforce will suffer as the invasions of privacy threaten the dignity and self-esteem of the worker; and the atmosphere of suspicion built up by the testing policy will result in worker resentment.

It is difficult to predict the future of drug testing in the workplace. If it is to be allowed—and, according to the surveys reported by Verespej, it should —more reliable tests are needed on the front line. There is now a very expensive test for which 99.9 percent accuracy is claimed, which is often used as a backup if an employee fails a drug test once. But generally, it is not used to screen candidates for employment, so there is still the risk of excluding good employees because of false positives or ruining credibility with too many false negatives. Primarily, drugs are not a company problem or an affliction of American business or capitalism. They are proliferating in the society at large, and until drugs are removed from the street, there is little hope of getting them out of the workplace. Under these circumstances, it seems that the certainty of invasion outweighs the possibility of preventing drug use. On the other hand, the corporations may be the perfect place to begin to confront drug abuse.

Suggested Readings

Rob Brookler, "Industry Standards in Workplace Drug Testing," *Personnel Journal* (April 1992).

Michael Janofsky, "Drug Use and Workers' Rights," *The New York Times* (December 28, 1993).

Laura Lally, "Privacy Versus Accessibility: The Impact of Situationally Conditioned Belief," *Journal of Business Ethics* (November 1996).

Rita C. Manning, "Liberal and Communitarian Defenses of Workplace Privacy," *Journal of Business Ethics* (June 1997).

On the Internet ...

DUSHKIN ONLINE

Marketing Today

This MarketWare Technologies site offers links to miscellaneous resources related to various forms of marketing, including direct mail, television and radio advertising, Internet marketing, and trade show marketing.

http://www.marketware-tech.com/advertising.htm

Advertising World

Advertising World, maintained by the Department of Advertising at the University of Texas at Austin, links to numerous sites on advertising. Among the many indexed topics are ethics and self-regulation, consumer interest, public relations, and market research.

http://advertising.utexas.edu/world/

Overlawyered.com

Overlawyered.com explores an American legal system that too often turns litigation into a weapon against guilty and innocent alike, erodes individual responsibility, rewards sharp practice, enriches its participants at the public's expense, and resists even modest efforts at reform and accountability. This page focuses on litigation over auto safety.

http://overlawyered.com/topics/auto.html

PART 4

Moving the Product: Marketing and Consumer Dilemmas

*W*hat *right does a consumer have to expect that the product he or she buys will cause no harm? At the start of the twentieth century, the buyer tended to be stuck with a purchase, however reached, and responsible for her or his own safety in using the product. This is no longer the rule governing product liability. This section looks at advertising in and of itself and the marketing of a car that may or may not have contained a dangerous design flaw (the Pinto).*

- Are Marketing and Advertising Fundamentally Exploitive?

- Product Liability: Was Ford to Blame in the Pinto Case?

Are Marketing and Advertising Fundamentally Exploitive?

YES: John P. Foley, from "Ethics in Advertising: A Look at the Report by the Pontifical Council for Social Communications," *Journal of Public Policy & Marketing* (Fall 1998)

NO: Gene R. Laczniak, from "Reflections on the 1997 Vatican Statements Regarding Ethics in Advertising," *Journal of Public Policy & Marketing* (Fall 1998)

ISSUE SUMMARY

YES: Archbishop John P. Foley summarizes and comments on the 1997 report of the Pontifical Council for Social Communications, which charges that advertising can be deceptive and improperly influential on media editorial policy and states that it often promotes a lifestyle based on unbridled consumption.

NO: Professor of marketing Gene R. Laczniak contends that many of the Pontifical Council report's conclusions are overstated, only partially true, economically naive, and socially idealistic. While sympathetic to its aims, he argues that the Church's contribution to the debate is vitiated by such errors.

$\mathbf{I}$n a film on Wall Street, made at the height of "merger mania" in the 1980s, investment banker Felix Rohatyn is asked his opinion of a contemporary statement by the American Bishops on the problems of capitalism and the need to share America's wealth with the poor. He was expected, apparently, to attack the Bishops as naive, ignorant, and possibly Communists—much as former secretary of the treasury William Simon did. But that was not Rohatyn's reply. Instead, he suggested that the Bishops had spoken well, they spoke out of concern for the poor, and that, he said, is what bishops are supposed to do. Who else would do it? Who else but the pastors of the beleaguered flock will recall that not every aspect of a plump American economy is good for absolutely everyone? There are many who agree that capitalism is a good system; it helps many people make a living and enjoy a prosperous life. But there are poor people, and they, too, have to be fed. The burden of speaking out on issues of social justice and of the welfare of those who have not been as fortunate as Rohatyn or Simon often falls on the Church.

The Pontifical Council for Social Communications, some say, is trying to tell advertisers how to do their business. The council seems to be worried about the possibility that advertisers may be promoting a lifestyle based on unbridled consumption. And the Council accuses advertisers of causing "people to feel and act upon cravings for items and services they do not need." Some would say that this is exactly the whole idea behind the business of advertising. According to Foley, what the Council is trying to do, however, is to direct people toward possibilities of living that do not include the pleasurable materialistic styles Americans have adopted within the capitalist system and to squire peoples energies to goals often forgotten, having to do with a communal life enjoyed for its own sake and for its potential to make us all into better people.

In many ways Gene R. Laczniak and the Council have visions of society that they do not share with each other. But the visions meet on the ground. Advertisers and marketers have to decide every day what sorts of advertising meet the moral minimal criteria of acceptable taste and adequate truth. How can one decide what violates taste (or human dignity) and what is overly untruthful unless one has some idea of the worth, basic human rights, and dignity of the audience? Can the Church and other moral advisors help to formulate sensible guidelines for advertising?

As you read the following selections bear in mind, that while Foley and Laczniak sometimes seem to be talking past each other, they present a genuine choice between views of human nature, as well as between views of what is desirable in business enterprise. As Foley suggests, even advertisers want to do the right thing and are occasionally grateful for suggestions as to how they might.

John P. Foley

 **YES**

Ethics in Advertising: A Look at the Report by the Pontifical Council for Social Communications

In February 1997, the cabinet-level Pontifical Council for Social Communications at the Vatican released a report on the state of advertising worldwide. To complete its review, the council solicited materials from advertising practitioners and scholars through a variety of venues, including a plea in the trade magazine *Advertising Age*. . . .

A Brief Summary of the Report

The report by the Pontifical Council for Social Communications (1997) is divided into five sections: introduction, benefits of advertising, harm done by advertising, ethical and moral principles, and conclusions. These sections build on one another and overlap in significant ways. A description of each follows, using quotes from the document whenever possible.

The introduction opens with the conclusion that "advertising has a profound impact on how people understand life, the world and themselves, especially in regard to their values and their ways of choosing and behaving" (p. 7). The media are described as "gifts from God" that can be employed to accomplish "his providential design, bringing people together and [to] help them to cooperate with his plan for their salvation" (p. 6). However, the council also "calls attention to moral principles and norms relevant to social communications" (p. 6) that should shape the content, target, and influence of advertising.

The next section, on advertising benefits, is divided into four segments. In the first segment, the council studies the economic benefits of advertising and notes that "advertising can be a useful tool for sustaining honest and ethically responsible competition that contributes to economic growth in the service of authentic human development" (p. 11). These benefits are accomplished in a variety of ways, including "by informing people about the availability of rationally desirable new products and services and improvements in existing ones" (pp. 11–12). The council examines the benefits of political advertising in the second segment and comes to a similar conclusion. The primary benefit is educational, "informing people about the ideas and policy proposals of parties and candidates, including new candidates not previously known to the public" (p. 13). In the third segment, the council discusses the cultural benefits of advertising, which comprise "a positive influence on decisions about media content" as well as "motivating [people] to act in ways that benefit themselves and others" (p. 13). The popular culture influence also is recognized as positive because "advertising can brighten lives simply by being witty, tasteful and entertaining" (p. 13). In the fourth and final segment, the council explores the moral and religious benefits of advertising, noting that advertising can deliver "messages of faith, of patriotism, of tolerance, compassion and neighborly service" (pp. 13–14), as well as others. From this perspective, advertising is viewed as essential to effective moral suasion and "a necessary part of a comprehensive pastoral strategy" (p. 14).

Section Three is titled "The Harm Done by Advertising," and it is divided into the same four segments as the previous section. Among the economic harms of advertising, the council includes deceptive advertising, the improper use of influence on media editorial content by advertisers, and the implicit promotion of a lifestyle built on unbridled consumption. It also argues against "brand-related advertising" that drives "people to act on the basis of irrational motives ('brand loyalty,' status, fashion, 'sex appeal,' etc.) instead of presenting differences in product quality and price as bases for rational choice" (p. 16). Furthermore, advertisers are indicted for causing "people to feel and act upon cravings for items and services they do not need" (p. 17).

With regard to the harms of political advertising, the council is concerned that "the costs of advertising limit political competition to wealthy political candidates or groups, or require that office-seekers compromise their integrity and independence by over-dependence on special interests for funds" (p. 18). In addition, political advertising is an "obstruction of the democratic process" when it "seeks to distort the views and records of opponents" or "appeals more to people's emotions and base instincts" (p. 19).

According to the council, the cultural harms of advertising are multi-faceted and include "cultural injury done to those nations and their peoples by advertising whose content and methods, reflecting those prevalent in the first world, are at war with sound traditional values in indigenous cultures" (p. 19). Advertisers also are blamed for pressure on the media to "ignore the educational and social needs of certain [market] segments" in favor of editorial content that "attracts ever larger audiences" through the delivery of editorial content that "lapses into superficiality, tawdriness and moral squalor" (p. 20). Furthermore, advertising is blamed for "invidious stereotyping of particular groups that places them at a disadvantage in relation to others," especially the "exploitation of women," which often ignores "the specific gifts of feminine insight, compassion, and understanding" (pp. 20–21).

Finally, the moral and religious harms of advertising include "appeals to such motives as envy, status seeking and lust," or those that "seek to shock and titillate by exploiting content of a morbid, perverse, pornographic nature" (p. 21). The council also finds advertising unacceptable "when it involves exploiting religion or treating it flippantly," or it "is used to promote products and inculcate attitudes and forms of behavior contrary to moral norms," "for instance, with the advertising of contraceptives, abortifacients, and products harmful to health" (p. 22).

The fourth section identifies "moral principles that are particularly relevant to advertising" (p. 25), and three in particular are discussed: truthfulness, the dignity of the human person, and social responsibility. The principle of truthfulness in advertising lobbies against advertisements that are "simply and deliberately untrue" or "distort the truth by implying things that are not so or withholding relevant facts" (p. 25). The principle of the dignity of the human person condemns advertisements that violate our right "to make a responsible choice" or "exploit man's lower inclinations" (e.g., "lust, vanity, envy and greed") (pp. 26–27). This principle is particularly relevant for vulnerable groups such as "children and young people, the elderly, the poor, the culturally disadvantaged" (p. 27). Finally, the principle of advertising and social responsibility criticizes "advertising that fosters a lavish life style which wastes resources[,] despoils the environment [, and] offends against important ecological concerns" (p. 28).

The fifth and final section is the conclusion. Much of this section is consumed with who is responsible for ensuring that advertising is "ethically correct." According to the council, the "indispensable guarantors" of such behavior are advertising professionals who "may be called upon to make significant personal sacrifices to correct [unethical practices]" (p. 34). The council recommends "voluntary ethical codes" before turning to government intervention, and these codes should be updated regularly by the industry, with feedback from "ethicists and church people, as well as representatives of consumer groups" (p. 31).

When all else fails, the government should intervene, especially in areas such as the "quantity" and "content of advertising directed at groups particularly vulnerable to exploitation, such as children and old people. Political advertising also seems an appropriate area for regulation: how much may be spent, how and from whom may money for advertising be raised" (p. 32). Furthermore, "besides avoiding abuses, advertisers also should undertake to repair the harm sometimes done by advertising, insofar as that is possible: for example, by publishing corrective notices, compensating injured parties, increasing the quantity of public service advertising, and the like" (pp. 33–34).

Remarks Made by Archbishop Foley at the 1998 Public Policy Conference

First of all, I wish to express my thanks to Dean Ron Hill of the School of Business Administration of the University of Portland for having arranged this session on ethics in advertising, with a special focus on the document of the same name published last year by our Pontifical Council for Social Communications in Rome. I also wish to thank Professors Brenkert, Laczniak, and Murphy for their generally favorable comments, and also for their constructive criticisms. Such dialogue is exactly what we wanted to happen, not only within the

Catholic Church, but also in the advertising and communications industries and in the academic community.

While a number of comments seem to imply that our document will have little or no effect within the advertising community, I must confess that I have been encouraged by the reaction of the advertising community. Not only have I been invited all over the world to comment on this document in various fora of advertisers, agencies, and associations, but the document has been translated into more than a dozen languages and distributed widely, either through advertising associations or the communications committees of bishops' conferences. At a meeting in Geneva of the World Federation of Advertisers, I was even asked to have our Council begin the development of a wider study on ethics in communications, and we are trying to do just that. In fact, I already invoke such ethical norms when I represent the Holy See at the council of Europe to recall that broadcast frequencies should be considered a public trust and should be required to serve the public interest and not merely private commercial interests.

It would be unrealistic, however, to think that our document, which we strove to keep brief, readable, and practical, would result in overnight world-wide conversion. After 2000 years, the world is not yet Christian, and Jesus was (and is) God! If we can get some people all over the world thinking about ethics in advertising, however, using some of the principles which we have articulated, we will consider that some progress had been made.

There were areas into which we did not enter, but well could have entered; for example, the failure in the United States to distinguish when commercial announcements are beginning or ending, so that one can confuse the news or the entertainment program with the advertising message; the use of product placement in films and television programs; [and] the promotion of products connected with programs being shown, so that there is a temptation to use programs which have product tie-ins.

As we know, there are also endorsements of products by famous persons—sometimes apparent endorsements without the knowledge or permission of the person in question. Let me give an example: When I went to Budapest to speak on this same theme, I saw a billboard on the way from the airport showing a yawning Pope saying something in Hungarian, obviously in support of RTL, Radio-TV Luxembourg, one of the continent's largest private broadcasters. I mentioned this in my talk and said that the use of a person's image to sell a product or service without that person's authorization is at least immoral, if not illegal. The head of the Hungarian Advertising Standards Council rose to say that the billboard would be removed, the Ambassador of Hungary to the Holy See called me to apologize, and the president of the RTL later saw me at a dinner and told me that they had canceled that campaign in all of Europe. Occasionally, invoking ethical standards has dramatic results.

I am in favor of advertising, and I am in favor of commercially supported media; after all, I was editor of a newspaper which depended upon advertising for its survival. I am also in favor of ethics in advertising; after all, I was a Professor of Ethics for 17 years. I am convinced, however, that most people want to do the right thing and that they appreciate some guidance and support, preferably through industry guidelines, and even, if necessary, regulations by public authority to guarantee that they will not be victimized by their competition for being ethical.

Our point is that ethics in advertising serves the truth, the authentic development of the human person, and the healthy progress of society. If that sounds idealistic, so be it; if the Catholic Church cannot articulate an ideal, who can? What is encouraging to me is that so many seem to be hungry to hear such ideals articulated and, as advertising executives might say, in promoting our document, we are meeting a felt need. In this, we are not claiming a monopoly on truth; we are merely trying to articulate a consensus—and I hope that, in large measure, we have succeeded.

NO

Gene R. Laczniak

Reflections on the 1997 Vatican Statements Regarding Ethics in Advertising

In February 1997, the Vatican Pontifical Council for Social Communications issued a 35-page pamphlet, which provides a religion-based commentary on the ethics of advertising. This document is composed of five sections that endeavor to treat the economic, political, cultural, and moral dimensions of advertising as they affect society. Although the thematic tone of the writing is difficult to capture by excerpting a few paragraphs, the following quotations sample the rhetorical sense of the essay:

> On advertising in developing countries: "serious harm can be done them if advertising and commercial pressure becomes so irresponsible that communities seeking to rise from poverty to a reasonable standard of living are persuaded to seek this progress by satisfying wants that have been artificially created" (Section 10).

> On the relationship of advertising and the media: "In the competition to attract ever larger audiences and deliver them to advertisers, communicators can find themselves tempted—in fact pressured, subtly and not so subtly—to set aside high artistic and moral standards and lapse into superficiality, tawdriness, and moral squalor" (Section 12).

> On the morality of advertising: "Advertising can be tasteful and in conformity with high moral standards, and occasionally even morally uplifting but it can also be vulgar and morally degrading. Frequently it deliberately appeals to such motives as envy, status seeking, and lust. Today, too, some advertisers conscientiously seek to shock and titillate by exploiting content of a morbid, perverse, pornographic nature" (Section 13).

The Vatican essay concludes with the postulation of three ethical principles, which are discussed subsequently. It pointedly calls for greater responsibility on the part of those involved in the advertising industry, especially advertising practitioners. The document states (Section 14), "advertisers—that is, those who commission, prepare or disseminate advertising—are morally responsible for what they seek to move people to do." This pamphlet was distributed in its entirety by the Vatican Office to all Catholic bishops for the purposes of pastoral teaching and reflection. Its explicit target market consists of more than 600 million Catholics worldwide, as well as the global advertising community, but it also is intended for all people of goodwill.

The Statement's Fundamental Structure and Method

The Vatican essay takes the form of an analytical commentary on the social implications of advertising. The pamphlet, drawing almost exclusively on Catholic religious sources, logically moves from a statement of purpose to a final explication of principles. It is composed of four parts and 23 sections and runs approximately 35 pages in length.

The bibliographic citations made throughout the essay are scripturally and religiously rooted. The majority of references are to papal encyclicals and the *Catechism of the Catholic Church* (1994). These footnoted sources, in turn, are referenced heavily with additional biblical and doctrinal citations and can be used to examine the full scope of religious teaching that is invoked as a basis for the statements made. This approach to source authority can be expected to receive negative comment in most academic circles. That is, many will argue that, to maximize the credibility and defensibility of the observations made in this document, its tenets should be supported not by sectarian, religious documents but mainly by references to the most current and reputable social science and business literature dealing with the social outcomes of advertising. Such criticism partially misses the point.

... [M]ost of the issues raised regarding the possible economic, political, and cultural harms for which the institution of advertising might be responsible have been dissected previously by serious academic analysis (Rotzoll and Haefner 1990). But elaborate discussion of the questions previously raised by advertising should not imply a consensus resolution of the issues. In the mid-1980s, Richard Pollay authored a now-classic article that examines the ever-evolving history of advertising criticism as perceived by significant humanities and social science scholars. Pollay (1986, p. 21) writes in summation, "They see advertising as reinforcing materialism, cynicism, irrationality, selfishness, anxiety, social competitiveness, powerlessness and/or the loss of self respect." As such observations suggest, the power and visibility of advertising breeds ongoing, critical commentary in some sectors of society, but often this criticism raises more issues than solutions. For example, one recent literature review, covering the period 1987 to 1993, found 127 articles published on the topic of advertising ethics alone (Hyman, Tansey, and Clark 1994). That the Catholic Church also might weigh in on this pervasive topic should not be astounding to anyone. Thus, the systematic elaboration of religious values and accompanying citation of supporting writings should be understood as a different and possibly valuable perspective on the impact of advertising in a complex society. For example, Protestant and Jewish academics have drawn on their own religious traditions to offer commentary on addressing and improving business ethics (Camenish 1998; Pava 1998).

The Statement's Likely Impact: Ideal and Actual

The Vatican pamphlet on advertising ethics will receive a modicum of discussion, especially in Catholic circles, given its source and purpose. For example, I already am aware of several faculty, teaching at Catholic business schools, who have incorporated it into classroom discussions that pertain to the social impact of marketing activities. More than likely, it also will be used by some members of the Catholic clergy as an inspiration for homilies or a possible theme in parish programs or youth education efforts that include social reflections. The Vatican essay also can be expected to fall on some sympathetic ears among nonsectarian audiences, especially those searching for novel ideas wherever they can be found. For example, business academics interested in the questions of public policy and social issues certainly would fall into this category. On the balance, however, I believe this statement will not have much visibility or impact, at least not without a concerted effort to publicize (dare I say advertise?) it to upper-level marketing and advertising executives. According to a *New York Times* (Charry 1997) article published approximately 30 days after the Vatican essay on advertising ethics had been released, few high-profile advertising practitioners even were aware of its existence. There is little evidence to suggest that awareness levels regarding the content of the document will increase among the advertising community at any time in the future.

Perhaps more disturbing is my contention that, even if the document comes to the attention of the advertising community, the opinions of the Catholic Church on such matters will not be welcomed. On what basis do I say this? Church leaders systematically have opined on other economic issues on previous occasions (Naughton and Laczniak 1993). These observations, directed at the Catholic laity in general, but at the broader business community as well, have not been received graciously by business. For example, in 1986, the U.S. Catholic bishops published a lengthy, thoughtful pastoral letter titled *Economic Justice for All* (1986). That document attempted to articulate the implications of Catholic social teaching (CST) for the U.S. economy. Specifically, the principles of CST were explicated, and their connections to various managerial issues, such as employment, poverty, and economic development, were laid out comprehensively. In a poll of 2000 randomly selected business executives, reported in *Chicago Studies* (McMahon 1989), the majority of the executives perceived that this Catholic bishops' letter on economics was a political statement, rather than a constructive contribution to the dialogue regarding social justice. This observation was made despite the majority of executives claiming that religious values significantly influenced their business decision making....

As a business professor at a Catholic university, who teaches classes in both competitive strategy and business ethics, I have been asked by corporate executives on several occasions my opinion regarding the standing of the Catholic Church to comment intelligently on economic matters. My standard reply has been to say that Catholic Church leaders probably have at least as much useful to say about "justice" and "fairness" in the operation of the economy as business executives do about the efficient running of universities.

Observations in the Vatican Ethics Statement Likely to Be Attacked

Almost any assertion pertaining to the social role of advertising has a high likelihood of engendering debate. The Vatican statement on ethics in advertising contains several observations that are likely to serve as lightening rods for controversy. Regrettably, a few of these remarks will bolster the position of those in the business community who contend that the clergy lack economic understanding. For purposes of illustration, I focus on three such postulations from the ethics document.

First, in Section 10, the statement criticizes brand-related advertising for often accentuating irrational buying motives by consumers and causing potentially serious, supposedly ethical, problems. This condemnation is blanket and without sufficient illustration. Presumably, unstated examples, such as targeting $180 basketball shoes at the poorest urban youth, would represent such egregious abuse. In these cases, the Vatican and most of us should be outraged appropriately. But, this superficial criticism of branding and brand-related advertising as often leading to product proliferation and irrational consumer choice is also naive. Although branding, at the extreme, has been subject to some marketing exploitation, the benefits of branding are well accepted and key elements in enhancing the social value of advertising (Wilkie and Moore-Shay, in press). Even many severe critics of advertising generally are willing to grant this and admit that branding is one of the net "pluses" of complex marketing systems. Branding enables consumers to accrue a shorthand form of product identification and provides them with a longitudinally consistent indicator of price and quality across product categories. My point here is that such hypercritical analysis of possible advertising shortcomings undermines the credibility of the entire Vatican document.

Second, in Section 11, there is an unfortunate foray into the dysfunctions of political advertising. More than likely, this commentary by the Vatican Office was well intended, given that contemporary political campaigns have evolved away from interpersonal communications campaigns to ones that feature mass communications and often contain destructive negative advertising (Laczniak and Caywood 1987). Nevertheless, political advertising, at least in the United States, remains a protected class of speech that arises from constitutional guarantees. For this reason, political advertising would have best been eliminated in the Pontifical discussion. I say this because, by questioning the ethics of political speech, the church raises a frightening specter. If the Vatican is willing to delimit the sacrosanct area of paid-for political debate, advertising executives will wonder how much else church leaders would want to censor quickly. Such issues would have been better addressed in a separate document on the ethics and morality of modern political campaigns.

Third, in Section 14, the Vatican essay raises a dichotomy that, in my opinion, is far too dramatic. Referencing the media in general, and advertising in particular, the essay portrays media practitioners as facing a forked choice: "Either they help human persons to grow in their understanding and practice of what is true and good, or they are destructive forces in conflict with human well-being." Is human nature really so black and white? Does the Vatican believe that all advertising is either all good or all bad? Such simplistic analysis again undermines the credibility of other useful and valuable insights contained in the essay.

Moral Principles Relevant to Improving Advertising Ethics

The most substantive portion of the document involves the postulation of three principles that should be used to adjudicate the ethics of advertising. According to the Vatican essay, these are the following:

1. A principle of *truthfulness.* It states that, "advertising may not deliberately seek to deceive, whether it does that by what it says, by what it implies, or what it fails to say" (Section 15).
2. A principle of *human dignity.* "There is an imperative requirement" that advertising "respect the human person, his right/duty to make a responsible choice, his interior freedom; all these goods would be violated if man's lower inclinations were to be exploited, or his capacity to reflect and decide compromised" (Section 16). In the explication of this principle, promotions that appeal to lust, vanity, envy, and greed are referenced specifically. In addition, advertising that is directed exploitatively at vulnerable groups, such as children, the elderly, and the poor, is mentioned as particularly troubling.
3. A principle of *social responsibility.* "Advertising that reduces human progress to acquiring material and cultivating a lavish lifestyle expresses a false, destructive vision of the human person harmful to individuals and society alike" (Section 17). Specifically noted in this principle, by way of explanation, are advertisements that encourage lifestyles that contribute to the waste of resources or the despoiling of the natural environment.

Taken together, the worth of these principles is that they cover important, fundamental, and necessary ground. They remind advertisers of their proactive duties to avoid deception and respect persons, particularly those who are vulnerable, and of the special requirement of enlightened stewardship that managers should embrace in constructing responsible marketing campaigns.

The principles serve as noteworthy moral commentary in the long-running debate about how advertising is moderated best from a social and public policy standpoint (e.g., Preston 1994).

However, it is also fair to note that most of the issues addressed by these principles have been brought previously to the attention of the advertising community. The sentiment of nondeception covered in the first principle, at least in its basic form (i.e., "do not intentionally deceive"), is included in most existing professional codes of advertising ethics, as well as in the law. For example, "avoidance of false and misleading advertising" is a specific provision of the American Marketing Association code of ethics (Laczniak and Murphy 1993). And regarding the third ethical principle, advertisers long have espoused a high level of social responsibility. For example, the document titled *Standards of Practice of the American Association of Advertising Agencies* begins with the following language:

> We hold that a responsibility of advertising agencies is to be a constructive force in business. We hold that to discharge this responsibility, advertising agencies must recognize an obligation, not only to their clients, but to the public, the media they employ, and to each other ... unethical competitive practices in the advertising agency business lead to financial waste, dilution of service, diversion of manpower, loss of prestige, and tends to weaken public confidence both in advertisements and in the institution of advertising (quoted in Laczniak and Murphy 1993).

If anything, these three Vatican principles might be faulted as too general. What may be needed more, perhaps, are midrange corollaries that address specific, documentable abuses in the advertising system.

The Professional Responsibilities of Advertising Educators and Practitioners

In the end, whether cleric, layperson, academic, or advertising practitioner, readers are left with the question: What social obligations are incumbent on advertising executives? Clearly, advertisers have some duties to contribute to the common good. The real debate comes regarding how broadly these social requirement parameters should be drawn and how aggressively practitioners should seek to fulfill their professional duties.

References

Camenish, Paul (1998), "A Presbyterian Approach to Business Ethics," in Perspectives in Business Ethics, L. P. Hartman, ed. Chicago: Irwin/McGraw-Hill, 229–38.

Catechism of the Catholic Church (1994). Chicago: Loyola University Press.

Charry, Tamer (1997), "Advertising: Roman Catholic Church Gets Mixed Review on Ads," New York Times, (March 31), Business Section, 1.

Economic Justice for All: Catholic Social Teaching and the U.S. Economy (1986). Washington, DC: National Conference of Catholic Bishops.

Hyman, Michael Richard, R. Tansey, and Jarvis W. Clark (1994), "Research on Advertising Ethics: Past, Present, and Future," Journal of Advertising, 23, 5–15.

Laczniak, Gene R. and Clarke L. Caywood (1987), "The Case For and Against Tele-vised Political Advertising: Implications for Research and Public Policy," Journal of Public Policy & Marketing, 6, 16–32.

——and Patrick E. Murphy (1993), Ethical Marketing Decisions. Boston, MA: Allyn & Bacon.

McMahon, Thomas F. (1989), "Religion and Business," Chicago Studies, 3–15.

Naughton, Michael and Gene R. Laczniak (1993), "A Theological Context of Work from the Catholic Social Encyclical Tradition," Journal of Business Ethics, 12, 981–94.

Pava, Moses L. (1998), "Developing a Religiously Grounded Business Ethics: A Jewish Perspective," Business Ethics Quarterly, 8, 65–83.

Pollay, Richard W. (1986), "The Distorted Mirror: Reflections on the Unintended Consequences of Advertising," Journal of Marketing, 50 (April), 18–36.

Pontifical Council for Social Communications (1997), Ethics in Advertising. Vatican City: Vatican Documents.

Preston, Ivan L. (1994), The Tangled Web They Weave: Truth, Falsity, and Advertisers. Madison, WI: University of Wisconsin Press.

Rotzoll, Kim and James Haefner (1990), Advertising in Contemporary Society. Cincin-nati, OH: Southwestern.

Wilkie, William and Elizabeth S. Moore-Shay (in press), "Marketing's Contributions to Society," Journal of Marketing, forthcoming.

POSTSCRIPT

Are Marketing and Advertising Fundamentally Exploitive?

We live in an age of rapid change in the communications business. Many are concerned over the directions that change is taking, and for good reason. How can one assess what proportion of the problems of society are traceable to advertising and the general marketing practices of corporations? For instance, if it turns out that ads for diet products and slim fashions, advertised by emaciated supermodels, are unduly influencing young girls to lose their self-esteem and self-confidence, ruin their health with fad diets, and sometimes even starve themselves, what, can or should be done about that? Is government regulation the answer? Is industry self-regulation the answer? As citizens and as consumers, you will be part of these serious decisions.

Suggested Readings

Stevan Alburty, "The Ad Agency to End All Agencies," *Fast Company* (December–January 1997).

George Brenkert, "Ethics in Advertising: The Good, the Bad, and the Church," *Journal of Public Policy and Marketing* (Fall 1998).

Carol Krol, "Pontifical Council Sets Guidelines for Making Ads," *Advertising Age* (vol. 68, no. 4, 1997).

James E. Liebig, *Merchants of Vision: People Bringing New Purpose and Values to Business* (Berret-Koehier, 1994).

Pontifical Council for Social Communications, *Ethics in Advertising* (Vatican Documents, 1997).

ISSUE 12

Product Liability: Was Ford to Blame in the Pinto Case?

YES: Mark Dowie, from "Pinto Madness," *Mother Jones* (September/October 1977)

NO: Ford Motor Company, from "Closing Argument by Mr. James Neal," Brief for the Defense, *State of Indiana v. Ford Motor Company*, U.S. District Court, South Bend, Indiana (January 15, 1980)

ISSUE SUMMARY

YES: Award-winning investigative journalist Mark Dowie alleges that Ford Motor Company deliberately put an unsafe car—the Pinto—on the road, causing hundreds of people to suffer burn deaths and horrible disfigurement. He argues that the related activities of Ford's executives, both within the company and in dealing with the public and the government, were criminal.

NO: James Neal, chief attorney for Ford Motor Company during the Pinto litigation, argues to the jury that Ford cannot be held responsible for deaths that were caused by others—such as the driver of the van that struck the victims—and that there is no proof of criminal intent or negligence on the part of Ford.

On August 10, 1978, three girls had stopped their car, a 1973 Ford Pinto, on U.S. Highway 22 near Goshen, Indiana, and were about to get under way again when they were struck from the rear at high speed by a van. The car immediately burst into flames, and the girls had no chance to escape before the flames reached them.

The blame for these girls' deaths fell not on the driver of the van but on the manufacturer of the Pinto. Questions that were asked were: What was wrong with the car? Why did it burst into flames so quickly? Mark Dowie, then–general manager of business operations of the magazine *Mother Jones*, had argued a year earlier that there was a great deal wrong with the Pinto. Dowie's argument, which is reprinted here, is based on data obtained for him by some disaffected Ford engineers. In it, he suggests that the Pinto had been rushed into production without adequate testing; that it had a vulnerable fuel system that would rupture with any rear-end collision; that even though the vulnerability was discovered before production, Ford had hurried the Pinto to the market anyway; and that successful lobbying thereafter had prevented government regulators from instituting a requirement for a safer gas tank. Most suggestive to the public was a document supplied by one of the engineers, an estimate of the probable costs of refitting valves to prevent fire in a rollover accident. It was a cost-benefit analysis that placed a dollar value on human life—among the estimates were the probability of a fatal accident, the amount of money needed to settle a lawsuit for the loss of a life, and the amount of money needed to do the refitting so that there would be less chance for that loss of life—and concluded that it was more economical to accept the higher probability of death occurring and then settle the suits as they come. The document caused serious damage to Ford Motor Company's reputation.

Ford endured two sets of court appearances as a result of Dowie's article. More common, and successful, were the civil suits, alleging culpable negligence that damaged the rights of other individuals. But the state of Indiana also brought a public prosecution for *criminal* negligence, and James Neal's brief, which also follows, was prepared for that trial.

The 1916 case *McPherson v. Buick* helps set the stage for this debate. In this case, McPherson successfully sued the Buick Motor Company for injury sustained as a direct result of a poorly manufactured product. This was the first instance of a consumer's suing a manufacturer (as opposed to the seller), and it marked the transfer of product liability cases from the form of action known as "contract" to the form of action known as "tort" (in this case, negligence). The logic is that not only is an individual agreement breached when a shoddy product injures a consumer but a general obligation on the part of a manufacturer (an implied "warrant of merchantability") to avoid putting an unsafe product on the market is not met. Given the myriad ways that people can injure themselves, that obligation seems to be very broad indeed.

With regard to the Pinto case, was Ford guilty of deliberate malfeasance? Was it a series of unlucky decisions made in good faith? Or was this just a very unfortunate accident? As you read these selections, ask yourself what conditions need to be satisfied in order to attribute "responsibility" to any person or company. Also, what kinds of risks do people assume when buying a car, a motorcycle, or a can of tuna fish? For what is the manufacturer responsible? Should we be willing to assume more risks in the enormously competitive market that prevails among small automobiles? Does the product liability suit unjustly cripple American efforts to compete in highly competitive industries? Is this something that we should be concerned about?

Mark Dowie  **YES**

Pinto Madness

One evening in the mid-1960s, Arjay Miller was driving home from his office in Dearborn, Michigan, in the four-door Lincoln Continental that went with his job as president of the Ford Motor Company. On a crowded highway, another car struck his from the rear. The Continental spun around and burst into flames. Because he was wearing a shoulder-strap seat belt, Miller was unharmed by the crash, and because his doors didn't jam he escaped the gasoline-drenched, flaming wreck. But the accident made a vivid impression on him. Several months later, on July 15, 1965, he recounted it to a U.S. Senate subcommittee that was hearing testimony on auto safety legislation. "I still have burning in my mind the image of that gas tank on fire," Miller said. He went on to express an almost passionate interest in controlling fuel-fed fires in cars that crash or roll over. He spoke with excitement about the fabric gas tank Ford was testing at that very moment. "If it proves out," he promised the senators, "it will be a feature you will see in our standard cars."

Almost seven years after Miller's testimony, a woman, whom for legal reasons we will call Sandra Gillespie, pulled onto a Minneapolis highway in her new Ford Pinto. Riding with her was a young boy, whom we'll call Robbie Carlton. As she entered a merge lane, Sandra Gillespie's car stalled. Another car rear-ended hers at an impact speed of 28 miles per hour. The Pinto's gas tank ruptured. Vapors from it mixed quickly with the air in the passenger compartment. A spark ignited the mixture and the car exploded in a ball of fire. Sandra died in agony a few hours later in an emergency hospital. Her passenger, 13-year-old Robbie Carlton, is still alive; he has just come home from another futile operation aimed at grafting a new ear and nose from skin on the few unscarred portions of his badly burned body. (This accident is real; the details are from police reports.)

Why did Sandra Gillespie's Ford Pinto catch fire so easily, seven years after Ford's Arjay Miller made his apparently sincere pronouncements—the same seven years that brought more safety improvements to cars than any other period in automotive history? An extensive investigation by *Mother Jones* over the past six months has found these answers:

• Fighting strong competition from Volkswagen for the lucrative small-car market, the Ford Motor Company rushed the Pinto into production in much less than the usual time.

• Ford engineers discovered in pre-production crash tests that rear-end collisions would rupture the Pinto's fuel system extremely easily.

• Because assembly-line machinery was already tooled when engineers found this defect, top Ford officials decided to manufacture the car anyway—exploding gas tank and all—*even though Ford owned the patent on a much safer gas tank.*

• For more than eight years afterwards, Ford successfully lobbied, with extraordinary vigor and some blatant lies, against a key government safety standard that would have forced the company to change the Pinto's fire-prone gas tank.

By conservative estimates Pinto crashes have caused 500 burn deaths to people who would not have been seriously injured if the car had not burst into flames. The figure could be as high as 900. Burning Pintos have become such an embarrassment to Ford that its advertising agency, J. Walter Thompson, dropped a line from the end of a radio spot that read "Pinto leaves you with that warm feeling."

Ford knows the Pinto is a firetrap, yet it has paid out millions to settle damage suits out of court, and it is prepared to spend millions more lobbying against safety standards. With a half million cars rolling off the assembly lines each year, Pinto is the biggest-selling subcompact in America, and the company's operating profit on the car is fantastic. Finally, in 1977, new Pinto models have incorporated a few minor alterations necessary to meet that federal standard Ford managed to hold off for eight years. Why did the company delay so long in making these minimal, inexpensive improvements?

• Ford waited eight years because its internal "cost-benefit analysis," *which places a dollar value on human life,* said it wasn't profitable to make the changes sooner.

Before we get to the question of how much Ford thinks your life is worth, let's trace the history of the death trap itself. Although this particular story is about the Pinto, the way in which Ford made its decision is typical of the U.S. auto industry generally. There are plenty of similar stories about other cars made by other companies. But this case is the worst of them all.

❦

The next time you drive behind a Pinto (with over two million of them on the road, you shouldn't have much trouble finding one), take a look at the rear end. That long silvery object hanging down under the bumper is the gas tank. The tank begins about six inches forward of the bumper. In late models the bumper is designed to withstand a collision of only about five miles per hour. Earlier bumpers may as well not have been on the car for all the protection they offered the gas tank.

Mother Jones has studied hundreds of reports and documents on rear-end collisions involving Pintos. These reports conclusively reveal that if you ran into that Pinto you were following at over 30 miles per hour, the rear end of the car would buckle like an accordion, right up to the back seat. The tube leading to the gas-tank cap would be ripped away from the tank itself, and gas would immediately begin sloshing onto the road around the car. The buckled gas tank would be jammed up against the differential housing (that big bulge in the middle of your rear axle), which contains four sharp, protruding bolts likely to gash holes in the tank and spill still more gas. Now all you need is a spark from a cigarette, ignition, or scraping metal, and both cars would be engulfed in flames. If you gave that Pinto a really good whack—say, at 40 mph—chances are excellent that its doors would jam and you would have to stand by and watch its trapped passengers burn to death.

This scenario is no news to Ford. Internal company documents in our possession show that Ford has crash-tested the Pinto at a top-secret site more than 40 times and that *every* test made at over 25 mph without special structural alteration of the car has resulted in a ruptured fuel tank. Despite this, Ford officials denied under oath having crash-tested the Pinto.

Eleven of these tests, averaging a 31-mph impact speed, came before Pintos started rolling out of the factories. Only three cars passed the test with unbroken fuel tanks. In one of them an inexpensive light-weight plastic baffle was placed between the front of the gas tank and the differential housing, so those four bolts would not perforate the tank. (Don't forget about that little piece of plastic, which costs one dollar and weighs one pound. It plays an important role in our story later on.) In another successful test, a piece of steel was placed between the tank and the bumper. In the third test car the gas tank was lined with a rubber bladder. But none of these protective alterations was used in the mass-produced Pinto.

In pre-production planning, engineers seriously considered using in the Pinto the same kind of gas tank Ford uses in the Capri. The Capri tank rides over the rear axle and differential housing. It has been so successful in over 50 crash tests that Ford used it in its Experimental Safety Vehicle, which withstood rear-end impacts of 60 mph. So why wasn't the Capri tank used in the Pinto? Or, why wasn't that plastic baffle placed between the tank and the axle—something that would have saved the life of Sandra Gillespie and hundreds like her? Why was a car known to be a serious fire hazard deliberately released to production in August of 1970?

~◈~

Whether Ford should manufacture subcompacts at all was the subject of a bitter two-year debate at the company's Dearborn headquarters. The principals in this corporate struggle were the then-president Semon "Bunky" Knudsen, whom Henry Ford II had hired away from General Motors, and Lee Iacocca, a spunky Young Turk who had risen fast within the company on the enormous success of the Mustang. Iacocca argued forcefully that Volkswagen and the Japanese were going to capture the entire American subcompact market unless Ford put out its own alternative to the VW Beetle. Bunky Knudsen said, in effect: let them have the small-car market; Ford makes good money on medium and large models. But he lost the battle and later resigned. Iacocca became president and almost immediately began a rush program to produce the Pinto.

Like the Mustang, the Pinto became known in the company as "Lee's car." Lee Iacocca wanted that little car in the showrooms of America with the 1971 models. So he ordered his engineering vice president, Bob Alexander, to oversee what was probably the shortest production planning period in modern automotive history. The normal time span from conception to production of a new car model is about 43 months. The Pinto schedule was set at just under 25.

... Design, styling, product planning, advance engineering and quality assurance all have flexible time frames, and engineers can pretty much carry these on simultaneously. Tooling, on the other hand, has a fixed time frame of about 18 months. Normally, an auto company doesn't begin tooling until the other processes are almost over: you don't want to make the machines that stamp and press and grind metal into the shape of car parts until you know all those parts will work well together. *But Iacocca's speed-up meant Pinto tooling went on at the same time as product development.* So when crash tests revealed a serious defect in the gas tank, it was too late. The tooling was well under way.

When it was discovered the gas tank was unsafe, did anyone go to Iacocca and tell him? "Hell no," replied an engineer who worked on the Pinto, a high company official for many years, who, unlike several others at Ford, maintains a necessarily clandestine concern for safety. "That person would have been fired. Safety wasn't a popular subject around Ford in those days. With Lee it was taboo. Whenever a problem was raised that meant a delay on the Pinto, Lee would chomp on his cigar, look out the window and say 'Read the product objectives and get back to work.'"

The product objectives are clearly stated in the Pinto "green book." This is a thick, top-secret manual in green covers containing a step-by-step production plan for the model, detailing the metallurgy, weight, strength and quality of every part in the car. The product objectives for the Pinto are repeated in an article by Ford executive F. G. Olsen published by the Society of Automotive Engineers. He lists these product objectives as follows:

1. TRUE SUBCOMPACT
   - Size
   - Weight
2. LOW COST OF OWNERSHIP
   - Initial price
   - Fuel consumption
   - Reliability
   - Serviceability
3. CLEAR PRODUCT SUPERIORITY
   - Appearance
   - Comfort
   - Features

- Ride and Handling
- Performance

Safety, you will notice, is not there. It is not mentioned in the entire article. As Lee Iacocca was fond of saying, "Safety doesn't sell."

Heightening the anti-safety pressure on Pinto engineers was an important goal set by Iacocca known as "the limits of 2,000." The Pinto was not to weigh an ounce over 2,000 pounds and not to cost a cent over $2,000. "Iacocca enforced these limits with an iron hand," recalls the engineer quoted earlier. So, even when a crash test showed that that one-pound, one-dollar piece of plastic stopped the puncture of the gas tank, it was thrown out as extra cost and extra weight.

People shopping for subcompacts are watching every dollar. "You have to keep in mind," the engineer explained, "that the price elasticity on these subcompacts is extremely tight. You can price yourself right out of the market by adding $25 to the production cost of the model. And nobody understands that better than Iacocca."

Dr. Leslie Ball, the retired safety chief for the NASA manned space program and a founder of the International Society of Reliability Engineers, recently made a careful study of the Pinto. "The release to production of the Pinto was the most reprehensible decision in the history of American engineering," he said. Ball can name more than 40 European and Japanese models in the Pinto price and weight range with safer gas-tank positioning. Ironically, many of them, like the Ford Capri, contain a "saddle-type" gas tank riding over the back axle. *The patent on the saddle-type tank is owned by the Ford Motor Co.*

Los Angeles auto safety expert Byron Bloch has made an in-depth study of the Pinto fuel system. "It's a catastrophic blunder," he says. "Ford made an extremely irresponsible decision when they placed such a weak tank in such a ridiculous location in such a soft rear end. It's almost designed to blow up—premeditated."

A Ford engineer, who doesn't want his name used, comments: "This company is run by salesmen, not engineers; so the priority is styling, not safety." He goes on to tell a story about gas-tank safety at Ford.

Lou Tubben is one of the most popular engineers at Ford. He's a friendly, outgoing guy with a genuine concern for safety. By 1971 he had grown so concerned about gas-tank integrity that he asked his boss if he could prepare a presentation on safer tank design. Tubben and his boss had both worked on the Pinto and shared a concern for its safety. His boss gave him the go-ahead, scheduled a date for the presentation and invited all company engineers and key production planning personnel. When time came for the meeting, a grand total of two people showed up—Lou Tubben and his boss.

"So you see," continued the anonymous Ford engineer ironically, "there *are* a few of us here at Ford who are concerned about fire safety." He adds: "They are mostly engineers who have to study a lot of accident reports and look at pictures of burned people. But we don't talk about it much. It isn't a popular subject. I've never seen safety on the agenda of a product meeting and, except for a brief period in 1956, I can't remember seeing the word safety in an advertisement. I really don't think the company wants American consumers to start thinking too much about safety—for fear they might demand it, I suppose."

Asked about the Pinto gas tank, another Ford engineer admitted: "That's all true. But you miss the point entirely. You see, safety isn't the issue, trunk space is. You have no idea how stiff the competition is over trunk space. Do you realize that if we put a Capri-type tank in the Pinto you could only get one set of golf clubs in the trunk?"

cᴏᴏ⠻

Blame for Sandra Gillespie's death, Robbie Carlton's unrecognizable face and all the other injuries and deaths in Pintos since 1970 does not rest on the shoulders of Lee Iacocca alone. For, while he and his associates fought their battle against a safer Pinto in Dearborn, a larger war against safer cars raged in Washington. One skirmish in that war involved Ford's successful eight-year lobbying effort against Federal Motor Vehicle Safety Standard 301, the rear-end provisions of which would have forced Ford to redesign the Pinto.

But first some background:

During the early '60s, auto safety legislation became the *bête-noire* of American big business. The auto industry was the last great unregulated business, and if *it* couldn't reverse the tide of government regulation, the reasoning went, no one could.

People who know him cannot remember Henry Ford II taking a stronger stand than the one he took against the regulation of safety design. He spent weeks in Washington calling on members of Congress, holding press conferences and recruiting business cronies like W. B. Murphy of Campbell's Soup to join the anti-regulation battle. Displaying the sophistication for which today's American corporate leaders will be remembered, Murphy publicly called auto safety "a hula hoop, a fad that will pass." He was speaking to a special luncheon of the Business Council, an organization of 100 chief executives who gather periodically in Washington to provide "advice" and "counsel" to government. The target of their wrath in this instance was the Motor Vehicle Safety Bills introduced in both houses of Congress, largely in response to Ralph Nader's *Unsafe at Any Speed.*

By 1965, most pundits and lobbyists saw the handwriting on the wall and prepared to accept government "meddling" in the last bastion of free enterprise. Not Henry. With bulldog tenacity, he held out for defeat of the legislation to the very end, loyal to his grandfather's invention and to the company that makes it. But the Safety Act passed the House and Senate unanimously, and was signed into law by Lyndon Johnson in 1966.

While lobbying for and against legislation is pretty much a process of high-level back-slapping, press-conferencing and speech-making, fighting a regulatory agency is a much subtler matter. Henry headed home to lick his wounds in Grosse Pointe, Michigan, and a planeload of the Ford Motor Company's best brains flew to Washington to start the "education" of the new federal auto safety bureaucrats.

Their job was to implant the official industry ideology in the minds of the new officials regulating auto safety. Briefly summarized, that ideology states that auto accidents are caused not by *cars*, but by 1) people and 2) highway conditions.

This philosophy is rather like blaming a robbery on the victim. Well, what did you expect? You were carrying money, weren't you? It is an extraordinary experience to hear automotive "safety engineers" talk for hours without ever mentioning cars. They will advocate spending billions educating youngsters, punishing drunks and redesigning street signs. Listening to them, you can momentarily begin to think that it is easier to control 100 million drivers than a handful of manufacturers. They show movies about guardrail design and advocate the clear-cutting of trees 100 feet back from every highway in the nation. If a car is unsafe, they argue, it is because its owner doesn't properly drive it. Or, perhaps, maintain it.

In light of an annual death rate approaching 50,000, they are forced to admit that driving is hazardous. But the car is, in the words of Arjay Miller, "the safest link in the safety chain."

Before the Ford experts left Washington to return to drafting tables in Dearborn they did one other thing. They managed to informally reach an agreement with the major public servants who would be making auto safety decisions. This agreement was that "cost-benefit" would be an acceptable mode of analysis by Detroit and its new regulators. And as we shall see, cost-benefit analysis quickly became the basis of Ford's argument against safer car design.

❧

Cost-benefit analysis was used only occasionally in government until President Kennedy appointed Ford Motor Company President Robert McNamara to be Secretary of Defense. McNamara, originally an accountant, preached cost benefit with all the force of a Biblical zealot. Stated in its simplest terms, cost-benefit analysis says that if the cost is greater than the benefit, the project is not worth it—no matter what the benefit. Examine the cost of every action, decision, contract, part, or change, the doctrine says, then carefully evaluate the benefits (in dollars) to be certain that they exceed the cost before you begin a program or—and this is the crucial part for our story—pass a regulation.

As a management tool in a business in which profits matter over everything else, cost-benefit analysis makes a certain amount of sense. Serious problems come, however, when public officials who ought to have more than corporate profits at heart apply cost-benefit analysis to every conceivable decision. The inevitable result is that they must place a dollar value on human life.

Ever wonder what your life is worth in dollars? Perhaps $10 million? Ford has a better idea: $200,000.

Remember, Ford had gotten the federal regulators to agree to talk auto safety in terms of cost-benefit analysis. But in order to be able to argue that various safety costs were greater than their benefits, Ford needed to have a dollar value figure for the "benefit." Rather than be so uncouth as to come up

Table 1

What's Your Life Worth? Societal Cost
Components for Fatalities, 1972 NHTSA Study

Component	1971 Costs
Future productivity losses	
Direct	$132,000
Indirect	41,300
Medical costs	
Hospital	700
Other	425
Property damage	1,500
Insurance administration	4,700
Legal and court	3,000
Employer losses	1,000
Victim's pain and suffering	10,000
Funeral	900
Assets (lost consumption)	5,000
Miscellaneous accident costs	200
Total per fatality: $200,725	

Here is a chart from a federal study showing how the National Highway Traffic Safety Administration has calculated the value of a human life. The estimate was arrived at under pressure from the auto industry. The Ford Motor Company has used it in cost-benefit analyses arguing why certain safety measures are not "worth" the savings in human lives. The calculation above is a breakdown of the estimated cost to society every time someone is killed in a car accident. We were not able to find anyone, either in the government or at Ford, who could explain how the $10,000 figure for "pain and suffering" had been arrived at.

with such a price tag itself, the auto industry pressured the National Highway Traffic Safety Administration to do so. And in a 1972 report the agency decided a human life was worth $200,725. (For its reasoning, see [Table 1].) Inflationary forces have recently pushed the figure up to $278,000.

Furnished with this useful tool, Ford immediately went to work using it to prove why various safety improvements were too expensive to make.

Nowhere did the company argue harder that it should make no changes than in the area of rupture-prone fuel tanks. Not long after the government arrived at the $200,725-per-life figure, it surfaced, rounded off to a cleaner $200,000, in an internal Ford memorandum. This cost-benefit analysis argued that Ford should not make an $11-per-car improvement that would prevent 180 fiery deaths a year. (This minor change would have prevented gas tanks from breaking so easily both in rear-end collisions, like Sandra Gillespie's, and in rollover accidents, where the same thing tends to happen.)

Ford's cost-benefit table [Table 2] is buried in a seven-page company memorandum entitled "Fatalities Associated with Crash-Induced Fuel Leakage and

Table 2

$11 vs. a Burn Death: Benefits and Costs Relating to Fuel Leakage Associated With the Static Rollover Test Portion of FMVSS 208

Benefits

Savings: 180 burn deaths, 180 serious burn injuries, 2,100 burned vehicles.

Unit cost: $200,000 per death, $67,000 per injury, $700 per vehicle.

Total benefit: 180 x ($200,000) + 180 x ($67,000) + 2,100 x ($700) = $49.5 million.

Costs

Sales: 11 million cars, 1.5 million light trucks.

Unit cost: $11 per car, $11 per truck.

Total cost: 11,000,000 x ($11) + 1,500,000 x ($11) = $137 million.

From Ford Motor Company internal memorandum: "Fatalities Associated with Crash-Induced Fuel Leakage and Fires."

Fires." The memo argues that there is no financial benefit in complying with proposed safety standards that would admittedly result in fewer auto fires, fewer burn deaths and fewer burn injuries. Naturally, memoranda that speak so casually of "burn deaths" and "burn injuries" are not released to the public. They are very effective, however, with Department of Transportation officials indoctrinated in McNamarian cost-benefit analysis.

All Ford had to do was convince men like John Volpe, Claude Brinegar and William Coleman (successive Secretaries of Transportation during the Nixon-Ford years) that certain safety standards would add so much to the price of cars that fewer people would buy them. This could damage the auto industry, which was still believed to be the bulwark of the American economy. "Compliance to these standards," Henry Ford II prophesied at more than one press conference, "will shut down the industry."

The Nixon Transportation Secretaries were the kind of regulatory officials big business dreams of. They understood and loved capitalism and thought like businessmen. Yet, best of all, they came into office uninformed on technical automotive matters. And you could talk "burn injuries" and "burn deaths" with these guys, and they didn't seem to envision children crying at funerals and people hiding in their homes with melted faces. Their minds appeared to have leapt right to the bottom line—more safety meant higher prices, higher prices meant lower sales and lower sales meant lower profits.

So when J. C. Echold, Director of Automotive Safety (which means chief anti-safety lobbyist) for Ford wrote to the Department of Transportation—which he still does frequently, at great length—he felt secure attaching a memorandum that in effect says it is acceptable to kill 180 people and burn another 180 every year, *even though we have the technology that could save their lives for $11 a car.*

Furthermore, Echold attached this memo, confident, evidently, that the Secretary would question neither his low death/injury statistics nor his high cost estimates. But it turns out, on closer examination, that both these findings were misleading.

First, note that Ford's table shows an equal number of burn deaths and burn injuries. This is false. All independent experts estimate that for each person who dies by an auto fire, many more are left with charred hands, faces and limbs. Andrew McGuire of the Northern California Burn Center estimates the ratio of burn injuries to deaths at ten to one instead of the one to one Ford shows here. Even though Ford values a burn at only a piddling $67,000 instead of the $200,000 price of life, the true ratio obviously throws the company's calculations way off.

The other side of the equation, the alleged $11 cost of a fire-prevention device, is also a misleading estimation. One document that was *not* sent to Washington by Ford was a "Confidential" cost analysis *Mother Jones* has managed to obtain, showing that crash fires could be largely prevented for considerably *less* than $11 a car. The cheapest method involves placing a heavy rubber bladder inside the gas tank to keep the fuel from spilling if the tank ruptures. Goodyear had developed the bladder and had demonstrated it to the automotive industry. We have in our possession crash-test reports showing that the Goodyear bladder worked well. On December 2, 1970 (*two years before* Echold sent his cost-benefit memo to Washington), Ford Motor Company ran a rear-end crash test on a car with the rubber bladder in the gas tank. The tank ruptured, but no fuel leaked. On January 15, 1971, Ford again tested the bladder and again it worked. The total purchase and installation cost of the bladder would have been $5.08 per car. That $5.08 could have saved the lives of Sandra Gillespie and several hundred others.

⚜️

When a federal regulatory agency like the National Highway Traffic Safety Administration (NHTSA) decides to issue a new standard, the law usually requires it to invite all interested parties to respond before the standard is enforced—a reasonable enough custom on the surface. However, the auto industry has taken advantage of this process and has used it to delay lifesaving emission and safety standards for years. In the case of the standard that would have corrected that fragile Pinto fuel tank, the delay was for an incredible eight years.

The particular regulation involved here was Federal Motor Vehicle Safety Standard 301. Ford picked portions of Standard 301 for strong opposition back in 1968 when the Pinto was still in the blueprint stage. The intent of 301, and the 300 series that followed it, was to protect drivers and passengers *after* a crash occurs. Without question the worst postcrash hazard is fire. So Standard 301 originally proposed that all cars should be able to withstand a fixed barrier impact of 20 mph (that is, running into a wall at that speed) without losing fuel.

When the standard was proposed, Ford engineers pulled their crash-test results out of their files. The front ends of most cars were no problem—with minor alterations they could stand the impact without losing fuel. "We were already working on the front end," Ford engineer Dick Kimble admitted. "We knew we could meet the test on the front end." But with the Pinto particularly, a 20-mph rear-end standard meant redesigning the entire rear end of the car. With the Pinto scheduled for production in August of 1970, and with $200 million worth of tools in place, adoption of this standard would have created a minor financial disaster. So Standard 301 was targeted for delay, and, with some assistance from its industry associates, Ford succeeded beyond its wildest expectations: the standard was not adopted until the 1977 model year. Here is how it happened:

There are several main techniques in the art of combating a government safety standard: a) make your arguments in succession, so the feds can be working on disproving only one at a time; b) claim that the real problem is not X but Y (we already saw one instance of this in "the problem is not cars but people"); c) no matter how ridiculous each argument is, accompany it with thousands of pages of highly technical assertions it will take the government months or, preferably, years to test. Ford's large and active Washington office brought these techniques to new heights and became the envy of the lobbyists' trade.

The Ford people started arguing against Standard 301 way back in 1968 with a strong attack of technique b). Fire, they said, was not the real problem. Sure, cars catch fire and people burn occasionally. But statistically auto fires are such a minor problem that NHTSA should really concern itself with other matters.

Strange as it may seem, the Department of Transportation (NHTSA's parent agency) didn't know whether or not this was true. So it contracted with several independent research groups to study auto fires. The studies took months which was just what Ford wanted.

The completed studies, however, showed auto fires to be more of a problem than Transportation officials ever dreamed of. Robert Nathan and Associates, a Washington research firm, found that 400,000 cars were burning up every year, burning more than 3,000 people to death. Furthermore, auto fires were increasing five times as fast as building fires. Another study showed that 35 per cent of all fire deaths in the U.S. occurred in automobiles. Forty per cent of all fire department calls in the 1960s were to vehicle fires—a public cost of $350 million a year, a figure that, incidentally, never shows up in cost-benefit analyses.

Another study was done by the Highway Traffic Research Institute in Ann Arbor, Michigan, a safety think-tank funded primarily by the auto industry (the giveaway there is the words "highway traffic" rather than "automobile" in the group's name). It concluded that 40 per cent of the lives lost in fuel-fed fires could be saved if the manufacturers complied with proposed Standard 301. Finally, a third report was prepared for NHTSA by consultant Eugene Trisko entitled "A National Survey of Motor Vehicle Fires." His report indicates that the Ford Motor Company makes 24 per cent of the cars on the American road, yet these cars account for 42 per cent of the collision-ruptured fuel tanks.

Ford lobbyists then used technique a)—bringing up a new argument. Their line then became: yes, perhaps burn accidents do happen, but rear-end collisions are relatively rare (note the echo of technique b) here as well). Thus

Standard 301 was not needed. This set the NHTSA off on a new round of an-alyzing accident reports. The government's findings finally were that rear-end collisions were seven and a half times more likely to result in fuel spills than were front-end collisions. So much for that argument.

By now it was 1972; NHTSA had been researching and analyzing for four years to answer Ford's objections. During that time, nearly 9,000 people burned to death in flaming wrecks. Tens of thousands more were badly burned and scarred for life. And the four-year delay meant that well over 10 million new unsafe vehicles went on the road, vehicles that will be crashing, leaking fuel and incinerating people well into the 1980s.

Ford now had to enter its third round of battling the new regulations. On the "the problem is not X but Y" principle, the company had to look around for something new to get itself off the hook. One might have thought that, faced with all the latest statistics on the horrifying number of deaths in flaming accidents, Ford would find the task difficult. But the company's rhetoric was brilliant. The problem was not burns, but... impact! Most of the people killed in these fiery accidents, claimed Ford, would have died whether the car burned or not. They were killed by the kinetic force of the impact, not the fire.

And so once again, as in some giant underwater tennis game, the ball bounced into the government's court and the absurdly pro-industry NHTSA began another slow-motion response. Once again it began a time-consuming round of test crashes and embarked on a study of accidents. The latter, however, revealed that a large and growing number of corpses taken from burned cars involved in rear-end crashes contained no cuts, bruises or broken bones. They clearly would have survived the accident unharmed if the cars had not caught fire. This pattern was confirmed in careful rear-end crash tests performed by the Insurance Institute for Highway Safety. A University of Miami study found an inordinate number of Pintos burning on rear-end impact and concluded that this demonstrated "a clear and present hazard to all Pinto owners."

Pressure on NHTSA from Ralph Nader and consumer groups began mounting. The industry-agency collusion was so obvious that Senator Joseph Montoya (D-N.M.) introduced legislation about Standard 301. NHTSA waf-fled some more and again announced its intentions to promulgate a rear-end collision standard.

Waiting, as it normally does, until the last day allowed for response, Ford filed with NHTSA a gargantuan batch of letters, studies and charts now arguing that the federal testing criteria were unfair. Ford also argued that design changes required to meet the standard would take 43 months, which seemed like a rather long time in light of the fact that the entire Pinto was designed in about two years. Specifically, new complaints about the standard involved the weight of the test vehicle, whether or not the brakes should be engaged at the moment of impact and the claim that the standard should only apply to cars, not trucks or buses. Perhaps the most amusing argument was that the engine should not be idling during crash tests, the rationale being that an idling engine meant that the gas tank had to contain gasoline and that the hot lights needed to film the crash might ignite the gasoline and cause a fire.

Some of these complaints were accepted, others rejected. But they all required examination and testing by a weak-kneed NHTSA, meaning more of those 18-month studies the industry loves so much. So the complaints served their real purpose—delay; all told, an eight-year delay, while Ford manufactured more than three million profitable, dangerously incendiary Pintos. To justify this delay, Henry Ford II called more press conferences to predict the demise of American civilization. "If we can't meet the standards when they are published," he warned, "we will have to close down. And if we have to close down some production because we don't meet standards we're in for real trouble in this country."

⋄◈⋄

While government bureaucrats dragged their feet on lifesaving Standard 301, a different kind of expert was taking a close look at the Pinto—the "recon man." "Recon" stands for reconstruction; recon men reconstruct accidents for police departments, insurance companies and lawyers who want to know exactly who or what caused an accident. It didn't take many rear-end Pinto accidents to demonstrate the weakness of the car. Recon men began encouraging lawyers to look beyond one driver or another to the manufacturer in their search for fault, particularly in the growing number of accidents where passengers were uninjured by collision but were badly burned by fire.

Pinto lawuits began mounting fast against Ford. Says John Versace, executive safety engineer at Ford's Safety Research Center, "Ulcers are running pretty high among the engineers who worked on the Pinto. Every lawyer in the country seems to want to take their depositions." (The Safety Research Center is an impressive glass and concrete building standing by itself about a mile from Ford World Headquarters in Dearborn. Looking at it, one imagines its large staff protects consumers from burned and broken limbs. Not so. The Center is the technical support arm of Jack Echold's 14-person anti-regulatory lobbying team in World Headquarters.)

When the Pinto liability suits began, Ford strategy was to go to a jury. Confident it could hide the Pinto crash tests, Ford thought that juries of solid American registered voters would buy the industry doctrine that drivers, not cars, cause accidents. It didn't work. It seems that juries are much quicker to see the truth than bureaucracies, a fact that gives one confidence in democracy. Juries began ruling against the company, granting million-dollar awards to plaintiffs.

"We'll never go to a jury again," says Al Slechter in Ford's Washington office. "Not in a fire case. Juries are just too sentimental. They see those charred remains and forget the evidence. No sir, we'll settle."

Settlement involves less cash, smaller legal fees and less publicity, but it is an indication of the weakness of their case. Nevertheless, Ford has been settling when it is clear that the company can't pin the blame on the driver of the other car. But, since the company carries $2 million deductible product-liability insurance, these settlements have a direct impact on the bottom line. They must therefore be considered a factor in determining the net operating profit on the

Pinto. It's impossible to get a straight answer from Ford on the profitability of the Pinto and the impact of lawsuit settlements on it—even when you have a curious and mildly irate shareholder call to inquire, as we did. However, financial officer Charles Matthews did admit that the company establishes a reserve for large dollar settlements. He would not divulge the amount of the reserve and had no explanation for its absence from the annual report.

Until recently, it was clear that, whatever the cost of these settlements, it was not enough to seriously cut into the Pinto's enormous profits. The cost of retooling Pinto assembly lines and of equipping each car with a safety gadget like that $5.08 Goodyear bladder was, company accountants calculated, greater than that of paying out millions to survivors like Robbie Carlton or to widows and widowers of victims like Sandra Gillespie. The bottom line ruled, and inflammable Pintos kept rolling out of the factories.

In 1977, however, an incredibly sluggish government has at last instituted Standard 301. Now Pintos will have to have rupture-proof gas tanks. Or will they?

<hr/>

To everyone's surprise, the 1977 Pinto recently passed a rear-end crash test in Phoenix, Arizona, for NHTSA. The agency was so convinced the Pinto would fail that it was the first car tested. Amazingly, it did not burst into flame.

"We have had so many Ford failures in the past," explained agency engineer Tom Grubbs, "I felt sure the Pinto would fail."

How did it pass?

Remember that one-dollar, one-pound plastic baffle that was on one of the three modified Pintos that passed the pre-production crash tests nearly ten years ago? Well, it is a standard feature on the 1977 Pinto. In the Phoenix test it protected the gas tank from being perforated by those four bolts on the differential housing.

We asked Grubbs if he noticed any other substantial alterations in the rear-end structure of the car. "No," he replied, "the [plastic baffle] seems to be the only noticeable change over the 1976 model."

But was it? What Tom Grubbs and the Department of Transportation didn't know when they tested the car was that it was manufactured in St. Thomas, Ontario. Ontario? The significance of that becomes clear when you learn that Canada has for years had extremely strict rear-end collision standards.

Tom Irwin is the business manager of Charlie Rossi Ford, the Scottsdale, Arizona, dealership that sold the Pinto to Tom Grubbs. He refused to explain why he was selling Fords made in Canada when there is a huge Pinto assembly plant much closer by in California. "I know why you're asking that question, and I'm not going to answer it," he blurted out. "You'll have to ask the company."

But Ford's regional office in Phoenix has "no explanation" for the presence of Canadian cars in their local dealerships. Farther up the line in Dearborn, Ford people claim there is absolutely no difference between American and Canadian Pintos. They say cars are shipped back and forth across the border as a matter of course. But they were hard pressed to explain why some Canadian Pintos were shipped all the way to Scottsdale, Arizona. Significantly, one engineer at the St. Thomas plant did admit that the existence of strict rear-end collision standards in Canada "might encourage us to pay a little more attention to quality control on that part of the car."

The Department of Transportation is considering buying an American Pinto and running the test again. For now, it will only say that the situation is under investigation.

ᴇᴬ◉ᴬᴥ

Whether the new American Pinto fails or passes the test, Standard 301 will never force the company to test or recall the more than two million pre-1977 Pintos still on the highway. Seventy or more people will burn to death in those cars every year for many years to come. If the past is any indication, Ford will continue to accept the deaths.

According to safety expert Byron Bloch, the older cars could quite easily be retrofitted with gas tanks containing fuel cells. "These improved tanks would add at least 10 mph improved safety performance to the rear end," he estimated, "but it would cost Ford $20 to $30 a car, so they won't do it unless they are forced to." Dr. Kenneth Saczalski, safety engineer with the Office of Naval Research in Washington, agrees. "The Defense Department has developed virtually fail-safe fuel systems and retrofitted them into existing vehicles. We have shown them to the auto industry and they have ignored them."

Unfortunately, the Pinto is not an isolated case of corporate malpractice in the auto industry. Neither is Ford a lone sinner. There probably isn't a car on the road without a safety hazard known to its manufacturer. And though Ford may have the best auto lobbyists in Washington, it is not alone. The anti-emission control lobby and the anti-safety lobby usually work in chorus form, presenting a well-harmonized message from the country's richest industry, spoken through the voices of individual companies—the Motor Vehicle Manufacturers Association, the Business Council and the U.S. Chamber of Commerce.

Furthermore, cost-valuing human life is not used by Ford alone. Ford was just the only company careless enough to let such an embarrassing calculation slip into the public records. The process of willfully trading lives for profits is built into corporate capitalism. Commodore Vanderbilt publicly scorned George Westinghouse and his "foolish" air brakes while people died by the hundreds in accidents on Vanderbilt's railroads.

The original draft of the Motor Vehicle Safety Act provided for criminal sanction against a manufacturer who willfully placed an unsafe car on the market. Early in the proceedings the auto industry lobbied the provision out of the bill. Since then, there have been those damage settlements, of course, but the only government punishment meted out to auto companies for non-compliance to standards has been a minuscule fine, usually $5,000 to $10,000. One wonders how long the Ford Motor Company would continue to market lethal cars were Henry Ford II and Lee Iacocca serving 20-year terms in Leavenworth for consumer homicide.

Closing Argument by Mr. Neal

If it please the Court, Counsel, ladies and gentlemen:

Not too many years ago our broad American Industry straddled the world like a giant.

It provided us with the highest standards of living ever known to man.

It was ended, eliminated, no more. Now it is an Industry weakened by deteriorating plants and equipment, weakened by lack of products, weakened by lack of manpower, weakened by inadequate capital, weakened by massive Government controls, weakened by demands on foreign oil and reeling from competition from foreign manufacturers.

I stand here today to defend a segment of that tattered Industry.

One company that saw the influx of foreign, small-made cars in 1967 and '68 and tried to do something about it, tried to build a small car with American labor that would compete with foreign imports, that would keep Americans employed, that would keep American money in America.

As State's witness, Mr. Copp, admitted, Ford Motor Company would have made more profit sticking to the bigger cars where the profit is.

That would have been the easiest way.

It was not the way Ford Motor Company took.

It made the Ford to compete. And this is no easy effort, members of the jury.

As even Mr. Copp admitted, the Automobile Industry is extremely regulated.

It has to comply with the Clean Air Act, the Safety Act, the Emissions Control Act, the Corporate Average Fuel Economy Act, the Safety Act, and OSHA as well as a myriad of Statutes and Regulations applicable to large and small businesses generally, and, again, as Mr. Copp admitted, it now takes twice as many Engineers to make a car as it did before all the massive Government controls.

Nevertheless, Ford Motor Company undertook the effort to build a subcompact, to take on the imports, to save jobs for Americans and to make a profit for its stockholders.

This rather admirable effort has a sad ending.

On August 10, 1978, a young man gets into a van weighing over 4,000 pounds and heads towards Elkhart, Indiana, on a bad highway called "U.S. 33."

From U.S. District Court, South Bend, Indiana, *State of Indiana v. Ford Motor Company* (January 15, 1980).

He has a couple of open beer bottles in his van, together with his marijuana which he may or may not have been smoking....

As he was cruising along on an open stretch of highway in broad daylight at at least 50 to 55 miles per hour, he drops his "smoke," ignores his driving and the road, and fails to see a little Pinto with its emergency flashers on stopped on the highway ahead.

He plows into the rear of the Pinto with enormous force and three young girls are killed.

Not the young man, but Ford Motor Company is charged with reckless homicide and arraigned before you.

I stand here to defend Ford Motor Company, and to tell you that we are not killers....

Mr. Cosentino gave you the definition of "reckless homicide" as "plain, conscious and unjustifiable disregard of harm, which conduct involves substantial deviation from acceptable standards of conduct."

This case and the elements of this case, strictly speaking, involve 40 days, July 1, 1978 to August 10, 1978, and the issue is whether, during that period of time, Ford Motor Company recklessly, as that term is defined, omitted to warn of a danger and repair, and that reckless omission caused the deaths involved....

[I]n my opening statement, I asked you to remember nine points, and I asked you to judge me, my client, by how well or how poorly we supported those nine points.

Let me run through briefly and just tick them off, the nine points, with you, and then let me get down to discussing the evidence and record with respect to those nine points.

One, I said this was a badly-designed highway, with curbs so high the girls couldn't get off when they had to stop their car in an emergency.

Two, I said that the girls stopped there with their emergency flashers on, and this boy in a van weighing more than 4,000 pounds, with his eyes off the road, looking down trying to find the "smoke," rammed into the rear of that Pinto at at least 50 miles an hour, closing speed.

And by "closing speed," I mean the differential speed.

That is Points 1 and 2.

Point 3, I said the 1973 Pinto met every fuel-system integrity standard of any Federal, State or Local Government.

Point No. 4, I said, Ford Motor Company adopted a mandatory standard dealing with fuel-system integrity on rear-impact of 20 miles per hour moving-barrier, 4,000 pound moving-barrier, and I said that no other manufacturer in the world had adopted any standard, only Ford Motor Company.

Five, I said that the Pinto, it is not comparable to a Lincoln Continental, a Cadillac, a Mercedes Benz or that Ascona, or whatever that exotic car was that Mr. Bloch called—but I did say No. 5, it is comparable to other 1973 subcompacts.

No. 6, I said that... we would bring in the Engineers who designed and manufactured the Pinto, and I brought them from the stand, and they would tell you that they thought the Pinto was a good, safe car, and they bought it for themselves, their wives and their children to drive.

No. 7, I told you that we would bring in the statistics that indicated to us as to our state of mind that the Pinto performed as well or better than other subcompacts.

And, No. 8, I said we would nevertheless tell you that we decided to recall the Pinto in June of 1978, and having made that decision for the reasons that I—that I told you I would explain, we did everything in our power to recall that Pinto as quickly as possible, that there was nothing we could have done between July 1, 1978 and 8-10-1978, to recall the Pinto any faster.

And finally, No. 9, I said we would demonstrate that any car, any subcompact, any small car, and even some larger cars, sitting out there on Highway 33 in the late afternoon of August 10, 1978 and watching that van roar down that highway with the boy looking for his "smoke"—any car would have suffered the same consequences.

Those are the nine points I ask you to judge me by, and let me touch on the evidence, now, with respect to those nine points. . . .

The van driver, Duggar, took his eyes off the road and off driving to look around the floor of the van for a "smoke."

Duggar had two open beer bottles in the car and a quantity of marijuana.

Duggar was not prosecuted for reckless homicide or for possession of marijuana, even though his prior record of conviction was:

November, '73, failure to yield right-of-way;

April, '76, speeding 65 miles an hour in a 45 mile an hour zone;

July, '76, running stop sign;

June, '77, speeding 45 in a 25 zone;

August, '77, driver's license suspended;

September, '77, driving with suspended license;

December, '77, license suspended again.

Mr. Cosentino, you got up in front of this jury and you cried.

Well, I cry, too, because Mr. Duggar is driving, and you didn't do anything about him with a record like that except say, "Come in and help me convict Ford Motor Company, and I will help you get probation."

We all cry.

But crying doesn't do any good, and it doesn't help this jury.

The big disputed fact in this case regarding the accident, ladies and gentlemen, is the closing speed. The differential speed, the difference between the speed the Pinto was going, if any, and the speed the van was going.

That is the big disputed fact in regard to this accident.

And whether the Pinto was stopped or not is relevant only as it affects closing speed. . . .

Mr. Duggar testified—I guess he is great about speed, because while he's looking down there for his "smoke," he knows he is going 50 miles per hour in the van.

But he said he was going 50 miles per hour at the time of impact, and he said the Pinto was going 15.

But here is the same man who admits he was going at least 50 miles per hour and looking around down "on a clear day," trying to find the "smoke" and looked up only to see the Pinto ten feet ahead of him.

Here is a witness willing to say under oath that the Pinto was going 15 miles per hour, even though he had one-sixth of a second—one-sixth of a second to make the judgment on the speed.

Here is a witness who says he had the time to calculate the speed of the Pinto but had no time even to try to apply brakes because there were no skid marks.

And here is a witness who told Dr. Galen Miller, who testified here, that—told him right after the accident that in fact the Pinto was stopped.

And here was a witness who made a deal with the State.

And here was a witness who's not prosecuted for recklessness.

And here is a witness who is not prosecuted for possession of marijuana.

So the State's proof from Mr. Alfred Clark through Mr. Duggar is kind of a smorgasbord or a buffet—you can go in and take your choice.

You can pick 15—5 miles per hour, if you want to as to differential speed, or you can take 35 miles per hour.

And the State, with the burden of proof says, "Here," "Here," "Here. I will give you a lot of choice."

"You want choices? I will give you choices. Here. Take 5. Take 15. 10, 15, 20, 25, 30, 35."

Because, ladies and gentlemen of the jury,—and I'm sure you are—the alternatives the State offers you are closing speeds of anywhere from 5 miles—on the low side—to 35 miles on the high side as a differential speed in this accident. . . .

Mr. Toms, the former National Highway Traffic Safety Administrator, told you that in his opinion the 20 mile per hour rear-impact moving-barrier was a reasonable and acceptable standard of conduct for 1973 vehicles.

Why didn't Ford adopt a higher standard?

Mr. MacDonald, a man even Mr. Copp—do you remember this? Mr. MacDonald sitting on the stand, the father of the Pinto, as Mr. Cosentino called him—and he didn't deny it.

He says, "Yes, it is my car."

Mr. MacDonald, a man even Mr. Copp—on cross examination I asked him, I said:

"Q Mr. Copp, isn't it a fact that you consider Harold MacDonald an extremely safety-conscious Engineer?"

And he said:

"A Yes, sir."

Mr. MacDonald, that extremely safety-conscious Engineer, told you he did not believe a higher standard could be met for 1973 cars without greater problems, such as handling, where more accidents and death occur.

Mr. Copp, let's take the State's witness, Copp.

Mr. Copp admitted that even today, seven years later, the Federal Government Standard is only 30 miles per hour, 10 miles higher than what Ford adopted—voluntarily adopted for itself for 1973.

And Mr. Copp further testified that a 30 mile an hour would be equivalent only to a 31.5 or 32 mile car-to-car.

So, ladies and gentlemen of the jury, Mr. Cosentino tells you about, "Oh, isn't it terrible to put these cars out there, wasn't it awful—did you know?"

Well, do you know that today, the—today, 1980 model cars are required to meet only a 30 mile an hour rear-impact moving-barrier standard? 1980 cars.

And that that is equivalent to a 32 mile an hour car-to-car, and yet Ford Motor Company, the only company in the world, imposed upon itself a standard and made a car in 1973, seven years ago, that would meet 26 to 28 miles an hour, within 5, 6 or 7 miles of what the cars are required by law to meet today.

Mr. Cosentino will tell you, frankly, the cars today, in his judgment, are defective and he will prosecute.

What a chaos would evolve if the Government set the standard for automobiles and says, "That is reasonable," and then Local Prosecutors in the fifty states around the country start saying, "I am not satisfied, and I am going to prosecute the manufacturer."

Well, Mr. Cosentino may say that the standard should be 40.

The Prosecutor in Alabama may say, "No, it should be 50."

The Prosecutor in Alaska may say, "No, it should be 60."

And the Prosecutor in Tennessee—they say—you know, "I am satisifed—I am satisfied with 30," or, "I think it should be 70."

How can our companies survive?

Point 5, the 1973 Pinto was comparable in design and manufacture to other 1973 subcompacts.

I say again, ladies and gentlemen, we don't compare the Pinto with Lincolns, Cadillacs, Mercedes Benz—we ask you to compare the Pinto with the other three subcompacts.

Let's take the State's witnesses on this point first.

Mr. Bloch—Mr. Cosentino didn't mention Mr. Bloch, but I don't want him to be forgotten.

Mr. Bloch and Mr. Copp complain about the Pinto, and that is easy.

Let's descend to the particulars. Let's see what they really said.

Well, they complain about the metal, the gage of the metal in the fuel tank; you remember that?

And then on cross examination it was brought out that the general range of metal in fuel tanks ranged between twenty-three-thousandths of an inch and forty-thousandths of an inch.

That is the general range. Twenty-three-thousandths on the low to forty-thousandths on the high, and lo and behold, what is the gage of metal in the Pinto tank?

Thirty-five-thousandths.

And Mr. Bloch admits that it is in the upper third of the general range.

And they complain about the bumper on the Pinto.

And, remember, I said we would show that the Pinto was comparable to other '73 subcompacts.

They complain about the bumper, but then they admit on cross examination the Vega, the Gremlin, the Colt, the Pinto and the Toyota had about the same bumper.

And they complain of a lack of a protective shield between the tank and the axle, but they admitted on cross examination that no other 1973 car had such a shield, and Mr. Copp admits that there was no significant puncture in the 1973—in the Ulrich accident caused by the axle, and you remember I had him get up here and say, "Point out where this protective shield would have done something, where this puncture source we are talking about—" and you remember, it is so small—I can't find it now.

So much for the protective shield.

And then they complained about the insufficient rear structure in the Pinto, but they both admit that the Pinto had a left side rail hat section and that the Vega had none, nothing on either side, that the Pinto had shear plates, these plates in the trunk, and that neither the Vega, the Gremlin or the Colt or Toyota had any of these.

And the Vega used the coil-spring suspension, when the Pinto had a leaf-spring, and that was additional structure.

I am not going through all those—well, I will mention one more thing.

They talked about puncture sources, there is a puncture source there, puncture source here, but on cross examination, they end up by admitting that the puncture sources on all subcompacts have about the same—and in about the same space. . . .

Mr. MacDonald testified, "Yes, I thought the Pinto was a reasonably safe car. I think the '73 Pinto is still a reasonably safe car, and I bought one, I drove it for years for myself."

Mr. Olsen—you remember little Mr. Frank Olsen?

He came in here, has his little eighteen-year-old daughter—he said, "I am an Engineer responsible for the Pinto. I think it is a safe car. I bought one for my little eighteen-year-old daughter, and she drove it for several years."

And Mr. Freers, the man who Mr. Cosentino objected to going over the fact that he was from Rose-Hullman, and on the Board of Trustees there—Mr. Freers said, "I like the Pinto. I am an Engineer responsible for the Pinto, and I bought a '73 Pinto for my young son and he drove it several years."

And then Mr. Feaheny says, "I am one of the Engineers responsible for the Pinto, and I bought one for my wife, the mother of my six children, and she drove it for several years."

Now, when Mr. Cosentino tried to say there was something phoney about that—he brought out their salaries.

And I—I don't know how to deal with the salary question.

It just seems to me to be so irrelevant, like some other things I am going to talk about in a minute that I am just going to simply say, "It is irrelevant," and go on.

But he said to these people—he suggested to you, suggested to these people, "Well, you make a lot of money, you can afford better than a Pinto."

Like, "You don't really mean you had a Pinto?"

And Mr. Feaheny says, "Yes, I could afford a more expensive car, but, you know, I—all of us, we have been fighting, we come out with something we thought would fight the imports, and we were proud of it, and our families were proud of it."

Do you think, ladies and gentlemen of the jury, that Mr. MacDonald was indifferent, reckless, when he bought and drove the Pinto?

He drives on the same roads, he has the—subject to the same reckless people that Mr. Cosentino didn't prosecute.

Do you think that Mr. Olsen was reckless and indifferent when he gave a Pinto to his eighteen-year-old daughter, a '73 Pinto?

Do you think that Mr. Freers was reckless when he gave one to his young son? . . .

Finally, ladies and gentlemen—not "finally," but Point No. 8: Notwithstanding all I have said, Ford Motor Company decided on June 8th, 1978, to recall the Pintos to improve fuel systems and did everything in its power to recall it as quickly as possible.

This is really what this case, I guess, is all about, because that period of time involved is July 1, 1978 until August 10, 1978.

And the Court will charge you, as I said, the elements are whether we recklessly failed to warn and repair during that period of time.

And whether that reckless omission, if any, caused the deaths.

And you may ask—and I think it is fair to ask—why recall the Pinto, the '73 Pinto, if it is comparable to other subcompacts, if statistics say it is performing as well as other '73 subcompacts?

And if Ford had a standard for '73 that no other manufacturer had?

And Feaheny and Mr. Misch told you why.

The Federal Government started an investigation. The publicity was hurting the Company.

They thought the Government was wrong, but they said, "You can't fight City Hall."

"We could fight and fight and we could go to Court and we could fight, but it's not going to get us anywhere. If we can improve it, let's do it and let's don't fight the Federal Government."

Maybe the Company should not have recalled the '73 Pinto.

Douglas Toms did not think, as he told you on the stand under oath, that the '73 Pinto should have been recalled.

He had information that the Pinto did as well as other cars;

That Pinto fire accidents equaled the total Pinto population or equaled the percentage of Pinto population to all car population.

And Mr. Bloch, on the other hand, says, "All of them should be recalled."

He said, "The Pinto should have been recalled."

He said, "The Vega should have been recalled."

He said, "The Gremlin should be recalled."

And he didn't know about the Dodge Colt.

Nevertheless, the Company did decide to recall the Pinto. And they issued widely-disseminated Press Releases on June 9, 1978.

It was in the newspapers, TV, radio, according to the proof in this case.

And thereafter the Government regulated what they did in the recall.

That is what Mr. Misch told you.

He said, "From the time we started—June 9, 1978—to August 10, Mr.—the Federal Government regulated what we did."

Now, Mr. Cosentino is prosecuting us.

And the Federal Government has regulated us.

Mr. Misch said, "The Federal Government reviewed what kind of Press Releases we should issue, what kind of Recall Letter we should issue, what kind of a Modification Kit that they would approve."

Even so—it is undisputed, absolutely undisputed that we did everything in our power to recall as fast as possible—nights, days, weekends.

And notwithstanding all of that, the first kit—the first complete kit was assembled August 1, 1978.

And on August 9, 1978, there were only 20,000 kits available for 1,600,000 cars.

And this was not Ford's fault. Ford was pushing the suppliers, the people who were outside the Company doing work for them.

And Mr. Vasher testified that he got the names of the current owners from R. L. Polk on July 17;

That the Ulrich name was not among them;

That he sent the Recall Letter in August to the original owner because he had no Ulrich name.

Now,—and he said he couldn't have gotten the Ulrich name by August 10.

Now, Mr. Cosentino said, "Well, the Ulrich Registration was on file with the State of Indiana and it is open to the public."

Well, Ford Motor Company doesn't know where these 1,600,000 cars are. It has to use R. L. Polk because they collect the information by the VIN Numbers.

If Ford Motor Company went to each state, they would go to fifty states and they would have each of the fifty states run through its files 1,600,000 VIN Numbers.

And Mr. Vasher, who is the expert in there, said it would take months and months to do that.

And, finally, ladies and gentlemen, the Government didn't approve the Modification Kit until August 15, 1978.

But the State says that we should have warned—we should have warned 1973 Pinto owners not to drive the car.

But the Government never suggested that.

Based on our information, and confirmed by the Toms testimony, our cars were performing as well—or better than—other '73 subcompacts.

As Mr. Misch so succinctly stated, "We would have been telling the Pinto owners to park their Pintos and get into another car no safer—and perhaps even less safe—than the Pinto." . . .

Well, we submit that the physical facts, the placement of the—the placement of the gasoline cap, where it is found, the testimony of Levi Woodard, and Nancy Fogo—demonstrate the closing speed in this case was at least 50 to 60 miles per hour.

Mr. Copp, the State's witness, testified that no small car made in America in 1973 would withstand 40 to 50 miles per hour—40 to 50 rear-impact. No small car made in America in 1973 would withstand a 40-plus mile per hour rear-impact.

The Dodge Colt would not have; the Vega could not have; the Gremlin would not have; and certainly even the Toyota would not have.

Mr. Habberstad told you that no small car—and some big cars—would have withstood this crash.

And he established by the crash-tests you have seen that the Vega could not withstand 50;

That the Gremlin could not withstand 50;

That the Toyota Corolla with the tank over the axle could not withstand 50;

And that even a full-sized Chevrolet Impala cannot withstand 50 miles per hour.

If it made no difference what kind of car was out there, members of the jury, how can Ford Motor Company have caused the deaths? . . .

I am not here to tell you that the 1973 Pinto was the strongest car ever built.

I'm not here to tell you it is equal to a Lincoln, a Cadillac, a Mercedes— that funny car that Mr. Bloch mentioned.

I'm not here to tell you a stronger car couldn't be built.

Most of us, however, learn early in life that there is "no Santa Claus," and, "There's no such thing as a free lunch."

If the public wanted it, and could pay for it, and we had the gasoline to drive it, Detroit could build a tank of a car—a car that would withstand practically anything, a car that would float if a careless driver drove it into the water.

A car that would be invulnerable even to the "Duggars" of the world.

But, members of the jury, only the rich could afford it and they would have to stop at every other gasoline station for a refill.

I am here to tell you that the 1973 Pinto is comparable to other '73 subcompacts, including that Toyota, that Corolla with the tank over the axle.

I am here to tell you it was not designed by some mysterious figure you have never seen.

It was designed and manufactured by Harold MacDonald, Frank Olsen and Howard Freers.

I am here to tell you these are the decent men doing an honorable job and trying to do a decent job.

I am here to tell you that Harold MacDonald, Frank Olsen, and Howard Freers are not reckless killers.

Harold MacDonald is the same man, State's witness, Copp, called an "extremely safety-conscious individual."

Frank Olsen is the same "Frank Olsen" Mr. Copp said was a "good Engineer."

And Howard Freers is the same "Howard Freers" Mr. Copp said was a "man of honesty and integrity."

I am here to tell you that these men honestly believe and honestly believed that the 1973 Pinto was—and is—a reasonably safe car—so safe they bought it for their daughters, sons and family.

Do you think that Frank Olsen believed he was acting in plain, conscious, unjustifiable disregard of harm?

When he bought a '73 Pinto for his eighteen-year-old daughter?

Or Howard Freers, when he bought one for his young son?

I am here to tell you that the design and manufacture of an automobile is not an easy task;

That it takes time to know whether a change in one part of the 14,000 parts of a car will or will not cause greater problems elsewhere in the car or its performance.

I am here to tell you that safety is a matter of degree;

That no one can say that a car that will meet a 26 to 28 mile per hour rear-impact is unsafe and one that will meet a 30 to 32 impact is safe.

I am here to tell you that if this country is to survive economically, it is really time to stop blaming Industry or Business, large or small, for our own sins.

I am here to tell you that no car is now or ever can be safe when reckless drivers are on the road.

I am here to tell you that Ford Motor Company may not be perfect, but it is not guilty of reckless homicide.

Thank you, members of the jury.

And God bless you in your deliberations.

POSTSCRIPT

Product Liability: Was Ford to Blame in the Pinto Case?

Was Ford guilty? The jury said no, but the larger issue remains: Who takes responsibility when many factors combine to bring about an injury?

Consider the following: Ford Motor Company obeyed the law, but the law may not have been all that it *should* have been. The reason for this is that the Ford Motor Company spent a great deal of money lobbying Congress to prevent the release of new and higher legal safety standards in order to be able to sell the Pinto for a lower price and thus increase its market share and its profits. Is the government, through its agencies, guilty for not fulfilling its role as protector of the consumer? Does government have some absolute duty in these cases, or are legislators asked only to bring about the greatest good for the greatest number?

Ford Motor Company found new structural allies when the criminal negligence case was brought against it. Under the U.S. Constitution, the legal system tends to protect the defendant in these cases. The tradition in the United States is to protect the rights of the individual against the interests of the community. In this case, the "individual" was one of the largest corporations in the world. However, legal traditions held true, and the rights of Ford were supported when the company was acquitted.

Manufacturers know how to make a safe car. They *could* build one like a tank and rig it to go no faster than 30 miles per hour, but very few people would buy it. So they make relatively unsafe cars that people will buy—lighter and faster, but more likely to crumple and burn in an accident. Is this trade-off acceptable to a nation that is used to making choices? Or should we be more diligent about eliminating threats to safety?

Suggested Readings

Lawrence A. Benningson and Arnold I. Benningson, "Product Liability: Manufacturers Beware!" *Harvard Business Review* (May–June 1974).

Richard T. DeGeorge, "Ethical Responsibilities of Engineers in Large Organizations: The Pinto Case," *Business and Professional Ethics Journal* (Fall 1981).

Richard A. Epstein, "Is Pinto a Criminal?" *Regulation* (March–April 1980).

On the Internet ...

Business Cycle Indicators

This site leads to the 256 data series known as the U.S. Business Cycle Indicators, which are used to track and predict U.S. business activity. The subjects of the data groups are clearly listed.

http://www.globalexposure.com

Voice of the Shuttle: Postindustrial Business Theory Page

This site links to a variety of resources on many subjects related to business theory, including restructuring, reengineering, downsizing, flattening, the team concept, outsourcing, business and globalism, human resources management, labor relations, statistics, and history, as well as information and resources on job searches, careers, working from home, and business start-ups.

http://vos.ucsb.edu/shuttle/commerce.html

Society, Religion and Technology Project

This is the home page on patenting living organisms of the Society, Religion and Technology Project (SRT) of the Church of Scotland. It provides a simple introduction to the issues involved, other SRT pages on patenting, and links to related pages.

http://dialspace.dial.pipex.com/town/terrace/
aa244/scsunpat.htm

TobaccoLeaf

TobaccoLeaf is the Web site of the International Tobacco Growers' Association, which is composed of thousands of tobacco farmers from all over the world. This site offers facts and figures about the production of tobacco as well as the economic and social importance of tobacco in many developed and developing countries.

http://www.tobaccoleaf.org/index.htm

PART 5

International Operations: Global Obligations

*M*ultinational businesses are driving a massive and unprecedented process of globalization. What obligations can they be held to in a world where capitalism has apparently triumphed? This section considers whether or not multinational corporations can be held responsible for conditions in their factories in the developing world and whether or not there are limits on the products that companies should be developing and exporting abroad.

- Are Multinational Corporations Free from Moral Obligations?

- Are Sweatshops Necessarily Evil?

- Should Patenting Life Be Forbidden?

- Should We Encourage International Trade in Tobacco Products?

- Should We Export Pesticides to Developing Nations?

ISSUE 13

Are Multinational Corporations Free from Moral Obligations?

YES: Manuel Velasquez, from "International Business, Morality and the Common Good," *Business Ethics Quarterly* (January 1992)

NO: John E. Fleming, from "Alternative Approaches and Assumptions: Comments on Manuel Velasquez," *Business Ethics Quarterly* (January 1992)

ISSUE SUMMARY

YES: Professor of business ethics Manuel Velasquez doubts that, in the absence of accepted enforcement agencies, any multinational corporation will suffer for violating rules that restrict business for the sake of the common good. He argues that since any business that tried to conform to moral rules in the absence of enforcement would cease to be competitive, moral strictures cannot be binding on such companies.

NO: Professor emeritus John E. Fleming asserts that multinational corporations tend to deal with long-term customers and suppliers in the goldfish bowl of international media and must therefore adhere to moral standards or lose business.

This issue is a complex one with many gray areas.

In the first selection, for example, Manuel Velasquez perceives the issue to be between the Hobbesian realists (those who adhere to the philosophies of Thomas Hobbes), who value the bottom line above all else, and those who believe that high moral thoughts influence world affairs. Velasquez concludes that a Hobbesian realist, knowing the worst about human nature, must acknowledge that moral obligations simply do not apply in the absence of moral community. John E. Fleming does not counter Velasquez's argument in the tone of lofty idealism but in that of a practitioner who has to keep an enterprise afloat from day to day. He concludes that the only way to serve the bottom line is through moral behavior.

Second, Velasquez perceives right action to be on trial. He asks, Can morality justify itself with regard to profit? Can we show that acting for the common good will not damage the profit picture or detract from the increase in shareholder wealth? If not, Velasquez suggests, then we will have to forgo morality. Fleming seems to say that right action is compatible with (in fact, necessary for) the health of the bottom line and the corporate enterprise in general. If Fleming is right, then the major premise of Hobbesian capitalism—that the sole social responsibility of business is to increase its profits—may be unworkable. Any activity that might be expected to follow from the injunction to serve the bottom line and increase profits, activity in total disregard of the moral persuasions of all others in society, may result in lost business, leaving shareholders with valueless promises.

Third, according to both Velasquez and Fleming, the dispute is over human behavior in business situations—both about the way humans *will* behave and the way they *should* behave. Both authors condition their predictions and advice on the nature of the international business community. Fleming claims that the international business scene is not at all how Velasquez portrays it—strangers interacting in strange lands on a one-time basis only—but is a place of custom, regular habits, and familiar people, where memories are long, word gets around, and tolerance for being taken advantage of is very low.

As you read the following selections, consider how international dealings differ from domestic dealings. Aren't folks abroad rather like folks at home, with just a few differences in manners? What are the real controls on human behavior—enforcement of laws or the simple social expectations of peers and colleagues?

Manuel Velasquez

International Business, Morality and the Common Good

During the last few years an increasing number of voices have urged that we pay more attention to ethics in international business, on the grounds that not only are all large corporations now internationally structured and thus engaging in international transactions, but that even the smallest domestic firm is increasingly buffeted by the pressures of international competition....

Can we say that businesses operating in a competitive international environment have any moral obligations to contribute to the international common good, particularly in light of realist objections? Unfortunately, my answer to this question will be in the negative....

International Business

... When speaking of international business, I have in mind a particular kind of organization: the multinational corporation. Multinational corporations have a number of well known features, but let me briefly summarize a few of them. First, multinational corporations are businesses and as such they are organized primarily to increase their profits within a competitive environment. Virtually all of the activities of a multinational corporation can be explained as more or less rational attempts to achieve this dominant end. Secondly, multinational corporations are bureaucratic organizations. The implication of this is that the identity, the fundamental structure, and the dominant objectives of the corporation endure while the many individual human beings who fill the various offices and positions within the corporation come and go. As a consequence, the particular values and aspirations of individual members of the corporation have a relatively minimal and transitory impact on the organization as a whole. Thirdly, and most characteristically, multinational corporations operate in several nations. This has several implications. First, because the multinational is not confined to a single nation, it can easily escape the reach of the laws of any particular nation by simply moving its resources or operations out of one nation and transferring them to another nation. Second, because the multinational is not confined to a single nation, its interests are not aligned with the interests of any single nation. The ability of the multinational to achieve its

From Manuel Velasquez, "International Business, Morality and the Common Good," *Business Ethics Quarterly* (January 1992). Copyright © 1992 by *Business Ethics Quarterly*. Reprinted by permission of The Philosophy Documentation Center, publisher of *Business Ethics Quarterly*. Notes omitted.

profit objectives does not depend upon the ability of any particular nation to achieve its own domestic objectives. . . .

The Traditional Realist Objection in Hobbes

The realist objection, of course, is the standard objection to the view that agents —whether corporations, governments, or individuals—have moral obligations on the international level. Generally, the realist holds that it is a mistake to apply moral concepts to international activities: morality has no place in international affairs. The classical statement of this view, which I am calling the "traditional" version of realism, is generally attributed to Thomas Hobbes. . . .

In its Hobbsian form, as traditionally interpreted, the realist objection holds that moral concepts have no meaning in the absence of an agency powerful enough to guarantee that other agents generally adhere to the tenets of morality. Hobbes held, first, that in the absence of a sovereign power capable of forcing men to behave civilly with each other, men are in "the state of nature," a state he characterizes as a "war . . . of every man, against every man." Secondly, Hobbes claimed, in such a state of war, moral concepts have no meaning:

> To this war of every man against every man, this also is consequent; that nothing can be unjust. The notions of right and wrong, justice and injustice have there no place. Where there is no common power, there is no law: where no law, no injustice.

Moral concepts are meaningless, then, when applied to state of nature situations. And, Hobbes held, the international arena is a state of nature, since there is no international sovereign that can force agents to adhere to the tenets of morality.

The Hobbsian objection to talking about morality in international affairs, then, is based on two premises: (1) an ethical premise about the applicability of moral terms and (2) an apparently empirical premise about how agents behave under certain conditions. The ethical premise, at least in its Hobbsian form, holds that there is a connection between the meaningfulness of moral terms and the extent to which agents adhere to the tenets of morality: If in a given situation agents do not adhere to the tenets of morality, then in that situation moral terms have no meaning. The apparently empirical premise holds that in the absence of a sovereign, agents will not adhere to the tenets of morality: they will be in a state of war. This appears to be an empirical generalization about the extent to which agents adhere to the tenets of morality in the absence of a third-party enforcer. Taken together, the two premises imply that in situations that lack a sovereign authority, such as one finds in many international exchanges, moral terms have no meaning and so moral obligations are nonexistent. . . .

Revising the Realist Objection: The First Premise

. . . The neo-Hobbsian or realist . . . might want to propose this premise: When one is in a situation in which others do not adhere to certain tenets of morality, and when adhering to those tenets of morality will put one at a significant competitive disadvantage, then it is not immoral for one to like-wise fail to adhere to them. The realist might want to argue for this claim, first, by pointing out that in a world in which all are competing to secure significant benefits and avoid significant costs, and in which others do not adhere to the ordinary tenets of morality, one risks significant harm to one's interests if one continues to adhere to those tenets of morality. But no one can be morally required to take on major risks of harm to oneself. Consequently, in a competitive world in which others disregard moral constraints and take any means to advance their self-interests, no one can be morally required to take on major risks of injury by adopting the restraints of ordinary morality.

A second argument the realist might want to advance would go as follows. When one is in a situation in which others do not adhere to the ordinary tenets of morality, one is under heavy competitive pressures to do the same. And, when one is under such pressures, one cannot be blamed—i.e., one is excused —for also failing to adhere to the ordinary tenets of morality. One is excused because heavy pressures take away one's ability to control oneself, and thereby diminish one's moral culpability.

Yet a third argument advanced by the realist might go as follows. When one is in a situation in which others do not adhere to the ordinary tenets of morality it is not fair to require one to continue to adhere to those tenets, especially if doing so puts one at a significant competitive disadvantage. It is not fair because then one is laying a burden on one party that the other parties refuse to carry.

Thus, there are a number of arguments that can be given in defense of the revised Hobbsian ethical premise that when others do not adhere to the tenets of morality, it is not immoral for one to do likewise. . . .

Revising the Realist Objection: The Second Premise

Let us turn, to the other premise in the Hobbsian argument, the assertion that in the absence of a sovereign, agents will be in a state of war. As I mentioned, this is an apparently empirical claim about the extent to which agents will adhere to the tenets of morality in the absence of a third-party enforcer.

Hobbes gives a little bit of empirical evidence for this claim. He cites several examples of situations in which there is no third party to enforce civility and where, as a result, individuals are in a "state of war." Generalizing from these few examples, he reaches the conclusion that in the absence of a third-party enforcer, agents will always be in a "condition of war." . . .

Recently, the Hobbsian claim . . . has been defended on the basis of some of the theoretical claims of game theory, particularly of the prisoner's dilemma. Hobbes' state of nature, the defense goes, is an instance of a prisoner's dilemma, and *rational* agents in a Prisoner's Dilemma necessarily would choose not to adhere to a set of moral norms. . . .

A Prisoner's Dilemma is a situation involving at least two individuals. Each individual is faced with two choices: he can cooperate with the other individual or he can choose not to cooperate. If he cooperates and the other individual also cooperates, then he gets a certain payoff. If, however, he chooses not to cooperate, while the other individual trustingly cooperates, the noncooperator gets a larger payoff while the cooperator suffers a loss. And if both choose not to cooperate, then both get nothing.

It is a commonplace now that in a Prisoner's Dilemma situation, the most rational strategy for a participant is to choose not to cooperate. For the other party will either cooperate or not cooperate. If the other party cooperates, then it is better for one not to cooperate and thereby get the larger payoff. On the other hand, if the other party does not cooperate, then it is also better for one not to cooperate and thereby avoid a loss. In either case, it is better for one to not cooperate.

... In Hobbes' state of nature each individual must choose either to cooperate with others by adhering to the rules of morality (like the rule against theft), or to not cooperate by disregarding the rules of morality and attempting to take advantage of those who are adhering to the rules (e.g., by stealing from them). In such a situation it is more rational ... to choose not to cooperate. For the other party will either cooperate or not cooperate. If the other party does not cooperate, then one puts oneself at a competitive disadvantage if one adheres to morality while the other party does not. On the other hand, if the other party chooses to cooperate, then one can take advantage of the other party by breaking the rules of morality at his expense. In either case, it is moral rational to not cooperate.

Thus, the realist can argue that in a state of nature, where there is no one to enforce compliance with the rules of morality, it is more rational from the individual's point of view to choose not to comply with morality than to choose to comply. Assuming—and this is obviously a critical assumption—that agents behave rationally, then we can conclude that agents in a state of nature will choose not to comply with the tenets of ordinary morality....

Can we claim that it is clear that multinationals have a moral obligation to pursue the global common good in spite of the objections of the realist?

I do not believe that this claim can be made. We can conclude from the discussion of the realist objection that the Hobbsian claim about the pervasiveness of amorality in the international sphere is false when (1) interactions among international agents are repetitive in such a way that agents can retaliate against those who fail to cooperate, and (2) agents can determine the trustworthiness of other international agents.

But unfortunately, multinational activities often take place in a highly competitive arena in which these two conditions do not obtain. Moreover, these conditions are noticeably absent in the arena of activities that concern the global common good.

First, as I have noted, the common good consists of goods that are indivisible and accessible to all. This means that such goods are susceptible to the free rider problems. Everyone has access to such goods whether or not they do their part in maintaining such goods, so everyone is tempted to free ride on the generosity of others. Now governments can force domestic companies to do their part to maintain the national common good. Indeed, it is one of the functions of government to solve the free rider problem by forcing all to contribute to the domestic common good to which all have access. Moreover, all companies have to interact repeatedly with their host governments, and this leads them to adopt a cooperative stance toward their host government's objective of achieving the domestic common good.

But it is not clear that governments can or will do anything effective to force multinationals to do their part to maintain the global common good. For the governments of individual nations can themselves be free riders, and can join forces with willing multinationals seeking competitive advantages over others. Let me suggest an example. It is clear that a livable global environment is part of the global common good, and it is clear that the manufacture and use of chlorofluorocarbons is destroying that good. Some nations have responded by requiring their domestic companies to cease manufacturing or using chlorofluorocarbons. But other nations have refused to do the same, since they will share in any benefits that accrue from the restraint others practice, and they can also reap the benefits of continuing to manufacture and use chlorofluorocarbons. Less developed nations, in particular, have advanced the position that since their development depends heavily on exploiting the industrial benefits of chlorofluorocarbons, they cannot afford to curtail their use of these substances. Given this situation, it is open to multinationals to shift their operations to those countries that continue to allow the manufacture and use of chlorofluorocarbons. For multinationals, too, will reason that they will share in any benefits that accrue from the restraint others practice, and that they can meanwhile reap the profits of continuing to manufacture and use chlorofluorocarbons in a world where other companies are forced to use more expensive technologies. Moreover, those nations that practice restraint cannot force all such multinationals to discontinue the manufacture or use of chlorofluorocarbons because many multinationals can escape the reach of their laws. An exactly parallel, but perhaps even more compelling, set of considerations can be advanced to show that at least some multinationals will join forces with some developing countries to circumvent any global efforts made to control the global warming trends (the so-called "greenhouse effect") caused by the heavy use of fossil fuels.

The realist will conclude, of course, that in such situations, at least some multinationals will seek to gain competitive advantages by failing to contribute to the global common good (such as the good of a hospitable global environment). For multinationals and rational agents, i.e., agents bureaucratically structured to take rational means toward achieving their dominant end of increasing their profits. And in a competitive environment, contributing to the common good while others do not, will fail to achieve this dominant end. Joining this conclusion to the ethical premise that when others do not adhere to the requirements of morality it is not immoral for one to do likewise, the realist can conclude that multinationals are not morally obligated to contribute to such global common goods (such as environmental goods).

Moreover, global common goods often create interactions that are not iterated. This is particularly the case where the global environment is concerned. As I have already noted, preservation of a favorable global climate is clearly part of the global common good. Now the failure of the global climate will be a one-time affair. The breakdown of the ozone layer, for example, will happen once, with catastrophic consequences for us all; and the heating up of the global climate as a result of the infusion of carbon dioxide will happen once, with catastrophic consequences for us all. Because these environmental disasters are a one-time affair, they represent a non-iterated prisoner's dilemma for multinationals. It is irrational from an individual point of view for a multinational to choose to refrain from polluting the environment in such cases. Either others will refrain, and then one can enjoy the benefits of their refraining; or others will not refrain, and then it will be better to have also not refrained since refraining would have made little difference and would have entailed heavy losses.

Finally, we must also note that although natural persons may signal their reliability to other natural persons, it is not at all obvious that multinationals can do the same. As noted above, multinationals are bureaucratic organizations whose members are continually changing and shifting. The natural persons who make up an organization can signal their reliability to others, but such persons are soon replaced by others, and they in turn are replaced by others. What endures is each organization's single-minded pursuit of increasing its profits in a competitive environment. And an enduring commitment to the pursuit of profit in a competitive environment is not a signal of an enduring commitment to morality.

John E. Fleming

 **NO**

Alternative Approaches and Assumptions: Comments on Manuel Velasquez

Introduction

I feel that Professor Velasquez has written a very interesting and thought-provoking paper on an important topic. His initial identification with a "strong notion of the common good" raises the level of analysis to a high but very complex plane. The author introduces the interesting and, from my view, unusual *realist objection* in the Hobbsian form. After a rigorous analysis of this concept Professor Velasquez reaches what I find to be a disturbing conclusion: "It is not obvious that we can say that multinationals have an obligation to contribute to the global common good...." He then finishes the paper with a strong plea for the establishment of "an international authority capable of forcing everyone to contribute toward the global good."

It would be presumptuous of me to question the fine ethical reasoning that appears in the paper. I am impressed with its elegance. However, in a topic of this complexity I would like to think that there might be alternative approaches and assumptions that would lead us to a different conclusion. The presentation of such alternatives will be the path that I will take, examining the conceptual and empirical underpinnings of the argument from a management viewpoint.

The Model of a Multinational Corporation

The profit-maximizing, rational model of a multinational corporation presented in the paper is consistent with traditional economics and serves as a useful approximation of the firm from a theoretical viewpoint. But it falls somewhat short in less than purely competitive environments and was never intended to describe the decision processes of actual managers. Empirical studies of firms can lead to a profit-sacrificing, bounded rational model. The importance of profit is still there, but the stockholder does not get all the benefits. Other stakeholders are considered and rewarded. Out of all this can come the important concept of corporate social responsibility, which can include such topics as concerns for the environment and for host country governments.

I also find the faceless and interchangeable bureaucrat a poor model for business executives, particularly the chief executive officers of large corporations. Many of these individuals have a personal impact on the organization, including such areas as business ethics and corporate responsibility. There are also important behavioral aspects of management, such as pride in the firm and corporate culture, that are fertile soil for the nurture of ethics.

Most large American multinational corporations have codes of ethics and some have well-developed programs concerned with ethical behavior worldwide. A number of these firms emphasize that their one code of conduct applies everywhere that they do business. At the GTE Corporation its vision and values statements have been translated into nine different languages and distributed to all its employees to ensure this world-wide understanding of how it conducts its business. This is a far cry from the situational ethics described in the model used by Professor Velasquez.

Model of the International Business Climate

The planning and decision environment of the managers conducting international business is different from that described in the paper. There is the very real problem of a lack of an overarching global government and enforceable laws for the international arena. Nevertheless, there are other very strong restraining forces on companies that prevent the "state of nature" (or law of the jungle) described in the paper. For example, the national governments that do exist influence the ethical behavior of companies acting within their boundaries and beyond. The Foreign Corrupt Practices Act of the United States has set a new standard of behavior in the area of bribery that dictates how American companies will behave world-wide. The financial practices of large banks and securities markets have added major constraints to global corporate behavior. There are also a number of regional and functional organizations in the areas of trade and monetary issues that provide limitations to managerial decision making.

The decisions of multinational executives are also constrained by such factors as public opinion and the pressures of special interest groups. In this area the media also plays a strong role. Examples of these forces are the actions of interest groups that forced marketing changes on infant formula manufacturers and the strong "green" movement that is affecting business decisions throughout many parts of the world. My own view is that considerable progress has been made in the area of limiting the manufacture and release of chlorofluorocarbons. This is a very complex issue involving tremendous social and economic changes that are far more critical, widespread and controlling than the profits of the producing companies. Even with the existence of an enforcing government there is no guarantee that the problem would be solved speedily. An example in point is the acid rain problem of the United States.

Model of the Prisoner's Dilemma

From the standpoint of managerial decision making the Prisoner's Dilemma model does not simulate a situation that is frequently found in international business. An executive generally would not be negotiating or making mutually beneficial decisions with competitors. I would see the greatest amount of effort of multinational decision makers devoted to the development of repeat customers. Such an accomplishment comes about through solving customer problems with better product/service at a lower cost. An emphasis on efficiency and excellence is a far more effective use of executive time than questionable negotiations with a competitor. I believe that the weakness Professor Velasquez identifies in the Prisoner's Dilemma model as a one-time event with competitors applies even more to negotiations with customers.

The author also points out a major weakness of the model in the signaling of intent that goes on between individuals. He then states that this same signaling is not found to any great extent between companies. I would disagree with this thought. An important part of corporate strategic planning is analyzing market signals. United States antitrust forbids direct contact between competitors on issues relating to the market. But there is no limitation on independent analysis of competitive actions and the interpretation of actions by competitors. When Kodak introduced its instant camera, both Kodak and Polaroid watched the other's actions to determine whether it signaled detente or fight.

Conclusion

For the reasons enumerated above I tend to question the models and assumptions that Professor Velasquez has used in his ethical analysis. And, with these underpinnings in jeopardy, I also tend to question the tentative conclusion of his moral reasoning as it relates to the managerial aspects of international business. I feel that multinationals *do* have a strong obligation to contribute to the global common good.

POSTSCRIPT

Are Multinational Corporations Free from Moral Obligations?

As we write, international business has sunk into a sea of troubles: the once-booming Asian economies seem to be self-destructing, prominent public figures such as movie stars and athletes are being accused of exploitation and owning sweatshops, and trade in securities has gone global and is running wild. What are the possibilities for the comprehensive set of international laws, guidelines, and the committees to enforce them, as suggested by Velasquez?

Is national sovereignty an idea whose time has come, gone, and gone south? While national boundaries between peoples are in violent dispute worldwide, and while the economy goes global with blinding speed, does the concept of national boundaries make any sense at all? How else would we know what each central government controls? What is the reason for the centrality of national sovereignty?

Suggested Readings

Corporate Ethics: A Prime Business Asset, Report of the Business Roundtable (1988).

Ashay B. Desai and Terri Rittenburg, "Global Ethics: An Integrative Framework for MNEs," *Journal of Business Ethics* (June 1997), pp. 791–800.

Thomas Donaldson, *The Ethics of International Business* (Oxford University Press, 1989).

W. Michael Hoffman, Ann E. Lange, and David A. Fedo, eds., *Ethics and the Multinational Enterprise* (University Press of America, 1986).

Kevin T. Jackson, "Globalizing Corporate Ethics Programs: Perils and Prospects," *Journal of Business Ethics* (September 1997), pp. 1227–1235.

ISSUE 14

Are Sweatshops Necessarily Evil?

YES: Susan S. Black, from "Ante Up," *Bobbin* (September 19, 1996)

NO: Allen R. Myerson, from "In Principle, a Case for More 'Sweatshops,'" *The New York Times* (June 22, 1997)

ISSUE SUMMARY

YES: Susan S. Black, publisher of *Bobbin*, argues that customers will not tolerate goods made by slave labor, children, or women working in inhumane conditions. She maintains that customers are willing to pay more to make sure that the goods they buy were not made in sweatshops.

NO: Allen R. Myerson, a writer for the *New York Times*, looks at the economies of less developed countries and finds that allowing their citizens to work in sweatshops may be the only option these nations have to accumulate capital.

The Scottish economist Adam Smith's recommendation regarding government regulation of the terms of commercial contracts was to let every player in the market make his or her own best bargain, and in the end everyone would be better off.

Consider the conditions for the "voluntary exchange": there must be no fraud or misrepresentation on either side—both parties must know what they are getting into—and there must be no coercion. Simply put, this means that there must be no gun held to the head of either party. Less obviously, there must be no economic coercion: one party may not be under absolute economic coercion to sign. For example, if someone takes a job for the money to buy a new car, that decision seems to be perfectly free. But if the person needs the job immediately just to feed his or her family, it could be argued that the individual is not "free" to turn it down—the offer of a job is impossible to refuse. When one party has enormous economic power, and the other has none, there cannot be a free or voluntary agreement—there must be a certain degree of economic equality between the contracting parties, not absolute but not nonexistent, or there is no voluntariness.

Smith probably never imagined that this situation could arise. In a society with many employers in competition with each other for labor and other resources, not one of which is large enough to dominate the market, the laborer can simply withhold his or her services until he or she finds the employer that is willing to pay the most. There was a time when independent craftspeople made their contracts with individual buyers and when many small farmers needed help at harvest time. Then perhaps the economic power of the contracting parties was approximately equal and all exchanges were voluntary. But in the day of the huge factory that dominates the town and of the replaceable unskilled worker, one side seems to hold all the chips, and the other side holds none.

It could be argued that sweatshops—huge mass-production facilities where hundreds work in barbaric conditions for subsistence wages—built the United States. Workers rendered vulnerable by their immigrant status, disorientation in unfamiliar urban settings, and irremediable poverty were forced to take whatever jobs were available; entrepreneurs with access to capital threw up factories, and so the sweatshop was born. The union movement in the United States is all about the abolition of the sweatshop and the development of the modern factory—clean, safe, pleasant, and paying its workers adequate wages and benefits.

Clean, safe, pleasant, and losing money, modern entrepreneurs might say. In many industries, like the garment industry, the major cost of manufacture is labor. As long as there is no alternative, consumers seem willing to pay whatever they have to for their merchandise. But as soon as less expensive products become available—and with the growth of Asian competition, they certainly have become available—consumers buy them instead. Some say that only by continuing to manufacture offshore, in the sweatshops of Asia, can America remain competitive.

Meanwhile, the nations in which America is building these sweatshops do not seem to be complaining. On the contrary, they complain when U.S. multinational corporations shut down the sweatshops in response to American protests against them. Because so many of these nations' people can obtain jobs in American sweatshops, these shops are considered by some to be the only way the nations can grow.

As you read the following selections by Susan S. Black and Allen R. Myerson, ask yourself whether or not the outrage over sweatshop conditions in the developing world is justified. Are we importing standards appropriate to the late-twentieth-century United States rather than putting these manufactures against a backdrop of the lives lived by the workers before the factory came? Should a country be allowed to oppress or exploit its people in an effort to get its economy started?

Susan S. Black

 **YES**

Ante Up

Another chapter in the U.S. Labor Department's self-proclaimed war on apparel industry sweatshops was played out in mid-July when Secretary of Labor Robert Reich hosted a group of some 300, including *Bobbin*, to discuss what could be done about the problem.

The "Fashion Industry Forum," held at Marymount University just outside of Washington, D.C., drew manufacturers and retailers, union leaders, industry association representatives and such celebrity endorsers at Kathie Lee Gifford and Cheryl Tiegs, many of whom participated in panel presentations.

While Reich said he didn't expect "major headlines" to result from the forum, he did say that he hoped it would be a "turning point" and that he expected it to foster a "renewed commitment" to battle sweatshops and child labor. Of course, the fact that such major players as Wal-Mart Stores, Kmart Corp., Nordstrom, Liz Claiborne, Patagonia Inc. and Levi Strauss & Co. participated in the forum is evidence in itself that Reich has managed to focus industry's attention on the subject of sweatshops. And whether one agrees with Reich's tactics or not—I don't—it seems almost certain that his momentum-gaining antisweatshop campaign is going to result in changes for our industry, namely that both retailers and manufacturers are going to have to incur additional expenses to prove to consumers that their goods are made under fair and legal labor conditions.

Among the options put on the table at the forum were "no-sweat" labeling programs, independent third-party monitoring of factories and increasing the duties of quality assurance personnel to encompass monitoring responsibilities —each of which undoubtedly comes with a price tag and such possible complex concerns as, "Who monitors the monitors?" If additional monitoring and labeling programs do come to fruition, the key question is who will pay the price. Opinions on the level of cost and who should bear responsibility for that cost varied at the forum, but my bet is that ultimately it will be the entire soft goods chain—and the consumer—that pays.

"The customer can't have its cake and eat it too," said Tiegs, who first licensed her name for an apparel line in the 1980s. "They must pay the price."

John Ermatinger, senior vice president of operations and sourcing for Levi Strauss North America, said it's time to stop placing blame and time to start finding solutions. "I would like to spend more time working on this issue and less time talking about it," he said. "It's unfair to focus on the retailer. It's a supply chain challenge and we will have to find flexible, non-mandated solutions. It's not a one-size-fits-all solution."

Levi's success in producing no-sweat goods (it first established standards for monitoring contractors in 1991) is a result of making monitoring an integral part of the business. "This is how we do business," Ermatinger said. "It's part of how we measure performance."

As part of its reengineering, Levi's also has cut its supplier base by 50 percent, said Ermatinger, "enabling us to focus more efficiently on our remaining base."

Roberta Karp, vice president of corporate affairs and general counsel for Liz Claiborne, agreed that there is no "recipe to follow" when it comes to monitoring. She said Claiborne has its own internal monitoring program, but might consider expanding it. "We must reach out to partnerships [in monitoring]," she said.

Warren Flick, president of merchandising for Kmart, said for its part, the merchant is "rebuilding" its entire buying organization. He said Kmart will have fewer vendors, and longer-term relationships with those vendors.

Flick also said Kmart has created a new executive position, based in Hong Kong, to oversee Kmart's global monitoring efforts. "Our eyes and ears are wide open," he added. "We know what products and regions where our focus needs to be."

Gale Cottle, executive vice president for Nordstrom who said that Nordstrom will not tolerate vendors who use illegal practices, also pointed to some of the challenges a retailer has in monitoring the conditions under which its goods are made. For starters, she said Nordstrom has 13,000 U.S. vendors, and 870 decentralized buyers who buy on a customized level according to changing fashion needs. She said: "A buyer cannot identify cost in a showroom... and even the right price doesn't guarantee the right conditions."

Also bringing a practical slant to the forum was Tracy Mullin, president of the National Retail Federation (NRF), who observed that while retailers cannot afford to jeopardize their reputations and want to take "aggressive steps forward," there are a myriad of considerations in handling sweatshop accusations. Noting that the problem of sweatshops often involves organized crime and immigration violations, she recommended coordinated efforts among the Internal Revenue Service, the Immigration and Naturalization Service and the Justice Department.

The granddaddy retailer of them all, Wal-Mart—around which much media attention has been generated after it was discovered that Kathie Lee Gifford apparel was being produced in a New York, NY, sweatshop—said at the forum that it never had inspected U.S. factories with whom it does business, but is doing so now. It also will be recertifying the overseas factories with whom it does business, and has studied an independent monitoring program used by The Gap, said Lee Scott, executive vice president of merchandise and sales for Wal-Mart.

Still, Scott cautioned that there could be a tendency to migrate toward using only large, well-established vendors, which would "keep out the young, innovative companies."

If the Fashion Industry Forum means that some companies will adopt more careful monitoring practices with their contractors and subcontractors, there's no question the results will be positive. After all, good manufacturing practices logically should result in better quality and higher profits. But it's important to note that behind the publicly spoken words at the forum were many forces at play, several with distinctly different motives. Government, unions, retailers, manufacturers, contractors—each has its own self-interests.

Let's just hope that as many of the already law-abiding businesses in our industry commit themselves to more thorough documentation of how their goods are made, the illicit businesses and sweatshops will fall by the wayside in greater numbers. Because the last thing this industry needs is more bad publicity based on the actions of a few.

One last thought. Did you know that the members of the American Apparel Manufacturers Association (AAMA)—which represent about two-thirds of the garments made in the United States—manufacture 85 percent of their goods in their own plants? And that the average U.S. apparel worker makes double the minimum wage, plus another 30 percent in benefits?

Those statistics came from AAMA president Larry Martin at the forum. I think they're worth remembering—and repeating.

NO

Allen R. Myerson

In Principle, a Case for More "Sweatshops"

CAMBRIDGE, MASS.

For more than a century, accounts of sweatshops have provoked outrage. From the works of Charles Dickens and Lincoln Steffens to today's television reports, the image of workers hunched over their machines for meager rewards has been a banner of reform.

Last year, companies like Nike and Wal-Mart and celebrities like Kathie Lee Gifford struggled to defend themselves after reports of the torturous hours and low pay of the workers who produce their upscale footwear or downmarket fashions. Anxious corporate spokesmen sought to explain the plants as a step up for workers in poor countries. A weeping Mrs. Gifford denied knowing about the conditions.

Now some of the nation's leading economists, with solid liberal and academic credentials, are offering a much broader, more principled rationale. Economists like Jeffrey D. Sachs of Harvard and Paul Krugman of the Massachusetts Institute of Technology say that low-wage plants making clothing and shoes for foreign markets are an essential first step toward modern prosperity in developing countries.

Mr. Sachs, a leading adviser and shock therapist to nations like Bolivia, Russia and Poland, is now working on the toughest cases of all, the economies of sub-Saharan Africa. He is just back from Malawi, where malaria afflicts almost all its 13 million people and AIDS affects 1 in 10; the lake that provided much of the country's nourishment is fished out.

When asked during a recent Harvard panel discussion whether there were too many sweatshops in such places, Mr. Sachs answered facetiously, "My concern is not that there are too many sweatshops but that there are too few," he said.

Mr. Sachs, who has visited low-wage factories around the world, is opposed to child or prisoner labor and other outright abuses. But many nations, he says, have no better hope than plants paying mere subsistence wages. "Those are precisely the jobs that were the steppingstone for Singapore and Hong Kong," he said, "and those are the jobs that have to come to Africa to get them out of their backbreaking rural poverty."

Rising Stakes

The stakes in the battle over sweatshops are high and rising. Clinton Administration officials say commerce with the major developing nations like China, Indonesia and Mexico is crucial for America's own continued prosperity. Corporate America's manufacturing investments in developing nations more than tripled in 15 years to $56 billion in 1995—not including the vast numbers of plants there that contract with American companies.

In matters of trade and commerce, economists like Mr. Sachs, who has also worked with several Government agencies, are influential. A consensus among economists helped persuade President Clinton, who had campaigned against President Bush's plan of lowered restrictions, to ram global and North American trade pacts through Congress.

Paradoxically, economists' support of sweatshops represents a sort of optimism. Until the mid-1980's, few thought that third world nations could graduate to first world status in a lifetime, if ever. "When I went to graduate school in the early to mid-1970's," Mr. Krugman said, "it looked like being a developed country was really a closed club." Only Japan had made a convincing jump within the past century.

Those economists who believed that developing nations could advance often prescribed self-reliance and socialism, warning against foreign investment as a form of imperialism. Advanced nations invested in the developing world largely to extract oil, coffee, bananas and other resources but created few new jobs or industries. Developing nations, trying to lessen their reliance on manufactured imports, tried to bolster domestic industries for the home market. But these protected businesses were often inefficient and the local markets too small to sustain them.

From Wigs to Cars

Then the Four Tigers—Hong Kong, Singapore, South Korea and Taiwan—began to roar. They made apparel, toys, shoes and, at least in South Korea's case, wigs and false teeth, mostly for export. Within a generation, their national incomes climbed from about 10 percent to 40 percent of American incomes. Singapore welcomed foreign plant owners while South Korea shunned them, building industrial conglomerates of its own. But the first stage of development had one constant. "It's always sweatshops," Mr. Krugman said.

These same nations now export cars and computers, and the economists have revised their views of sweatshops. "The overwhelming mainstream view among economists is that the growth of this kind of employment is tremendous good news for the world's poor," Mr. Krugman said.

Unlike the corporate apologists, economists make no attempt to prettify the sweatshop picture. Mr. Krugman, who writes a column for Slate magazine called "The Dismal Scientist," describes sweatshop owners as "soulless multinationals and rapacious local entrepreneurs, whose only concern was to take advantage of the profit opportunities offered by cheap labor." But even in a nation as corrupt as Indonesia, he says, industrialization has reduced the portion of malnourished children from more than half in 1975 to a third today.

In judging the issue of child labor also, Mr. Krugman is a pragmatist, asking what else is available. It often isn't education. In India, for example, destitute parents sometimes sell their children to Persian Gulf begging syndicates whose bosses mutilate them for a higher take, he says. "If that is the alternative, it is not so easy to say that children should not be working in factories," Mr. Krugman said.

Not that most economists argue for sweatshops at home. The United States, they say, can afford to set much higher labor standards than poor countries—though Europe's are so high, some say, that high unemployment results.

Labor leaders and politicians who challenge sweatshops abroad say that they harm American workers as well, stealing jobs and lowering wages—a point that some economists dispute. "It is especially galling when American workers lose jobs to places where workers are really being exploited," said Mark Levinson, chief economist at the Union of Needletrades, Industrial and Textile Employees, who argues for trade sanctions to enforce global labor rules.

Yet when corporations voluntarily cut their ties to sweatshops, the victims can be the very same people sweatshop opponents say they want to help. In Honduras, where the legal working age is 14, girls toiled 75 hours a week for the 31-cent hourly minimum to make the Kathie Lee Gifford clothing line for Wal-Mart. When Wal-Mart canceled its contract, the girls lost their jobs and blamed Mrs. Gifford.

No Jobs in Practice

Mr. Krugman blames American self-righteousness or guilt over Indonesian women and children sewing sneakers at 60 cents an hour. "A policy of good jobs in principle, but no jobs in practice, might assuage our consciences," he said, "but it is no favor to its alleged beneficiaries."

POSTSCRIPT

Are Sweatshops Necessarily Evil?

As the troubles now afflicting Asia remind us, no economic powerhouse is forever. Before the current crumbling of Asian economies, Americans had watched in fascination while the once-invulnerable Japan went through a "miniature U.S. history": workers clamoring for better conditions, people spending more on consumer goods and saving less, and wages rising steadily. Then, of course, manufacture shifted to Thailand and other places where labor was very inexpensive.

Suggested Readings

"Watching the Sweatshops," *The New York Times* (August 20, 1997).

David R. Henderson, "The Case for Sweatshops," *Fortune* (October 28, 1996), pp. 48–52.

Mark Henricks, "Labor Says No Sweat," *Apparel Industry Magazine* (January 1996), pp. 68–70.

James Mamarella, "Decent Labor Standards Should Be the Standard," *Discount Store News* (April 1, 1996), p. 2.

Jack A. Raisner, "Using the 'Ethical Environment' Paradigm to Teach Business Ethics: The Case of the Maquiladoras," *Journal of Business Ethics* (September 1997), pp. 1331–1346.

ISSUE 15

Should Patenting Life Be Forbidden?

YES: Jeremy Rifkin, from "Should We Patent Life?" *Business Ethics* (March/April, 1998)

NO: William Domnarski, from "Dire New World," *Intellectual Property Magazine* (January 1999)

ISSUE SUMMARY

YES: Jeremy Rifkin, president of the Foundation on Economic Trends, fears that genetic engineering extends human power over the rest of nature in ways that are unprecedented and whose consequences cannot be known. He urges a halt to such research, especially research whose aim is profit for the company that "owns" the results.

NO: William Domnarski, an intellectual property lawyer, finds the patenting of genes or genetic discoveries no different than patenting any other ideas. The purpose of patents is to reward and encourage useful invention, he argues, and there is no doubt that the modifications we introduce to the genetic material of plants and animals are useful to feed a starving world.

There is an apocryphal story that at a meeting of the gentlemanly Scientific Society of the seventeenth century, one of the members proposed a toast to the next scientific discovery, to which another of the members immediately added a fervent wish "that it may be of no use to anyone." The story illustrates well the ambivalence of scientific research that informs this issue.

Why do we seek knowledge? Some answer this question by saying that the Lord created our minds, and a fascinating world to study, and that in seeking wisdom and insight into the ways of Nature we honor our creator and raise our minds closer to the Divine mind.

But Francis Bacon, an early seventeenth-century philosopher of science, suggested another reason: "The end of our foundation is the knowledge of causes, and secret motions of things; and the enlarging of the bounds of human empire, to the effecting of all things possible." Knowledge is power, and the reason we pursue knowledge, some argue, is to increase the power of human beings. It is the mission of science to expand the domain of human understanding precisely so that in knowing all things, we might do all things.

Shall we pursue knowledge of the genetic factors in animal and plant life, including knowledge of the human genome? As one reflects on the problem, Monsanto Inc. is going forward with genetically engineered agricultural plant germ lines for export. Europe has firmly said that no genetically modified organisms (GMOs) shall appear on its tables, and in many places farmers have refused to grow them. Already a controversy has exploded in the grocery market: may GMOs grown without fertilizers or pesticides be labeled "organic"? Enthusiasts point out that GMOs, because they are better plants, often do not need any fertilizers or pesticides, so that should make organic farmers and their customers very happy. Critics point out that the reason they do not need chemical fertilizers or pesticides is that they have the bug repellent and who knows what other chemicals engineered into their skins. For example, Monsanto came up with a "terminator gene," a genetic modification that sets only sterile seeds and cannot naturally reproduce. Why do this? Monsanto explained that it did not want genetically inserted bug repellent spreading to the natural weeds, which would make it harder to keep them under control; opponents of Monsanto suggested that the technique made it impossible for farmers to collect and set their own seed from the harvest, so ensuring that the farmers would have to come back to Monsanto year after year for refills.

Why is Monsanto investing so much time and money to develop new lines of plants? One obvious reason is to make money. But if the company is going to make money, there have to be patents on the new seeds it develops, or they will immediately be outflanked and undersold by similar firms, which can duplicate their seeds without all of the expensive investment. So patents are necessary in order to protect the enterprise. Meanwhile, Monsanto maintains that all it wants to do is provide more food for a hungry world, a goal that we can only applaud, and that it needs the protection of patents to keep up the good work.

Where is technology taking us in this case? Can we separate out the genuine altruism from the scientific curiosity and from the selfish desire to make a very large amount of money very quickly?

As you read the following selections, bear in mind that you are looking at a real cutting-edge issue. For most of biotechnology, no one knows the empirical consequences 10 years down the road—that is how recent the science is. Should we calculate costs versus benefits, as far as they may be known? Or, should we adopt the precautionary principle and put off all introduction of this technology? Shall we allow the entrepreneur inventor to reap the fortunes associated with a good patent or two on the most recent developments? Or, shall we decide that life in all its forms is sacred and not open to private claim or profit?

Jeremy Rifkin  **YES**

Should We Patent Life?

A handful of companies are engaged in a race to patent all 100,000 human genes. In less than a decade, the race will be over. The genetic legacy of our species will be held in the form of private intellectual property. The genes inside your cells will belong not to you, but to global corporations. Welcome to the world of the biotech revolution.

While the 20th century was shaped by breakthroughs in physics and chemistry, the 21st century will belong to the biological sciences. Scientists are deciphering the genetic code, unlocking the mystery of millions of years of evolution. Global life science companies, in turn, are beginning to exploit these new advances. The raw resources of the new economic epoch are genes—already being used in businesses ranging from agriculture and bioremediation to energy and pharmaceuticals.

By 2025, we may be living in a world remade by a revolution unmatched in history. The biotech revolution raises unprecedented ethical questions we've barely begun to discuss. Will the artificial creation of cloned and transgenic animals mean the end of nature and the substitution of a bio-industrial world? Will the release of genetically engineered life forms into the biosphere cause catastrophic genetic pollution? What will it mean to live in a world where babies are customized in the womb—and where people are stereotyped and discriminated against on the basis of their genotype? What risks do we take in attempting to design more "perfect" human beings?

At the heart of this new commercial revolution is a chilling question of great ethical impact, whose resolution will affect civilization for centuries to come: *Should we patent life?* The practice has already gotten a green light, through a controversial Supreme Court decision and a subsequent ruling by the Patent and Trademark Office in the 1980s. But if the question were put directly to the American people, would they agree? If you alter one gene in a chimpanzee, does that make the animal a human "invention"? If you isolate the gene for breast cancer, does that give you the right to "own" it? Should a handful of global corporations be allowed to patent all human genes?

On the eve of the Biotech Century, we do still have an opportunity to raise ethical issues like these—although the window is rapidly closing.

From Jeremy Rifkin, "Should We Patent Life?" *Business Ethics* (March/April 1998), pp. 15–17. Copyright © 1998 by *Business Ethics*. Reprinted by permission of *Business Ethics*, P.O. Box 8439, Minneapolis, MN 55408.

We've only completed the first decade of a revolution that may span several centuries. But already there are 1,400 biotech companies in the U.S., with a total of nearly $13 billion in annual revenues and more than 100,000 employees. Development is proceeding in an astonishing number of areas:

At Harvard University, scientists have grown human bladders and kidneys in laboratory jars. Monsanto hopes to have a plastic-producing plant on the market by the year 2003—following up on the work of Chris Sommerville at the Carnegie Institution of Washington, who inserted a plastic-making gene into a mustard plant. Another biotech company, the Institute of Genomic Research, has successfully sequenced a microbe that can absorb large amounts of radioactivity and be used to dispose of deadly radioactive waste. The first genetically engineered insect, a predator mite, was released in 1996 by researchers at the University of Florida, who hope it will eat other mites that damage strawberries and similar crops.

At the University of Wisconsin, scientists have genetically altered brooding turkey hens to increase their productivity, by eliminating the "brooding" instinct: the desire to sit on and hatch eggs. Other researchers are experimenting with the creation of sterile salmon who will not have the suicidal urge to spawn, but will remain in the open sea, to be commercially harvested. Michigan State University scientists say that by breaking the spawning cycle of chinook salmon, they can produce seventy-pound salmon, compared to less than eighteen pounds for a fish returning to spawn. In short, the mothering instinct and the mating instinct are being bred out of animals.

With genetic engineering, humanity is extending its reach over the forces of nature far beyond the scope of any previous technology—with the possible exception of the nuclear bomb. At the same time, corporations are assuming ownership and control over the hereditary blueprints of life itself. Can any reasonable person believe such power is without risk?

⋙⟐⟐⋘

Genes are the "green gold" of the biotech century, and companies that control them will exercise tremendous power over the world economy. Multinational corporations are already scouting the continents in search of this new precious resource, hoping to locate microbes, plants, animals, and humans with rare genetic traits that might have future market potential. Having located the desired traits, biotech companies are modifying them and seeking patent protection for their new "inventions."

The worldwide race to patent the gene pool is the culmination of a 500-year-odyssey to enclose the ecosystems of the Earth. That journey began in feudal England in the 1500s, with the passage of the great "enclosure acts," which privatized the village commons—transforming the land from a community trust to private real estate. Today, virtually every square foot of landmass on the planet is under private ownership or government control.

But enclosure of the land was just the beginning. Today, the ocean's coastal waters are commercially leased, the air has been converted into commercial airline corridors, and even the electromagnetic spectrum is considered commercial property—leased for use by radio, TV, and telephone companies. Now the most intimate commons of all—the gene pool—is being enclosed and reduced to private commercial property.

The enclosure of the genetic commons began in 1971, when an Indian microbiologist and General Electric employee, Ananda Chakrabarty, applied to the U.S. Patents and Trademark Office (PTO) for a patent on a genetically engineered microorganism designed to consume oil spills. The PTO rejected the request, arguing that living things are not patentable. The case was appealed all the way to the Supreme Court, which in 1980—by a slim margin of five to four —ruled in favor of Chakrabarty. Speaking for the majority, Chief Justice Warren Burger argued that "the relevant distinction was not between living and inanimate things," but whether or not Chakrabarty's microbe was a "human-made invention."

In the aftermath of that historic decision, bioengineering technology shed its pristine academic garb and bounded into the marketplace. On Oct. 13, 1980 —just months after the court's ruling—Genentech publicly offered one million shares of stock at $35 per share. By the time the trading bell had rung that first day, the stock was selling at over $500 per share. And Genentech had yet to introduce a single product.

Chemical, pharmaceutical, argribusiness, and biotech startups everywhere sped up their research—mindful that the granting of patent protection meant the possibility of harnessing the genetic commons for vast commercial gain. Some observers, however, were not so enthused. Ethicist Leon Kass asked:

> "What is the principled limit to this beginning extension of the domain of private ownership and dominion over living nature . . . ? The principle used in Chakrabarty says that there is nothing in the nature of being, not even in the patentor himself, that makes him immune to being patented."

While the Supreme Court decision lent an air of legal legitimacy to the emerging biotech industry, a Patent Office decision in 1987 opened the floodgates. In a complete about-face, the PTO ruled that all genetically engineered multicellular living organisms—including animals—are potentially patentable. The Commissioner of Patents and Trademarks at the time, Donald J. Quigg, attempted to calm a shocked public by asserting that the decision covered every creature except human beings—because the Thirteenth Amendment to the Constitution forbids human slavery. On the other hand, human embryos and fetuses as well as human genes, tissues, and organs were now potentially patentable.

What makes the Supreme Court decision and Patent Office ruling suspect, from a legal point of view, is that they defy previous patent rulings that say one cannot claim a "discovery of nature" as an invention. No one would suggest that scientists who isolated, classified, and described the properties of chemical elements in the periodic table—such as oxygen and helium—ought to be granted a patent on them. Yet someone who isolates and classifies the properties of human genes can patent them.

The European Patent Office, for example, awarded a patent to the U.S. company Biocyte, giving it ownership of all human blood cells which have come from the umbilical cord of a newborn child and are being used for any therapeutic purposes. The patent is so broad that it allows this one company to refuse the use of any blood cells from the umbilical cord to any individual unwilling to pay the patent fee. Blood cells from the umbilical cord are particularly important for marrow transplants, making it a valuable commercial asset. It should be emphasized that this patent was awarded simply because Biocyte was able to isolate the blood cells and deep-freeze them. The company made no change in the blood itself.

A similarly broad patent was awarded to Systemix Inc. of Palo Alto, Calif., by the U.S. Patent Office, covering all human bone marrow stem cells. This extraordinary patent on a human body part was awarded despite the fact that Systemix had done nothing whatsoever to alter or engineer the cells. Dr. Peter Quisenberry, the medical affairs vice chairman of the Leukemia Society of America, quipped, "Where do you draw the line? Can you patent a hand?"

⋯⟨◉⟩⋯

The life patents race is gearing up in the wake of government and commercial efforts to map the approximately 100,000 human genes that make up the human genome—a project with enormous commercial potential. As soon as a gene is tagged its "discoverer" is likely to apply for a patent, often before knowing the function of the gene. In 1991, J. Craig Venter, then head of the National Institute of Health Genome Mapping Research Team, resigned his government post to head up a genomics company funded with more than $70 million in venture capital. At the same time, Venter and his colleagues filed for patents on more than 2,000 human brain genes. Many researchers on the Human Genome Project were shocked and angry, charging Venter with attempting to profit off research paid for by American taxpayers.

Nobel laureate James Watson, co-discoverer of the DNA double helix, called the Venter patent claims "sheer lunacy." Still, it's likely that within less than ten years, all 100,000 or so genes that comprise the genetic legacy of our species will be patented—making them the exclusive intellectual property of global corporations.

The patenting of life is creating a firestorm of controversy. Several years ago, an Alaskan businessman named John Moore found his own body parts had been patented, without his knowledge, by the University of California at Los Angeles (UCLA), and licensed to the Sandoz Pharmaceutical Corp. Moore had been diagnosed with a rare cancer and underwent treatment at UCLA. A researcher there discovered that Moore's spleen tissue produced a blood protein that facilitates the growth of white blood cells valuable as anti-cancer agents. The university created a cell line from Moore's spleen tissue and obtained a patent on the "invention." The cell line is estimated to be worth more than $3 billion.

Moore subsequently sued, claiming a property right over his own tissue. But in 1990, the California Supreme Court ruled against him, saying Moore had no such ownership right. Human body parts, the court argued, could not be bartered as a commodity in the marketplace.

The irony of the decision was captured by Judge Broussard, in his dissenting opinion. The ruling "does *not* mean that body parts may not be bought or sold," he wrote. "[T]he majority's holding simply bars *plantiff*, the source of the cells, from obtaining the benefit of the cell's value, but permits *defendants*, who allegedly obtained the cells from plaintiff by improper means, to retain and exploit the full economic value of their ill-gotten gains."

◄◉►

A battle of historic proportions has also emerged between the high-technology nations of the North and the developing nations of the South, over ownership of the planet's genetic treasures. Some Third World leaders say the North is attempting to seize the biological commons, most of which is in the rich tropical regions of the Southern Hemisphere, and that their nations should be compensated for use of genetic resources. Corporate and governmental leaders in the North maintain that the genes increase in value only when manipulated using sophisticated gene-splicing techniques, so there's no obligation to compensate the South.

To ease growing tensions, a number of companies have proposed sharing a portion of their gains. Merck & Co., the pharmaceutical giant (often considered a leader in social responsibility), entered into an agreement recently with a research organization in Costa Rica, the National Biodiversity Institute, to pay the organization a paltry $1 million to secure the group's plant, microorganism, and insect samples. Critics liken the deal to European settlers giving American Indians trinkets in return for the island of Manhattan. The recipient organization, on the other hand, is granting a right to bio-prospect on land it has no historic claim to in the first place—while indigenous peoples are locked out of the agreement.

Such agreements are beginning to meet with resistance from countries and non-governmental organizations (NGOs) in the Southern Hemisphere. They claim that what Northern companies are calling "discoveries" are really the pirating of the indigenous knowledge of native peoples and cultures. To defuse opposition, biotech corporations are seeking to impose a uniform intellectual property regime worldwide. And they've gone a long way toward achieving that with the passage of the Trade Related Aspects of Intellectual Property Agreements (TRIPS) at the Uruguay Round of the General Agreement on Tariffs and Trade (GATT). Sculpted by companies like Bristol Myers, Merck, Pfizer, Dupont, and Monsanto, the TRIPS agreement makes no allowance for indigenous knowledge, and grants companies free access to genetic material from around the world.

Suman Sahai, director of the Gene Campaign—an NGO in New Delhi—makes the point, "God didn't give us 'rice' or 'wheat' or 'potato.' " These were once wild plants that were domesticated over eons of time and patiently bred by generations of farmers. Sahai asks, "Who did all of that work?" Groups like his argue that Southern countries should be compensated for their contribution to biotech.

Still others take a third position: that neither corporations nor indigenous peoples should claim ownership, because the gene pool ought not to be for sale, at any price. It should remain an open commons and continue to be used freely by present and future generations. They cite precedent in the recent historic decision by the nations of the world to maintain the continent of Antarctica as a global commons free from commercial exploitation.

The idea of private companies laying claim to human genes as their exclusive intellectual property has resulted in growing protests worldwide. In May of 1994, a coalition of hundreds of women's organizations from more than forty nations announced opposition to Myriad Genetics's attempt to patent the gene that causes breast cancer in some women. The coalition was assembled by The Foundation on Economic Trends. While the women did not oppose the screening test Myriad developed, they opposed the claim to the gene itself. They argued that the breast cancer gene was a product of nature and not a human invention, and should not be patentable. Myriad's exclusive rights to such a gene could make screening more expensive, and might impede research by making access to the gene too expensive.

The central question in these cases—Can you patent life?—is one of the most important issues ever to face the human family. Life patenting strikes at the core of our beliefs about the very nature of life and whether it is to be conceived as having sacred and intrinsic value, or merely utility value. Surely such a fundamental question deserves to be widely discussed by the public before such patents become a ubiquitous part of our daily lives.

The biotech revolution will force each of us to put a mirror to our most deeply held values, making us ponder the ultimate question of the purpose and meaning of existence. This may turn out to be its most important contribution. The rest is up to us.

William Domnarski

 **NO**

Dire New World

With an authorial voice that only a conspiracy maven such as Oliver Stone could love, Jeremy Rifkin is back, this time to warn us about the dangers inherent in our idea of so-called "progress," as Rifkin puts it.

Rifkin—the president of the Foundation of Economic Trends and the author of many books on economic trends relating to science, technology, and culture—is especially worried about the implications of the biotech century that will not wait two years to begin. It's here now, and unless we heed Rifkin's warnings and keep ourselves from temptation by agreeing with him that progress is too fraught for mischief to be acceptable, we'll end up in a genetically polluted world in which genetic discrimination reigns—though you will be able to go down to your local laboratory when the time comes to be fitted with that new vital organ you've had cloned in the expectation that you might need it.

The advances in genetic engineering in medicine—to say nothing of the advances in plant genetics—have been staggering. Now knowing most of the code, we can identify and even act on various types of diseases and disabilities before birth. We have added a range of new treatments in which genetically engineered cells are introduced into the body to take hold and combat disease. Alzheimer's disease and Parkinson's disease are not on the verge of being conquered, but we are closer to victory than ever because of genetic research.

But where some see the advances that genetic engineering has produced, Rifkin sees a new wave of eugenic zealots eager to use our genetic makeup as even more revealing of our true nature than the SAT.

Ripped from the Headlines

Rifkin relies primarily on national news magazines and newspapers to sketch both the developments in and the predictions for various aspects of this scientific revolution, and, in that sense, his story is one ripped from the headlines. His persistent complaint is that journalists fail to present balanced coverage because of a delight in describing the often dazzling possible uses of the technology at issue. What's left out, he argues, are the myriad ethical issues that coalesce around the question of whether progress, by itself, is a good thing.

Trying to interpret the scientific breakthroughs that are changing the way we think of both ourselves as individuals and the dominant species on the planet, Rifkin details seven strands of what he calls the new operational matrix of the biotech century. It's not the evil that men do that outlives them; it's the mischief that computers and genetic research can get us into when they are spliced together that we need to worry about.

Four strands of the biotech century's matrix encompass recombinant DNA techniques; the wholesale reseeding of the planet with genetically enhanced and devised plants; gene mapping; and computers that can probe and manage the vast genetic resources of our bodies and our planet. The other strands include the ideological, philosophical, and cultural structures supporting the new research and its application.

In Rifkin's view, the courts are primarily to blame for this state of affairs because they have allowed for the patenting of genetically altered cells, thus creating a slippery slope that we will be unable to negotiate. Going further, however, he argues that a new cultural context has emerged that favors the new biotechnologies. Underpinning all of this is a new cosmological narrative that sees evolution as an improvement in information processing, rather than as a random process of selection winnowing its way through passive natural elements.

They Know Not What They Do

Rifkin complains that the scientists know not what they do, unwittingly creating Frankensteins at every turn. He objects that their sheer ability to do something seems to them justification enough to just do it. They are too little concerned with the collateral effects of genetic engineering.

It's clear that Rifkin is writing for an audience already persuaded by his general thesis and by his credentials as a prophet of doom. And he wants us to know that he was right in all the predictions on genetic engineering that he began making 20 years ago. But the world still hasn't caught on to the issue as he has framed it—that progress is generally bad—so he's back for more hectoring. What Rifkin does not want to accept is that as a culture we desire and embrace progress.

The press does not seem guilty of the one-sided reporting that Rifkin ascribes to it. Recently, for example, *The New York Times* featured two reports on a new technique in genetic engineering that allows scientists to take embryonic human stem cells before they have distinguished themselves as the type of cell they will be, such as a brain cell or heart cell; the technique then coaxes those cells to morph into the type of cell that is needed. The result is that heart cells can be grown and then used to heal the heart when it fails—all rather heady—or should I say hearty—stuff.

The use of such new cell technology has been condemned by some because it comes perilously close to infringing on our notion of what constitutes an individual. As opponents see it, there is a great difference between using stem cells from miscarried fetuses, which a spokesperson for the Catholic

Church finds acceptable, and using cells derived from pre-implantation embryos that were created in fertility clinics. To use the latter cells is to use humans for research, the opponents stress.

Annoying Disingenuousness

One senses, however, that Rifkin would not have been satisfied with the coverage that the ethical issues received, because the heart of the story emphasizes that scientists are all but dancing with excitement over this new technology. There is, at the core of Rifkin's book, an annoying disingenuousness. He poses himself in a neutral posture that pretends to provide us with the information we need to decide if this biotech century is for us; at the same time, Rifkin urges us to think that the problems created by the new technologies outweigh the possible benefits.

Two lines of reasoning in particular show how, despite his good intentions, Rifkin seems out of touch with reality, at least as it is defined by law. The first is the supposed exploitation of indigenous peoples by agribusiness and pharmaceutical companies that search the world, especially the world in the southern hemisphere, for new plants that yield new drugs or new strains of foodstuffs. The indigenous peoples, the argument does, have done all the work in cultivating the plants over time, which makes the genetic manipulations of the big companies a negligible contribution at best, certainly not one entitling them to patent protection and profits. What Rifkin does not want to acknowledge is that patents are hard earned and necessary for research to continue. Rifkin wants a world that does not privilege the capacity of science to make productive what otherwise wouldn't be. His is a politically correct world, blissfully ignorant of law's contribution to society.

The second and perhaps more revealing line of misguided reasoning is Rifkin's unwillingness to accept patent law for what it is. The Supreme Court has recognized that the distinction is not between living and inanimate things, but between products of nature, whether living or not, and human-made inventions. Rifkin's argument is that scientists cannot be said to create anything patentable because the life they manipulate was already there. That is a narrow and misguided view of both the law and of what scientists do. The law sides with progress; Rifkin sides against it. What Rifkin cannot accept is what Justice William O. Douglas wrote in *The Great A&P Tea Co. v. Supermarket Corp.*, 340 U.S. 147 (1950)—30 years before the celebrated oil-eating bacteria case of 1980: That the inventions that most benefit mankind are those that "push back the frontiers of chemistry, physics and the like."

As his book makes all too clear, Rifkin does not want to explore the frontier. He wants to circle the wagons and hold off, through the pouting in his book, that which cannot be held back. Those concerned with the ethical implications of genetic research are with us and are heard. That we as a society want to search the frontier should not be dismissed, as Rifkin so keenly wants to dismiss them, as ignorant, selfish or misguided.

POSTSCRIPT

Should Patenting Life Be Forbidden?

In general, the United States has adopted the "cost-benefit approach" to problems with new products. If Americans cannot foresee the consequences of a new technology, they tend to make educated guesses about the benefits of all kinds and the probable costs and balance the one against the other. Engineered seeds seem to have the potential to increase crop yields, cut labor costs, and not inconsequentially, lower the use of fertilizers and pesticides. Those are benefits. Costs may be negligible. Is this a good argument for going ahead with the new life forms and allowing the companies the patents they need to make them profitable?

In Europe, on the other hand, the custom is to use the "precautionary approach" toward new technology. Europe's strategy is if the costs are unknown, then try the seeds in a small controlled area for a long time and see what develops. Only after the seeds are proven safe over generations will Europeans make them publicly available. Which approach do you think is the best for such new technologies?

Suggested Readings

Lester R. Brown, "Struggling to Raise Cropland Productivity," *State of the World 1998* (Norton, 1998).

Charles C. Mann, "The Brave New World of Science and Business," *Foreign Policy* (December 1998).

Ho Mae-Wan, *Genetic Engineering: Dream or Nightmare?* (Gateways Books, 1998).

G. Tyler Miller, *Living in the Environment,* 11th ed. (Brooks/Cole Publishing, 2000).

ISSUE 16

Should We Encourage International Trade in Tobacco Products?

YES: International Tobacco Growers Association, from *ITGA Issues Papers Nos. 2, 14, and 3* (April 1996)

NO: Simon Chapman, from "Tobacco Control," *British Medical Journal* (July 13, 1996)

ISSUE SUMMARY

YES: The International Tobacco Growers Association is ecstatic about the success in spreading tobacco growing into developing nations. The Association argues that tobacco is a product that is easier to grow than many other agricultural products and promises substantial economic progress for people who desperately need it.

NO: Associate professor Simon Chapman, assuming that the goal of reducing tobacco use worldwide takes first priority, suggests stopping the export of tobacco products and of tobacco-growing technology. He states that now that we have discovered the damage done by tobacco, it is wrong to spread that damage abroad for the sake of profit.

The normal form of an ethical controversy in business features one side making and selling a product, blissfully unaware of anything controversial, aiming only to make an honest profit out of an honest enterprise, while the other side cries "Halt!" on account of the consequences unnoticed by the promoters of the enterprise.

In the case of tobacco, the voices crying "Halt!" have been heard at least since 1964, when Luther Terry, U.S. Surgeon General and a heavy smoker himself, first presented the grim findings of a strong association between tobacco use and serious disease—especially lung cancer. Following that presentation, debate continued for some years on the truth of those findings, with the health care industry generally arguing that tobacco is a serious threat to human health and the Tobacco Institute, hastily cobbled together by the tobacco industry to present a solid front to a hostile world, arguing that Terry's charges were unproved. Thirty-five years later, the charges are accepted by most to be true—too late for Terry himself, who made several unsuccessful attempts to stop smoking and eventually died of lung cancer. Now the question becomes, What obligations should there be to minimize smoking among the populations of the world, given the knowledge that smoking is terribly dangerous?

Here, the International Tobacco Growers Association is delighted to find an international market for its product. At a time when every company that hopes to survive into the next century must "go global," and when tobacco use is falling in the United States, the discovery of an international market must be good news for the industry. Isn't it? Of course, the reason that tobacco use is falling in the United States is that Americans realize that tobacco kills its users. Even the Tobacco Institute agrees with that now. If something kills people, should they be allowed to have it? Or, if it is something they might choose to have, even knowing how really bad it is, should we refrain from pushing it on them and attempting to profit from the sale of it? The ethical dilemma involving the marketing and sale of dangerous products is made more complicated if the people to whom a product is sold do not know how dangerous the product is. An example is the small-pox laden blankets that some unscrupulous settlers gave the Native Americans, who were so grateful for this deadly favor. Is the tobacco industry doing the same thing when it sells tobacco to developing nations and persuades them to use it, pushing on them the means of their own death, them all unknowing? The International Tobacco Growers Association and Chapman are coming at the subject from very different perspectives, and they may seem at first glance to be talking past each other. They are not—this is a moral argument in the very first stages of its existence, when a nonbusiness orientation toward a subject runs directly counter to the usual business, or business-as-usual, orientation.

As you read the following selections, bear in mind that tobacco was America's first export crop when the country was very young and that it has always played a role in the country's image and prosperity. Yet, it kills. Some say, enough regulation, let the world make a choice and let the farmers make a profit for a change. Others say, How can tobacco growers set out in all innocence to poison the world?

275

International Tobacco
Growers Association

 YES

ITGA Issues Papers

Tobacco—A Major World Crop

Tobacco, the world's most widely cultivated non-food crop, is a major contributor to the global economy. China leads the field of more than 100 countries in which it is grown, followed by the United States, Brazil, India and Turkey. That these top five countries span four continents graphically illustrates how successfully it is grown around the world.

In 1994, global production reached 6.388 million tonnes greenweight, a decrease of 23 per cent on 1993. Despite this one-year down turn, the trend looks set to continue upward in the light of the UN Food & Agriculture Organisation's (FAO) forecast of a 1.5–2 per cent rise in annual leaf tobacco production and consumption between now and 2000—a projection based both on population growth and improvements in disposable income.

It has become increasingly evident that the developing world is building its share of global tobacco production. This evidence is apparent from production figures for the 1980s, showing growth of 3.4 per cent a year for developing countries, compared with a decline of 0.9 per cent elsewhere. In the remaining years of the 20th century, the largest growth rates are expected in Indonesia (up 4.3 per cent), China (3.1 per cent) and Zimbabwe (2.4 per cent), while developed countries will return a more modest one per cent growth rate.

Looked at another way, developing countries 30 years ago accounted for 53 per cent of world production; today, they account for more than 80 per cent, as they respond to world-wide demand for quality tobaccos.

International Trade

About 25 per cent of total global production is traded internationally; the rest meets domestic demand. The ratio is slowly changing, however, and about 30 per cent of production is expected to be traded internationally by 2000.

Despite the projected increase in production, the total area of land under tobacco is reducing, as better cultivation methods lead to higher productivity. There are approximately 4.3 million hectares under tobacco today, but they account for a mere 0.3 per cent of the world's arable and permanent crop areas —less than half the area (0.7 per cent) devoted to coffee, for example.

Global Employment

Tobacco cultivation, being highly labour intensive, is a major global employer. Estimates suggest that, if workers' families, seasonal workers and landless labourers are included, some 33 million people are currently employed. If all tobacco-related industries and processes are added, the figure is at least 100 million.

By comparison, only about 1.65 million are involved in the cultivation of maize or sugar cane. Change is unlikely, at least in the developing countries where mechanisation can be expensive and often of limited benefit....

Balance of Payments

Tobacco can often make a considerable contribution to a developing country's balance of payments, particularly one with few viable alternative sources of foreign exchange. Kenya, for example, though better placed than many, with tea, coffee and horticultural produce accounting for about half its export revenue, began a tobacco growing programme in 1974. Then, annual tobacco production accounted for only five per cent of domestic needs.

Today, Kenya is not only self-sufficient but a small exporter. Compared with other crops, tobacco provides markedly higher gross margins to farmers than maize and cotton. While tobacco's share of exports is still small in absolute terms, growth has helped to diversify the national export base, reduce economic risk and provide more market opportunities for farmers.

In Latin America the position is different. Here, developing countries are less dependent on primary commodities than they are in Africa, as can be seen when tobacco earnings as a proportion of national export income are compared. Taking the two extremes, 1992 figures show that in Brazil tobacco accounted for 2.2 per cent of export income, while in Zimbabwe tobacco accounted for a 36.4 per cent share.

Foreign Exchange

Without tobacco revenue, the social and economic development plans of many developing countries might be postponed or simply shelved. Imports of basic foodstuffs, particularly in periods of shortage, might not be affordable. A recent case study from Zimbabwe illustrates how important tobacco's contribution can be.

As with several African countries, where population growth has outstripped food supply, severe drought in 1992 accentuated its dependence on food imports. Traditionally self-sufficient in basic foodstuffs, Zimbabwe had to import large quantities of maize, wheat and sugar, much of which was paid for by the foreign exchange earnings of tobacco exports.

Tobacco is attractive to farmers because it is traded on a simple supply and demand basis. Production and price are based on manufacturers' predictions of demand, bearing in mind the quality of the crop and residual stocks they hold. The result is a relative price stability not enjoyed by other crops. UNCTAD [United Nations Conference on Trade and Development] figures show that over the ten years to 1993 tobacco prices were more stable than any of 30 or so agricultural commodities, except beef.

Pricing

World Bank figures show that between 1985 and 1993 tobacco prices fell by 29 per cent which, without explanation, may appear to contradict UNCTAD. A look at other agricultural commodities, however, shows greater falls over the same period, so that among the non-foods were rubber (58 per cent), cotton (36 per cent) and jute (35 per cent); among the foods were coffee (68 per cent), cocoa (67 per cent) and maize (40 per cent). Further, the World Bank forecast an increase in the price (in current $US terms) of tobacco of 21 per cent between 1990 and 2005, compared with 15 per cent for maize.

According to the EIU [Economist Intelligence Unit], tobacco consumption is likely to rise faster in the final four years of this century than between 1990 and 1995. Clearly, this forecast offers no logical reason for farmers to switch from tobacco to other high-yield complementary crops. But these are scarce and, if the forecast proves incorrect, developing countries would either be forced to place greater reliance upon aid flows, or suffer a decline in socio-economic standards....

World Tobacco Leaf Data

Tobacco is grown in more than 120 countries. In 1997, total production was 7.3 million metric tons (dry weight), of which 1.9 million tons (26 per cent) was exported from the country of production.

Tobacco leaf is grown in developed and developing countries, in both northern and southern hemispheres, and in a wide range of climatic and soil conditions.

China, the United States, India, Brazil, Turkey, Zimbabwe, Indonesia, Italy, Greece and Malawi are the leading producers, with China the biggest of all at 3.1 million tons in 1997—42.5 per cent of worldwide output....

The Economic and Social Value of Tobacco in Grower Countries

Abstract: Tobacco growing provides developing countries with foreign income and work both for growers and in the post cultivation chain. (April 1996)

...Developing countries account for about 75 of the world's tobacco producers and for many of them the cultivation, processing and export of tobacco is of major economic and social significance. Coincidentally, these countries are also responsible for about 80 per cent of world production. Some, particularly Brazil, Bulgaria, China, Malawi and Zimbabwe, are heavily dependent on the crop as a leading source of foreign income. In other countries, such as India and Turkey, tobacco has an important regional significance.

World-wide leaf production reached about 6.388 million tonnes (green-weight) in 1993, an increase of nearly 40 per cent since 1987. Yet through ever-improving technology and rising productivity, the total area under cultivation amounts to a mere 0.3 per cent of all arable land world-wide, less than half that under coffee, for example.

Socio-Economic Infrastructure

The importance of tobacco growing can be demonstrated by looking at the part it plays in the socio-economic infrastructure of producer countries, beginning with employment figures. A current estimate suggests that tobacco growing world-wide sustains at least 33 million full-time or seasonal workers, while another 70 million or so are employed in tobacco-related industries.

The majority of these jobs are in developing countries, where tobacco cultivation is particularly suitable for women and unskilled labourers who would otherwise find work difficult or impossible to obtain. Where husbands and wives are both involved in cultivation, family prosperity is boosted as a consequence. Family farming is an essential part of the rural society structure in developing country agriculture.

In Malawi, for instance, which is the world's twelfth largest producer, tobacco growing provides a living for over half the farming population. This, in turn, means that fruitless job-seeking migrations to the cities, the "urban drift" seen all too often elsewhere, are averted.

Even in developed countries, where greater mechanisation has reduced the number of jobs, the tobacco industry still provides employment and prosperity for more than 1.5 million people.

Gross Domestic Product

The economic worth of tobacco leaf and manufactures can be expressed as a ratio of a country's earnings to its Gross Domestic Product (GDP). According to UNCTAD, Malawi's tobacco exports between 1989 and 1991 represented a massive 14 per cent of its GDP, ahead of Zimbabwe at 6.2 per cent and Bulgaria at 3.5 per cent. For most developing countries tobacco's share ranges from 0.1 to 2.5 per cent of GDP.

Foreign exchange earnings from tobacco can also be significant to developing countries. Many rely on these earnings to help reduce their balance of trade deficits, as well as to finance essential domestic advancement programmes. A 1992 International Tobacco Growers Association study of the tobacco industry in central and southern Africa showed, for example, that Zimbabwe generated 20 times as much in foreign exchange per hectare from tobacco as it did from cotton, and 59 times as much from soya.

Further, the production and manufacture of tobacco for home consumption also produces domestic income, while governments are able to derive significant taxation revenue from its production, sale and export.

Cash Crop

For the individual grower, tobacco is one of the most remunerative, reliable and stable short-term cash crops. Despite the careful husbandry tobacco needs at all stages of growth, net returns per hectare are generally several times greater than those obtained from industrial crops such as cotton and sugar, as well as from cereals and other staple foodstuffs. Other crops can be successfully grown in a rotation with tobacco.

Tobacco's relative price stability is another point in its favour. UNCTAD figures show that over the ten years to 1993 tobacco prices were more stable than any of 30 or so other agricultural commodities, with the exception of beef. Its price stability exceeded that of sugar, tea and wheat by factors of roughly four, three and two respectively. Looking ahead, the World Bank forecasts that while maize prices are likely to rise 15 per cent by 2005, the price of tobacco is projected to rise by 21 per cent.

Employment Chain

But it is not just the growers for whom tobacco cultivation brings benefits. Once the crop has left the fields it must be prepared for home consumption or export. Leaving manufacturing aside, tobacco must be sorted and graded, stored, marketed, insured, packaged and transported to factories or docks; export crop has to be shipped. In fact, it has been estimated that for every five people involved in growing tobacco, another individual is employed in the post-cultivation chain.

Increasingly, the prosperity of tobacco growers is shared by the communities in which they operate. The larger tobacco farms, for example, contribute substantially to improving local infrastructure, as well as being a means of private capital formation. Another feature in many countries is the development of on-farm health and education services which bring normally town-based facilities to rural communities. Individuals are able to buy more food and other goods and services from stores, thus contributing directly to their local economy.

The Economist Intelligence Unit (EIU) has forecast that tobacco production will need to grow faster between now and 2000, a view that emphasises the certainty of a continuing role for tobacco cultivation. The stark alternatives would be either that developing countries would place greater reliance on aid, or suffer a decline in socio-economic standards. As the EIU says: *"Other crops . . . can provide many of the benefits of tobacco cultivation . . . (but) few, if any, can rival tobacco overall."*

NO ↩

Simon Chapman

Tobacco Control

T he world now has an estimated 1.1 billion smokers—that is, about one third of the global population aged 15 years and over. Most of these smokers (800 million) live in developing countries. China alone has 300 million smokers (90% men), about the same number as in all the developed countries combined. About one third of regular smokers in developed countries are women, compared with only about one in eight in the developing world.(1)

During 1990–2 smokers consumed some 6.05×10^{12} cigarettes per year,(1) with an estimated three million deaths annually, a figure which is expected to rise to 10 million a year by the 2020s or early 2030s. Seventy per cent of these deaths will occur in developing countries.(2)

With such huge numbers, advances in tobacco control worthy of the name must have potential to make major inroads into those factors that promote current rates of smoking. Otherwise they risk being marginalised as largely irrelevant to efforts to address seriously what is without doubt a global pandemic....

Tobacco Taxation

Tobacco products have a price elasticity in Western nations of approximately −0.5, meaning that a 10% rise in price causes a 5% fall in demand.(3) In recognition of this, tobacco companies regularly wage price wars with each other and are implacable in their opposition to rises in tax on tobacco. With smoking typically being more common in income groups with lower disposable income and evidence that cessation in low income groups is much more responsive to price rises than in higher income groups,(4) price policy is widely considered to be of the highest priority among tobacco control strategies. Given the lack of resources and infrastructure devoted to tobacco control in most developing countries, price policy holds enormous but largely unexplored potential as a cost free means of reducing demand.(5) However, because cheaper, "tax unpaid," smuggled cigarettes are widely available in many developing nations,(6) tax policy may not prove to be as feasible in such countries.

Regulation of Tobacco

Historically, all nations have treated tobacco as if it were a simple grocery item, with minimal regulation often applying to its availability, packaging, and advertising. In the United States the Food and Drug Administration has proposed to regulate tobacco as a drug delivery device(7) and has consequently been the target of an unprecedented lobbying campaign by the tobacco industry.(8) The administration's recommendations are being strongly supported by President Clinton. If legislation goes ahead, it will allow (by other national standards) the modest regulation of tobacco advertising and access by minors. The real implication of this development, however, lies in the Pandora's box of possibilities that will open both for the United States and for other nations in areas such as generic (plain) packaging,(9) full disclosure of additives, and serious restrictions on the number of retail outlets.

Tobacco Advertising and Promotion

There are encouraging signs of substantial momentum in the hitherto glacial acceptance by governments that tobacco advertising is of critical importance in influencing children to start smoking and in the willingness of governments to act to control advertising. Several Asian nations, including China, have recently implemented new restrictions on tobacco advertising. The tobacco industry has had considerable success with its strategy of arguing that, unlike every other industry, its advertising is not directed at recruiting new consumers. The poverty of this argument has recently come under further pressure from recent research showing the greater responsiveness of children than current smokers to advertising.(10),(11),(12)

Over 100 nations now restrict tobacco advertising to some degree.(13) In recent years Australia, New Zealand, and Canada have introduced all but total bans on tobacco advertising, exempting point of sale advertisements. Canada's ban was overturned by the High Court in 1995 but is expected to be reintroduced when the government reclassifies tobacco as a restricted product, subject to the same sort of controls as pharmaceuticals.

In the United States, Philip Morris, the world's largest tobacco company, has offered to cooperate with one of the Food and Drug Administration's recommendations that tobacco advertising should not be sited within 1000 feet (300 m) of schools or playgrounds.(14) The amusing logic here—that a billboard at 999 feet could influence children but at 1001 feet would be benign— is none the less of symbolic importance as an industry admission that tobacco advertising can influence children.

Major concern remains about the potential of satellite television to deliver tobacco advertising to international audiences. National laws on tobacco advertising may become historic irrelevancies in the era of satellite communication.

The Trojan Horse of Passive Smoking

Concern about the effects of passive smoking on the health of non-smokers has widened the tobacco debate fundamentally from "my smoking is dangerous to my health" to include "your smoking is dangerous to my health," thereby transforming the ethical justification for smoking control policies from paternalism to Millian precepts.(15) The implacable worldwide efforts by the tobacco industry to discredit the epidemiological evidence on passive smoking and to support "smokers' rights" movements(16) is explicable in terms of the loss of sales caused by smoking bans.(17) When people cannot smoke at work their daily consumption falls by up to 25%(18),(19)—a level unprecedented in any other intervention. Cessation is also promoted by workplace bans.(20) As smoking bans in the workplace and on public transport proliferate,(21) the number of cigarettes forgone will correspondingly increase.

Harm Reduction

Other areas of drug policy have long embraced a harm reduction philosophy, where population-wide goals of "zero use" are seen as largely unrealistic, obviating the need for policies that can at least reduce harm. By contrast, international tobacco control has always been dominated by absolutist precepts, where slogans such as "no safe level of use" have assumed inviolate status. Those supporting this position argue that policies that in any way facilitate reduced tobacco use are both dangerous and naive distractions from policies that are cessation oriented. This absolutism has tended to dampen enthusiasm for policies that reduce either smoking or the delivery of harmful tobacco constituents to smokers. This debate seems certain to be tested by the development of new tobacco products such as Eclipse—a largely smokeless cigarette that delivers carbon monoxide and vaporised nicotine to the smoker, but not tar.(22) R [J] Reynolds, Eclipse's manufacturer, has sought dialogue with the tobacco control community, resulting in considerable debate between absolutists and those who are more pragmatic. Critics of this development point to the market failure of similar prototypes and caution that tar free cigarettes may serve merely to divert smokers from stopping smoking, maintaining nicotine addiction before likely reversion to routine cigarette smoking. With evidence from several nations that the decline in adult smoking has stalled, the harm reduction debate is likely to increase, with many challenging questions arising for researchers about reducing the risks for continuing smokers.

Nicotine Replacement Therapy

Nicotine gum and patches are now widely regarded as important innovations in smoking cessation, with meta-analyses finding rates of cessation in users in a variety of settings that are two to three times higher than with placebo or no nicotine replacement therapy.(23),(24) With several countries now ending the prescribing monopoly and rescheduling nicotine replacement therapy to make it available over the counter, higher rates of use are expected because of easier access.(25) Rescheduling can also allow nicotine replacement therapy to be advertised to the public, leading to the broadcast and publication of many more motivational messages about cessation. Important research questions will arise about the comparative skills of physicians and pharmacists in counselling smokers about cessation.(26),(27)

Legal Actions

The 1990s will be remembered in the history of tobacco control as the decade when legal actions against the tobacco industry became turbocharged with state initiated actions, private class actions, and personal injury lawsuits. These include:

- Seven US states suing tobacco companies for recovery of health care Medicaid costs in treating diseases caused by tobacco in the indigent (one tobacco company, Liggett, has agreed to pay 5% of pretax income —to a maximum of $50m (pound 33.3m) a year—for 25 years(28));
- A Florida class action on behalf of non-smoking current and former flight attendants who assert that they have diseases caused by their exposure to tobacco smoke in aircraft cabins;
- The Castano class action—a case filed by a consortium of 60 prominent American law firms on behalf of "all nicotine-dependent people in the United States... who have purchased and smoked cigarettes manufactured by the defendants." The case focuses on addiction and is based on recent statements by the Food and Drug Administration's commissioner, David Kessler, that tobacco companies intentionally sell cigarettes with an addictive level of nicotine.(29),(30) The plaintiffs claim that tobacco companies manipulate the level of nicotine in cigarettes so that it is addictive and allege that the defendants engaged in, among other things, fraud, deceit, negligent misrepresentation, and violation of consumer protection statutes.

Whistleblowing and Leaks

In the past two years the United States has seen an unprecedented series of whistleblowers come forward from the tobacco industry with both extensive documentation(31) and testimony (32),(33),(34) covering the industry's knowledge and tactics on health effects, nicotine addiction, passive smoking, and marketing strategies. Whatever the outcome of the legal testimonies of these individuals in the various cases to which they are contributing, their revelations have caused huge and unprecedented negative media coverage about the tobacco industry, from which the industry is unlikely to recover politically.

References

(1) World Health Organisation. The tobacco epidemic: a global public health emergency. Tobacco Alert 1996 (special issue): 1–26.

(2) Peto R., Lopez, A. D., Boreham, J., Thun M., Heath C. Mortality from tobacco in developed countries: indirect estimation from national vital statistics. Lancet 1992; 339: 1268–78.

(3) Townsend, J. Price and consumption of tobacco. Br Med Bull 1996; 52: 132–42.

(4) Townsend, J., Roderick, P., Cooper, J. Cigarette smoking by socioeconomic group, sex, and age—effects of price, income, and health publicity. BMJ 1994; 309: 923–7.

(5) Chapman, S., Richardson, J. Tobacco excise and declining tobacco consumption: the case of Papua New Guinea. Am J Public Health 1990; 80: 537–40.

(6) Joossens, L., Raw M. Smuggling and cross border shopping of tobacco in Europe. BMJ 1995; 310: 1393–7.

(7) Food and Drug Administration. Regulations restricting the sale and distribution of cigarettes and smokeless tobacco products to protect children and adolescents: proposed rule. United States Federal Register 1995; 60: 41314–75.

(8) Arno, P. S., Brandt, A. M., Gostin, L. O., Morgan, J. Tobacco industry strategies to oppose federal regulation. JAMA 1996; 275: 1258–62.

(9) Cunningham, R., Kyle, K. The case for plain packaging. Tobacco Control 1995; 4: 80–6.

(10) Evans, N., Farkas, A., Gilpin, E., Berry C., Pierce, J. Influence of tobacco marketing and exposure to smokers on adolescent susceptibility to smoking. J Natl Cancer Inst 1995; 87: 1538–45.

(11) Pierce, J., Gilpin, E. A historical analysis of tobacco marketing and the uptake of smoking by youth in the United States: 1890–1977. Health Psychol 1995; 14: 500–9.

(12) Pollay, R. W., Siddarth, S., Siegel, M., Haddix, A., Merritt, R. K., Giovino, G. A., Eriksen, M. P. The last straw? Cigarette advertising and realized market shares among youths and adults, 1979–1993. Journal of Marketing 1996; Apr: 1–16.

(13) Chapman, S. The ethics of tobacco advertising and advertising bans. Br Med Bull 1996; 52: 121–31.

(14) Thanks but, no, thanks to Philip Morris' offer. Government should not compromise with cigarette giant editorial. Los Angeles Times 1996; May 17.

(15) Goodin, R. E. The ethics of smoking. Ethics 1989; 99: 574–624.

(16) Cardador, M. T., Hazan, A. R., Glantz, S. A. Tobacco industry smokers' rights publications: a content analysis. Am J Public Health 1995; 85: 1212–7.

(17) Chapman, S., Borland, R., Hill, D., Owen, N., Woodward, S. Why the tobacco industry fears the passive smoking issue. Int J Health Services 1990; 20: 417–27.

(18) Borland, R., Chapman, S., Owen, N., Hill, D. Effects of workplace bans on cigarette consumption. Am J Public Health 1990; 80: 178–80.

(19) Woodruff, T. J., Robbrook, B., Pierce, J., Glantz, S. A. Lower levels of cigarette consumption found in smoke-free workplaces in California. Arch Intern Med 1993; 153: 1485–93.

(20) Longo, D. R., Brownson, R. C., Johnson, J. C., Hewett, J. E., Kruse, R. L., Novotny, T. E., et al. Hospital smoking bans and employee smoking behavior. JAMA 1996; 275: 1252–7.

(21) Kyle K., Du Melle, F. International smoke-free flights: buckle up for take-off. Tobacco Control 1994; 3: 3–4.

(22) Feder B. J. A safer smoke? Or just another smokescreen? New York Times News Service 1996; Apr 12.

(23) Silagy, C., Mant, D., Fowler, G., Lodge, M. Meta-analysis on efficacy of nicotine replacement therapies in smoking cessation. Lancet 1994; 343: 139–42.

(24) Fiore, M. C., Smith, S. S., Jorenby, D. E., Baker, T. B. The effectiveness of the nicotine patch for smoking cessation. A meta analysis. JAMA 1994; 271: 1940–7.

(25) Ramstrom, L. M. Use of nicotine replacement therapy with and without prescription. Proceedings of future directions in nicotine replacement therapy, Paris, October 1993. Chester: ADIS International, 1994.

(26) Morgall, J. M. Pharmacists helping smokers to quit. An evaluation of a Danish initiative. Copenhagen: Department of Social Pharmacy, Royal Danish School of Pharmacy, (nd).

(27) Silagy, C., Muir, J., Coulter, A., Thorogood, M., Yudkin, P., Roe, L. Lifestyle advice in general practice: rates recalled by patients. BMJ 1992; 305: 871–4.

(28) Feder, B. J. A united front by big tobacco starts to crack: Liggett agrees to settle class-action lawsuit. New York Times 1996; Mar 14: A1, D6.

(29) Kessler, D. A. Statement on nicotine-containing cigarettes. Tobacco Control 1994; 3: 148–58.

(30) Kessler, D. A. The control and manipulation of nicotine in cigarettes. Tobacco Control 1994; 3: 362–70.

(31) Glantz, S. A., Slade, J., Bero, L. A., Hanauer, P., Barnes, D. E. The cigarette papers. Berkeley: University of California Press, 1996.

(32) Freedman, A. M., Hwang, S. L. Three ex-employees say Philip Morris deliberately controlled nicotine levels. Wall Street Journal 1996; Mar 19: B1.

(33) Skolnick, A. A. Cancer converts tobacco lobbyist: Victor L. Crawford goes on the record. JAMA 1995; 274: 199–202.

(34) Prey M. A mole's tale. American Lawyer 1995; Jul/Aug: 86–93.

POSTSCRIPT

Should We Encourage International Trade in Tobacco Products?

In perspective, the tobacco problem is a product of America's success, pure and simple. Tobacco may be enjoyable to many, but it is risky in a world that has become increasingly averse to risk. When the life expectancy of the people of the world was 40 years, and a healthy adult might hope to live to 60 years, the threat of cancer did not seem so oppressive—there were hundreds of other things of which to die before cancer. As America has cleaned up the risks—wiping out infections with antibiotics, forcing employers to make the workplace safer, banking roads, requiring seatbelts for automobiles and helmets for riding horses and motorcycles, and reconstructing playgrounds with strap swings and rubber floors—Americans have become accustomed to safe lives. The risks remaining, one by one, have become unacceptable. But has society gone too far?

Meanwhile, Americans are rich, and tobacco is a luxury. When people live at the subsistence level, they do not buy tobacco. But prosperity has spread worldwide, for the present. That is why the United States is finding an export market for tobacco. With wealth comes choices. With choices come bad choices. Purchasing tobacco is considered a bad choice. Should people nonetheless be free to make it? And should American products be available when the choice is made?

Suggested Readings

P. S. Arno, A. M. Brandt, L. O. Gostin, and J. Morgan, "Tobacco Industry Strategies to Oppose Federal Regulation," *JAMA* (vol. 275, 1996).

Centers for Disease Control and Prevention, "Tobacco Use and Usual Source of Cigarettes Among High School Students" (United States, 1995).

Simon Chapman, "The Ethics of Tobacco Advertising and Advertising Bans," *British Medical Bulletin* (vol. 52, 1996).

David A. Kessler, "Statement on Nicotine-Containing Cigarettes" and "The Control and Manipulation of Nicotine in Cigarettes," *Tobacco Control* (vol. 3, 1994).

A. A. Skolnick, "Cancer Converts Tobacco Lobbyist: Victor L. Crawford Goes on the Record," *JAMA* (vol. 274, 1995).

World Health Organization, "The Tobacco Epidemic: A Global Public Health Emergency," *Tobacco Alert* (1996).

ISSUE 17

Should We Export Pesticides to Developing Nations?

YES: Kenneth E. Goodpaster and Laura L. Nash, from *Policies and Persons: A Casebook in Business Ethics,* 3rd ed. (McGraw-Hill, 1998)

NO: Jefferson D. Reynolds, from "International Pesticide Trade: Is There Any Hope for the Effective Regulation of Controlled Substances?" *Journal of Land Use & Environmental Law* (1997)

ISSUE SUMMARY

YES: Professor Kenneth E. Goodpaster and professor Laura L. Nash state that due to its increasing population, the world will need all the food that can be grown to feed the people. This pertains mostly to the people of the developing world, where population growth is the highest. They concede that pesticides can be dangerous if abused but assert that the risks are outweighed by the certainty of death by starvation if pesticides are not used.

NO: Captain Jefferson D. Reynolds of the United States Air Force argues that developing countries lack the resources to protect their people from dangerous chemical exports. He considers pesticide exposure to be a major health problem, which is simply not getting the attention it deserves, and urges more regulation.

Certain claims about trade may be accepted without reservation: First, we are living in an increasingly interconnected world, in which international trade plays an increasingly large part; second, much of the manufacturing traditionally done in the United States can now be done better offshore, threatening U.S. jobs and balance of trade; third, it follows that the United States should be eager to engage in as much export trade as possible. Pesticides have proven a profitable product in the past. Now that other nations want pesticides, should the United States supply them?

Proponents of pesticides argue that we have 6 billion people walking this earth right now, and they all have to be fed. There are places in this world, as in developing nations, where food shortages are chronic, and at least part of the reason for this is that each crop must be shared with insects.

If the developing world needs pesticides to combat famine, should the United States assist these countries by exporting pesticides? Opponents argue that pesticides can hurt, maim, or kill many organisms besides insects, and historically, we have seen them do just that. The most effective pesticides kill everything that lives, in sufficient quantities, and linger in the environment long enough to kill their eggs. Rachel Carson's book *Silent Spring* (1962) proved the danger of unregulated use of DDT to bird populations, especially to the large raptors highest on the food chain. Without adequate regulation —to eliminate the most dangerous of the pesticides and to control carefully the application of the ones that are left—the use of pesticides poses significant dangers to the environment and to the humans that work with them. The United States has undertaken such regulation, pursuant to Carson's warnings, and many once-popular pesticides are no longer in use there.

There is a peculiar wrinkle in the profitable pesticides export trade. Many of the pesticides that America exports are banned for use in the United States, because they are dangerous for birds or people. The bans lead to idle manufacturing capacity and sometimes large inventories of pesticides that cannot be sold. But often there is no law against exporting them. Just as often, the developing nations to which pesticides are sent are glad to have them.

What is the United States doing when pesticides banned for use in America are exported to a developing nation? Are Americans simply making a deal, a very advantageous trade for both sides? Or, are Americans taking advantage of the inability of many developing nations to regulate for the health and safety of their own people? On the one hand, these nations need pesticides; on the other, they may suffer the respiratory diseases, liver complications, and birth defects that have been associated with pesticide poisoning. Should that concern Americans?

As you read the following selections, bear in mind that the United States is not the only nation that has a chemical industry and that if Americans seize the moral high ground by refusing to export substances that might harm somebody somewhere, other nations' industries will likely undertake to make up for that supply. U.S. pesticides may actually be safer than theirs. On the other hand, do Americans want to be party for profit to this very dangerous activity?

Kenneth E. Goodpaster
and Laura L. Nash

 **YES**

Note on the Export of Pesticides from the United States to Developing Countries

From the 1940s to the late 1970s the pesticide industry, driven by the frequent introduction of new products, experienced rapid growth. Investment of R&D [research and development] was high to sustain innovation and cheaper manufacturing processes. In 1981 R&D budgets were 8% of sales. The industry also required high capital investment because of the rapid obsolescence of plant and equipment; thus, capital expenditures were 7.2% of sales. These high technology costs, as well as high regulation and marketing costs, posed significant barriers to entry.

Sales of U.S. producers steadily increased from $1.2 billion in 1972 to $5.4 billion in 1982.... Exports steadily rose from $220 million in 1970 to about $1.2 billion in 1980. Production of pesticides in the U.S. rose from 675 million pounds in 1960 to a peak of 1.7 billion pounds in 1975 and declined to 1.3 billion pounds in 1980.

Prices and profits for pesticides depended largely on whether or not patents were involved. Pretax profit margins on proprietary products that had a market niche were about 48%. Older products, like DDT and 2,4–D, functioned more like commodities and returned considerably less on investment. Even though a product was patented, competing companies often developed similar products not covered by the original patent. Prices of pesticides tripled between 1970 and 1980; in 1981 herbicides had the highest price and accounted for 60% of sales.

The pesticide industry was a mature industry and U.S. markets had become saturated. As demand in the U.S. slowed, exports increased. In 1978 exports were 621 million pounds and were 36% of total shipments. In 1990, it was predicted, exports would be 855 million pounds and would be 43% of total pesticide shipments. Dollar volume of U.S. exports was projected to reach $2.6 billion by 1990.[1]

Industry analysts agreed that exports would provide the fastest growth for U.S. producers, since the U.S. markets were saturated. Farmers were also using fewer pesticides because of increased costs, declining acreage under cultivation, a slowing of growth in farm income, and increased use of integrated pest management (IPM) techniques which relied more on cultural and biological controls and less on pesticides.

There were 35 producers of pesticides worldwide with sales of more than $100 million per year. In 1982 total worldwide sales were $13.3 billion, up from $2.8 billion in 1972. Six countries—United States, West Germany, France, Brazil, the USSR, and Japan—accounted for 63% of worldwide sales. All of the developing countries combined accounted for 15% of the worldwide market in dollar volume. A report by the U.S. General Accounting Office (GAO) estimated that pesticide requirements in dollar value for these countries were expected to increase fivefold from 1979 to 1985.[2]

The Benefits of Pesticides

The pesticide industry and many agricultural scientists defended the sale of pesticides to developing countries, declaring that pesticides were necessary to feed an ever-increasing world population, most of it poor, and that pesticides were of great value in fighting diseases which primarily affected the poor. They also argued that there were important secondary benefits.

In 1979 the world population reached approximately 4.4 billion people. Using a minimum-intake level for survival, with no allowance for physical activity, the Food and Agricultural Organization (FAO) of the United Nations estimated that there were 450 million chronically malnourished people in the world. Using a higher standard, the International Food Policy Research Institute put the figure at 1.3 billion.[3]

World population doubled from A.D. 1 to A.D. 1650; a second doubling occurred after 200 years; the next took 80 years; and the last doubling took place in 1975, requiring only 45 years. Given the 1980 worldwide average birthrate of 2.05%, according to Norman Borlaug the next doubling would occur in 2015, when world population would total 8 billion. At that birthrate, 172 people would be born every minute, resulting in an additional 90 million people each year. David Hopper of the World Bank stated that developing countries accounted for 90% of this increase.[4]

In 1977, Borlaug noted, world food production totaled 3.5 billion tons, 98% of which came directly or indirectly from plants. On the basis of rates of population growth and projected income elasticities for food, Hopper emphasized the necessity for an increase in food availability of about 3% per year, requiring a doubling of world food production to 6.6 billion tons by 2015. Increasing demand for food by developing countries was reflected in the fact that imports of grains to these countries rose from 10 million tons in 1961 to 52 million tons in 1977, according to Maurice Williams, and food shortages were projected to reach 145 million tons by 1990, of which 80 million tons would be for the low-income countries of Asia and Africa.[5]

A major cause of these shortages was that food production in developing countries had not kept pace with the increased demand for food. While per capita production of food for developed countries had steadily increased since 1970, per capita production in developing countries *decreased* by an average of 50%, with the economies of Africa and Latin America showing the greatest drop.

Although experts agreed that it was important to attack the world food problem by lessening demand, they also concurred that deliberate efforts to slow population growth would not produce any significant decline in demand for food for the next decade or so. It was argued, then, that ameliorating the world food problem depended on increasing the food supply. Norman Borlaug, recipient of the 1971 Nobel Peace Prize for the development of the high-yield seeds that were the basis for the Green Revolution, argued that developed countries would not make significant additional increases in yields per acre and that developing countries had to increase their per capita food production. Due to the scarcity of easily developed new land, Borlaug concluded that increases in world food supply could come only from increased yields per acre in these countries, and that this required the widespread use of pesticides.[6]

There was little argument, even from critics, that pesticides increased food production. The technology of the Green Revolution, which depended on pesticides, had enabled scientists in the tropics to obtain yields of 440 bushels of corn per acre versus an average yield of 30 bushels per acre by traditional methods.[7] The International Rice Research Institute in the Philippines had shown that rice plots protected by insecticides yielded an average of 2.7 tons per hectare (2.47 acres) more than unprotected plots, an increase of almost 100%. They also found that the use of rodenticides resulted in rice yields up to three times higher than those of untreated plots.[8] (*Only* producing more food would not end world hunger. What kinds of foods people eat and the quantity are correlated with income. Thus, many experts maintain that economic development is equally important in eliminating world hunger.)

Even with the use of pesticides, worldwide crop losses because of pests before harvest averaged about 25% in developed countries and around 40% in undeveloped countries. In 1982, GIFAP estimated that total crop losses due to pests for rice, corn, wheat, sugar cane, and cotton were about $204 billion. Most experts (quoted in Ennis et al.) estimated an additional loss of 20–25% of food crops if pesticides were not used.[9]

Pesticides also contributed to reducing losses after harvesting. A National Academy of Sciences study identified most postharvest loss resulting from pests and observed that "conservative estimates indicate that a minimum of 107 million tons of food were lost in 1976; the amounts lost in cereal grains and legumes alone could produce more than the annual minimum caloric requirements of 168 million people." Postharvest losses of crops and perishables through pests were estimated to range from 10% to 40%. Insects were a major problem, especially in the tropics, because environmental conditions produced rapid breeding. The National Academy of Sciences noted that "50 insects at harvest could multiply to become more than 312 million after four months." In India, in 1963 and 1964, insects and rodents attacked grain in the field and in storage and caused losses of 13 million tons. According to Ennis et al., this amount of wheat would have supplied 77 million families with one loaf of bread per day for a year.[10]

Many developing countries also relied on the sale of agricultural products for foreign exchange that they needed for development or to buy the commodities they could not produce. Cotton, for example, was an important cash crop for many of these countries. Several experimental studies in the United States had shown that untreated plots produced about 10 pounds of seed cotton per acre, but over 1,000 pounds were produced when insecticides were used.[11] It was estimated that 50% of the cotton produced by developing countries would be destroyed if pesticides were not used.

It was also argued that major indirect benefits resulted from the use of an agricultural technology that had pesticide use as an essential component. This "package" was more efficient not only because it increased yields per acre, but also because it decreased the amount of land and labor needed for food production. In 1970 American food production, for example, required 281 million acres. At 1940 yields per acre, which were generally less than half of 1970 yields, it would have taken 573 million acres to produce the 1970 crop. This was a savings of 292 million acres through increased crop yields.[12] The estimated 300% increase in per capita agricultural production from 1960 to 1980 also meant that labor resources could be used for other activities. Other experts estimated that without the use of pesticides in the United States, the price of farm products would probably increase by at least 50% and we would be forced to spend 25% or more of our income on food.[13] It was held that many of these same secondary benefits would accrue to developing countries through the use of pesticides.

Pesticides also contributed both directly and indirectly to combating disease; because of this, their use in developing countries had increased. Pesticides had been highly effective in reducing such diseases as malaria, yellow fever, elephantiasis, dengue, and filariasis. Malaria was a good example. In 1955, WHO initiated a global malaria eradication campaign based on the spraying of DDT. This effort greatly reduced the incidence of malaria. For example, in India there were approximately 75 million cases in the early 1950s. But in 1961 there were only 49,000 cases. David Bull estimated that by 1970 the campaign had prevented 2 billion cases and had saved 15 million lives. In 1979 Freed estimated that one-sixth of the world's population had some type of pest-borne disease.[14]

Notes

1. "Pesticides: $6 Billion by 1990," *Chemical Week,* May 7, 1980, p. 45.
2. *Better Regulation of Pesticide Exports and Pesticide Residues in Imported Foods Is Essential* (Washington, DC: General Accounting Office, 1979), p. 1.
3. Maurice J. Williams, "The Nature of the World Food and Population Problem," in *Future Dimensions of World Food and Population,* ed. by R. G. Woods (Boulder, CO: Westview Press, 1981), p. 20.
4. Norman Borlaug, "Using Plants to Meet World Food Needs," *Future Dimensions,* p. 180; David Hopper, "Recent Trends in World Food and Population," *Future Dimensions,* p. 37.
5. Borlaug, pp. 118, 128; Hopper, p. 39; and Williams, p. 11.
6. Borlaug, p. 114 and pp. 129–34.

7. Hopper, p. 49.

8. Bull, p. 5.

9. *GIFAP Directory* 1982–1983, p. 19; W. B. Ennis, W. M. Dowler, W. Klassen, "Crop Protection to Increase Food Supplies," in *Food: Politics, Economics, Nutrition, and Research,* ed. P. Abelson (Washington, DC: American Association for the Advancement of Science, 1975), p. 113.

10. E. R. Pariser et al., *Post-Harvest Food Losses in Developing Countries* (Washington, DC: National Academy of Sciences, 1978), pp. 7, 53; Ennis et al., p. 110.

11. William Hollis, "The Realism of Integrated Pest Management as a Concept and in Practice—with Social Overtures," paper presented at Annual Meeting of Entomological Society of America, in Washington, DC, December 1, 1977, p. 7.

12. Borlaug, p. 106.

13. Ennis et al., p. 113.

14. Bull, p. 30; Virgil Freed, in *Proceedings,* in p. 21.

NO

Jefferson D. Reynolds

International Pesticide Trade: Is There Any Hope for the Effective Regulation of Controlled Substances?

Introduction

... In the last decade, the international community has grown increasingly concerned with pesticides and their effects on human health and the environment, with particular emphasis on the threat posed in developing countries. Workers in developing countries are exposed to pesticides in the course of their work to provide produce for domestic consumption as well as for export to developed countries like the United States (U.S.). Because export dollars are so valuable to developing countries, there is added pressure to produce a higher yield of produce. These countries often obtain a higher yield through the use of pesticides considered too dangerous to use in developed countries. Therein lies the crisis, large international corporations are able to sell pesticides abroad that cannot be sold in the U.S. These corporations sell pesticides that are classified as so harmful to human health and the environment, that their use cannot be justified for any purpose. In response to worldwide concerns, the United Nations has advanced some important initiatives to regulate the international pesticide trade. For example, in 1985 the United Nations Food and Agriculture Organization (FAO) published the International Code of Conduct (Code) on the Distribution and Use of Pesticides, giving participating countries a formal method to refuse or consent to hazardous imports. FAO designated this method the "Prior Informed Consent" (PIC) procedure. Developed and developing countries alike welcomed PIC because this procedure possesses a common sense approach to the problem by providing an important link in the transfer of information on pesticides to developing countries that otherwise would not have access to the information....

From Jefferson D. Reynolds, "International Pesticide Trade: Is There Any Hope for the Effective Regulation of Controlled Substances?" *Journal of Land Use & Environmental Law*, vol. 13, no. 1 (Fall 1997). Copyright © 1997 by *Journal of Land Use & Environmental Law*. Reprinted by permission. Notes omitted.

Adverse Effects of Pesticides

Pesticides play a vital role in protecting crops and livestock, as well as in controlling vector-borne diseases. In many countries, pesticides also present significant dangers to people and the environment. The danger to people arises from residues in food crops and livestock, as well as from the handling of pesticides by farmers. Farm workers suffer from pesticide exposure the most, with an estimated 20,000 deaths each year. Ninety-nine percent of these deaths occur in developing countries due to farming practices, storage of pesticides in living areas, location of residential areas near application sites, method of application and type of equipment used. Pesticides also cause water pollution, soil degradation, insect resistance and resurgence, and the destruction of native flora and fauna.

Of all the potential hazards of pesticides, the most serious is the risk to human health. Adverse effects of exposure include cancer, reproductive impairment, mutation and neuro-toxicity. Recently, pesticides have also been found to cause endocrine disruption. The pesticide bio-accumulates in human tissue, mimicking estrogen and disrupts regular hormonal activity.

The high incidence of injury in developing countries primarily results from inadequate information on proper application methods, insufficient government resources to monitor pesticide use, and the greater availability of highly toxic substances than in developed nations. For example, field and packing plant workers in Chile have little knowledge about the hazards of pesticides. The workers wear no protective clothing and continue to work in the fields while airplanes or tractors pass by spraying produce. The workers are primarily young, transient, uneducated individuals with little political influence to improve the situation.

Common environmental problems associated with pesticides include contamination of water resources and insect resistance and resurgence. Some pesticides deplete the ozone and exacerbate the greenhouse effect. Further, diffuse aerial spraying of fields damages non-target crops and may destroy non-target species. Pesticides that enter the waterways through run-off result in fish kills. Wild animals and domestic livestock also ingest pesticides by drinking contaminated water or by eating smaller animals and vegetation in which toxic chemicals exist. Persistent pesticides like DDT do not dissolve, and concentrate in the fatty tissue of animals. DDT bio-accumulates, moving up the food chain until it finally becomes part of the human diet.

Excessive use of pesticides leads to the destruction of natural enemies and the resurgence of pest species, which in turn leads to increased spraying. This process is commonly known as the "pesticides treadmill," which leads to the resistance of pesticides. In extreme cases, a pesticide can create a more destructive "super pest" by altering the genetic composition of the insect. In India, the introduction of DDT to reduce malaria resulted in the number of cases dropping from 7.5 million to 50,000; however, increased resistance eventually raised the number back to 6.5 million. Although only 182 existed in 1965, there are now more than 900 pesticide and herbicide resistant species of insects, weeds, and plant pathogens, while seventeen insects show resistance to all major categories of insecticides. In addition, resistant species of weeds have grown from twelve to eighty-four.

The foregoing information illustrates that agrichemicals have a profound and significant impact on human health and the environment. However, a solution must also objectively evaluate why these substances are so highly valued. Pesticides increase the food yield for an ever-increasing populace. Measuring the environmental and health damage that results from pesticide exposure against the famine that would result without pesticides is a model not yet constructed.

DDT probably best illustrates the double-edged nature of pesticides. Although restricted from use in the U.S. in 1972, several developing countries still use it as an effective defense against vector-borne diseases like malaria, yellow fever, river blindness, elephantiasis and sleeping sickness. Developing countries must consider what is more beneficial to public health by balancing the disabling or fatal effects of vector-borne disease with the disabling or fatal effects of DDT use. This is particularly important since DDT is a known carcinogen found to increase the risk of breast cancer in women exposed to the pesticide by a magnitude of four.

Vietnam exemplifies the abuse of pesticides. Since Vietnam's shift to a free market economy in 1988, agricultural exports have been increasing with the use of pesticides. Emphasizing agriculture, Vietnam has enjoyed steady economic growth. To maintain yield, farmers have applied increasing amounts of DDT to fight pest resistance. Unfortunately, this practice shows little sensitivity to the long-term adverse effects on the environment and sustainable economic development. Soil acidification and salinization has occurred in conjunction with contamination of fisheries and water resources. The U.S. exhibits little sensitivity to the issue. The Pesticide Action Network (PAN), a special interest group tracking pesticide exports, reported that the U.S. exported fifty-eight million pounds of banned pesticides between 1991 and 1994, making the U.S. a key contributor to the degradation of human health and the environment in Vietnam.

The "Circle of Poison"

As early as 1981, various pesticides restricted in the U.S. were exported to developing countries, only to return as residues concentrated in imported foods. This problem has been termed the "circle of poison." In 1989, the General Accounting Office (GAO) reported that the circle of poison was a concern because the EPA was not monitoring the content, quantity, or destination of exported, unregistered pesticides under sections 17(a) and 17(b) of the Federal Insecticide, Fungicide and Rodenticide Act (FIFRA). Specifically, the GAO found that the EPA "does not know whether export notices are being submitted, as required under FIFRA" and that "notices were not sent for three pesticides (out of four) that were voluntarily canceled [by the manufacturer] because of concern about toxic effects."

The U.S. is a leading producer of pesticides, contributing fourteen percent of the world's export market. At least twenty-five percent of the four to six hundred million pounds of pesticides exported annually are not registered with the EPA. The EPA canceled or suspended some of these chemicals because of the dangers they pose to human health and the environment, and in some cases manufacturers voluntarily withdrew their products. Because the U.S. exports a high percentage of unregistered pesticides, these chemicals have a high potential to reenter this country as residues on imported foods. For example, Chile is a large market for U.S. manufacturers of pesticides. Included in the 1,460 pesticides used by Chile are Lindane, a substance banned in the U.S.; Paraquat, which contains dioxin; and Parathion, a toxic organic phosphate that has restricted use in the U.S. In addition, Chile uses Methyl Bromide. Ironically, these pesticides are either banned or restricted in the U.S., but may be used on produce that is eventually imported by the U.S. . . .

Conclusion

The current unregulated practice of exporting chemicals to developing countries has yielded unfortunate consequences. Although the developed world feels the effects of pesticide trade, a majority of the detrimental impacts on human health and the environment afflict the developing world. Unfortunately, developing countries generally lack the resources, information and expertise to protect their people from dangerous chemical exports that are banned or severely restricted in developed countries. The incidence of pesticide exposure worldwide suggests that a major public health problem is not receiving the attention it deserves. New methods for estimating the true incidence of pesticide poisoning must be explored. The fact that exposure is almost exclusively in developing countries, even when pesticide consumption is so low in comparison to developed countries, would suggest research needs to be conducted to develop exposure intervention programs.

There is also a critical shortage of information on pesticide exposure, resulting in an inability to evaluate the true environmental and human health impacts of pesticides. Little is known about the effects of long term exposure to pesticide residues in food. Further, the lack of exposure data internationally makes the problem difficult to evaluate. As this [selection] illustrates, exposure data is outdated and available only through special interest groups or from international organizations that currently suffer from budget shortfalls. For example, the most recent comprehensive exposure study was conducted by the World Health Organization in 1988. That report conservatively estimated over one million exposures occur annually. Many developing countries do not keep track of exposure data, and those that do often fail to report the data to central organizations like the United Nations. There are indications of a worldwide pesticide exposure crisis, but there is little data to confirm or deny the conclusion. The situation can be associated with a patient who would rather not be examined for fear of hearing the news of a costly diagnosis. If reliable exposure data were available, perhaps there would be more interest in the problem leading to firm and decisive regulation.

One approach certain to bring responsibility to pesticide trade is to outlaw or severely restrict the export of those pesticides the U.S. has banned, withdrawn registration or severely restricted. Furthermore, pesticides that have no registration could also be included among those outlawed for export. This is probably the most unlikely resolution because the U.S. has a significant share of the global pesticide industry. Chemical lobbies and politicians alike have long recognized that foreign pesticide manufacturers would be more than satisfied to obtain the U.S. share of pesticide exports.

Although domestic and international efforts are moving toward full disclosure of the dangers and proper use of pesticides, no single set of rules can ensure the safe use of pesticides under every condition. Instruction and restriction apply to specific pesticides, formulations, application methods and commodities. In an effort to help resolve this problem, governments and industry alike should follow strict PIC procedures. Demanding good conduct on the part of industry in exchanging toxicological information between states, and having rules on trading, labeling, packaging, storage and disposal will have a beneficial impact. The current trend in the pesticide industry involves more training time for agricultural workers and greater company efforts to monitor pesticide use.

Current initiatives to curb pesticide trade problems offer little assistance in resolving exposure problems without a firm commitment by the world's key chemical exporting countries. The voluntary nature of international "soft law" schemes render them virtually unenforceable in today's lucrative international chemical market. Moreover, until the international market reflects a level economic playing field, powerful domestic lobbies will likely defeat U.S. initiatives on a legislative level. Incentives greater than money must exist before key chemical producing countries would submit to a convention mandating responsible trade. Perhaps proponents should stress the potential loss of life and the danger of domestic food safety, in hopes that ethical and moral motivations will prevail.

POSTSCRIPT

Should We Export Pesticides to Developing Nations?

Pesticides kill things and then persevere in the environment to kill things in the future. That is what is good about them and bad about them. At this writing, the continued export of pesticides and other lethal substances (including tobacco and guns) is of intense concern to business ethicists and many legislators.

Suggested Readings

Pesticides: For Export Only, film, Richter Productions (1981).

William Hollis, "The Realism of Integrated Pest Management as a Concept and in Practice With Social Overtures," presented at the Annual Meeting of the Entomological Society of America (1977).

Lake Sagaris, "Conspiracy of Silence in Chile's Fields: Pesticide Spraying of Fruit Results in High Levels of Birth Defects," *Montreal Gazette* (November 27, 1995).

World Health Organization, Division of Health and Environment, *Pesticides and Health in the Americas,* Environmental Series #12.

Food and Agriculture Organization, *International Code of Conduct on the Distribution and Use of Pesticides,* U.N. Document MIR8 130.

Executive PayWatch

Executive PayWatch, sponsored by the AFL-CIO, is a working families' guide to monitoring and curtailing the excessive salaries, bonuses, and perks in CEO compensation packages.

http://www.aflcio.org/paywatch/

FAQs About Free-Market Environmentalism

Sponsored by the Thoreau Institute, this site lists and answers frequently asked questions about free-market environmentalism. It is the institute's position that a free-market system can solve many environmental problems better than more government regulation can.

http://ti.org/faqs.html

Pennsylvania Department of Environmental Protection

This home page of the Pennsylvania Department of Environmental Protection monitors environmental responsibility.

http://www.dep.state.pa.us

PART 6

Environmental Policy and Corporate Responsibility

*M*ankind's attempts to protect the environment have involved many conflicts over fundamental values. We know that the environment must be protected, but the natural environment cannot participate in our political processes as an interest group nor can it buy itself protection on the open market. So we have to put aside the fundamental model of human action as rule-governed competition; nature cannot compete. This section considers a debate on strategies for preventing the destruction of the tropical rain forests. In exploring corporate responsibility, this section also features a debate on whether or not CEO compensation is justified by performance.

- Is CEO Compensation Justified by Performance?

- Can Green Marketing Save Tropical Rain Forests?

ISSUE 18

Is CEO Compensation Justified by Performance?

YES: Kevin J. Murphy, from "Top Executives Are Worth Every Nickel They Get," *Harvard Business Review* (March/April 1986)

NO: Lisa H. Newton, from "The Care and Feeding of the Truly Greedy: CEO Salaries in World Perspective," An Original Essay Written for This Volume (1999)

ISSUE SUMMARY

YES: Professor of finance and business economics Kevin J. Murphy argues that chief executive officers (CEOs) are simply paid to do what they were hired to do—bring up the price of the stock to increase shareholder wealth. He concludes that for large increases in shareholder wealth, CEOs deserve large compensation.

NO: Professor of philosophy Lisa H. Newton finds the ultimate effect of large compensation packages on U.S. business to be negative. She asserts that the disparity between CEOs' wealth and the pay of their workers—let alone the poverty-stricken developing world—is unjust and a case of bad stewardship of resources.

CEOs are paid a lot to face facts, however unpleasant," writes Geoffrey Colvin in *Fortune* (1992), "so it's time they faced this one: The issue of their pay has finally landed on the national agenda and won't be leaving soon." He ticks off the sources of national discontent with the enormous sums (and stocks, etc) paid to the corporate chiefs: layoffs continue; the lowest paid workers advance only slowly; Japanese CEOs are paid much less for much more productivity; but mostly, paying one person more money than he can ever spend on anything worthwhile for himself or his family, while the world's millions struggle, just seems to be wrong.

According to John Cassidy's *New Yorker* article, "Gimme" (November, 1997), since Colvin wrote, CEO compensation has gone much higher—by a factor of 4 for the average compensation up to factors of 15 and 20 for fortunate individuals. The reason for the increase is clear enough to Cassidy: stock prices have gone up; shareholder wealth has increased enormously; and for reasons detailed in the following selections, shareholders wish to compensate managers of their companies according to the increase in the price of the stock. Is this right? The shareholders' interests legitimately dictate some aspects of corporate policy, and the salaries have been agreed upon by the legally appropriate parties, but if the result is substantially unjust, should not the people as a whole step in and rectify the situation?

That possibility is precisely what troubles Colvin. If CEOs will not regulate their own compensation, Congress and the Securities and Exchange Commission (SEC) will surely step in and do a bit of regulating on their own. The prospect is not enticing to the business community. On the other hand, is this not exactly why we have government—so that when private motives get out of hand, the people can step in and defend their long-term interests?

As you read the following selections, bear in mind that the corporation was set up as a private enterprise; it is a voluntary contract among investors to increase their wealth by legal means. But it is chartered and protected by the state, in the service of the state's long-term interest in a thriving economy. Economist Adam Smith would be pleased; he argued that leaving investors to make money as best they could for their own selfish interests would best increase the welfare of the whole body of the people. The question is, At what point do we conclude that the legal means set up for private parties to serve our interests by serving their own have failed of their purported effect and should be modified or revised? Or, do we have any right to make such a judgment?

Kevin J. Murphy

 **YES**

Top Executives Are Worth
Every Nickel They Get

Each spring, critics, journalists, and special-interest groups devour hundreds of corporate proxy statements in a race to determine which executive gets the most for allegedly doing the least. They're running the wrong race.

The "excessive" compensation paid these greedy types, we are told, gouges the nation's 30 million shareholders. Their salaries are arbitrarily set at outrageous levels without regard to either profitability or performance. Moreover, the six- and seven-digit base salaries are just the tip of the compensation iceberg—executives fatten their already sizable paychecks severalfold through bonuses, stock options, and other short- and long-term incentive plans. As a result, the public view prevails that executives are paid too much for what they do and that compensation policies are irrational and ignore the needs of shareholders.

Simply put, the public view is wrong and based on fundamental misconceptions about the managerial labor market. One reason for these misconceptions is that executive compensation is an emotional issue. And because critics become wound up in their emotions, they rely on a blend of opinion, intuition, and carefully selected anecdotes to prove their points.[1] Of course, such anecdotal evidence is not useless and may even be valuable in identifying abuses in the compensation system when carefully interpreted. Critics cannot use such evidence, however, to show compensation trends or to support across-the-board condemnations of compensation policies.

I have devised a better way to test the validity of the complaints about executive pay by subjecting each proposition to a series of logical and statistical tests. My data are drawn, in part, from an examination of the compensation policies of almost 1,200 large U.S. corporations over ten years and are supplemented by the findings of a 1984 University of Rochester symposium, "Managerial Compensation and the Managerial Labor Market."[2] My results paint a very different picture of executive compensation by showing that:

- The pay and performance of top executives are strongly and positively related. Even without a direct link between pay and performance, executives' incomes are tied to their companies' performance through

stock options, long-term performance plans, and, most important, stock ownership.
- Compensation proposals like short- and long-term incentive plans and golden parachutes actually benefit rather than harm shareholders.
- Changes in SEC reporting requirements and a shift toward compensation based on long-term performance explain most of the apparent compensation "explosion." This shift links compensation closely to shareholder wealth and motivates managers to look beyond next quarter's results.

Of course, some executives are overpaid or underpaid or paid in a way unrelated to performance. But, on average, I have found that compensation policies encourage executives to act on behalf of their shareholders and to put in the best managerial performance they can.

Pay & Performance

Because shareholders are the owners of the corporation, it makes sense to analyze the executive compensation controversy from their perspective. One way to motivate managers is to structure compensation policies that reward them for taking actions that benefit their shareholders and punish them for taking actions that harm their shareholders. Shareholders measure corporations in terms of stock price and dividend performance. Thus a sensible compensation policy would push an executive's pay up with good price performance and down with poor performance.

A common criticism of compensation policies is that they encourage executives to focus on short-term profits rather than on long-term performance. Assuming efficient capital markets, current stock price reflects all available information about a company, thus making its stock market performance the appropriate measure of its long-term potential. My analysis... indicates that compensation gives executives the incentive to focus on the long term since it is implicitly or explicitly linked to their companies' stock market performance.

The statistics in *Table 1* compare the rate of return on common stock (including price appreciation and dividends) with percentage changes in top executives' salaries and bonuses over ten years. I have grouped the data, which represent sample averages, by the companies' stock price performance, but experiments with alternative measures like sales growth and return on equity yield similar qualitative results.

Throughout the ten-year period, executives received inflation-adjusted average annual increases in salary and bonus of 7.8%; more important is the positive relationship shown between the rate of return on common stock and average percentage changes in salary and bonus. When returns were less than −20%, executives received pay increases of only .4%; when performance exceeded 40%, pay increases averaged 13.8%.

As *Table 1* shows, the relationship between pay and performance has remained positive over time and has actually become stronger in recent years.

Table 1

Relationship Between Rate of Return on Common Stock and Percentage
Changes in Executive Salary and Bonus 1975–1984

	1975-1984		1975-1979		1980-1984	
Annual rate of return on common stock	Number of executive-years in sample	Average annual change in salary and bonus	Number of executive-years in sample	Average annual change in salary and bonus	Number of executive-years in sample	Average annual change in salary and bonus
Entire sample	6,523	7.8%	3,314	6.9%	3,209	8.8%
Less than -20%	639	0.4%	257	0.5%	382	0.4%
-20% to 0%	1,734	5.3%	1,002	5.5%	732	4.9%
0% to 20%	1,917	8.3%	989	7.5%	928	9.2%
20% to 40%	1,212	9.6%	538	7.1%	674	11.6%
More than 40%	1,021	13.8%	528	11.1%	493	16.6%

Note: Rates of return and percentage pay increases have been adjusted for inflation. As an example of how the rate of return is calculated, suppose that a share of stock worth $10 at the beginning of the year had increased in price to $12 by the end of the year and that the company paid cash dividends of $1 per share during the year. The holder of a share of the company's common stock would have realized a return of $3, or 30% for the year. Salary and bonus data were constructed from *Forbes* annual compensation surveys from 1975 to 1984. The sample consists of 1,948 executives in 1,191 corporations.

Chief executives in companies with returns greater than 40% received inflation-adjusted average annual increases in salary and bonus of 11.1% from 1975 to 1979 and 16.6% from 1980 to 1984....

As measured by the rate of return on common stock, a strong, positive statistical relationship exists between executive pay and company performance. These results are sharply at odds with recent studies that compare pay levels with measures of profitability and conclude that compensation is independent of performance.[3] The problem with such studies is that they look at the level of executive compensation across companies at a particular time instead of considering the extent to which compensation varies with companies' performance *over time*. This is an important distinction. Whether a company has well-paid—or low-paid—executives tells us nothing about the sensitivity of pay to performance.

To illustrate, consider two well-documented relationships—the positive relationship between company size and executive compensation and the negative one between company size and the average rate of return realized by shareholders.[4] From these it follows that a large company would have low rates of return and well-paid executives, while a small company would have high rates of return and low-paid executives. You'd conclude that pay and performance didn't correlate, and you'd be right if you took this kind of snapshot of the relationships. But if you took a moving picture—that is, looked at the results over time—you'd see that the pay of individual executives and the performance of their companies are strongly and positively related.

It is better to study how executive pay varies from year to year in a given company. *Table 1* ... show[s] that changes in executive pay mirror changes in shareholders' wealth. Two studies presented at the Rochester symposium corroborate this result. The first was based on a sample of 461 executives in 72 manufacturing companies over 18 years; in it I examined salary, bonus, stock options, deferred compensation, total compensation, and stock ownership. It shows that executive compensation parallels corporate performance as measured by the rate of return on common stock.[5]

Another study of 249 executives from as many companies from 1978 to 1980 reaches the same conclusion. It found a strong, positive correlation between changes in executive compensation and stock-price performance (adjusted for marketwide price changes). Ranking companies on the basis of their stock-price performance, it suggests that those in the top 10% will raise their executives' compensation by an inflation-adjusted 5.5% and those in the bottom 10% will lower pay by 4%. In addition, the study finds that chief executives in the bottom 10% of the performance ranking are almost three times more likely to leave their companies than executives in the top 10%.[6]

The Expanded Compensation Package

... Most studies in the financial press consider *only* salary and bonus and ignore potentially crucial variables like restricted stock, stock options, and long-term performance plans. In fact, these plans have become increasingly important. By their very nature, these plans tie executives' ultimate compensation directly to their companies' performance.

Executives' holdings of their companies' common stock constitute a large part of their wealth. The value of these stock holdings obviously goes up in good years and down in bad ones, quite independently of any relationship between performance and base pay. Suppose an executive with $4 million of stock sees the share price drop 25%. Because of his company's poor performance in the securities market, he has lost a million dollars—a loss that trivializes anything a board of directors might do to his base pay.

To assess the importance of inside stock ownership, I collected a 20-year time series of chief executive officer data from the proxy statements of 73 *Fortune* "500" manufacturing companies. Executives in this sample, which covered fiscal years 1964 through 1983, held an average (in 1984 constant dollars) of almost $7 million in their companies' common stock. Although this sample does not include shares held by family members and outside trusts, it does include a few executives with extraordinary stock holdings; the median stock holding for executives in this 20-year period is $1.5 million. That is, 50% of the chief executives in the 73 sample companies held more than $1.5 million in their companies' common stock....

Does Generosity Backfire?

Executive employment contracts are determined by the board of directors, which in turn is elected by shareholders. A cooperative relationship between executives and their directors is usually required for corporate success, and some have incorrectly interpreted this fact as evidence that executives can set their own salaries by pushing their compensation plans past "captive" directors. A friendly relationship between executives and their boards does not mean that the executives are free of constraints; rather, constraints usually operate in subtle yet powerful ways.

For example, some corporations have adopted short- and long-term compensation plans that pay off only if the executives meet a certain performance standard. Golden parachutes, which compensate executives if they leave their company after a takeover, have also grown in popularity. If, as some critics contend, these plans benefit executives and harm shareholders, you would expect stock prices to fall at the announcement of the plan. Likewise, if these plans benefit shareholders, you would expect prices to rise.

Three symposium studies examined market reaction. One found that average stock prices rise by about 11% when companies make the first public announcement of bonus and other plans that reward short-term performance.[7] Another concluded that shareholders realize a 2% return when companies adopt long-term compensation plans.[8] A third study found that, on average, stock prices increase by 3% when companies announce the adoption of a golden parachute provision.[9] This favorable reaction supports the contention that golden parachutes benefit shareholders by removing managers' incentives to block economically efficient takeovers. The price increase may also indicate that takeovers are more likely when golden parachutes are adopted but does not indicate that these provisions harm shareholders.

In each study, stock values not only increase when companies announce compensation plans but also continue to trade at the new, higher levels. The studies thus support the idea that such plans help align the interests of executives and shareholders and signal "good times ahead" to the market. They refute the view that executives "overreach" when they adopt lucrative compensation schemes.

On average, executives do not harm shareholders when they alter employment-contract provisions nor do they arbitrarily set their own salaries. If executives were truly able to set their salaries, why wouldn't they make them comparable with those of rock stars like Michael Jackson, whose income is many times that of even the highest paid executive? The only way the "set-their-own-salaries" argument works is if you assume that these salaries are somehow within some reasonable range of the competition—what other executives in similar industries are paid.

What's Out of Hand?

"Top management pay increases have gotten out of hand," warns Arch Patton, citing an apparent "explosion in top management compensation."[10] Indeed, a casual (but careless) look at compensation totals published in the business press seems to justify such concern. *Figure 1* shows the total compensation received by the nation's best paid executives from 1974 to 1984 using *Forbes* data (unadjusted for inflation). Before 1977, the fattest paycheck hovered around $1 million but then jumped to $3.4 million in 1978, $5.2 million in 1979, and $7.9 million in 1980. Warner Communications' Steven Ross shattered the eight-digit barrier with a total compensation of $22.6 million in 1981; in 1982, Frederick Smith of Federal Express received a total package of $51.5 million. The figure "plummeted" in 1983 to the mere $13.2 million received by NCR's retiring William Anderson but rebounded in 1984 to the $23 million received by Mesa's T. Boone Pickens, Jr.

A closer look at the data reveals that the apparent increase stems, in part, from a shift in the structure of compensation and has been exaggerated by changes in SEC reporting requirements. Moreover, the increase does not indicate that the conflict of interest between executives and their shareholders has worsened. Rather, the trend reflects a growing reliance on stock options and other long-term performance plans designed to link compensation more closely with shareholder wealth. The often spectacular payoffs are a once-in-a-lifetime experience.

For example, Frederick Smith's 1982 salary and bonus of $413,600 accounted for less than 1% of his $51.5 million total compensation; if the ranking had been based on salary and bonus alone, he wouldn't have made the top 300. NCR's William Anderson received only 8% of his 1983 compensation in the form of salary and bonus; his salary and bonus of $1,075,000 was only the nation's thirty-seventh highest. (Mr. Pickens's 1984 salary and bonus of $4.2 million was indeed the nation's highest but included $3 million for services provided in 1982 and 1983 when bonuses were not awarded.) In any given year, only a small percentage of executives enjoy big gains from stock options or other performance plans. The overwhelming majority get most of their compensation in the form of salaries and cash bonuses.

Even so, the great popularity of stock options and other long-term performance plans has several implications. First, an executive's pay in any given year reflects amounts actually accrued or earned over several years and tends to increase the maximum compensation observed, just as a switch from weekly to monthly pay periods will increase the maximum compensation observed in any given week (for example, the last week of the month).

Second, long-term performance plans give high rewards for excellent performance but are neutral toward poor or mediocre performance. It's the same as designing a state lottery with one grand prize of $1 million rather than a hundred prizes of $10,000 each; you increase the amount paid to the winner but not the total amount awarded. If the chief executives of ten different companies were each awarded stock options at the beginning of the year, their value at the

Figure 1

Total compensation received by the nation's highest paid executives
1974–1984

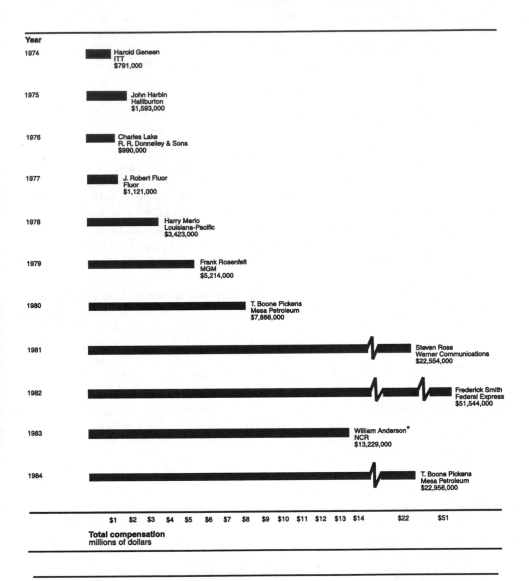

Year

1974 — Harold Geneen / ITT / $791,000

1975 — John Harbin / Halliburton / $1,593,000

1976 — Charles Lake / R. R. Donnelley & Sons / $990,000

1977 — J. Robert Fluor / Fluor / $1,121,000

1978 — Harry Merlo / Louisiana-Pacific / $3,423,000

1979 — Frank Rosenfelt / MGM / $5,214,000

1980 — T. Boone Pickens / Mesa Petroleum / $7,866,000

1981 — Steven Ross / Warner Communications / $22,554,000

1982 — Frederick Smith / Federal Express / $51,544,000

1983 — William Anderson* / NCR / $13,229,000

1984 — T. Boone Pickens / Mesa Petroleum / $22,956,000

$1 $2 $3 $4 $5 $6 $7 $8 $9 $10 $11 $12 $13 $14 $22 $51

Total compensation
millions of dollars

Note: Data are not adjusted for inflation. Total compensation before 1978 does not include gains from exercise of stock options.

Source: Forbes, various issues.
*Forbes does not include Anderson in its 1984 compensation survey since he retired just prior to the end of the 1983 fiscal year.

date of grant might be similar. By the end of the option period, however, only a few would be worth a great deal of money; the others would be worthless.

Third, most long-term performance plans are based on stock prices. The stock market boom produced high payoffs from 1981 to 1983, while the market decline in the 1970s produced low or zero payoffs. Thus an executive awarded an equal number of stock options or performance plan units each year would have realized zero gains during the stock market decline and large gains during the boom; cyclical movements produced increases in the dollar amounts realized even though the amounts granted under these plans remained relatively constant.

Finally, before 1978, the payoffs from stock options and other long-term plans were reported in a somewhat incomprehensible table at the back of corporate proxy statements. Changes in SEC reporting rules have moved these payoffs to the front of the statement, where they are much more accessible to the media. Compensation totals published in *Forbes* (see *Figure 1*) and other business periodicals before 1978 exclude option realizations; data published after 1978 include them. The editors of these compensation surveys warn against making year-to-year comparisons when the definitions have changed. Unfortunately, critics have often ignored these warnings.

Why Such Controversy?

The recent attacks on executive compensation come mainly from a few individuals and special-interest groups who use the controversy to further their own agendas. In 1984, for example, former U.S. Trade Representative William Brock assailed "excessive" auto executive bonuses to argue against Japanese import quotas. Labor unions have used the executive pay issue to bolster demands for higher wages for their members. Mark Green's condemnation of "overreaching" executives continues the general Nader-Green attack on the corporation. In each case, the executive compensation question is virtually unrelated to the ultimate objectives of the attackers.

Such highly publicized assaults cause confusion about executive compensation, a confusion exacerbated by the second-rate research conducted and reported by most media commentators. How compensation is determined is complex; current performance is only one of the many factors that affect executive pay. Thus performance cannot explain all or even most of an individual's compensation even though the relationship between pay and performance is strong, positive, and statistically significant. In any case, estimating the relationship between pay and performance is tricky and cannot be done by making simple cross-sectional comparisons....

The nation's shareholders need not fear that they are being swindled by greedy executives. Compensation policies normally make a great deal of sense. Companies are, moreover, adopting compensation plans that benefit shareholders by creating better managerial incentives.

Author's note: I am indebted to Michael Jensen and Jerold Zimmerman for their help. I gratefully acknowledge financial support from the Managerial Economics Research Center.

References

1. See, for example, Joseph E. Muckley, " 'Dear Fellow Shareowner'," HBR March–April 1984, p. 46; Mark Green and Bonnie Tenneriello, "From Pay to Perks to Parachutes: The Trouble with Executive Compensation," Democracy Project Report No. 8, March 1984.
2. Papers presented at the symposium are published in the *Journal of Accounting and Economics,* April 1985.
3. See, for example, Carol Loomis, "The Madness of Executive Compensation," *Fortune,* July 1982, p. 42.
4. The relationship between compensation and sales is reported by Harland Fox, *Top Executive Compensation,* Report No. 854 (New York: Conference Board, 1985). Evidence relating company size and shareholder return appears in the Symposium on Size and Stock Returns, published in the *Journal of Financial Economics,* June 1983.
5. Kevin J. Murphy, "Corporate Performance and Managerial Remuneration: An Empirical Analysis," *Journal of Accounting and Economics,* April 1985, p. 11.
6. Anne T. Coughlan and Ronald M. Schmidt, "Executive Compensation, Management Turnover, and Firm Performance: An Empirical Investigation," *Journal of Accounting and Economics,* April 1985, p. 43.
7. Hassan Tehranian and James Waegelein, "Market Reaction to Short-Term Executive Compensation Plan Adoption," *Journal of Accounting and Economics,* April 1985, p. 131.
8. James Brickley, Sanjai Bhagat, and Ronald C. Lease, "The Impact of Long-Range Managerial Compensation Plans on Shareholder Wealth," *Journal of Accounting and Economics,* April 1985, p. 113.
9. Richard A. Lambert and David F. Larcker, "Golden Parachutes, Executive Decision Making, and Shareholder Wealth," *Journal of Accounting and Economics,* April 1985, p. 179.
10. Arch Patton, "Those Million-Dollar-A-Year Executives," HBR January–February 1985, p. 56.

NO ↩

Lisa H. Newton

The Care and Feeding of the Truly Greedy: CEO Salaries in World Perspective

In 1996, Jack Welch, CEO of General Electric, received $21.4 million in salary and performance bonuses (and about $18 million in stock options); Lawrence Coss of the Green Tree Financial Corporation received $102.4 million in salary and bonus (plus stock options worth at least $38 million). Michael Eisner of Disney added $196 million in stock to his previous holding, somewhere around a third of a billion. The list goes on: Intel's Andrew Grove took home $97.6 million, Traveler's Group Sanford Weill made $94.2 million, and Citicorp's John Reed got $43.6 million. (These figures from John Cassidy's piece, aptly titled "Gimme," in *The New Yorker* of April 21, 1997; See also "The Top Ten List" in *The Nation,* December 8, 1997.) According to a preliminary study of 60 companies by Pearl Meyer & Partners, the CEO of a multibillion-dollar company received an average of $4.37 million in compensation in 1995. That was a 23% increase from 1994. (That number from an anonymous squib, "Checking in on the CEO's Pay," in *HR Focus,* May 1996, p. 15.) As Cassidy points out, we're not supposed to think those figures excessive:

> But, according to *Business Week,* when you add together salary, bonuses, and options packages the typical C.E.O. at a large company saw his pay envelope grow by just fifty-four per cent—barely eighteen times the increase necessary to keep pace with the cost of living. (All told, his paycheck was only two hundred and nine times as big as the average factory employee's.)

Meanwhile, World Resource Institute figures from a few years earlier show that average annual compensation for a citizen (or Gross Domestic Product per capita, which is as close to the same thing as we can get in largely non-cash economies), in U.S. dollars, was less than $100 in Mozambique and Tanzania, less than $200 in seven other African countries (Burundi, Chad, Malawi, Rwanda, Sierra Leone, Somalia, Uganda), plus Nepal and Vietnam, under $300 in another 15 countries worldwide. (That list from *World Resources 1996–1997,* published by the World Resources Institute, p. 166.) We are not living in a rich world. But some CEO's are rich, very rich.

How, the untaught observer might ask, is this kind of disparity justified? How can it be that one of the world's inhabitants has a yearly compensation equal to the combined resources of 43,700 other of the world's inhabitants? We can understand that some people are lucky (born with perfect pitch) and others are not (born without arms). But the agreement to compensate an executive to the tune of tens of millions is not a matter of luck. It's a human decision if ever there was one. What on earth could make it the right human decision?

Justifications abound. Justifications are products, and like all products, are for sale for a fair market price. They are not always necessary or desirable, but become so very quickly if something not quite right—something that just doesn't *smell* very good—is happening. Having an annual compensation 209 times that of your employees, and 43,700 times that of fellow humans across the world, is one of those conditions that assaults the nostrils, so CEO's need justifications; and with that much money to spend, there's bound to be some left after the mortgage and the groceries to splurge on a justification or two. It's a perfect free market situation: a willing buyer (the CEO and his loyal staff) meets a willing seller (a well-educated and articulate wordsmith who really needs money), and a justification changes hands. A rudimentary knowledge of human psychology tells you that the wordsmith will instantly convince himself (or herself: this is an equal opportunity sellout) that CEO's really are worth the enormous amount of money they're getting, and that the CEO will instantly convince himself (never herself: equal opportunity has not yet reached this level) that the justification is sound. But it isn't. As we might expect of products turned out at such speed in such an uncritical market, the quality isn't the best. It might be worthwhile to count some of the errors.

It won't do, for instance, to claim that the CEO contributes 43,700 times as much value to the world as the shepherd in Tanzania or the farmer in Chad. Even if the movies, or software, or candy bars produced by the CEO's company are really worth that many times the wool or corn produced by the Africans, they are not made by the CEO, who never goes near the production floor, but by the minions of the company, making 1/209 their CEO's annual pay. Whatever value the company produces, in short, could equally well be produced with a CEO making half that annual compensation, or, most likely, no CEO at all. (That suggestion might be worth examining.)

Nor will it do to claim that a company simply *has* to pay that much for such rare talent, that you really *can't* get a good CEO these days for under that price, given all the competition. The reason why that rings somehow false is that these decisions are made by the Board of Directors of the company, being a very small club of similarly compensated executives (on whose Boards of Directors the CEO will also sit), and the whole decision stays within that little overpaid group. One wonders if, given another Search Committee, someone could not have been found to do the job for, say, $2,000,000 per annum. Or maybe $650,000, which will pay most of the bills that a CEO might run up in the course of a year.

Comparisons with other high-paid talent also ring false. Entertainers, to be sure, make big bucks, singing or acting or shooting baskets. But here we have direct value for money, paid by those who are entertained. The entertainers make a lot of money: but their careers come to an end as soon as *our* tastes change or attention wanders, and for the time being, they are at least fun to watch. Careers can also end in a minute with a car accident or even a badly twisted knee. But the CEO is not at all fun to watch, and he seems to be immune to the changing of consumer tastes or accidental assaults on the body; he can write his memos from a wheelchair.

Now we come to the crux of the value! He writes memos. What is he *writing*, in those memos, that makes him so valuable? For an answer to that question, a review of the incentive structures of the publicly held corporation is needed:

The Corporation from Cradle to Grave

How does the corporation get started? An investor, or a group of investors, decide that there is a good market for a good or service (i.e. a high demand coupled with the money to buy that which will fill the demand), and that the revenue from sales will exceed the cost of making the good or service available by a healthy margin (i.e. they're going to make a lot of money), so they buy the machinery and supplies and office space and talent required for the production of this good or service, and the production and marketing and advertising begin. In a magic metaphysical moment the articles of incorporation are signed, and a bouncing baby company is launched. Pretty soon the money's rolling in and the investors are very happy.

Now, it's always possible for one of these investors to decide he wants his money back, possibly to invest in some other enterprise; he can try to sell out his share in the enterprise, to one of the other investors or to a stranger. He may have problems doing that if the enterprise is not doing well or if he owns a very large share. To make a long story very short, that problem and myriads of others were solved by a common Stock Market where all such shares can be bought and sold. In the present day, if an investor decides he no longer wants to be a shareholder, an investor, in Acme Corporation, he can sell his shares on the open market and invest instead in Beter Corporation. His choice.

Why would a shareholder want to sell out? The reason he bought in was to make money, and the company he set up is doing fine. If he wants continuing income, he'll do better to hang on to the stock and continue collecting dividends. But suppose he just wants lots of cash right now: fine, he sells his shares, "liquidates" his share of the assets of the company, and he gets the cash. Now of course, if all the original investors early in the company's history decided to do that at once, the whole company would be liquidated. But that's not likely to happen. (In the contemporary stock market, it's almost impossible, just because of the huge volume of stock traded; some mutual funds turn over their entire portfolio in the course of the year, and stray stocks are likely to be picked up.)

Why is it not likely to happen, at least in the original model of shareholdership? Because a funny thing happens when you put your money into a company as an investor. You begin to think of the company as "yours," which is appropriate, because it is, in part. You become anxious for its fortunes, not only for the monetary value of your initial investment, but for its own sake, as you would be anxious for the fortunes of a nephew. You watch its coverage in the press, cheering when it is favorable, grousing when it is not. You get attached to the company. You don't call your broker and have him sell it if it goes down a few points. For one thing, by the time you got hold of your broker and he got the stock offered for sale, the whole situation would have changed; for another, his fee would wipe out any gains; but for a third, your sense of ownership has become tinged with loyalty: you don't "sell out" until something really big, college or retirement or a new house, comes along. Besides, the individual shareholder is important in the company. If you are the owner of the company, even a part owner, you are the "principal," and all the company's employees are your "agents"—they act for you and for your interests. The CEO has to please you or (in theory: it almost never happened) you can wage a proxy fight at the annual meeting, bring about the election of your own Board of Directors, and have them hire a new CEO who will represent your interests more perfectly. So the CEO wants to keep you happy. But what does the CEO of your company have to do to please you? Not much: keep the company on an even keel, no scandals, distribute profits regularly, but remember to keep some of those profits to reinvest for the long term, because the long term is what you're in for.

That was the American shareholder up into the 1960's. There were mutual funds, of course, that owned stock, effectively pooling the investment funds of small shareholders to give them a diversified portfolio. Mutual funds did not operate like individual shareholders, for their managers, under the same fiduciary obligation to *their* shareholders, were not permitted to get attached to the companies they held—their job was to increase the total amount of stock value in the fund, and they didn't care what companies they had to hold shares in, in order to do that. But the funds were not really big players at the time.

They could become big players if they were joined by the vast money salted away in huge trust funds—pension funds and the like, and the endowments of not-for-profit institutions of all kinds. But these funds always invested in bonds, for the sake of safety; they didn't buy stocks. Until the 1960's, that is. Then these huge funds decided that 1929 was a long time ago, that stocks were quite as safe as bonds, and that it was time to trade in creditorship for ownership. Slowly they moved into the market, and took it over.

Again: what a fund manager wants from the investments he makes is rapid growth, the swift increase in the total amount of money in the fund. If it is a pension fund, that money is what the workers are going to retire on, and he (or she) works for the workers. If the fund is an investment pool, the manager works for the investors; if it is the endowment fund of a University, the manager works for the University. He will keep his huge funds invested in a company for the long term only if it is pouring money into his fund at a rate unmatched anywhere else in the market, or if he really has no choice. For a long time, the customs of the market and the available technology kept the funds' money moving slowly through the market, as well-weighted decisions moved the cash from blue chip to blue chip. But in the 1980's, the established ways of the market broke down, the white-shod country clubbers were shoved aside by the new breed of traders and arbitragers, and computer technology advanced to the point of allowing program trading (programming your computer to make trades automatically, in a split second, in response to certain changes in the market) and otherwise very rapid shifts of money from one stock to another.

Then it all came together. The new breed of trader talked the managers of the huge slowmoving funds into becoming players in a new rapid-fire market, and their money funded the leveraged buyouts, the mergers and acquisitions, and the infamous hostile takeovers for which the 1980's became famous. In the process a new breed of fund manager was born, one who is acutely aware, first, that his fund (for instance, my favorite pension fund), CREF, owns very large chucks of (say) Acme Company, second, that the Acme Board of Directors had therefore better take CREF's interests seriously or he'll have them replaced (he may even demand, and get, his own Director on the Board), third, that his obligation is to increase the amount of money in CREF as rapidly as possible, fourth, that therefore the Acme Board of Directors must instruct the Acme CEO to run the company in such a way that CREF's stock position appreciates, and fifth, that if the CEO is unresponsive to that instruction, the Board must fire him and get a more responsive one. This is what we call an "active" investor: no longer does the fund manager simply sell Acme and buy Beter when Acme is not running the way he wants it to run. He gets in there and makes it do what he wants. (Oh, but doesn't CREF offer a "social responsibility" track, in which only stocks in socially responsible corporations are purchased, for conscientious investors? Yes indeed; and CREF's fund manager manages those funds just as aggressively as all the others.)

Once a CEO is on board who promises to extract money from the company's workings and move it into shareholder hands faster than ever, the Board kind of makes *sure* he doesn't forget what to do by structuring incentives to help his memory: the more the dividends flow and the price per share of the stock goes up, the greater his bonus.

That, of course, is the link between the new way of doing business and the CEO's compensation.

Now, what was on that memo? How does the CEO suddenly put lots more money into shareholder hands? We know that the size profit to be divided among the shareholders is based in part on the ratio of corporate revenue to corporate costs—best understood as a fraction with revenue as a numerator and costs as the denominator—so the CEO has to increase the numerator, the revenue stream, or cut costs, the denominator, or, preferably, both. Let me count the ways he might do that: (1) He can discover that the company's operations were rife with waste, inefficiency, theft, whatever; tighten it up, get things working the way they should, and the company saves oodles of money, squeezing down the denominator, without changing operations at all. He'll always say that's what he's doing, but it's unlikely that much savings will be got that way. (2) He can try to raise the numerator, the revenue, by raising price. In some markets he can get away with that for awhile, but in a highly competitive market that's just likely to reduce sales, theoretically to zero. (3) He can try to raise revenue by developing new products, new markets, or both. That's a good idea, but it requires more investment, therefore lower distributions of profits right now. CREF is not interested in waiting. It wants money now. (4) There aren't any other ways to raise revenue, so he has to cut costs. He can cut the paper clip budget and pick up cheaper raw materials for his manufacturing, and he'll do that, but it's not enough. The big item in any company is payroll, not only for the meager salaries and wages the workers make, but also for those infinitely expensive medical and other insurance plans the company signed on for and now can't back out of. Fire a worker, and you save all that money. Fire (lay off) lots of workers, and you save lots of money. The denominator goes way down, raising profits, and the stock price goes way up. And that was the object of the expedition.

So that's what the memo was about. The CEO was setting the ball in motion to lay off thousands of workers. CREF will see the stock price go way up, and will be happy when the Board of Directors presents the CEO with a wonderful year-end bonus. That's why CEO compensation is so high, millions of dollars for successfully pink-slipping the company.

What does CREF do next? Sells the stock, obviously. After all, the prospects for the company are not good. They've cut way back on the quality of their materials, refused to reinvest in better plant or equipment, and laid off the folks who were doing the work, all to cut costs and send the price of the stock way up. In effect, they sold off some fraction of the value of the company, "liquidated" it, for quick cash, and distributed the cash. Now the company is worth a lot less, and CREF has no intention of holding on to worthless goods. Seeing the stock go up, investors who do not know why it went up will buy into Acme now on the expectation that it will go higher. CREF will take their cash and invest in the stock of (say) Beter, and promptly insist that Beter go through the same round of liquidation—cost-cutting, laying off, and neglecting reinvestment. Then Beter's stock will go up, CREF will sell it, and repeat the process. And all other funds are doing the same thing. In theory, the process could lead to the liquidation of the entirety of American industry. The grave of the productive corporation is already prepared; we await the death rattle. However long it takes, the CEO's will be well paid throughout.

In the Public Interest

What's wrong with very high CEO compensation? Two things: First, it is bad stewardship for people to take more than they can use, and unjust that some people should be making 43,700 times what other people make, especially when at least some of those other people are starving. John Locke, high priest of private property, put the case for the morality of private property very simply: each man may take from the commons (the world resources available to all) only as much as he can use, and only as long as enough and as good is left for others. The CEO fails on both counts.

Second, this compensation system is destroying American industry. It is commonplace by now that our cost-saving schemes have cost us the economy: our products made obsolete by foreign companies that invested in R & D [research and development] when we did not, and invested in new plants when we did not, our industrial jobs lost as our obsolete plants have to be shuttered, as pink slips flutter from the corner offices in the most recent "downsizings" and "rightsizings," as the actual work is assigned to East Asian and Mexican factories and American workers are handed over to unemployment. We are moving, we are told, from an era of manufacturing to an era of information-driven service industries. These are precisely the industries for which the vast majority of the population is not prepared and from which they cannot profit. We are condemning a majority of working-age adults to temporary, underpaid, service jobs, while the tiny minority feeds off the global wealth generated by the exploitation of the rest of the world. The entire system is unjust, and cries out to heaven, and to an informed citizenry, for remedy. The compensation of the truly greedy might be a good place to start.

POSTSCRIPT

Is CEO Compensation Justified by Performance?

In 1992, when Colvin wrote the article bringing the problem of CEO compensation to public attention, he was worried about America's perception of annual outlays of $1.7 million average total CEO compensation for almost 300 large companies, with pay going up to a whopping $3.2 million annually for the really big companies. By 1995, the CEO of a multibillion-dollar company received an average of $4.37 million in compensation in 1995, up 23 percent from 1994. With 1996 figures going through the roof, many have asked how on earth could General Electric CEO Jack Welch spend the $21.4 million in salary and performance bonuses (and about $18 million in stock options) that he received or Green Tree Financial Corporation's Lawrence Coss spend his $102.4 million in salary and bonuses (plus stock options worth at least $38 million)?

The political impact of CEOs' salaries may be muted for the present, but the moral dimensions of the problem have not changed since the days of the prophet Amos of the Hebrew Scriptures: What right have the rich to enjoy their warm palaces and mansions, dining plentifully on the best food from all the world, while the poor suffer from hunger and cold? But the political dimensions are volatile and dependent upon the rest of the system to provide context and opportunity. This issue will likely be with us for a while.

Suggested Readings

AP Dispatch, "Welch Defends Pay: Ratio Proposal Rejected by Shareholders," *Connecticut Post* (April 22, 1999).

John A. Byrne, "Gross Compensation?" *Business Week* (March 18, 1996).

Jack Lederer and Carl R. Weinberg, "CEO Compensation: Share the Wealth," *Chief Executive* (September 1996).

Dana Wechsler Linden and Vicki Contavespi, "Incentivize Me, Please," *Forbes* (May 27, 1991).

Mike Maharry, "AFL-CIO Launches Web Site to Expose CEO Pay Levels," *The News Tribune* (April 11, 1997).

Peter Passell, "A Theory of Capitalism: Lonely, and Rich at the Top," *The New York Times* (August 27, 1995).

Frederick Schmitt, "Study Finds CEO Salaries Tracking Performance," *National Underwriter* (October 21, 1996).

Thomas A. Stewart, "CEO Pay: Mom Wouldn't Approve," *Fortune* (March 31, 1997).

Peter Truell, "Another Year, Another Bundle: Billions in Bonuses Are Expected to Fall on Wall Street," *The New York Times* (December 5, 1997).

ISSUE 19

Can Green Marketing Save Tropical Rain Forests?

YES: Thomas A. Carr, Heather L. Pedersen, and Sunder Ramaswamy, from "Rain Forest Entrepreneurs: Cashing in on Conservation," *Environment* (September 1993)

NO: Jon Entine, from "Let Them Eat Brazil Nuts: The 'Rainforest Harvest' and Other Myths of Green Marketing," *Dollars and Sense* (March/April 1996)

ISSUE SUMMARY

YES: Economics professors Thomas A. Carr and Sunder Ramaswamy and mathematics teacher Heather L. Pedersen describe three projects to promote sustainable use of rain forest products, which they argue help to preserve the forest and support the local economy.

NO: Investigative reporter Jon Entine asserts that most green marketing programs do nothing to slow forest destruction and, moreover, frequently result in the mistreatment of employees, vendors, and customers.

T he tropical rain forests of the world, spread in rapidly decreasing pockets over South America (especially in Brazil's Amazon region), Africa, and Malaysia, are the home of most of the species in the world. Due to the favorable climate and stability over many centuries, the speciation of the dominant varieties of life has progressed to degrees only imaginable elsewhere. Some whole species of insect, for instance, live on *only one tree* in the Amazonian forest. Each species —or rather, the DNA of each species—is a parcel of information that may be irreplaceably valuable in the human scheme of things. (The rosy periwinkle of Madagascar, for instance, found nowhere else, is the source of methetrexate and vincristine, two very effective cancer therapies.) There is no way we could invent for ourselves the variety of effective chemicals that are supplied free of charge by the rain forest.

More than that, the tropical rain forest, a huge green canopy spread under the hottest sun, is the lungs of the world. Every leaf in the canopy carries on the endless task of absorbing carbon from the air (in the form of the most problematic "greenhouse gas," CO_2, or carbon dioxide) and releasing oxygen. That huge canopy supplies a significant amount of the oxygen for the world's air-breathers.

With all these functions for our good, how can it be that the rain forest would be destroyed? Tragically, the interests of a few people, in the absence of worldwide concerted action to protect it, conspire to cut down the trees of the rain forest. Tropical rain forests once covered 14 percent of the planet. Less than half remain, most of the loss occurring in the last 50 years; an area the size of Germany is lost every year.

As much as one-third of the annual contribution to the increase in atmospheric carbon dioxide, which contributes to global warming, comes from deforestation. The global warming connection comes from the fact that the cutting and combustion of trees release carbon dioxide that can only be balanced by an equal number of new trees removing that same amount of carbon dioxide as they grow. Not only do we lose the canopy that breathes for us, but we contribute to the greenhouse gases by allowing the forest to be cut. On the other hand, since global warming is an issue of concern to many, there is hope among environmentalists that it will serve to mobilize the enormous number of people needed to save the forests.

Tropical forests supply many useful commercial products and are the source of a wide variety of chemicals, including natural products that are used in the pharmaceutical industry. Among the serious consequences of rain forest destruction would be the loss of a principal source of organic chemicals used in medical research.

Designing and implementing appropriate and effective strategies for reducing or reversing rain forest decimation has produced heated controversy, both within the tropical nations where the destruction is occurring and in the international community. Among the proposals that have been advanced, along with the "debt for nature" swaps that would allow debtor nations to get rid of their national debt by promising to preserve forests, are many "green marketing" strategies whose goal is to enhance the economic worth of goods that can be produced from the forests in a sustainable manner. This is a means of motivating entrepreneurs to favor forest preservation over using forest land for profit.

In the following selections, Thomas A. Carr, Heather L. Pedersen, and Sunder Ramaswamy describe two projects involving the use of forest products and one ecotourism initiative, which they argue are the types of endeavors that "may be key to preserving the vital and fragile resources of the tropical rain forests." Jon Entine discusses green marketing "schemes," such as Ben and Jerry's promotion of Rainforest Crunch ice cream and Body Shop International's tropical skin and hair care products. He argues that, while encouraging consumers to "shop for a better world," these enterprises frequently mistreat employees, vendors, and customers, and do little or nothing to help preserve the forests or support the indigenous peoples.

Thomas A. Carr, Heather L. Pedersen, and Sunder Ramaswamy

Rain Forest Entrepreneurs: Cashing in on Conservation

Each year, nearly 17 million hectares of rain forest—an area roughly equal to that of Wisconsin—are lost world-wide as a result of deforestation. Because more than half of all species on the planet are found in rain forests, this destruction portends serious environmental consequences, including the decimation of biological diversity. Another threat lies in the fact that rain forests serve as an important sink for carbon dioxide, a greenhouse gas that contributes to global warming. The Amazon region alone stores at least 75 billion tons of carbon in its trees. Furthermore, when stripped of its trees, rain forest land soon becomes inhospitable and nonarable because the soil is nutrient-poor and ill-suited to agriculture. Under current practices, therefore, the forests are being destroyed permanently.

Economic forces result in exploitation of the rain forest to extract hardwood timber and fuel and in clearcutting the land for agriculture and cattle ranching, which are primary causes of the devastation. Mounting evidence shows that these conventional commercial and industrial uses of the rain forest (see Table 1) are not only ecologically devastating but also economically unsound. These findings have inspired an innovative approach to save the rain forest. Environmental groups are now targeting their efforts toward developing commercially viable and sustainable uses of the rain forest. Their strategy is to create economic incentives that encourage local inhabitants to practice efficient stewardship over the standing forests. These environmental entrepreneurs no longer view the market as their nemesis but as an instrument to bring about constructive social and environmental change. In theory, the strategy promotes win-win solutions: Environmentalists gain by preserving the rain forests, and local inhabitants gain from an improved standard of living that is generated by enlightened, sustainable development. In practice, the challenge lies in implementing such programs.

Three applications of environmental entrepreneurship in the rain forests have been particularly successful. Conservation International's "The Tagua Initiative," Shaman Pharmaceutical's search for useful drugs in the rain forest, and the management of ecotourism in Costa Rica are three projects that together

Table 1

Commercial and Industrial Products Derived from Tropical Rain Forests

Product	Value of imports by region (millions of U.S. dollars)	Marketshare of rain forest products (percent)	Region receiving imports	Year of estimate
Commercial products				
Fruit and vegetable	4,000	100	World	1988
Cut flowers	2,500	100	World	1985
Food additives	750	100	United States, European Community	1991
Spices	439	small	United States	1987
Nuts	216	100	World	1988
Food colorings	140	10	World	1987
Vitamins	67	small	United States	1990
Fiber	54	100	United States	1983/4
Industrial Products				
Fuel	60,000	<1	United States	1984
Pesticides	16,000	1	World	1987
Natural rubber	666	100	United States	1978
Tannins	170	large	United States	1980
Construction material	12	1	United States	1984
Natural waxes	9.3	100	United States	1985

Note: James Duke, an economic botanist at the U.S. Department of Agriculture, has been compiling estimates of the economic value of hundreds of key commercial and industrial rain forest products. Some of the important estimates are summarized here. Although not all of the imported products are derived from tropical rain forest countries, Duke claims that they all have the potential to be sustainably harvested from these regions.

Source: James Duke, "Tropical Botanical Extractives" (Unpublished manuscript, U.S. Department of Agriculture, Washington, D.C., April 1989).

provide an interesting cross section of the efforts under way to promote sustainable use of rain forest products. A number of common issues and challenges confront these environmental entrepreneurs.

Responding to Deforestation

Although people everywhere may benefit from preserving the rain forest, the costs of preservation are borne mainly by the local inhabitants. Usually, the inhabitants' immediate financial needs far outweigh the long-term benefit gained by forgoing the traditional extractive methods of forestry or land conversion for agriculture. In many of these countries, high levels of poverty, rapid population growth, and unequal distribution of land encourage migration into the forest regions. Local inhabitants, confronted with the tasks of daily survival, cannot be expected to respond to appeals for altruistic self-sacrifice. Consequently, forests are cut and burned for short-term economic gains. This problem is often exacerbated by misguided government policies in many countries, such as government-sponsored timber concessions that promote inefficient harvest levels, tree selection, and reforestation levels. Governments may charge a royalty far below the true economic value of the standing forest. Such low royalties and special tax breaks raise the profits of logging companies, which thereby stimulate timber booms. In addition, some governments provide special land tenure rules or tax benefits to individuals who "improve" the land by clearing the forest. These rules encourage development in the rain forest region because they impel poor settlers to seek land for agriculture and wealthy landowners to look for new investments.

Environmental entrepreneurs can create commercial alternatives to the traditional damaging uses of rain forest resources, but several factors must first be taken into consideration. For example, commercial development cannot be allowed to harm the ecological integrity of the ecosystem. This can be a difficult challenge as the scale of production increases for many projects. Also, if existing firms are profitable, new firms will be attracted into the industry, thus placing additional pressure on the fragile ecosystem. Of course, the product must also pass the test of the market; consumers must be willing to pay a price that covers the full cost of production. Some environmentally conscious consumers may be willing to pay a premium for sustainably harvested rain forest products. The size of this "green premium" would depend upon these consumers' willingness and ability to pay, as well as on the prices of other products competing with the rain forest products. To maintain the green premium over time, environmental entrepreneurs need to devise a strategy that differentiates their products from others through advertising and some type of institutionalized labeling system. These entrepreneurs must also anticipate the effect of expanding output on market prices. Previous studies have examined the market value of sustainable products from a single hectare. One study in the Amazonian rain forest in Peru found that sustainably harvested products such as fruit, nuts, rubber latex, and selectively logged timber yield more net value than do plantation forestry and cattle ranching. If harvests are expanded, however, market prices may be pushed down, and the profitability of the program reduced. Another consideration is that entrepreneurs may be able to avoid the expense of developing extensive distribution networks and other marketing costs by forming alliances with established commercial firms. These firms typically have retail outlets and experienced business personnel that can assist the small entrepreneur.

Finally, the environmental entrepreneur must channel income back to the effective owners of the rain forests—the local indigenous people. This return raises the issue of rain forest property rights. The property rights over rain forest resources are not well defined or enforced. Rain forest land is often held collectively, and government-owned land marked as a reserve is not always protected. Even private landowners have a difficult time preventing landless squatters from using their property. Without the enforcement of property rights, rain forests become an open-access resource that is overexploited. This result is not inevitable, however. History suggests that, when the benefits of establishing new property rights exceed the costs, societies often devise new ways to define property rights and improve the allocation of resources.

In addition to the question of physical property rights, there is the problem of defining intellectual property rights. Indigenous people possess a wealth of esoteric knowledge about local plants and animals and their usages. Conservation groups argue that the wisdom of the local inhabitants must be given an economic value or else that knowledge will disappear amidst the destruction of the forest. At the same time, scientists and entrepreneurs also contribute value to rain forest products by discovering useful medicinal compounds in the plants. If these interests are not protected, there will not be sufficient economic incentive to develop new products. During the Earth Summit in Rio de Janeiro [in June 1992], the Bush administration refused to sign an international treaty on biodiversity on the grounds that it would harm the interests of biotechnology firms. (The Clinton administration signed the biodiversity treaty on 4 June 1993.) A key challenge is to develop an institutional mechanism that recognizes the value of both the natives' knowledge and the scientists' and entrepreneurs' contributions, and therefore rewards both types of intellectual property rights in the development of rain forest products.

The Tagua Initiative

Conservation International is an environmental organization based in Washington, D.C., that works to conserve biodiversity by supporting local rain forest communities world-wide. Through a project entitled "The Tagua Initiative," Conservation International is attempting to synthesize "the approaches of business, community development, and applied science to promote conservation through the marketing of non-timber forest products." The tagua nut is an ivory-like seed that is harvested from tropical palm trees to make buttons, jewelry, chess pieces, carvings, and other arts and crafts. Conservation International links button manufacturers in the United States and other countries with rural tagua harvesters in the endangered rain forests of Esmeraldas in Ecuador. The organization works independently with participating companies to design unique marketing strategies tailored to those companies' individual images, product offerings, and marketing campaigns.

In 1990, Conservation International began expanding the market for tagua products and developing a local industry around tagua. Today, tagua buttons are being used by 24 clothing companies, including such major manufacturers as Smith & Hawken, Esprit, J. Crew, and L. L. Bean. The current distribution network links the Ecuadorian tagua producers to the clothing companies through four wholesale button manufacturers. Conservation International collects a royalty based on a percentage of sales to wholesale button manufacturers and uses the proceeds to support local conservation and community development programs in the rain forest. It has also focused its efforts on developing a viable local tagua industry that includes harvesting and manufacturing. A primary objective of The Tagua Initiative is to provide the 1,200 local harvesters with an attractive price for tagua so that they have an economic incentive to protect the standing forest. Recent figures indicate that the price paid to tagua collectors has risen 92 percent since the program began (a 32 percent real price increase after adjusting for the estimated inflation rate). To increase the flow of income to the native economy, Conservation International encourages the development of new tagua products that can be manufactured locally. Currently, the tagua production line has expanded to include eight manufacturers of jewelry, arts and crafts, and other items.

The Tagua Initiative provides a tremendously successful example, at least in the initial stages of development. Since February 1990, 850 tons of tagua have been delivered directly to factories, and the program has generated approximately $2 million in button sales to manufacturers in North America, Europe, and Japan. According to Robin Frank, tagua product manager at Conservation International, the organization is collaborating with about 50 companies worldwide, and many others have expressed interest. Moreover, The Tagua Initiative in Ecuador has become a role model for new projects in Colombia, Guatemala, Peru, the Philippines, and a number of other countries. In all of these cases, Conservation International is working with local organizations to identify and develop sustainable commercial products in a manner that protects sensitive ecosystems. These projects are expanding the rain forest product line to Brazil nuts and pecans from Peru, fibers for textiles, and waxes and oils for the personal health and hygiene market.

In addition to creating marketable rain forest products, Conservation International cooperates with conservation and community development programs, such as the Corporacion de Investigaciones para el Desarrollo Socio/ Ambiental (CIDESA) in Ecuador. Ecologists, economic botanists, and conservation planners affiliated with Conservation International help CIDESA to identify critical rain forest sites and monitor harvesting practices to ensure their sustainability, among other things. The province of Esmeraldas in Ecuador is considered a critical "hot spot" because it contains some of the highest levels of biodiversity in Latin America and harbors some of Ecuador's last remaining pristine tracts of western Andean rain forest. Coincidentally, it is one of Ecuador's poorest communities, with a meager annual average per-capita income of $600, about one-half of the national average. The community of Comuna Rio Santiago in Esmeraldas has a population of 70,000, which grows dramatically at an annual rate of 3.7 percent. Four out of every 10 children suffer from malnutrition, and the infant mortality rate is 60 per 1,000 births. There is a high level of alcoholism, and drug addiction is a growing problem. Life expectancy is just 50 years, and the illiteracy level is near 50 percent. All of these actualities indicate an urgent need to protect the natural resources found in this region, not only to maintain biodiversity but also to ensure the economic welfare of the local inhabitants. If these needs are addressed, the program will have the potential to change the current low standard of living in Ecuador by promoting both conservation and economic development.

Over the next 10 years, Conservation International plans to increase the use of numerous rain forest products, such as medicines, furniture, and baskets. These efforts can serve as a role model for firms in the industrial world that seek to create rain forest products and improve the well-being of rain forest inhabitants.

Shaman Pharmaceuticals

Shaman Pharmaceuticals, Inc., draws its name from rain forest *shamans*, traditional medicine men who possess a vast amount of knowledge about the use of plants for medicinal purposes. The shamans' ability to cure a variety of illnesses is founded on centuries of practice and an intimate association with, and dependence upon, indigenous plants. By tapping the knowledge of the shamans, scientists hope to reduce the research costs of identifying plants with beneficial medicinal properties. Furthermore, investigating plant species already known to possess healing characteristics yields a much higher chance of success in the screening process. This ethnobotanical approach—which combines the skills of anthropology and botany to study how native peoples utilize plants—is the basic premise by which Shaman Pharmaceuticals functions. By innovatively combining the disciplines of ethnobotany, isolation chemistry, and pharmacology with a keen market-driven strategy, the company hopes to create a more efficient drug-discovery program.

Shaman has formed strategic alliances with the pharmaceutical industry to enhance its prospects of turning a pharmaceutical discovery into a financial gain. "Shaman feels it is in a strong position to strike such alliances because the company is not only formed around a handful of products, but also around an efficient, ongoing process for generating compounds with a greater likelihood of being active in humans." The company has two main objectives in building these alliances: generating research funds through cooperative arrangements and gaining access to a larger marketing network. Three major pharmaceutical manufacturers have entered into agreements with Shaman: Inverni della Beffa, an Italian manufacturer of plant-derived pharmaceuticals, has signed licensing and marketing agreements and invested $500,000 in Shaman; Eli Lilly committed $4 million to Shaman and collaborates in developing drugs for fungal infections; and Merck & Company is working with Shaman on projects targeting analgesics and medicines for diabetes. (For more on this topic, see "Making Biodiversity Conservation Profitable: A Case Study of the Merck/INBio Agreement," by Elissa Blum, in the May 1993 issue of *Environment.*)

To address the question of intellectual property rights and needs of the indigenous population, Shaman Pharmaceuticals created a nonprofit conservation organization called "The Healing Forest Conservancy" to protect global plant biodiversity and promote sustainable development. The company initially donated 13,333 shares of its own stock to the conservancy and plans to channel future product profits into projects that benefit the people of the source country. The first conservancy project provided health care benefits for the indigenous peoples of Amazonian Ecuador, a region that supplies valuable medicinal plants to Shaman. In return for information about these plants, physician Charles Limbach extended his medical services to three communities and treated 30 children during a whooping cough epidemic. Additionally, the conservancy seeks to create sustainable harvesting techniques for plants with commercial medicinal value. These programs have the task of reconciling the ecological constraints on plant extraction with the economic realities of producing a marketable product. This strategy reflects Shaman's concern that both the physical and intellectual property rights of the indigenous population are protected and that the inhabitants benefit from the research on these products.

As a result of its research efforts over the past few years, Shaman Pharmaceuticals has a pipeline full of active plant leads. Two antiviral products are currently being tested in clinical trials and are expected to reach the market in 1996: Provir is an oral treatment for respiratory viral infections that are common in young children; Virend is a topical treatment for the herpes simplex virus. Both products use the ingredient known as SP-303, a compound that was derived from a medicinal plant that grows in South America and was isolated by the company's discovery process. Patents have been filed on both the pure compounds and the methods of use for these products, which have a target market greater than $1 billion worldwide. Another consequential find is an antifungal agent found in an African plant that is traditionally ingested to treat infections. Shaman is using this compound to make a product that treats thrush, a fungal infection of the mouth, esophagus, and gastrointestinal tract. Given this discovery, the company hopes to find new treatments for other types of fungal infection. Shaman has strategically targeted its product development to address problems for which few effective treatments exist, such as viral and fungal infections. Moreover, there is a growing demand to find treatment for herpes and thrush because the increasing population of immunocompromised patients (including AIDS, chemotherapy, and transplant patients) is particularly vulnerable to these ailments. A third promising line of product development is in the area of analgesics. Shaman has found two plants exhibiting special binding properties that raise the prospect of creating a nonaddictive pain-relief drug. The company is conducting laboratory tests to identify the pure compounds responsible for this analgesic activity and is expanding its screening process by collaborating with Merck.

The raw materials for the screening all come from plants that are either presently harvested or sustainably collected. This discovery process has been quite successful at identifying plants with potential medicinal properties. Based on thousands of field samples collected by ethnobotanical field researchers and on reviews by a scientific strategy team, the company has screened 262 plants and found 192 to be active—a "hit rate" of 73 percent in the discovery process. Future products will be developed from some of these "hits."

According to company president Lisa Conte, "Shaman's well-defined strategic focus and outstanding, dedicated scientists will create a successful business by uniquely combining the newest in technology with the oldest of tribal lore." As a leader in ethnobotanical investigations, Shaman hopes that its initial success will translate into the development of a market for plant-based drugs from rain forest countries. The goal here is to use the revenue generated by these medicines as an economic incentive to preserve the forests and the wisdom of the native healers.

Ecotourism in Costa Rica

Ecotourism has been defined as "purposeful travel that creates an understanding of cultural and natural history, while safeguarding the integrity of the ecosystem and producing economic benefits that encourage conservation." Successful ecotourism creates economic opportunities in terms of both employment and income for the local people. These benefits furnish the local community with a strong incentive to practice good stewardship over their natural resources.

In Costa Rica, ecotourism has become a large and growing industry. In 1986, tourism generated $132.7 million and ranked as Costa Rica's third largest source of foreign exchange. In 1989, more than 375,000 tourists visited Costa Rica, 36 percent of whom were motivated by ecotourism. Tourism to Costa Rica's parks increased 80 percent between 1987 and 1990 and surged another 25 percent in 1991. Costa Rica offers the ecotourist diverse rain forests, abundant biodiversity, and breathtaking scenery. To protect these valuable resources, a national park system was established in 1970, which now comprises 34 parks and covers 11 percent of the total Costa Rican land area. Some of the most popular sites for ecotourism in Costa Rica, such as the Monteverde Cloud Forest Reserve and the La Selva Biological Station, are also centers for important biological research. Recently, these areas have attracted thousands of visitors each year, primarily because of the rich flora (more than 2,000 plant species) and fauna (some 300 animal species).

During the mid 1980s, the Costa Rican government sought to reconcile conservation and development interests by pursuing a strategy of sustainable development. Ecotourism was viewed as a clean source of development that might facilitate the preservation of the natural resource base. The actual implementation of this strategy was left to the private sector. The early environmental entrepreneurs in Costa Rica's ecotourism industry included Costa Rica Expeditions, Tikal, Horizontes, and the Organization for Tropical Studies. The growth of the ecotourism industry has since put strains on the fragile resource base. For example, the large number of visitors at popular parks is causing such problems as erosion and water pollution. Given the attraction of tourist revenues and the danger of overcrowding, environmental entrepreneurs are finding it difficult to create ecotourism programs that are consistent with the principles of sustainable development. Efforts to control ecotourism in Costa Rica are still in the early stages, and more research is needed soon if the industry is to serve its original purpose.

One firm that is striving to attain this balance is International Expeditions. This 11-year-old, Alabama-based company operates 30 travel programs on 6 continents. Company president Richard Ryel and Tom Grasse, the director of marketing and public relations, contend that the ecotourism industry needs to forgo short-run profits and adopt a four-part conservation ethic that includes increasing public awareness about the environment, maximizing economic benefits for local people, encouraging cultural sensitivity, and minimizing the negative impacts on the environment. International Expeditions applies these principles to business practices: For example, to create a flow of money into the local economy, the company uses the host country's airline when possible, employs local tour operators, and uses other services within the rain forest community. The company's tour of Costa Rica begins in San Jose and proceeds through the country's national parks. The tour organizers hire

Costa Rican guides who are familiar with the local habitat, and both guides and tourists stay at accommodations close to the parks whenever possible. These steps are designed to prevent tourist revenue from leaking outside the local communities that live near the parks.

To minimize detrimental impacts on the ecosystem and to promote respect for the rain forests, International Expeditions arranges small, manageable groups, educates participants about the ecosystem, avoids fragile habitats, and minimizes disruptions to the wildlife. In keeping with its objective of promoting natural history and conservation education, International Expeditions has designed a series of workshops in Costa Rica. The workshops are led by some of the world's leading experts on life in the rain forest, including Alwyn Gentry of the Missouri Botanical Garden, Donald Wilson of the National Museum of Natural History, and James Duke of the U.S. Department of Agriculture. Participants join in small group sessions to engage in hands-on field experience, such as nature walks, boat trips, and bird watching, and visit such sites as the Monteverde Cloud Forest and Tortuguero National Park on the Caribbean coast. Various sites feature canopied walkways up to 125 feet off the forest floor, which allow participants to walk among the treetops and closely observe the flora and fauna. The local guides also educate tourists about the history, culture, and socioeconomic conditions of indigenous peoples.

During the 1992 season, the cost of the 10-day, general nature tour throughout Costa Rica was $1,998 per person, and the 8-day workshop cost $1,498 per person. Because roughly 50 percent of these expenditures go to Costa Rica, these trips create the dual benefits of educating the nature traveler and generating income for the local economy.

A Key to Preservation

Clearly, sustainable development of rain forest products has the potential to bring about positive change, preserve biodiversity, and improve the welfare of local communities. Because deforestation is spiraling out of control, the efforts of organizations like Conservation International, Shaman Pharmaceuticals, Inc., and International Expeditions have become imperative. E. O. Wilson of the Museum of Comparative Zoology at Harvard University calculates that deforestation of the rain forest is responsible for the loss of 4,000 to 6,000 species a year—an extinction rate 10,000 times higher than the natural extinction rate before the emergence of humans on Earth. Furthermore, the unwritten knowledge of forest peoples is rapidly disappearing. Thomas Lovejoy, assistant secretary for external affairs at the Smithsonian Institution, asserts that the rain forest "is a library for life sciences, the world's greatest pharmaceutical laboratory, and a flywheel of climate. It's a matter of global destiny." The need to develop methods to deal with the issue is urgent, and environmental entrepreneurs may be key to preserving the vital and fragile resources of the tropical rain forests.

NO ☜   Jon Entine

Let Them Eat Brazil Nuts: The "Rainforest Harvest" and Other Myths of Green Marketing

Business is our new universal community," says the speaker, and there is an immediate murmur of agreement. With eyes closed, the scene echoes of a Rotary Club luncheon in a genial, Midwestern town. There is an air of optimism that everyone seems to share.

"Religion and government no longer work as forces for community and change. We are in the era of business, it defines our relationships and values, and it doesn't have to be driven by the bottom line." The burly, ruby-faced speaker is clearly taken by his own message. The all-white, well-heeled crowd is entranced. "We are the leaders who can turn business into a positive social force."

The audience rises from its seats and breaks into applause. Although the words ring of Des Moines, the audience is forty-something L.A. Aging baby boomers in khaki sportcoats and designer jeans mix with business executives in Ann Taylor power suits. One man with stylishly long hair, a black silk shirt, black pants and sunglasses whispers into a cellular phone. Judging by the cars in the parking lot, this crowd long since traded in its Beetles for BMWs and Broncos.

This was a June celebration to open the Los Angeles chapter of Business for Social Responsibility, a trade group that promotes itself as environmentally and socially progressive, and they have come to hear their hero. The slightly rumpled, three-time college dropout holds the audience spellbound with his prescription for 'saving the world through business.' Their affection, indeed the adulation, is tangible.

The object of their rapt attention is Ben Cohen, who, in the late 1970s, started mixing batches of ice cream at an abandoned gas station in Burlington, Vermont, with his high school buddy Jerry Greenfield. Today, Ben & Jerry's Rainforest Crunch, Chunky Monkey, and Cherry Garcia are indulgences of choice for baby boomers. Although he no longer runs the company day-to-day, Cohen, 44, remains Chairman and eccentric corporate symbol of Ben & Jerry's Homemade, the 18-year-old, $160 million publicly traded company.

Ben & Jerry's is the best known of the "good guy" entrepreneurs with quixotic corporate personas and New Age social philosophies. Skin-and-hair-care franchiser The Body Shop International (BSI), eco-friendly apparel makers Patagonia and Esprit, Tom's of Maine natural toothpaste and personal-care wholesaler, and Reebok athletic shoes are a few of the companies which have sliced a sizable niche out of the retail pie by turning "green" issues—such as the rainforest, "natural" ingredients and an opposition to animal testing—into their points-of-difference in a fickle, ultra-competitive consumer market. Many of these companies started with non-existent advertising budgets but were run by executives with an intuitive understanding of how to play the media dominated by baby boomers like themselves. And no company has benefited more from friendly press coverage than Ben & Jerry's.

In Los Angeles, Cohen rails on about the greedy, soulless character of Corporate America, and then boasts about his special flavor of New Age business. "Rainforest Crunch," he says, "shows that harvesting Brazil nuts is a profitable alternative for Amazon natives who have seen their lands ravaged to create grazing areas or for mining." The crowd is on its feet.

Yet, Ben & Jerry's own annual report carries the not-so-socially responsible details of what some anthropologists now call the rainforest fiasco. Despite Cohen's rhetoric that buying Rainforest Crunch helps preserve the fragile Amazon environment and the aboriginals who live there—a theme repeated uncritically by most of the media—his Third World project offers a lesson in the dangers of paternalistic capitalism. In fact, many anthropologists believe the rainforest harvest has led to the worst possible scenario: an increase in clear-cutting and mining, and a greater dependence among Amazon natives on selling land for subsistence income.

Green Marketing or Green Washing?

Cohen & Company preach an oxymoronic message: the generation that wanted to change the world now encourages consumers to "shop for a better world," the title of a best-selling "green" consumer guide. It's a two-for-one sale that rings up big profits: 'buy our not-tested-on-animals Brazil nut hair rinse or ice cream and get social justice for free.'

U.S. consumers spend upwards of $110 billion on products from companies they perceive as socially or environmentally progressive. According to a study last summer by the Social Investment Forum, $150 billion in teacher, union, church and other pension funds is held by investment managers using social screens; another $12 billion is invested in mutual funds which follow various "ethical" or "green" formulas. More than 45 funds in the U.S. alone screen out companies for manufacturing "sin" products such as cigarettes, while they include firms that promote social policies such as making "cruelty-free" products.

For years, The Body Shop was the favorite of the ethical investing community. Its founder, Anita Roddick, is the most visible and outspoken of the green marketing executives. Since opening a tiny shop in 1976 offering "one-stop ear piercing" and a range of natural-sounding lotions, Roddick has grown

BSI into an $800 million multinational company with 1300 mostly-franchised stores in 45 countries. She has cultivated a reputation for promoting the latest politically-correct social campaign: saving the whales, recycling, animal rights, AIDS research, and most prominently, preserving the environment and indigenous cultures by sourcing ingredients from the Third World. Roddick dubbed these micro-projects "Trade Not Aid," popularizing the eco-liberal concept of using capitalism instead of aid projects to reduce Third World dependency.

Despite rhetoric of good intentions, BSI has had a string of fair trade fiascos. For instance, over a year ago in Ghana, The Body Shop bought $20,000 worth of shea-butter from 10 villages for use in its creams. According to a front-page article in the *Toronto Globe & Mail*, the creams didn't sell, and today, the project is abandoned and the local economy is in tatters. BSI made no follow-up orders and left villages with thousands of dollars of unsold butter and no buyers.

The Body Shop's fair trade program has been plagued with problems. Richard Adams, who has founded two fair trade organizations, remembers seeing leaflets at BSI's stores in 1987 promoting its first import, foot massagers made by orphan boys in India. As director of Traidcraft in the early 1980s, Adams had briefly carried wood carvings made by the same group of orphans, who lived in a home called The Boys' Town. "Joe Homan, its director, was sourcing carvings from child labor sweat shops," he recalls discovering after poor quality shipments prompted an investigation. Worse, the local community said boys were being molested. Adams immediately sent the Roddicks a letter. "I never heard back," he says. Homan, it turns out, had been kicked out of a Christian Brothers sect. Two alarmed members of the Jesuit order visited the Roddicks after getting wind of the project. Still, nothing was done.

"Gordon [Roddick] was aware of his reputation," says Anne Downer, former head BSI franchisee for much of Asia. Downer, who attended the christening of The Boys' Town with the Roddicks in 1987, remembers Gordon saying that he had heard the rumors but didn't believe them. "He didn't seem unduly concerned and didn't seem to take it seriously."

Over the next few years, as Homan went about stealing charity funds and molesting orphan boys, the Roddicks sent out glowing reports to their franchisees. "Joe's work in The Boys' Town is ceaseless, he cares for the boys and girls and they really appreciate what he is doing for them," gushed one account in 1989. The roof caved in the next year when the English and Indian press ran exposes of Homan's escapades. The Roddicks first tried to suppress the scandal and then attempted to turn it into a public relations advantage by claiming credit for exposing him. "This story has not hit the Canadian Press yet but could erupt at any time," read one memo. "It is important that you know your facts. Anita... blew the whistle on Joe." A similar bulletin went to all of its American franchisees.

Not one of The Body Shop's dozen "Trade Not Aid" projects has been accurately promoted. And by its own statistics, they represented just 0.165% of the company's business as recently as 1993, at the height of its self-promoting rhetoric. Yet, despite their tiny size and frequent problems, these projects have generated overwhelmingly favorable media coverage—including much of the 10,000 positive mentions the company says it averages each year.

Rainforest Fiasco

Over the past decade, the "rainforest harvest," as it has come to be called, has been the most publicized international fair trade program and a defining symbol of social activism. The marketing of the rainforest blends three cultural trends: the environmentalist struggle to protect the forest against clear-cutting, the movement to preserve indigenous peoples, and baby boom narcissism.

The rainforest movement gathered momentum after the annual Brazilian Peoples Conference in 1989. Roddick and various journalists, environmentalists and eco-celebrities, from Jane Fonda to Sting, gathered in Altamira for the event, which garnered headlines around the world. Not long after, BSI introduced rainforest bath beads made with babassu nut oil, and hair conditioner from nuts harvested and processed by two Kayapo villages in the eastern Amazon.

BSI attached a bright Trade Not Aid sticker to its rainforest bead display, although babassu nuts are not grown in the Amazon, and the beads were made mostly from super-refined oil sourced from the Croda Chemical company—tested on animals in 1986. The hair conditioner uses a tiny fraction of Brazil nut oil at what cosmetic experts say are ineffective levels. According to a study by UK-based Survival International, BSI pays the workers $1.33 per kilo of nuts collected—an average of $500 for a five month harvesting season. Yet in its public relations hand-outs, BSI has claimed that workers in its projects are paid "first world wages." Little money trickles down to the villages. The young Kayapo leaders ("socios") who run the project continue to sell off land rights to profiteers cutting down mahogany trees. The village has been nicknamed Kayapo, Inc. for cashing in their timber dollars for cars, Western-style homes and even an airplane.

Harvest Moonshine

Ben & Jerry's rainforest project, which was more ambitious, has a serendipitous history. In 1988, at a party after a Grateful Dead rainforest fundraising concert, Ben Cohen casually mentioned that he was developing a new brittle for an ice cream using something more exotic than peanuts. According to those present, Jason Clay, an ambitious anthropologist with the Cambridge indigenous rights group Cultural Survival, lit up like a video game. He regaled Cohen with his pet project to market renewable non-timber rainforest products such as fruits, nuts and flowers. A few days after the concert, Cohen's new friend headed to Vermont carrying a 50-pound bag of rainforest nuts. "We mixed up the first batch of Brazil nut crunch in Ben Cohen's kitchen and served it to the board of directors that night," recalled Clay, "and we were off."

Within months, Cohen founded and became half-owner of Community Products Inc. CPI was set up to source Brazil nuts from Cultural Survival (CS) and turn them into brittle for ice cream, and cosmetic products and candy made by other companies. His intentions were no doubt benevolent; CPI promised to pay harvesters a 5% "environmental premium" and give 60% of any profits to charity, a third of that to Cultural Survival.

Ben & Jerry's has long been a favorite of both green-oriented consumers and investors. It does set an impressive standard of ethical innovation: it has published state-of-the-art social audits, gives an astonishing 7.5% of pre-tax profits to charity and buys local dairy products to help preserve the family farm. But the company is most readily identified with its flagship Rainforest ice cream.

Ben & Jerry's launched Rainforest Crunch early in 1990. "Money from these nuts," read the label, "helps to show that rainforests are more profitable when cultivated for traditional harvest than when their trees are cut and burned for short-term gain." The Third World ice cream was an overwhelming, overnight success—for Ben & Jerry's, which reaped tens of millions of dollars in profits and free publicity. But the view from Amazonia was not nearly so sanguine.

Critics found little evidence to support the central premise of the harvest—that foraging for nuts could ever approximate the income natives collect by selling off land rights to miners and foresters. "Marketing the rainforest... perpetuates the process of leaving to the forest dwellers the resources of the least interest to the broader society," wrote anthropologist Michael Dove for the East-West Center in Honolulu, in a typical critique.

Outside of Cultural Survival, where founder David Maybury-Lewis and Jason Clay were positioned to reap fame and perhaps fortune as consultants if the harvest took off, anthropologists quietly urged a go-slow strategy on Ben & Jerry's and BSI, but were ignored.

The worst case scenario was soon realized. There was no established supply chain for Amazon nuts. Most natives such as the Kayapo, long since corrupted by Western interests and fighting a losing battle to alcoholism, were not about to stop selling land rights to meet the expectations of social activists in London and Cambridge. Ben & Jerry's anticipated source for the nuts, the Xapuri cooperative (which had no native workers but was comprised of white rubber tappers, mostly of Portuguese ancestry) in western Brazil, never could meet the quality standards or quantity demands of the fad product.

To meet the sudden explosion in demand, market forces took hold and agri-businesses were drawn in to meet it. The harvest proved to be a windfall for landowners, who have long monopolized trade in this region. "That first year, we had to source all of our nuts from commercial suppliers," concedes Michelle McKinley, the former general manager of CS who left in November after reassembling the pieces of an organization nearly bankrupted by the ill-conceived harvest. Agri-barons elbowed out native suppliers and flooded the market. Nut prices, already soft, plummeted, cutting the incomes of tribes who did collect nuts. Amanakáa, a Brazilian peoples rights group, took Ben & Jerry's to task for sourcing directly from the Mutran family, a notorious Latin American agri-business convicted of killing labor organizers.

While the project was spinning out of control, harvest hype developed into a New Age business mantra. Sting set up the now-defunct Rainforest Foundation and began singing the praises of the free market. Usually-vigilant social critic Alexander Cockburn even became a convert; he attacked the UK-based indigenous rights organization Survival International after its director, Stephen Corry, published "Harvest Moonshine," a meticulously documented critique of the project which criticized Cockburn's friends at Cultural Survival.

Based in large measure on Roddick's self-promotion as a fair trade leader, Ralph Nader dubbed her "the most progressive business person I know," *Mother Jones* invited her onto its board, *USA Today* called her "The Mother Theresa of Capitalism," and the yuppie business magazine *Inc.* put Roddick on its cover with the headline, "This Woman Has Changed Business Forever."

The Brazilian and Bolivian governments took advantage of the harvest hype to justify cutting expensive, politically unpopular financial aid to native populations. A confidential report by the Alliance of Forest Peoples (a coalition including the Xapuri) attacked Cultural Survival for its "minimal" concrete support. "Their negative repercussions have been enormous," read the report. "We have not seen any return." Brazilian peoples groups, cowed at first by the Cohen-Roddick marketing barrage, gradually became more vocal. "A thriving market in forest products," said Julia Barbosa, president of the national Rubber Tappers Council which represented the Xapuri workers, "is no substitute for a political program that protects the forests and people who live in it."

To cover the economic shortfall, some native communities even sold off more land rights. In the end, the celebrated harvest has created a Brazil nut business dominated by some of Latin America's most notorious capitalists. Over the years, more than 95% of Ben & Jerry's Brazil nuts have been purchased on agribusiness dominated markets; today, almost 100% are commercially sourced. According to Cultural Survival's McKinley, the so-called progressive retailers had been increasingly unwilling to pay the 5% environmental premium; last year only $22,000 was collected. "We rushed into this project recklessly," she now says. "We created a fad market overnight and the hard sell promotions have contributed to a lot of confusion. The harvest just didn't work."

In retrospect, early optimistic projections by rainforest capitalists seem almost ridiculous. Clay had estimated a $20–25 million market by 1996 with the benefits flowing to the rubber tappers and native communities. The business peaked in 1991 at $1.3 million, dropped to $250,000 in 1995, and has nearly sunk Cultural Survival. Clay was forced out. By the spring of '94, the Xapuri had cut off all supplies to CS. The project has run in the red for four years, generating no profits for Community Products and no charity.

No Whales Have Been Killed by My Company

Ironically, despite Ben Cohen's attempts to brush off the fiasco, his company did release an independent social audit documenting it. Paul Hawken, the environmentalist, author and businessman, published his analysis as part of Ben & Jerry's annual report released last summer. "It is a legitimate question," wrote Hawken, "whether representations made on Ben & Jerry's Rainforest Crunch package give an accurate impression to the customer." He quoted sharp criticism from Amazon rights groups, then concluded: "There have been undesirable consequences which some say were predictable and avoidable."

So, why have social activists, academics and journalists been caught off guard by the ethical contradictions of socially responsible business and New Age adventures such as the rainforest fiasco? Does buying ice cream or hair rinse with Brazil nuts promote progressive social change or merely inure the public to the profligacy, and elitism, that has gradually coopted the green consumer movement?

The Sixties did inspire a new morality-based social philosophy that emphasizes the individual's responsibility to speak out against injustice and corruption. It drew its social vision from the civil rights movement, anti-Vietnam activism, environmental consciousness and feminism, and it continues to inspire social and environmental reforms. But there is an underside to the legacy of the counterculture: narcissism, arrogance and self-indulgence.

Baby boomers—people born from the mid-1940s to 1960—are beginning to dominate the business and political landscape. Since 1990, their share of national leadership—Congress and governorships—has more than doubled from 21% to 45%, and will reach more than 70% within the decade. They are gradually becoming the American political and business establishment.

Yet, many conspicuous baby boom business leaders seem convinced of their socially responsible credentials, in large measure because they came of age in the Sixties. The visionaries at the vanguard of this movement—from Cohen and Roddick to Mo Siegel at Celestial Seasonings and Paul Fireman at Reebok—are loath to admit that "social responsibility" is in part a margin game. When profits are rolling in, as they were in the 1980s, progressive gestures are painless.

But facing growing pains and intense worldwide competition, many are firing workers, closing inner city stores, cutting back on charity projects, and making their products in overseas sweatshops. Just last November, Reebok received reams of positive press when it gave a Human Rights Award, an annual event. Yet, it was curiously silent a few days later when reports surfaced that its workers in Thailand make 25 cents an hour for 18 hour days. Asked about the contradiction, Reebok's Paul Fireman told the UK newspaper *The Observer* that he will not "impose U.S. culture on other countries... 'when in Rome, do as the Romans.'" In other words, Reebok, BSI and other New Age entrepreneurs frequently act much like any business with bottom line challenges.

The not-so-pristine consequences of green consumerism have been largely absent from business reporting, since many journalists who have so slavishly profiled these successful entrepreneurs share with them common cultural pretensions. Many have convinced themselves that growing up protesting Vietnam and supporting Earth Day forever marks them as progressives, though today their closest brush with social responsibility may consist of little more than enjoying a Ben & Jerry's Peace Pop.

On close scrutiny, progressive business is often a land of alchemy where promises are easy to make, workers are frequently treated with indifference, and environmental reforms are superficially attempted. At best, the relatively small number of consumers with a high tolerance for high-priced goods—most of the products in question command a hefty premium over ordinary brands—play a modest role in raising awareness of social problems. (And even so, it's just a prosperous sliver of baby boomers affected.) At worse, cause-related marketing, as it is called, is little more than baby boom agitprop, masking serious ethical lapses. "Many socially responsible companies have noble corporate philosophies," observes Jon Lickerman, a social researcher with the Calvert Group of socially responsible mutual funds, "but mistreat their own employees, vendors, and customers."

They've also inspired a wave of green marketing by mainstream firms. Guardians of free speech and public health such as Philip Morris take out full-page ads decrying the sale of cigarettes to minors while railing against Big Government; Chevron brags that its sunken oil rigs are havens for Gulf fisheries; oil drillers, developers and natural gas companies band together to form the National Wetlands Coalition, complete with a logo featuring a duck flying over marshes, to front their attacks on environmental reform. Madison Avenue has embraced greenwashing with a vengeance, and the green business movement, with its facile posturing on complex issues, must bear some of the responsibility.

Ice Cream Politics

"It's really a disingenuous marketing strategy to say if you spend $2.99, you'll help save the rainforest," warns Michelle McKinley, formerly of Cultural Survival, which no longer sources Brazil nuts for Ben & Jerry's. But her criticism hasn't dampened Ben Cohen's enthusiasm for hawking Rainforest Crunch. Today, Cohen and co-founder Jerry Greenfield spend little time running the company that has grown far beyond their managerial expertise. They can be found on a college ice cream tour. At the Wharton Business School in Philadelphia, Ben and Jerry sermonized on their usual topics: the crazy fun of starting a business, corporate ethics and of course Rainforest Crunch. "After the speech, I talked with both Ben and Jerry personally," wrote Ritu Kalra, an MBA graduate, in a recent e-mail discussion about the controversy. "Neither of them knew much about the harvest. When it came down to it, they didn't want to comment on it and didn't feel responsible at all for any misleading labeling or for telling half-truths to about 300 college students."

In the case of the rainforest, Cohen still seems oblivious to or afraid to admit the real impact of his now-collapsed pet project. "We have created demand for rainforest products," he boasted at the annual meeting of Business for Social Responsibility in San Francisco in November. There was no mention of the rapacious agri-businesses that supply most of his nuts.

The BSR members—many personal friends of Cohen and part of an informal intelligentsia of the "progressive" business community—were reluctant to press their wounded hero. They were far more eager to munch on Ben & Jerry's Rainforest Crunch donated for the event. "It's so inspiring," one BSR member was heard to say as she licked her spoon clean, "to know that business can make money and still do so much good."

POSTSCRIPT

Can Green Marketing Save Tropical Rain Forests?

It could be argued that this issue's antagonists, the professors and the journalist, are arguing past each other. On the one hand, optimistic innovation, both scientific and economic, will be required to cut through the political barriers protecting the destroyers of the rain forests, so Carr, Pedersen, and Ramaswamy should be encouraged to continue their work. On the other hand, hope does not justify hype, nor do good intentions justify false promises. The journalistic skepticism of Entine is helpful in sorting out the self-serving environmental promotion from solid efforts to use the tremendous potential of the free enterprise system to save a precious global resource.

The rain forest issue is not one of government (and the environmentalists) versus the market (the ranchers). The opinion of many is that the long-term economic opportunity in preserving and harvesting the rain forests easily surpasses any economic gain to be realized in cutting it down. It can be argued that the difficulty in preserving the forest arises because the political powers in place at this time would prefer to use the forest in nonproductive ways for the stabilization of their regimes (through homesteading of the urban poor) and the benefit of political cronies. For centuries, the only means of overwhelming personal political interests has been the higher force of personal economic interests. When we can convince the rulers of the forest that they have more to gain from joining the world in the preservation of the forest than from their present destructive course, optimism on the ultimate fate of the forests will be justified.

Suggested Readings

Erik Eckholm, "Secrets of the Rainforest," *The New York Times Magazine* (November 17, 1988), p. 20.

Sandra Hackman, "After Rio—Our Forests, Ourselves," *Technology Review* (October 1992).

Andrew Revkin, *The Burning Season* (Houghton Mifflin, 1990).

Alex Shoumatoff, *The World is Burning* (Little, Brown, 1990).

Contributors to This Volume

EDITORS

LISA H. NEWTON is a professor of philosophy and director of the Program in Applied Ethics at Fairfield University in Fairfield, Connecticut. She received a B.S. in philosophy, with honors, from Columbia University in 1962 and a Ph.D. from Columbia in 1967. She was an assistant professor of philosophy at Hofstra University in Hempstead, New York, from 1967 to 1969, and she began teaching at Fairfield University in 1969. Professor Newton's articles have appeared in *Ethics* and the *Journal of Business Ethics*, among other publications. She is a member of the American Philosophical Association, the Academy of Management, and the American Society of Law and Medicine. Professor Newton currently serves as president of the Society for Business Ethics.

MAUREEN M. FORD is an associate for the Program in Applied Ethics at Fairfield University in Fairfield, Connecticut. She received a B.S. in business management and applied ethics from Fairfield University. Active as a consultant to community agencies, Mrs. Ford is a former president of the YWCA in Bridgeport, Connecticut, and was for several years vice president–secretary for JHLF, Inc., a marketing and consulting firm in Westport, Connecticut.

STAFF

Theodore Knight   List Manager
David Brackley   Senior Developmental Editor
Juliana Poggio   Developmental Editor
Rose Gleich   Administrative Assistant
Brenda S. Filley   Production Manager
Juliana Arbo   Typesetting Supervisor
Diane Barker   Proofreader
Lara Johnson   Design/Advertising Coordinator
Richard Tietjen   Publishing Systems Manager
Larry Killian   Copier Coordinator

AUTHORS

KEN BINMORE is a professor of economics at University College London in London, United Kingdom, and director of the ESRC Centre for Economic Learning and Social Evolution. He has also taught at the University of Michigan, the University of Pennsylvania, and the State University of New York. His publications include *Game Theory and the Social Contract: Just Playing* (MIT Press, 1998) and *Frontiers of Game Theory*, coauthored with Alan Kirman and Piero Tani (MIT Press, 1993).

SUSAN S. BLACK is publisher of *Bobbin* magazine.

SISSELA BOK is a faculty member of the Center for Advanced Study in the Behavioral Sciences in Stanford, California, and a former associate professor of philosophy at Brandeis University in Waltham, Massachusetts. Her publications include *Lying: Moral Choice in Public and Private Life* (Random House, 1979); *Secrets: On the Ethics of Concealment and Revelation* (Vintage Books, 1983); and *A Strategy for Peace: Human Values and the Threat of War* (Pantheon Books, 1989).

THOMAS A. CARR is an assistant professor in the economics department at Middlebury College in Middlebury, Vermont.

SIMON CHAPMAN is an associate professor of public health advocacy at the University of Sydney in Australia. His research interests include tobacco control policy research, mass media coverage of public health, public health advocacy analysis, and risk communication. His publications include *Over Our Dead Bodies: Port Arthur and Australia's Fight for Gun Control* (Pluto Press, 1998) and *The Last Right? Australians Take Sides on the Right to Die*, coedited with S. Leeder (Mandarin, 1995).

WILLIAM DOMNARSKI is an attorney in private practice in Minneapolis, Minnesota. His articles have appeared in such journals as *American Scholar* and *Virginia Quarterly*, and he is the author of *In the Opinion of the Court* (University of Illinois Press, 1995).

MARK DOWIE is an investigative journalist and a former editor of *Mother Jones* magazine. He is the author of *Losing Ground: American Environmentalism at the Close of the Twentieth Century* (MIT Press, 1996) and coauthor, with David T. Hanson and Wendell Berry, of *Waste Land: Meditations on a Ravaged Landscape* (Aperture Foundation, 1997).

WILLIAM R. EADINGTON is a professor of economics and director of the Institute for the Study of Gambling and Commercial Gaming at the University of Nevada, Reno.

FRIEDRICH ENGELS (1820–1895), a German socialist, was the closest collaborator of Karl Marx in the foundation of modern communism. The "official" Marxism of the Soviet Union relies heavily on Engels's contribution to Marxist theory. After the death of Marx in 1883, Engels served as the foremost authority on Marx and Marxism, and he edited volumes 2 and 3 of *Das Kapital* on the basis of Marx's incomplete manuscripts and notes. Two major works by Engels are *Anti-Duhring* and *Dialectics of Nature*.

JON ENTINE is a journalist specializing in business ethics, journalism ethics, sports, and society. His reporting over 20 years has earned him many awards, including two Emmys. He has served as adjunct professor of journalism at New York University, and he has lectured at Columbia University.

JOHN E. FLEMING is a professor emeritus at the University of Southern California, where he taught for 24 years and where he served as director of the doctoral program and chairman of the Department of Management. His research focuses on strategy and business ethics, and he has been published in the *Academy of Management Journal,* the *California Management Review,* and the *Journal of Business Ethics.*

JOHN P. FOLEY, an archbishop, is president of the Pontifical Council for Social Communications and Vatican media director for Pope John Paul II.

WILLIAM A. GALSTON is a professor in the School of Public Affairs at the University of Maryland at College Park and director of the university's Institute for Philosophy and Public Policy. A political participant as well as an academic, he is executive director of the National Commission on Civic Renewal, and he served as deputy assistant to President Bill Clinton for domestic policy from January 1993 through May 1995. He is coauthor, with Karen J. Baehler, of *Rural Development in the United States: Connecting Theory, Practice, and Possibilities* (Island Press, 1995).

KENNETH E. GOODPASTER holds the Koch Endowed Chair in Business Ethics in the Graduate School of Business at the University of St. Thomas in St. Paul, Minnesota.

LaRUE TONE HOSMER is a professor of corporate strategies in the Graduate School of Business Administration at the University of Michigan in Ann Arbor, Michigan.

INTERNATIONAL TOBACCO GROWERS ASSOCIATION is a coalition of tobacco farmers from 20 countries working to promote and develop their common interests throughout the world.

GENE R. LACZNIAK is the Wayne R. and Kathleen E. Sanders Professor in Marketing in the School of Business Administration at Marquette University in Milwaukee, Wisconsin. His research interests include marketing strategy, business ethics, and marketing and society. He has taught executive development classes in Europe and Asia, as well as in the United States. He is coauthor, with Patrick E. Murphy, of *Ethical Marketing Decisions* (Allyn & Bacon, 1992).

ROBERT A. LARMER is an associate professor of philosophy at the University of New Brunswick in Fredericton, New Brunswick, Canada. His research interests focus on the philosophy of religion, the philosophy of the mind, and business ethics. He has written numerous articles in these fields, and he is the editor of *Questions of Miracle* (McGill-Queen's University Press, 1996). He received his Ph.D. from the University of Ottawa.

KARL MARX (1818–1883) was the revolutionist, sociologist, and economist from whom the movement known as Marxism derives its name and many of its ideas. Together with Friedrich Engels he published *Manifest der Kommunistischen Partei* (1848), commonly known as *The Communist Manifesto.* His most important theoretical work is *Das Kapital,* an analysis of the economics of capitalism. He also became the leading spirit of the International Working Men's Association, later known as the First International. His works became the intellectual basis of European socialism in the late nineteenth century.

DAVID M. MESSICK is the Morris and Alice Kaplan Professor of Ethics and Decision in Management at the J. L. Kellogg Graduate School of Management at Northwestern University. He was an Eastern European Exchange Fellow of the National Academy of Science in 1990. A former editor of the *Journal of Experimental Social Psychology,* he is the author of more than 100 articles and chapters and has been published in many prominent academic journals. He is coeditor of a number of books, including *Codes of Conduct: Behavioral Research into Business Ethics,* with Ann E. Tenbrunsel (Russell Sage Foundation, 1996), and *Negotiation as a Social Process,* with Roderick M. Kramer (Sage Publications, 1995).

MERTON H. MILLER is the Robert R. McCormick Distinguished Service Professor Emeritus of Finance in the Graduate School of Business at the University of Chicago in Chicago, Illinois. He and William F. Sharpe were awarded the Nobel Prize in Economics in 1990 for their pioneering work in the theory of financial economics. He is the author of *Merton Miller on Derivatives* (John Wiley, 1997) and *Financial Innovations and Market Volatility* (Blackwell, 1991).

JENNIFER MOORE, a former assistant professor of philosophy at the University of Delaware in Newark, Delaware, has done teaching and research in business ethics and business law. She is the author of *Math Bridge* (Rainbow Bridge, 1999) and coauthor, with Karen Musalo and Richard A. Boswell, of *Refugee Law and Policy: Selected Statutes, Regulations and International Materials* (Carolina Academic Press, 1998).

KEVIN J. MURPHY is a professor of finance and business economics in the Marshall School of Business at the University of Southern California. He has also taught at the Harvard Business School and the University of Rochester. He is chairman of the Academic Research Committee of the American Compensation Association and associate editor of the *Journal of Financial Economics,* the *Journal of Accounting and Economics,* and the *Journal of Corporate Finance.* His publications include *Ecosystems,* coauthored with Gordon Dickinson (Routledge, 1997).

ALLEN R. MYERSON is a contributing journalist for the *New York Times.*

LAURA L. NASH is director of the newly formed Institute for Values-Centered Leadership at Harvard Divinity School. In addition to running the institute's programs, she teaches and writes on business ethics, religious values, and corporate culture. She has also been a senior research associate at Boston University's Institute for the Study of Economic Culture. She is the author of *Believers in Business* (Thomas Nelson, 1994) and coauthor, with

David A. Krueger and Donald W. Shriver, Jr., of *The Business Corporation and Productive Justice* (Abingdon Press, 1996).

JAMES NEAL is a lawyer who has served in many mass disaster and product liability cases, including the Ford Pinto suit and the *Exxon Valdez* environmental suit.

FRANK PARTNOY is an assistant professor of law at the University of San Diego Law School, where he teaches in the areas of corporations, Latin American finance, and white-collar offenses. He is the author of *Fiasco: The Inside Story of a Wall Street Trader* (Viking Penguin, 1999) and *F.I.A.S.C.O.: Blood in the Water on Wall Street* (W. W. Norton, 1997).

HEATHER L. PEDERSEN is a mathematics teacher at the Colorado Springs School in Colorado.

PHARMACEUTICAL MANUFACTURERS ASSOCIATION, founded in 1958 and located in Washington, D.C., is an association of over 100 manufacturers of pharmaceutical and biological products that are distributed under their own labels. It encourages high standards for quality control and good manufacturing practices, research toward the development of new and better medical products, and the enactment of uniform and reasonable drug legislation for the protection of public health.

SUNDER RAMASWAMY is chairman of the economics department at Middlebury College in Middlebury, Vermont. He received his Ph.D. from Purdue University. He is coauthor, with John H. Sanders and Barry I. Shapiro, of *The Economics of Agricultural Technology in Semiarid Sub-Saharan Africa* (Johns Hopkins University Press, 1996).

ARNOLD S. RELMAN is a professor of medicine and of social medicine at Harvard Medical School and a senior physician at Brigham and Women's Hospital in Boston. He was the editor in chief of the *New England Journal of Medicine* from 1977 to 1991.

JEFFERSON D. REYNOLDS is deputy regional environmental counsel, eastern region, for the U.S. Air Force. He earned his J.D. from Hamline University in 1990 and his LL.M. from George Washington University in 1995.

JEREMY RIFKIN is president of the Foundation on Economic Trends. His publications include *The End of Work: The Decline of the Global Labor Force and the Dawn of the Post-Market Era* (Jeremy P. Tarcher, 1996) and *The Biotech Century: Harnessing the Gene and Remaking the World* (Putnam, 1998).

ADAM SMITH (1723–1790) was a Scottish philosopher and economist and the author of *An Inquiry into the Nature and Causes of the Wealth of Nations*, 2 vols. (1776).

ROBERT C. SOLOMON is the Quincy Lee Centennial Professor of Philosophy and Management at the University of Texas at Austin and a member of the Academy of Distinguished Teachers. A specialist in post-Kantian continental philosophy, he has also published extensively on ethics, business ethics, and the emotions. His books include *Accountability in the Information Age, vol. 1* (South-Western, 2001) and *The Joy of Philosophy: Thinking Thin and the Passionate Life* (Oxford University Press, 1999).

RICHARD A. SPINELLO is associate dean of faculties and an adjunct assistant professor of philosophy at Boston College in Chestnut Hill, Massachusetts. He has published numerous articles on business ethics and ethical theory and on the social implications of new information retrieval technologies. He is the author of a textbook on computer ethics entitled *Ethical Aspects of Information Technology* (Prentice Hall, 1994).

MANUEL VELASQUEZ is the Charles Dirksen Professor of Business Ethics at Santa Clara University, where he teaches courses in the legal, political, and social environment of the firm; in business strategy; and in business ethics. He has published numerous articles in journals such as the *Academy of Management Review*, the *Business Ethics Quarterly*, *Social Justice Research*, and the *Business and Professional Ethics Journal*, and he is the author of *Business Ethics: Concepts and Cases*, 4th ed. (Prentice Hall, 1998). He received his B.A. from Gonzaga University and his Ph.D. from the University of California at Berkeley.

MICHAEL A. VERESPEJ is a writer for *Industry Week.*

DAVID WASSERMAN is a research scholar at the Institute for Philosophy and Public Policy in the School of Public Affairs at the University of Maryland at College Park. He has written about legal evidence and statistical inference, the moral underpinnings of criminal law and legal practice, the concept of discrimination, and various issues in procedural and distributive justice. His present research focuses on ethical and policy issues in genetic research and technology and on justice for people with disabilities. He is coauthor, with Anita Silvers and Mary Mahowald, of *Disability, Difference, Discrimination: Perspectives on Justice in Bioethics and Public Policy* (Rowman & Littlefield, 1998).

ANDREW C. WICKS is an assistant professor in the Department of Management and Organization at the University of Washington School of Business. He has a Ph.D. in religious studies, and his interests are in normative business ethics and the connections between medical ethics and business ethics. His articles have been published in such journals as *Soundings* and the *Journal of Business Ethics.*

Index